The Celts

The Celts

A history from earliest times to the present

Bernhard Maier

Translated from the German by Kevin Windle

University of Notre Dame Press
Notre Dame, Indiana

© C. H. Beck'sche Verlagsbuchhandlung, 2000

English translation © Kevin Windle, 2003

Published in North America by the University of Notre Dame Press, 2003

This edition first published 2003 by Edinburgh University Press

First published as *Die Kelten* 2000 by Verlag C. H. Beck, Munich

University of Notre Dame Press
310 Flanner Hall
Notre Dame, Indiana 46556
http://www.undpress.nd.edu

Typeset in 11/13pt Ehrhardt
by Hewer Text Ltd, Edinburgh, and
printed and bound in Great Britain by
MPG Books Ltd, Bodmin, Cornwall

A Cataloging-in-Publication record for this book is available from the Library of Congress

ISBN 0-268-02360-3 (cloth)
ISBN 0-268-02361-1 (paperback)

Contents

Preface

The history presented in this book seeks to do justice to the term 'Celt' in all its aspects, and therefore spans the entire field, from a time before written records to the present, from the westernmost manifestation of Celtic culture in Ireland to the easternmost in Asia Minor. It aims to help the general reader to make historical sense of the various facets of Celtic culture, while offering the specialist reader an overview of the present state of knowledge by means of detailed references to all sources. Following the historical sequence of events, the presentation is divided into three parts.

Part I deals with the continental Celts of antiquity, on whom there is little native documentary evidence and who are known chiefly from the evidence of archaeology and the observations of classical commentators. The first chapters present the culture and history of the Celts of Central Europe from the late West Hallstatt culture to the civilisation of the *oppida* in the immediately pre-Roman period. This is followed by a brief survey of the history of the Celts in northern Italy and the most westerly and easterly branches of Celtic culture in the Iberian peninsula and Asia Minor. Part I concludes with a chapter on the Romanisation of Gaul, which marked the end of the political independence of the Celtic peoples on the European mainland.

Part II covers the medieval history of the Celtic peoples of Ireland, Britain and Brittany, which was colonised from Britain. These chapters focus on the effects of the Celts' conversion to Christianity, the foundations of their political, legal and social order, and the evolution of their languages and literatures. They also analyse the contribution of the insular Celts to the culture of medieval Europe, which can be seen particularly clearly in the Irish mission and in the reception of Celtic materials and motifs in courtly literature. Part II ends by describing the transformation of traditional social, cultural and legal structures that resulted from the loss of political independence.

Part III is devoted to the modern age. It deals first with the later history of the Celtic languages and literatures, and secondly with the rediscovery of the ancient Celts and how this has affected the self-view of contemporary speakers of Celtic tongues. Here the focus is on developments in economic, demographic and cultural policy, the influence of the Christian denominations on language and literature, and lastly how romantic and nationalist tendencies have led to the creation of a timeless and imaginary Celtic world. The book concludes with some reflections on the question of our modern use of the term 'Celtic' and the role of the Celts in western culture.

It is my pleasant duty to record my gratitude to three bodies which, through their material support, have made possible my long-lasting engagement with Celtic culture and thus also this book: the German Research Foundation for a three-year post-doctoral scholarship for research into Celtic religious history; the Gerda Henkel Foundation for a two-year research grant to investigate the phenomenon of Interpretatio Romana; and Professor Geraint Jenkins of the Centre for Advanced Welsh and Celtic Studies in Aberystwyth for the Lady Amy Parry-Williams Memorial Scholarship, which made possible an extended period of study in summer 1998 in the National Library of Wales. I am grateful to Dr Stefan von der Lahr (Munich) and Dr Harald Krahwinkler (Klagenfurt) for their painstaking editorial report, and to Professor Herwig Wolfram for finding a place for this volume in his series on early peoples.

In the present English edition, the Bibliography and corresponding references have been brought up to date and adapted to the needs of English-speaking readers. I have taken the opportunity to add two short paragraphs on Manx and Cornish and to correct a number of minor inconsistencies and errors. For pertinent suggestions I am grateful to Dr Anja Gunderloch (Glasgow) and, above all, to Dr Kevin Windle (Canberra) who suggested a number of improvements and succeeded in translating an often difficult German text into readable English. Thanks are also due to Sarah Burnett for her extremely skilled and tactful editing.

Bernhard Maier

Translator's acknowledgements

For generous advice and assistance with linguistic, cultural, geographical and historical matters, the translator wishes to thank Robert Barnes, Jennifer Hendriks, Marian Hill, Peter Hill, Roger Hillman, Hans Kuhn, Elizabeth Minchin, Mary-Jane Mountain, Gabriele Schmidt and Clare Slater.

James Grieve devoted much time and effort to a close critical scrutiny of a draft of the translation. His sharp eye for detail and unerring feel for stylistic niceties have done much to enhance its accuracy and readability.

Finally, the author's close interest in the translation, his sure grasp of English nuances and readiness to help with all points of difficulty have helped to make the translation process easier and more enjoyable than it might otherwise have been.

Kevin Windle

Introduction

PEOPLE, LANGUAGE AND CULTURE IN THE HISTORY OF THE TERM 'CELTIC'

More than most names which have come down to us from classical antiquity, the name 'Celts' evokes a wealth of different associations. For some it may mean a museum exhibition of archaeological finds such as those from the Hochdorf barrow; for others it will be the vivid depictions of Celtic warriors by Posidonius, Caesar and other classical authors, classical sculptures like 'the dying Gaul', the distinctive patterns of early medieval book illumination, the heroes of medieval legends such as Arthur and Cú Chulainn, or personal experience of the language and customs of Ireland, Scotland, Wales or Brittany.

When we look more closely at the subject, we find that the term 'Celt' is applied in three distinct ways. First, in the ethnographical writing of antiquity, the word 'Celt' (Greek *Keltoí*, *Kéltai* and *Galátai*, Latin *Celtae* and *Galli*) stands for a variety of central European peoples with whom the Greeks and Romans came into contact from the sixth century BC, first through trading relations and later in armed conflict.[1] Unlike general usage in modern times, the term was also applied (above all by those writing in Greek) to those peoples commonly known today as Germanic. On the other hand, the inhabitants of Britain and Ireland were never termed 'Celts' by the writers of the classical period.

The Celts were probably known by name as early as the sixth century BC, when Hecataeus of Miletus wrote his geography of the world, of which only fragments have survived. The first clearly attested use of the name occurs in the writings of Herodotus (*Histories* 2, 33, 3–4), and he placed the Celts in the area of the source of the Ister, that is, the Danube (see Fischer 1972). Brief references to the Celts appear in the work of the historian Xenophon and the philosophers Plato and Aristotle, but the writings of Polybius in the second century BC are the first to give relatively extensive information about the Celts of the northern Italian region (see Urban 1991, Berger 1995). Early in the first century BC the Stoic philosopher Posidonius of Apamea included in the twenty-third book of his now lost *Histories* a description of Gaul and its inhabitants, based on his own exploratory travels, that pointed the way for later writers. This description can be roughly reconstructed from quotations and borrowed material in the work of the historian Diodorus Siculus (first century BC), the geographer Strabo (first century BC/first century AD) and the writer Athenaeus of Naucratis (second and third centuries AD).[2]

In the middle of the first century BC, Julius Caesar describes the Celts very differently from Posidonius, in keeping with the political and propagandist bias of his account of his campaigns, giving particular emphasis to the difference between them and the Germani (*De Bello Gallico* 6, 11–28).[3] The great significance of the Celts as military adversaries, first of the Greeks, then of the Romans, means that the ancient depictions of them are heavily overlaid with ethnographic clichés. All statements about their culture and religion are stereotyped, sometimes to the point of caricature, while there is no mention of a phenomenon as conspicuous as Celtic art in all of classical literature.

The second application of the term occurs in comparative philology, as it emerged in the early nineteenth century. And here, in contrast to the broad use of the term in the classical period, the term 'Celtic' referred exclusively to linguistic facts.[4] 'Celtic' was the designation for a group of related languages which had evolved from a common ancestor. All are characterised by a set of typical features, including the shift from 'ē' to 'ī' (eg. Latin *rēx* 'king' and Irish *rí*), and the loss of 'p' in initial position and before vowels (Latin *pater* 'father' and Irish *athair*). In this use of the word, Celtic forms the westernmost branch of the Indo-European family of languages, which includes (from west to east) Germanic, Romance (including Latin), Baltic, Slavonic, Albanian, Greek, Armenian, Hittite in Asia Minor, Iranian (including Persian), Indic (including Sanskrit) and Tocharian in Central Asia. For a long time it was usual to divide

Celtic according to the development of the sound k^u, inherited from the Indo-European parent language, into P-Celtic and Q-Celtic sub-groups. This diagnostic development is clearly apparent in the word for 'each', which yields *cách* in Old Irish (from an older form $k^u\bar{a}k^uos$) but *pawb* in Welsh (from an older form $p\bar{a}pos$). Nowadays, however, it is usual to apply geographical and chronological criteria and to distinguish two sub-groups: the continental Celtic recorded in antiquity (Gaulish in ancient Gaul, Galatian in Asia Minor, Lepontic in northern Italy, and Celtiberian in the Iberian peninsula), and insular Celtic, attested since the early medieval period in vernacular literature. The insular Celtic tongues are generally divided into the Goidelic sub-group (Irish, Scots Gaelic in the Scottish Highlands and the Hebrides, and Manx on the Isle of Man) and Brythonic (Welsh in Wales, Cumbrian in northern England, Cornish in Cornwall, and Breton in Brittany). Whereas the continental languages had died out by the early Middle Ages, Irish, Scots Gaelic, Welsh and Breton, which was transplanted from Cornwall to the continent in the early Middle Ages, have survived to the present day. Cumbrian was still spoken in the north of England in the Middle Ages, while Cornish remained alive until the eighteenth century and Manx until the twentieth.

The third application of the term Celt is in modern archaeology and here its use remains far from uniform.[5] The early historians of the seventeenth and eighteenth centuries had attributed practically all deposits and monuments from pre-Roman times to the Celts they knew from classical sources. However, in the nineteenth century, following the example of the Danish scholar Christian Jürgen Thomsen (1788–1865), they began to distinguish the three successive periods of the prehistory of central and northern Europe – the Stone Age, Bronze Age and Iron Age – and to restrict the term 'Celtic' to the last of these periods. Later, the Swedish archaeologist Hans Hildebrand (1842–1913) first separated the pre-Roman Iron Age in central Europe into an early period – the Hallstatt period – and a later one – the La Tène period – basing this distinction on finds from a burial ground discovered in 1846 near Hallstatt, in the Upper Austrian Salzkammergut, and others from the La Tène sandbar at the northern tip of Lake Neuchâtel in Switzerland.

It remains customary to this day to identify the bearers of the La Tène culture with the Celts known from classical sources. The Iron

Age Hallstatt culture, on the other hand, is attributed to the Celts for the most part only in its latter stage and in its western manifestation. This is because, first, the writers of antiquity never use the term 'Celtic' for earlier centuries or neighbouring cultures and, secondly, the last stage of the Hallstatt culture is clearly distinguished from preceding centuries by archaeological evidence, for example the fact that graves are richly furnished with imported wares from the Mediterranean area. It is also important to note that, on the evidence of place names, the use of the Celtic language was more widespread than La Tène culture, while on the other hand certain artefacts may have been familiar to non-Celtic speakers. Conjectures concerning the ethnic origins of the Celts earlier than the sixth century BC rely primarily on the archaeologically demonstrable continuity of isolated cultural features in finds from this period and earlier periods, and on the geographical situation of Celtic in the Indo-European language group. Thus far these conjectures have not led to any generally accepted theories.[6]

If, in view of these three different uses of the term 'Celt', we seek to establish what lends unity to the subject of this book, we must first confront several objections. As far as we can ascertain today, any such unity has no anthropological or cultural foundation, nor any foundation in the consciousness of the Celts themselves. The perspective of physical anthropology does not suggest a closely linked group since bone remains show considerable variation in body weight and head shape and provide no convincing evidence for any distinction between the Celts and their neighbours.[7] Nor can the Celts be defined on the basis of their material and spiritual culture: La Tène art, which is held to be typically Celtic, played hardly any role in Ireland and the Iberian peninsula; the Greeks' early Celtic trading partners of Herodotus's time had quite different forms of settlement and economic life from the Celtic peoples of Caesar's time; and the Celtic gods, most of whom are known only from inscriptions, had purely local or regional importance.

Much the same holds for the sense of community of the peoples we now term Celtic. What picture the Celts of antiquity had of their origins lies far beyond our reach: even in the early medieval period the Irish, Scots, Bretons and Welsh had lost all awareness of the continuity of their language and culture with that of the ancient Celts. It was the humanist scholars of the sixteenth century, among them the Scottish historian George Buchanan (1506–82), who first discovered the relationship between the surviving insular Celtic tongues and the Celts of antiquity. It was only even later, in the nineteenth century, that the romantic revival of the national and regional heritage awoke in the last speakers of Celtic languages a sense of historical and cultural community.[8]

Language seems, at first sight, to be the unifying link between the time before written records and the present, but here too we must raise reservations. The Goidelic and Brythonic branches of insular Celtic had grown so far apart by the early Middle Ages that the Irish and the Welsh could no longer communicate easily, and consequently their literatures followed their own widely divergent paths. The position is further complicated by the fact that modern insular Celtic tongues, their connection with the ancient continental Celtic tongues notwithstanding, in many respects resemble the Hamitic-Semitic languages of North Africa and the Near East (for example Arabic, Berber and ancient Egyptian) more closely than they do Greek and Latin. The pre-Celtic population of Ireland and Britain could possibly have come from North Africa, and if so these typological resemblances may be due to the effects of a pre-Indo-European substrate and the lingering influence of pre-Celtic speech habits.[9]

The application of the term 'Celtic' to different phenomena from prehistory to the present thus owes more to the subjective viewpoint of the modern observer than to any fundamental inner unity between them. Only with great reservations can we infer a Celtic nationhood or links with the proto-Celtic tongue from the archaeological data of prehistoric or early historical times. Furthermore, medieval Irish and Welsh literature cannot simply be described as 'Celtic'. For one thing, we can see many creative innovations and adaptations of foreign cultural influences alongside the archaic and conservative features; for another, the medieval Irish, Scots, Welsh and Bretons lacked precisely that sense of cultural unity and specialness that sometimes colours modern understanding of these literatures.

The application of the term 'Celtic' in modern usage is thus qualitatively quite different in different fields: a Celtic language may be identified by characteristic phonological and morphological features, but 'Celtic' here is really an arbitrary modern designation, and does not indicate a resemblance between these languages or any strong sense of community among their speakers. The use of the name 'Celt' to mean a unified ethnic group is easily shown to be a fiction of classical ethnography. That it is dubious is clear from the mistaken view that the Germani were Celts, or the barely tenable separation of the Celtic inhabitants of Britain and Ireland. At the same time, this use of the term fully merits closer consideration, as the fiction of a united Celtic nation played a considerable role in the minds of the Greeks and Romans and is therefore not to be under-estimated in understanding ancient history. The same applies to the notion, much in favour today, of 'Celtic spirituality'. While the concept thus designated is certainly as baseless as that of a unified Celtic nation, statements and suppositions referring to it fully repay closer investigation, as they may say little about the ancient Celts but a great deal about western intellectual history in the modern era.

For a history of the Celts, these reflections yield two conclusions. The first is that the proper focus in any study should be central and western European antiquity, where Celtic culture shows notable unity and also displays its greatest historical significance when set against the cultures of the Mediterranean area. The second is that the history of the Celts should not be seen as ending with the Romanisa-tion of Gaul and the advance of Germanic tribes into the former Celtic homeland. While it is certainly possible to understand the medieval cultures of the Irish, Scots, Welsh and Bretons outside their common Celtic origins, it is also legitimate to trace the continuing existence of Celtic traditions and their significance for the history of these peoples from their conversion to Christianity until the dawn of the modern era. The fact that the modern era itself cannot be excluded should be apparent from the foregoing, for this era was the first to give rise to a sense of community among the modern speakers of Celtic tongues, as well as the modern image of the ancient Celts and their history.

Let us now turn to the beginnings of this history.

PART I

The Celtic Cultures of the Ancient World

CHAPTER I

The Beginnings of Celtic History

LIFE IN THE IRON AGE: ECONOMY AND SOCIETY IN WEST HALLSTATT CULTURE

The period from the Greek geographers' and historians' first mention of the Celts by name until the political decline of the continental Celts, as a result of the expansion of the Roman empire and Germanic pressure, spans the last six centuries BC. Within this period we meet the Celts in an area extending from the Iberian peninsula in the west, across present-day France and northern Italy and the Balkans into Asia Minor in the east. The writings of antiquity and archaeological evidence form the main sources of our knowledge of the Celts of that era, but written sources mostly skim lightly over long stretches of time, so archaeology often provides our only information. To archaeology we also owe the greater part of our knowledge of daily life, forms of economic activity and settlement, and the structure of society and religion in those centuries.

The first archaeological evidence of the Celts of central Europe appears in the late West Hallstatt culture, which in the sixth and fifth centuries BC extended from southern France across Switzerland into south-western Germany.[1] The material underpinnings of this civilisation were provided mainly by agriculture and animal husbandry, but crafts and trade were also important. Evidence of these areas is seen clearly in archaeological remains, and from these we can also draw valuable conclusions concerning the organisation of society, the world-view and the religious outlook of the period. Naturally, the environment in which the early Celts lived differed in many respects from our own. Compared with modern conditions, the landscape

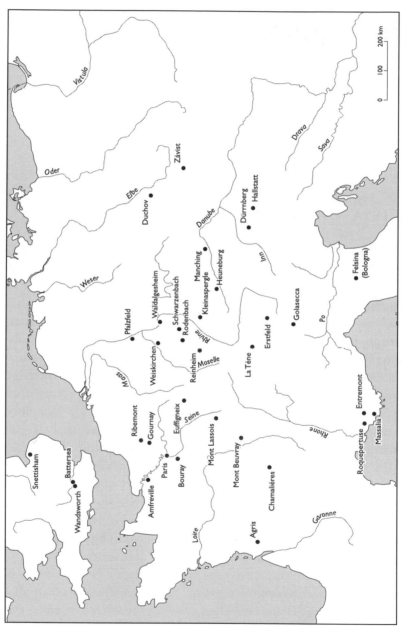

Map 1: Celtic sites in Europe

they inhabited was largely untouched, except for larger settlements. There was no developed network of land routes, and natural water-courses provided the chief means of transporting merchandise. No streams and rivers were controlled, and vast forests harboured a great variety of animals. The mobility of the greater part of the population was limited, and most people's lives ran on well defined tracks and within a relatively restricted cultural area.

With regard to land use, the early Celts of central Europe belong in a tradition that can be traced, using archaeological deposits, from the Neolithic, through the Bronze and Iron Ages, and into the Middle Ages.[2] The wooden plough was introduced into early European farming as far back as the third millennium BC, and the Celts knew a much improved version with an iron ploughshare. Crops such as barley, rye, oats, emmer, spelt and wheat, fibrous plants such as hemp and flax, and legumes such as peas, lentils and horse beans were cultivated, as well as woad for dying fabrics.

The most widespread domestic animal of the period was the ox, which could be used as a draught animal in the fields and for transporting heavy loads. The meat was eaten and the hide made into leather, while the cows provided milk and butter. Pig-rearing was most significant inland, as woodland pasture was the pig's most important food source until the introduction of the potato in the early modern age, and herds of swine could be kept only close to large beech and oak forests. Bone remnants show that both cattle and pigs were markedly smaller than the corresponding wild species and smaller than modern breeds, a fact which is attributed to the difficulty of caring for the beasts during the winter. Goats and sheep were less widespread than cattle and pigs. Sheep were reared mainly for their wool and played only a secondary role as a source of meat. Dogs were probably used as watch and guard animals, and to control vermin such as rats. In addition, according to later accounts by Greek and Roman authors, specially trained hunting dogs were used to track, hunt down and kill game. The Celtic name of a hunting dog especially prized for its speed, *vertragos*, was noted by the Greek author Arrian in the second century BC in his *Kynegetika* (*On Hunting*) and also occurs in Old French texts in the forms *veltre* or *viautre*. In the first century AD the Greek geographer Strabo (*Geography* 4, 5, 2) and in 283–4 AD the Roman poet Nemesianus (*Cynegetica* 219) report the export of British hunting dogs to Rome.

Unlike dogs, the cat was not introduced into central Europe until the influence of the Roman conquest was felt. The domestic fowl, descended from the red jungle fowl of India, was introduced at the beginning of the Iron Age to the regions north of the Alps from the Mediterranean area and may have been considered somewhat exotic by the early Celts. Hens had little economic importance, perhaps because they did not yet lay an egg every day. The prominence of cocks in the archaeological evidence has given rise to the view that at first poultry were kept primarily as ornamental fowl, on account of their brightly coloured plumes. Deposits of wild animals' bones in settlements show the wide variety of animals hunted by the early Celts: in addition to big game such as aurochs, bison, bear, red deer and wild boar, smaller animals such as roe deer, badgers, beavers, hares, wolves, foxes and many kinds of birds were hunted. Hunting, however, was probably motivated by the need to protect livestock or prevent damage to crops, rather than a need for meat. In view of the small returns for the large expenditure of time, hunting must have been mainly a privilege of the upper stratum of society.

Crafts were highly developed and specialised.[3] Celtic pottery belongs to a tradition which in central Europe reaches back as far as the fifth millennium BC. At first the slow-turning potter's wheel was used, with today's fast-turning wheel encroaching from the Mediterranean towards the end of the Hallstatt period and being universally adopted in the centuries that followed. The multiple uses of Hallstatt ceramics can be seen from the great variety of types of vessel. The pots were often decorated with incised or stamped geometrical patterns, or painted with black, white, grey and red dye. Woodwork was also much prized. It was needed above all for the construction of dwellings and fortresses, and for the production of barrels, vats and pails, as well as for building four-wheeled carts with spoked wheels. Glass is found, among the West Hallstatt Celts, almost exclusively in the form of (imported) coloured beads in the graves of women and children. The oldest Celtic glass-making workshops date from the fourth century BC and existed primarily to produce ornaments. The use of glass for tableware, mirrors and windows was unknown among the ancient Celts. Only occasional specimens of weaving have survived, pointing to a highly developed technique, practised in special workshops. The materials used in spinning and weaving included fibrous bark, flax and wool, of which wool has survived better than the others. The fibres were spun into yarn and worked into cloth on tall frame-shaped looms. Natural vegetable and mineral dyes were used as colouring agents, and brightly patterned cloth could be produced using the dyed yarn. The bones of wild animals and the antlers of stags, also worked by hand, yielded decorative articles in addition to tool handles, combs, awls and needles. The decorative articles included strings of threaded beads and slides, with which individual threads of beaded necklaces were separated and held apart.

Metalwork was of overriding importance. The early Celts worked iron, bronze, gold and, less commonly, silver, and it is possible to see a distinction between the manufacture of weapons, coarse work and artistic work. Iron, which unlike bronze was forged rather than smelted, was used in weapons (spear- and arrow-heads, swords and shield mountings), tools (axes, hammers, tongs), household utensils (knives, shears, meat forks, roasting spits, fire-dogs), agricultural implements (shovels, hoes, sickles, scythes) and clothing accessories such as clips (or brooches) and belt buckles. The high technical level is illustrated by a dagger found in Lake Neuchâtel near Estavayer-le-Lac in the Swiss canton of Fribourg. The handle, blade and scabbard consist of forty-five components, ingeniously joined together by twenty-nine rivets and two solderings (see Spindler 1996, 229).

Bronze was used in articles of clothing and jewellery, tableware and ornamental fittings. For casting bronze, the *cire perdue* (lost wax) method was utilised, in which the object to be cast was first modelled in wax, then coated in clay. The mould thus produced was then heated to melt the wax, and the molten bronze poured into the cavity. A form of intarsia, in which iron objects were decorated with fine inlaid bronze wire, was also popular. Gold, which was found in rivers and mined in both open-cast and underground mines, was used primarily for making jewellery.

Since reliable representations of the early Celts are lacking, an impression of their costumes and appearance can be formed only from grave goods. There are difficulties in this, since in many cases the grave goods may have been made solely for burial while others must have remained in the possession of the living. However, it is still possible to draw a few general conclusions (see J. Biel in Bittel et al. 1981, 138–59 and Spindler 1996, 265–99). The fibula – a bronze or iron clasp constructed on the principle of the safety pin – is the most widespread and typical item, and first appears in the late West Hallstatt culture (known to archaeologists as Hallstatt D), as a replacement for the earlier pin. As fibulae underwent much change in size and shape, they provide archaeologists with a useful point of reference for dating their finds when other indications are lacking. Characteristic items in the graves of females are hairpins, found singly, in pairs or in larger numbers in the area of the head. They presumably served as decorative fastenings for caps, veils or head-bands, to which the bronze rings often found in elaborately furnished graves may also belong. Tubular or solid cast bronze torcs, as well as necklaces of beads made of glass, amber, bone, horn, agate and bronze, served as neck adornments. The arm rings, bracelets and armlets, found mostly in pairs, display a great variety of types. Barrel-type armlets made of bronze plate or sapropelite (a glossy black bituminous coal), covering almost the entire forearm, are characteristic of richly appointed female graves. Belts, sometimes with decorative buckles or bronze chains, were used to gather clothes at the waist. The wearing of finger rings was apparently not customary in West Hallstatt culture. Instead, bronze anklets, worn mostly in pairs, are often found.

The evidence of excavated graves shows, on the other hand, that men's dress was relatively unadorned. Bronze, iron and gold torcs are occasionally found, but these must have been a mark of superior status. Unlike women, men never wore arm rings in pairs, and the anklets so often found in female graves are totally absent in male graves. As for the weapons of the early Celts, graves provide little information. Isolated lances or swords have been found, while the short daggers typical of rich graves seem to have been worn as marks of status and not actually used. However, it is unlikely that the graves reflect reality here, since not only swords but also defensive items such as helmets, shields, breastplates and greaves seem to have existed in central Europe even in the Bronze Age, so no doubt were also known to the early Celts.

The majority of the population lived in small open villages, which often lay among tilled fields close to streams or rivers.[4] As fertile land was preferred for this purpose, subsequent land use means that these settlements can rarely be located. We therefore know much more about the fortified hilltop settlements, which were in fact far fewer in number, than we do about small villages, hamlets and farmsteads. Dwellings usually had a single storey and were mostly built of timber and wattle and daub. The floor was often of beaten clay, and the roof made of straw, rushes or bark. An open fire provided warmth, and the smoke escaped through an opening in the roof.

Trade and commerce played a major role in the Celtic economy. Both raw materials and finished goods were sometimes conveyed over distances of hundreds of kilometres (see Kimmig 1985 and Spindler 1996, 316–54). One such trading commodity was amber, which in ancient times was found mostly on the coasts of West Jutland and East Prussia. Known in the Bronze Age from the south of England to Greece, amber was much prized by the early Celts, above all in the form of beads, rings, pendants and inlaid work. Most finds of amber come from graves, and it is only rarely discovered in the excavation of settlements. Another valuable trading commodity was salt, which in prehistoric times was used chiefly to preserve meat and to work hides and metals. In central Europe at the beginning of the first millennium BC, an increase in demand can be observed, resulting perhaps from changes in climatic conditions. One of the first and most important salt-mining centres from the ninth to the fifth century BC was the Upper Austrian Salzkammergut, near Hallstatt on the west bank of Lake Hallstatt. Another important salt-trading point developed around 600 BC at the Dürrnberg, on the west bank of the Salzach about fifteen kilometres south of Salzburg. In about 500 BC a hill fort was established on the precipitous mountain ridge now known as the Ramsauerkopf, while less advantageous sites were used as burial grounds and numerous workshops were established in the Ramsautal.[5]

What gives the early Celtic, late Hallstatt culture its distinctive character and separates it fundamentally from previous centuries is the active trade with the civilisations of the Mediterranean, especially with the Greek colony of Massalia (Marseilles), the Veneti of the northern Adriatic and the Etruscans in central and northern Italy (see Fischer 1973, W. Kimmig in Bittel et al. 1981, 248–78 and Kimmig 1992). From there the Celts imported handicraft wares such as bronze vessels and ceramics, raw materials such as coral, and luxury foodstuffs, in particular wine. In many cases not only the products but also the traders must have found their way from the south over the Alps into the centres of Celtic culture. How the Celts paid for such goods exceeds our knowledge, but raw materials such as gold, iron or pelts, and perhaps even slaves, may have been used. The distribution of the remains of these wares shows that these Mediterranean imports were in no sense everyday necessities, but rather costly luxuries, the preserve of a small elite.

PRINCELY GRAVES AND PRINCELY CENTRES: THE SELF-IMAGE OF A SOCIAL ELITE

In 1876, agricultural work near Hundersingen on the upper Danube uncovered gold jewellery and bronze vessels in prehistoric burial mounds. The Stuttgart curator of antiquities immediately embarked on further investigation at the site and termed these richly furnished burial sites '*Fürstengräber*' or 'princely graves'. Since that time German-speaking archaeologists have applied this term to a series of burial sites with precious grave goods from the sixth and fifth centuries BC. These count among the earliest evidence of Celtic culture in central Europe.[6]

The prime characteristic of the princely graves of the late Hallstatt period is the outward extravagance and often monumental scale evident in their construction, which required a large measure of communal organisation and considerable man-hours. They are further characterised by the presence of valuable commodities, including Mediterranean imports and objects made of precious metals, especially gold. It is also worth noting the conspicuous proximity of these graves to fortified hill settlements, which also often differ from those in less prominent situations in that they contain the remains of Mediterranean imports. All the evidence indicates that the denizens of these so-called *Fürstensitze*, or 'princely centres', and those buried in the nearby graves, were members of a politically influential and economically powerful tribal aristocracy, which maintained wide-ranging trading relations. The large area of the settlements and in part also the existence of later building have meant that exploration of the early Celtic princely centres of the late Hallstatt period has been most incomplete. In addition, many of the graves had already been robbed in ancient times, while others were excavated with the most modest of equipment and intentions in the nineteenth century and therefore incompletely documented. Only those sites excavated in the most recent past provide a graphic picture of the original appearance of these settlements and graves and the lives of those who built them.

The most studied early Celtic princely centre is the Heuneburg, which lies on the upper Danube between Hundersingen and Binzwangen, and whose original Celtic name we do not know (see the surveys by S. Schiek and W. Kimmig in Bittel et al. 1981, 369–90; also Kimmig 1983a). In 1921 the first exploratory excavations here discovered the traces of a late Hallstatt settlement. Earlier excavators had put forward a hypothesis that the builders of the large neighbouring burial mound lived here, and the extensive archaeological investigations between 1950 and 1977 established this with much greater certainty. Today the history of the Heuneburg can be traced from the Bronze Age to the early Middle Ages, and all the evidence suggests that the period of early Celtic settlement from the beginning of the sixth century until about the end of the fifth century BC represents a splendid high point. The artificially levelled area of the Heuneburg forms a rough triangle, 300 metres long and 150 metres across. In keeping with native tradition, the whole site was originally fortified with a wall of timber and earth. Early in the sixth century BC, however, it was completely redesigned in a fashion most unusual in central Europe, when a three-to-four metre wall of dried mud-bricks was built on footings of limestone blocks, in a style reminiscent of contemporary Greek city defences. To do this, several thousand cubic metres of squared stones had to be transported from a limestone quarry six kilometres away. The continuous wall had two gates, and at least ten projecting bastions provided additional protection. Although these fortifications probably stood for over half a century, the mud-brick wall was demolished, for reasons unknown to us, following a devastating fire towards the end of the sixth century BC. After this the Heuneburg regained its original central European aspect following the construction of a timber and earthen rampart.

Like the external fortifications, the internal construction was based on a precise plan. The individual structures were separated from each other by narrow alleyways, and surrounding guttering collected some of the rainwater in butts and channelled the rest of it out under the wall. All the buildings, from the smallest to the largest farmsteads and halls with several naves, were built entirely of wood.

The sole archaeological remains to be seen, however, are the foundations, while all details of the buildings themselves, their windows, doors and roofs are largely unknown. The great quantity of iron and bronze debris, broken casting moulds, crucibles and corresponding fixtures in the dwellings in the south-east corner of the site have led archaeologists to conclude that it was probably occupied by the artisans' quarters. In the north of the site stood buildings which, instead of the usual earthen floor, had a tiled floor of neatly fitted mud-bricks. It is likely that the homes of the elite were situated here, with perhaps also a place of worship or a meeting-place. In the environs of the fortified area, numerous burial mounds may still be seen to this day and, unlike the settlement, these were excavated in the mid-nineteenth century.

Hohmichele, two kilometres west of the settlement, is one of the largest burial mounds in central Europe, measuring almost eighty metres in diameter and fourteen metres in height (see Riek and Hundt 1962). It was partially excavated for the first time in 1937–8, when it turned out that the central burial chamber, timber-built and carpeted with an ox-hide, had been plundered in antiquity. However, some twelve metres south-east of the central chamber, in a timber-lined chamber, the sumptuously appointed grave of a man and his wife was found intact, complete with a four-wheeled cart, harness fittings for a pair of horses and a large bronze cauldron, given as burial gifts.

The masters of the Heuneburg owed their economic power to the extraction of raw materials like iron ore and clay on the one hand, as well as to their control over the important long-distance trade routes that led along the Danube and through the valleys of the Wutach and the upper Rhine to the west, and over the Hegau and central Switzerland across the Alpine passes to Italy. It is not only the Mediterranean influences in the construction of the fortifications that testify to wide-ranging and active contact with the Mediterranean area, but also the numerous fragments of imported ceramics from the South of France, Italy and Greece, which came to light during the excavations. Herodotus's report of the source of the Danube being 'among the Celts' (*Histories* 2, 33), who may have come from the Heuneburg area and been trading partners of the early Greeks, is perhaps a direct echo of these contacts.

The early Celtic princely centre of Mont Lassois, in the far west of the West Hallstatt culture, also lay on one of the important long-distance trade routes.[7] Situated on a steep hill on the left bank of the upper Seine, this site, fortified by a rampart and ditch, may have been one of the first trading points for the much prized Cornish tin. This could no longer be taken across the Straits of Gibraltar, following the victory of the Carthaginians over the Greeks in the naval battle of Alalia in 535 BC, and instead had to be transported to the Greek colonies in the South of France, including Massalia, by a land route through the valleys of the Seine and Rhône. The artefacts in the settlement deposits imported directly from the south include the remains of black-figure Attic pottery, wine amphorae and raw coral, which was fashioned into jewellery in local workshops. Further evidence of close contact with the Mediterranean littoral is provided by the pottery made in the Mont Lassois area, which shows traces of its southern origins in its style of painting, ornamentation, shaping and treatment of the surface.

In the vicinity of Mont Lassois four burial barrows were investigated as early as the nineteenth century, but only sparsely documented, owing to the archaeological practices of the time. A bronze cauldron and an iron tripod have been partially preserved, along with the remains of several four-wheeled carts, pieces of harness and gold bracelets and earrings, and these, together with the monumental scale of the barrows, indicate the high standing of the individuals buried here. The most significant discovery at Mont Lassois occurred in January 1953, when an exploratory excavation on the completely flat meadowland close to the bank of the Seine, not far from Vix, revealed a princely burial site from the mid-fifth century BC, as yet undisturbed. Beneath a burial mound about forty-two metres in diameter, which had later been levelled, in a pit more than two metres deep, excavators found a timber-lined burial chamber, measuring about three by three metres. In addition to a poorly preserved skeleton, it contained the metal remains of an elaborately finished four-wheeled cart and an extensive collection of drinking wares. Of the personal belongings of the person interred, there remained eight fibulae, several beads of stone and amber from a necklace, arm rings and anklets, and a decorated tubular gold torc with two figures of Pegasus, the winged horse of Greek mythology. The drinking set comprised two Attic ceramic cups, a hemispherical silver vessel, a beaked flagon, two cups with handles, a bronze basin and a huge bronze krater, or wine-mixing vessel, over 1.6 metres high and weighing 208 kilogrammes, and with a capacity of 1,100 litres, the largest metal vessel to survive from antiquity.

Comparable with the Heuneburg and Mont Lassois is the Hohenasperg, to the west of Ludwigsburg, where no archaeological investigation has been possible on the mountain itself owing to extensive subsequent building. It is accepted, however, that one of the most important early Celtic princely centres lay here, first because of its commanding topographical situation, and secondly because of its proximity to several rich burials.[8] The barrow to the south of Ludwigsburg, now known as the Römerhügel ('Roman barrow'), was investigated in the nineteenth century. Two graves were found, and their contents included the remains of a four-wheeled cart plated with sheet-bronze fittings, together with harness trappings, a gold torc and several bronze vessels. Another rich burial, the Grafenbühl, was excavated in 1964–5, but it emerged that the central burial chamber had been plundered soon after the burial. Of the original furnishings, there remained only a few items, including two gold-plated bronze brooches, fragments of drinking equipment, and pieces of a cart with iron fittings, in addition to sundry objects of ivory, bone and amber, which were evidently components of furniture imported from the Mediterranean.

A princely grave in Eberdingen-Hochdorf, discovered in 1968 and investigated in 1978–9, provides a vivid picture of the original wealth of such rich graves.[9] Here, beneath an almost completely levelled grave mound in a field, the archaeologists came upon an undisturbed central burial chamber containing the well preserved skeleton of a man aged about forty. Several of his personal effects, including a birch-bark hat, three fish-hooks and a quiver with arrows, had been buried with him. Moreover, his clothing had been adorned with gold jewellery especially for the burial. He had been laid on a couch of punch-dotted bronze plate, of a type that had never been seen in any previously discovered burials. Among the grave goods was a four-wheeled cart with harness, an extensive range of tableware, including nine drinking horns (one made of iron, the others from aurochs' horns), and a bronze cauldron with a capacity of 500 litres, imported from the Mediterranean. Thanks to favourable atmospheric conditions, the organic material was unusually well preserved and it was possible to draw numerous conclusions about living and

environmental conditions, for example the quiver and arrows provided information about the kinds of wood used, which had been
selected with expert knowledge. The cauldron still contained a
residue of mead, the analysis of which yielded information on its
ingredients and the plant life in the area of the grave, while a study of
the fabric remains provided insights into the material, manufacture
and colouring of the cloth used. In 1985 the Hochdorf barrow was
rebuilt at its original size, six metres high and sixty metres in
diameter, with 7,000 cubic metres of earth and 280 tons of stone.
Following painstaking conservation and restoration work, the original finds are now on display in the Württemberg Landesmuseum in
Stuttgart, and the Hochdorf/Enz Celtic Museum at the site includes
reconstructions of the burial artefacts.

LIFE AFTER DEATH: PRINCELY GRAVES AS A REFLECTION OF BELIEF IN THE HEREAFTER

It is beyond question that the prominent social position of the early
Celtic 'princes' or chieftains rested on their control of wide-ranging
trade routes and thus on economic and political power. It is likely
that this power had a religious and judicial basis as well, although
we can only conjecture on this, in the absence of contemporary
documentary sources. Many of the grave goods, particularly the
four-wheeled carts – sometimes richly decorated – point to the
likelihood that the early Celtic chieftains played a religious or ritual
role. These carts, being lightly built, were ill-suited to the trans-
portation of heavy goods, but the iron felloes and nails indicate that
they were kept in constant readiness for use. It is probable that they
were not merely for prestige, but also for use in ritual or ceremonial
parades. The tillage implement unearthed during the excavation of
the princely grave at Magdalenenberg, near Villingen, probably also
had ritual importance. This consists of two wooden beams, 2.2
metres long, cut straight and squared and joined by five cross-
members 1.5 metres long. We know from parallels in ethnography
that this implement, drawn by oxen, was used to close the furrows
after ploughing and the sowing of seed, to protect the seed against
birds. As the spruce-bole implement from Magdalenenberg shows no
signs of use, it may well be a burial gift connected with a perception

that the ruler had some responsibility for the fertility of the land (see Spindler 1996, 302–4).

The practice, adopted from northern Italy, of placing a stone effigy of the deceased on the top of the burial mound may be connected with a form of the cult of the dead. Perhaps the most impressive Hallstatt era specimen is the effigy discovered in 1963–4 in Hirschlanden near Ludwigsburg (see Spindler 1996, 172–85). It shows the deceased standing upright, naked, with phallus erect. Besides a neck ring, he is wearing a belt with a narrow-bladed dagger thrust into it, as a mark of status, and a flattish head-covering, possibly a representation of a birch-bark hat like the one found later in the Hochdorf barrow. The face appears to be slightly displaced downwards and may show the deceased in a mask. Two limestone figures found in 1992 at the entrance to a cult site close to the Vix burial should probably also be seen as representing an ancestral cult, or cult of heroes (see B. Chaume et al. in Haffner 1995, 43–50).

The scarlet cloak in which the body in the Hochdorf chieftain's grave was wrapped is worthy of special attention. Investigations have shown that this is a product of local weavers' art, but one treated with red dye extracted from the Kermes oak insect, imported from the Mediterranean and no doubt expensive. Whatever symbolic significance the cloak might have had lies beyond our knowledge, owing to the lack of recorded evidence. On the one hand, it may be related to the funerary tradition since red, being the colour of blood, played an important role in prehistoric times. On the other, it might be a token of sovereignty, like the crimson raiment of the Persian and later Hellenic rulers. The nine gold-bound drinking horns interred in the Hochdorf mound also had some symbolic meaning that cannot be determined. The practice of drinking from lavishly decorated ox horns is encountered in central Europe from the second half of the sixth century BC. It probably dates back, through Greek intermediaries, to the drinking customs of nomadic Near Eastern horsemen, but among the Celts such finds are known only from exceptionally rich burials. It is likely that an iron drinking horn was meant to mark the departed as a sovereign, since in the medieval literature of the insular Celts the drinking horn still stood as a metaphor for a ruler.[10]

Taken all together, the princely graves of the West Hallstatt culture known to us so far create the impression that the early Celts perceived the hereafter as a continuation of earthly life, in which the political, economic and very likely the religious elite maintained their leading positions even after death. The opulence of their burial furnishings, unchanged through many generations, cannot fail to astonish. How the early Celts endured the loss of these undoubtedly valuable materials we cannot know. We may only suppose that the economic burden created within their hierarchically structured society led to growing tensions. It is therefore no surprise that a mere 200 years after the rise of the princely centres, with their enormous concentration of political and economic power in the hands of a small elite, far-reaching changes can be seen in the world of the early Celts.

CHAPTER 2

The Early La Tène Culture

SOCIETY IN CRISIS: THE END OF THE HALLSTATT CULTURE

In central Europe during the fifth century BC, there were great social, economic and religious changes, and their causes and circumstances emerge only in broad outline from the archaeological data (see O.-H. Frey in Brun and Chaume 1997, 315–20). It is clear that almost all the late Hallstatt princely centres mentioned in the previous chapter lost their importance at this time, and some of them were completely abandoned. This development is particularly well documented in the case of the Heuneburg, which was abandoned by its inhabitants after a devastating fire in the second half of the fifth century BC and remained largely uninhabited until the early Middle Ages. The fact that the central burial chambers of many late Hallstatt barrows, especially in south-western Germany, were entered and looted soon after the interment may be related to the abandonment of the settlements (see Driehaus 1978).

In parallel with the decline of the old princely centres, grave deposits suggest the formation of new centres of power in what had previously been the fringes of the West Hallstatt culture. One such region is the area between the Maas and the Rhine, where numerous princely burials were laid out in the fifth and fourth centuries BC, in the area of the late Hunsrück-Eifel culture.[1] In 1849 both the princely graves of Schwarzenbach near Idar-Oberstein were discovered; in 1851 and 1866 the two Weiskirchen princely graves near Merzig-Wadern were found, and in 1869 the grave of the princess in Waldalgesheim, near Bingen was found.[2] Our knowledge of the original state of these graves is strictly limited, however, owing to unsatisfactory methods of extracting and restoring the finds, to say nothing of inadequate documentation of the excavation. A clear picture of the furnishing of such graves emerged only in 1954, with the discovery of the Reinheim grave on the Franco-German border (see Keller 1965 and Echt 1999). Here, about twenty kilometres south-east of Saarbrücken, in a layer of sand and gravel, archaeologists came upon a richly furnished female tomb dating from the middle of the fourth century BC. Although the skeleton had decayed completely in the acidic soil, the grave goods left no doubt that this was a woman from the elite. She wore a gold torc and gold arm- and finger-rings, as well as two bracelets, one made of glass, the other of black shale. On her right lay a bronze hand-mirror, which had originally been placed in a finely woven fabric pouch, and on her left lay several items of jewellery, made of amber, glass and metal, which had presumably been in a container of organic material. In addition, the grave contained a table- and drinking-set, consisting of a gilded bronze flagon, two bronze platters and the remains of two drinking vessels. Most of these early La Tène princely graves in the area of the late Hunsrück-Eifel culture are found singly or in groups of up to three burial mounds. Occasionally a princely necropolis of up to sixteen mounds occurs, but these are always situated at some distance from the burial grounds of the general population. The princely barrows were mostly situated on ranges of hills with a good view, close to main roads and important trade routes, as well as to hill forts.

Another region where several thousand Celtic graves from the fifth century BC have been found since the second half of the nineteenth century is northern Champagne (see P. Roualet in Moscati et al. 1991, 147–54). These graves, from the so-called Marne culture, are usually in burial grounds of varying size, outside the settlements or along what were once main routes. The bones of animals and the richly decorated ceramic vessels testify to the fact that many of the deceased were buried with supplies of solid and liquid sustenance. Women were often buried with their jewellery and men with their weapons. In the least elaborate graves the range of weapons was limited to two or three javelins, while the richer graves held a sword, a dagger and a helmet as well. Members of the leading military elite were interred with a light two-wheeled war chariot, of which only the bronze fittings of the wheels, axles and harness have survived. One of the most famous of these chariot burials is the Somme-Bionne tumulus, roughly thirty kilometres north-east of Châlons-sur-Marne

(see I. M. Stead in Moscati et al. 1991, 174–5). Besides the possessions and chariot of the deceased, it contained an Etruscan beaked
flagon and a red-figure Greek cup from about 420 BC, evidence of
ongoing contact between the Celts and the Mediterranean.

From the fifth and fourth centuries BC, rich burials are also known
in regions to the east of the large late Hallstatt seats of princely
power. For example, at the Dürrnberg near Hallein in 1932, in a
grave already plundered in antiquity, a beaked flagon from the
second half of the fifth century BC, modelled on an Etruscan pattern,
was found next to a two-wheeled chariot (see Moosleitner 1985).
Another princely grave was discovered in 1959 on the Moserstein,
the central hilltop in the Dürrnberg settlement area. Besides a sword,
helmet, arrowheads and spearheads, the grave goods included the
remnants of a two-wheeled chariot, a bronze canteen, a large bronze-
plated bucket, and a Greek clay cup which had been used as a
scooping and drinking vessel (see *Kelten* 1980, 227–8 and F.
Moosleitner in Moscati et al. 1991, 170). Over 200 other graves bear
witness to the considerable prosperity enjoyed by the Celtic inhabitants of the Dürrnberg, principally after the decline of salt-mining
in Hallstatt, further to the east. Several burials in western Bohemia
are comparable in their furnishings, including that at Chlum, discovered at the beginning of the twentieth century (see J. Michálek in
Moscati et al. 1991, 186–7).

If a new cultural and economic upsurge can be seen in the fifth
century BC in the erstwhile periphery of the world of the early Celts,
in parallel to the decline of the princely centres, there is also evidence
that at least some of the old power centres shared in the early stages
of this development. The best known example of this is the
Kleinaspergle burial mound to the south of Asperg, near Ludwigsburg (see Kimmig et al. 1988). Although the central burial chamber
had been robbed in ancient times, the archaeologists nevertheless
found another rich burial in a neighbouring chamber, containing
some pieces of jewellery and a large drinking service. This included
two red-figure Greek cups, from about 450 BC, which had been
decorated with gold-plating. While the Kleinaspergle, like the
Grafenbühl and Hochdorf barrows, bears a relation to the late
Hallstatt chiefdom at Hohenasperg, the burial discovered in 1879
is more closely comparable with the barrows of the Middle Rhine-
land mentioned above. Whereas the late Hallstatt tombs usually

contain a four-wheeled wagon and at most a dagger as a weapon, one finds in the early La Tène rich burials a light two-wheeled war chariot, and the weapons often include spears, a sword and a helmet. Further clear differences are apparent in the composition of the drinking paraphernalia and in the decoration of the metal objects, which show a previously unknown artistic style.

A WORLD VIEW IN TRANSITION: THE BIRTH OF CELTIC ART

The later phase of the pre-Roman Iron Age, now known as the La Tène period, takes its name from a sandbar near Marin at the northern end of Lake Neuchâtel (Neuenburger See) in Switzerland (see C. Dunning in Moscati et al. 1991, 366–8). Here, from 1857 on, historians discovered more and more iron weapons and items of clothing, in addition to the remains of timber structures. After the initial excavations in 1880–1900, the site was thought to be a shore settlement of the Celtic Helvetii, but modern archaeologists incline to the view that these were sacrificial sites, largely because of the deposits of bones of domestic animals and humans. Interpretations of the overall findings differ widely, but it was soon realised after the first finds that the handwork of the artefacts from La Tène diverged fundamentally from those from the Hallstatt cemetery. Thus, as early as 1874 the name 'La Tène' came into use as a synonym for the last phase of the pre-Roman Iron Age and the emergence of an independent Celtic art.

While Greek, Roman and medieval art has been studied for several centuries, research into Celtic art began much later, in the period between the two world wars. One reason for this is that the history of the pre-Roman Iron Age in central Europe began to take shape only with the rise of modern archaeology, at the end of the nineteenth century and the beginning of the twentieth. Another reason is that the Celts modified the stylistic features of classical art in such an unconventional manner that for a long time observers, accustomed to classical models, viewed Celtic works as aesthetically unsatisfying imitations, devoid of any independent worth. Seen in this light, the Greek and Roman characteristic of measuring the whole of Celtic culture by the standards of classical antiquity became even more apparent. The classical archaeologist Paul Jacobsthal (1880–1957) was the first to point out the artistic independence of the Celts and appreciate it critically, in his *Early Celtic Art*. This work, which appeared while he was in exile in England in 1944, remains a fundamental study to this day.[3]

What strikes the modern observer most forcefully about Celtic art is the absence of those means of artistic expression that play such an important role in medieval, Greek, Roman and early oriental art. There is no monumental building in stone, for example, and specimens of large three-dimensional work in wood, stone or metal are rare. Graphic representations of action and movement are also scarce, as are realistic portraits of humans or animals. The great majority of examples of Celtic art are the product of small-scale work, showing the artists' ability to create jewellery, weapons, and household utensils of all kinds with great devotion to detail and technical perfection. The artists applied above all a highly developed ornamental technique, marked by abstraction and multiplicity of meaning.

In the early La Tène period, that is the fifth and fourth centuries BC, soft and fluid forms were preferred to the stiff geometrical patterns of the late Hallstatt period. Thus, plant motifs and representations of animals, fabulous creatures and human faces were worked into the ornamentation. The stimuli for these innovations came, to some extent, from Etruscan art, while in other cases the influence of the peoples of the eastern steppes, like the Scythians, is possible (see R. Rolle in Brun and Chaume 1997, 243–9). The Waldalgesheim burial near Bingen, mentioned previously, is seminal in the second phase of Celtic art in the fourth and third centuries BC. The so-called 'running tendril' or Waldalgesheim style that takes its name from it is distinguished from earlier works by its intertwined flowing tendrils and coils. In contrast, the so-called Later or Plastic Style, from the third to the first century BC, is characterised by its strongly abstract, three-dimensional ornamentation.

On the European mainland the history of Celtic art ends with the Roman conquest of Gaul in the mid-first century BC, and after that only isolated stylistic features were adopted in provincial Roman art of the imperial period. In Britain and Ireland, on the other hand, Celtic art experienced a flowering in the new era (this is described in Part II of this book). In conjunction with the stylistic features of

Germanic art, Celtic art attained the summit of its development in medieval Irish book-illumination, in metalwork and sculpture in stone. Now, following this introduction to Celtic art, we shall turn our attention to certain works of art which are particularly representative of this period.

While the early Celts of the sixth century BC maintained close contacts with the Greek colony of Massalia, in the fifth century BC trade with the Etruscans of central and northern Italy increased in volume and importance (see Dobesch 1992 and several contributions in *Etrusker* 1992, 158–217). Clear evidence of this is seen in the beaked flagons which were introduced in great numbers from Etruria and imitated or adapted to native tastes by Celtic artisans. One such copy, which can give the modern observer a clear impression of the independence of Celtic craft, was unearthed when the Kleinaspergle barrow was excavated in 1879 (see Megaw 1970, no. 50, and O.-H. Frey in *Hundert Meisterwerke* 1992, 13–16). Unlike the bulbous Etruscan model, the Celtic flagon tapers towards its base, so that the shoulders appear more sharply accentuated and the vessel as a whole produces a more streamlined and dynamic effect. The broader lower end of the handle, where it joins the body, is decorated with the face of a satyr over a palmette, as in Etruscan flagons, but here the craftsman has adapted the model in his own individual manner. The satyr's pointed ears no longer lie to the side, but are right at the top of the head, and the beard is parted and flows into the palmette below. At the upper end of the handle, where a lion's head sometimes appears in Etruscan beaked flagons, the Celtic master has introduced a fabulous creature with pointed ears, protruding eyes and puffed-out cheeks.

Another beaked flagon, discovered in 1932 on the Dürrnberg near Hallein, is similar in shape, although with different decoration (see Megaw 1970, no. 72 and Moosleitner 1985). The body of the vessel is adorned with a raised pattern, repeated nine times, with a semicircular ending at the top and a three-leaved palmette at the bottom. On the handle is a stylised, cat-like beast of prey with round, bulging eyes and cheeks, clasping a human head in its jaws. The strongly protruding eyes with clearly marked pupils and the hair, which is firmly marked by parallel lines on the head resting on the rim of the flagon, are striking. The lower end of the handle is decorated with another, similar head, framed with spiral ornamentation. On the top, at each side of the handle, sit two small predatory quadrupeds, with the twisted tails of some animal hanging from their jaws.

A striking parallel to the form and surrounding raised pattern of the Dürrnberg flagon can be seen in a partially restored beaked flagon, which was found in 1994–5 during the excavation of the Glauberg princely grave near Büdingen in Hessen (see Herrmann and Frey 1996). In this case too a small human head sits at the lower joint of the handle, although the decorative work on this handle is in less prominent relief. The fragility of the handle leads one to suspect that the vessel was not designed for everyday use, but intended only for cult functions or prestige purposes. In several places the flagon is adorned with fine ornamental engraved figures, including lyres, palmettes, spirals and vegetal designs and representations of animals on the lower part of the body and on both sides of the spout. The three-dimensional decoration of the flagon, dominated by a triad at the top, is also striking. The outer figures are two seated animals with human heads, looking back over their shoulders at the shape between them. This figure is a clean-shaven man sitting cross-legged, who may represent a living person, god or deified ancestor. He is bare-headed and dressed in short breeches, an undergarment with half-length sleeves, and leather armour. The realistic reproduction of the leather armour, strongly reminiscent of Greek illustrations from the sixth century BC, is noteworthy, as is the meticulous representation of the man's hair, trimmed short, with ringlets on the forehead and temples, a style also derived from Greek models.

The so-called spouted flagon from the Reinheim princess's tomb, mentioned above (see Megaw 1970, 76–7, and O.-H. Frey in *Hundert Meisterwerke* 1992, 105–9), also illustrates the great importance of ornate metal vessels in burial customs. Its gently rounded body is made of gold-covered bronze plate, and the tubular spout and handle are attached by rivets. The body is ringed by several compass-work relief patterns showing flowers, lyres and ornamental lines in triangular shapes, zigzag lines and diagonal crosses. The decorative figures on the flagon comprise a bearded face at the lower end of the handle, and a man's head directly above a ram's head at the upper end, and a horse with a human head, as shown in later times on Celtic coins, as a pommel on the lid. Similar ornamentation and figures can be seen on the spouted flagon from the Waldalgesheim tomb, which features a three-dimensional image of a horse as a cover piece, a ram's head at the top of the handle, and a man's head at the lower end (see Megaw 1970, no. 78 and Joachim et al. 1995, 38–53). The existence elsewhere of this combination of a human head with a ram's head leads to the hypothesis that this motif had some clearly defined mythological significance which we cannot now determine.

Among the best known and most impressive specimens of Celtic art are the richly decorated finger rings, armlets and neck rings of bronze, iron and gold.[4] They display a wide variety of motifs, including geometric patterns, plant motifs, masks and grotesque faces, and figures of animals and fabulous creatures. The evidence of the deposits shows that the neck rings were worn with the opening at the front, with the ornamentation concentrated on the sides, where it could best be seen. The Rodenbach armlet, whose decoration includes drop-shaped forms, stylised human heads and figures of crouching four-pawed beasts looking backwards, dates from about 400 BC (see Megaw 1970, no. 55, and Eluère 1987, 135–7).

A roughly contemporary gold bracelet from a princely grave at Bad Dürkheim shows six human heads, arranged in pairs amidst decorative features, while the neck ring and arm rings from the Waldalgesheim grave are decorated with stylised faces surrounded by abstract decoration (see Megaw 1970, no. 54, and Joachim et al. 1995, 60–70). Four torcs and three arm rings, found in the summer of 1962 at Erstfeld in the Swiss canton of Uri, amid the high peaks on the road to the St Gotthard pass, probably date from the late fifth or early fourth century BC. Abstract ornaments and entwined bird, human and animal heads form the decoration of the rings, which may have been deposited in these inhospitable heights as a votive offering to a deity.[5]

Outstanding examples of the ornamental decoration of Celtic arms are provided by the two hemispherical ceremonial helmets dating from the fourth century BC, from Amfreville-sous-les-Monts and Agris. The circumstances of the finds indicate that they do not belong to the burial furnishings but probably represent votive offerings for a deity.

The Amfreville helmet was discovered in an old stream bed of the Seine in the department of Eure, south-west of Rouen. On the chased-bronze dome, at about the halfway point, a bronze band runs round the helmet, attached by gold-plated bronze rivets. The main form of decoration on the band consists of running coils. Before being attached, this band was covered with fine gold leaf, which was then pressed so firmly onto the bronze that the decorative pattern came through onto it. On both sides of the band, iron clasps were attached with iron rivets, and are adorned with round enamel inlays. The rim and neck-guard are decorated with a network of iron wires, with the spaces filled mosaic-style by inlaid enamel platelets (see Megaw 1970, no. 110, Eluère 1987, 141–5, and Megaw and Megaw 1989, 112).

The separate parts of the Agris helmet were found between 1981 and 1986 in the cave of Les Perrats near the village of Agris in the department of Charente in western France. The helmet consists of an iron bell with four broad gold-plated bronze bands attached. The ornamentation consists mainly of palmettes, some of which are encrusted with coral. The cheek-guards display a particularly lavish form of decoration in gold and coral, with various floral motifs and the image of a horned serpent set on an iron base (see Eluère 1987, 141–6 and 160 and J. Gomez de Soto in Moscati et al. 1991, 292–3).

The horned serpent also appears in Gallo-Roman sculptures of the imperial period, and doubtless had a mythological significance which we cannot now determine. It is highly likely that Celtic art in many areas bore the stamp of a religious or magical turn of mind, but as yet archaeologists have not identified any generally recognised correspondence between the pre-Roman archaeological and the much later literary legacy.[6] The pictorial language of Celtic art remains largely closed to us, and our knowledge of the religious outlook of the early Celts rests almost exclusively on the few clues provided by the numerous graves.

THE CULT OF THE ANCESTORS AND THE USE OF AMULETS: ASPECTS OF EARLY CELTIC RELIGION

When we examine the graves of the Celtic peoples of central Europe, we are struck first of all by the communal nature of their society and the continuity of their sites. Archaeological research has shown that, in the early Celtic late Hallstatt culture, the grave mounds of the earlier Hallstatt culture (or even of the late Urnfield culture which preceded it) were often in continuous use. The use of the

Bressey-sur-Tille barrow (Côte-d'Or), which was steadily expanded from the late Hallstatt to the early La Tène period, extended over a period of 250 to 300 years (see Spindler 1996, 98–101, 136–45 and 170–1). The Eislfeld graves on the Dürrnberg, which date from the period between 570 and 300 BC, display similar continuity, while the burial ground of Hochgerichtsheide near Wederath, the ancient Belginum, remained in use from the fourth century BC to the end of the fourth century AD (see *Gräber* 1989).

A comparative study of grave deposits shows that while burial rites may have differed from one region to another, they often remained constant for long periods within the generally restricted confines of tightly organised communities. The archaeological data show that most attention was given to the class of person to be buried, the choice of burial site, the choice of cremation or burial, the selection and range of burial gifts, and the position and orientation of the body. Particularly striking is the small proportion of children's graves, which seems low in relation to the undoubtedly high infant mortality rate. One can suppose that only upon attaining a certain age were young men treated as full members of society with the right to a burial (see A. Haffner in *Gräber* 1989, 96–8).

Of the rites which may have accompanied burial, archaeological remains again mostly provide only a hazy picture. The shards of at least thirty shattered clay vessels at the foot of the Hallstatt period burial mound at Tübingen-Kilchberg are probably the remnants of a funeral feast, but they reveal little about the circumstances, the religious motivation or the group of people involved (see S. Schiek in Bittel et al. 1981, 121). The remains of vegetation on the floor of the central chamber at Hochdorf point to the conclusion that the body was preserved for at least four weeks before its final interment, but we know nothing of the religious rites performed during this period (see Biel 1985, 34). It is possible that we have evidence here of the notion, widespread in ancient cultures, that the deceased does not depart from the circle of the living at the moment of death, but only after a certain time has elapsed and special ceremonies have been performed. In view of the parallels with ancient Greek culture, one such ceremony may perhaps be the subject of the picture of a wagon-ride and sword-dance on the bronze burial couch from Hochdorf. However, evidence of actual use shows that this couch was not intended merely to furnish the tomb but also served a real purpose for a long period (see Biel 1985, 36 and 92–113). The surviving evidence is rarely sufficient for us to determine which attitudes accompanied the performance of the traditional burial rites. The fact that before the Hochdorf interment the gold plaques specially prepared for the deceased's shoes were damaged and that the left and right plaques were confused may point to the reverential awe felt by the persons responsible when confronted with death. However, it might also point to their 'professional lack of feeling', as the excavating archaeologists put it (Biel 1985, 82).

The conclusion that everyday items and utensils from this life remained important after death is most clearly supported by the practice of providing burial furnishings for the dead. The difference between burial and cremation may often be merely a question of how the transition from the world of the living to that of the dead was perceived, whereas the view of the afterlife itself may in many cases have been similar. In view of the function of the grave goods, it seems reasonable to posit a real and a symbolic distinction between the two possibilities, although a clear dividing line can hardly be drawn. Thus the five unprepossessing amber beads found at the neck of the Hochdorf chieftain may have served not only as adornments but perhaps as a protective amulet. Weight is lent to this theory by the fact that remnants of worked amber were discovered under the workshop detritus in the barrow, suggesting that the beads were specially prepared for the burial, just like some of the gold jewellery (Biel 1985, 68). Burial goods were clearly not expected to be in the same working order in every case, for example the Hochdorf grave contained two gold serpent fibulae, which, unlike bronze fibulae, could not have functioned effectively owing to the properties of the material (Biel 1985, 78–9). Clearly the symbolic nature of the grave goods was often all-important, regardless of their practical utility. This is supported by the fact that some objects could stand for some larger entity, on the principle of *pars pro toto*: for example instead of a complete set of harness, only the decorative bronze bridle discs might be placed in the grave (see H. Müller-Karpe in *Gräber* 1989, 153–5).

One reason why the Celtic grave monuments have survived so well is that in most cases they were separated from human habitation. The practice of marking off a grave site from its surroundings by means of a ditch or a stone circle, often observed in excavations, may derive from the underlying idea of a division between the dominion of the living and that of the dead (see S. Schiek in Bittel et al. 1981, 120 and Spindler 1996, 162). Confirmation of the observance of a strict separation between the worlds of the living and the dead is found in the fact that objects used in the interment ceremony were often removed from subsequent profane use by being smashed and/or buried.

Side by side with those arguments for a clear separation, there are strong indications that the ancient Celts believed the dead to be linked in some degree with the world of the living. In this connection, we must point first of all to the choice of burial site, which is frequently in close proximity to a settlement (see A. Haffner in *Gräber* 1989, 44–5). An important reason for treating the dead in this manner lies no doubt in the significant role allocated to them in the living's perception of themselves. It could be the case that a community as a whole presented itself to outsiders in a certain way, or it could be that a social elite claimed legitimacy through its origins and registered its privileged position by its burial sites. The prominence of the legitimacy question is particularly striking in the case of the early La Tène princely grave discovered from the air in 1987 beneath the Glauberg hill fort and explored in 1994–6. From the south-eastern side a parade 350 metres long and seven metres wide, lined by deep ditches, runs towards the mound, and preliminary archaeological studies show that this must have been part of a large central shrine with other structures, as yet undiscovered. In June 1996, a life-size sandstone sculpture of an early Celtic warrior with sword and shield was found at the edge of the barrow, and this may have been an idealised representation of the man buried. The warrior has distinctive headgear, which has been described as a leaf-crown, owing to its similarity with mistletoe leaves. Similar headgear is seen on the mask-like heads on a roughly contemporary pillar from Pfalzfeld, which may have originally stood on a grave mound.[7]

Alongside the desire to commemorate the dead, early Celtic burial customs also point to a feeling that the dead represented a threat to those left behind. Indications of this are offered above all by those graves where there is clear evidence of manipulation of the body. One of the Eislfeld graves on the Dürrnberg contained, in addition to two infants in a crouching position, the skeleton of a man, with no burial gifts, whose head and chest had been crushed with a large block of stone. In another grave in the same burial ground, the pelvis of a grown man had been removed and laid on his chest. Furthermore, both the man's thighbones lay unnaturally close together, which might suggest ritual binding (see K. Zeller in *Kelten* 1980, 166). Indications of the use of protective amulets and lucky talismans bear some relation to these practices. It is true that there is no reflection of this in the writings of the classical authors or the medieval literature of the insular Celts, but it is well attested as part of the Celtic burial tradition of pre-Roman central Europe (for extensive documentation see Pauli 1975). A comparison with some well preserved grave furnishings from other regions and eras suggests that amulets were often made of organic material which in most cases has decayed, leaving no trace. Among the items which have survived, there is a preponderance of noise-producing objects such as rattles and metal clappers, miniature representations of small wheels, shoes or feet, axes and human figures, unfinished jewellery or jewellery later rendered unusable such as bracelets or rings, and a wide assortment of objects with no apparent practical purpose, such as pieces of rock crystal, flint arrowheads, fossils, boars' tusks or beads and slides made of bone. That glass and amber objects were not worn primarily as jewellery, but more often as amulets, can be deduced from the fact that they are frequently found with other amulets but are otherwise seldom seen in graves. The fact that the iron objects found in the graves of infants would usually be made of bronze in adult graves suggests that many iron items are amulets. Signs of wear and tear point to the conclusion that many amulets placed in graves had been the personal effects of the deceased. This applies particularly to the numerous objects with holes or eyelets in them, which were often worn on a thread round the neck. On the other hand, amulets found with new-born and stillborn children, and with unusable clothing accessories, are more likely to have been burial gifts, probably manufactured only for the burial.

Statistical studies have shown that in pre-Roman central Europe amulets are especially common in the graves of children and young women and that their use often accompanies manipulations of the corpse. Ethnographic parallels from other cultures suggest that these individuals were seen as having died 'before their time' and should not therefore be interred in the customary fashion. Here the amulets might have served less to protect the dead than those who remained behind. If we consider the pre-Roman graves of central Europe as a whole, the use of amulets appears to be far from uniform in different periods. The fact that it reached a peak in the early La Tène burials may be related to a crisis in Celtic society, and the effects of this crisis will be discussed in the next chapter.

CHAPTER 3

Celtic Expansion

THE THRUST TO THE SOUTH: CELTIC MIGRATIONS AS SEEN BY THE CLASSICAL AUTHORS

> The Gauls, imprisoned as they were by the Alps as by an insurmountable barrier, first found a motive for overflowing into Italy from the circumstance of a Gallic citizen from Switzerland named Helico, who had lived in Rome because of his skill as a craftsman, [and] brought with him when he came back some dried figs and grapes and some samples of oil and wine.

Thus does Pliny the Elder, in the mid-first century AD, explain the advance of the Celts into the Mediterranean region (*Natural History* 12, 2, 5). In the third century AD the historian Justin puts forward a different motivation in his summary of the world history written at the time of Christ by Pompeius Trogus, a historian born in southern Gaul:

> The reason the Gauls came to Italy and sought new areas to settle in was internal unrest and ceaseless fratricidal strife. When they tired of this and made their way to Italy they drove the Etruscans from their homeland and founded Milan, Como, Brescia, Verona, Bergamo, Trento and Vicenza.
>
> (*Epitome of the Philippic History* 20, 5, 7–8)

A third explanation is given by the historian Livy, a contemporary of Pompeius Trogus.

We have learned the following about the migration of the Gauls into Italy: when Tarquinius Priscus reigned in Rome, the Celts, who form one of the three parts of Gaul, were under the domination of the Bituriges, and this tribe supplied the Celtic nation with a king. This was Ambigatus, who had distinguished himself in public affairs by his ability and his golden touch. Under his rule the harvests in Gaul were so rich and the population so great that the great numbers seemed hardly governable. As the king was already advanced in years and wished to relieve his kingdom of a burdensome throng, he announced that he meant to send Bellovesus and Segovesus, his sister's sons, two enterprising young men, to find such homes as the gods might assign to them by augury. They were to take with them as many men as they pleased, so that nobody would be capable of holding them up. Whereupon to Segovesus were by lot assigned the Hercynian highlands; but to Bellovesus the gods proposed a far pleasanter road, into Italy.

(*History of Rome* 5, 34, 1–4)

The sources on which these reports are based cannot now be identified. While Livy in his remark about the threefold division of Gaul is patently relying on a similar statement by Caesar (*De Bello Gallico* 1, 1, 1), the story of King Ambigatus and his two nephews may date back to a local tradition of the Celts of northern Italy. Whatever the case, in seeking the causes of the migration of the Celts into the Mediterranean region, modern scholarship can only point to the theories of the classical historians. A degree of overpopulation, inner unrest and social tension, as well as the attractions of the southern regions and their material culture, may in fact have provided the decisive motivation for the population movements that caused much anxiety in the ancient world in the fourth and third centuries BC.

A detailed picture of the migrations of the Celtic peoples cannot be inferred from the reports of the classical writers or the archaeological deposits. It is highly likely that 'Celt' is merely a collective appellation, denoting land-hungry settlers and marauding warrior hordes from the north and embracing population groups of different ethnic and linguistic provenance. Our understanding of the progress of the

Celtic migrations is complicated by the fact that most of the surviving documentary sources begin their accounts only with the initial contact with the peoples of the Mediterranean. This means that events in the Celtic heartland of central Europe remain largely without illumination. The Celtic presence in the Iberian peninsula, northern Italy and Asia Minor is discussed in Chapters 5 to 7 of this book, while the history and culture of the Celtic peoples in Britain and Ireland will be the subject of Parts II and III. The following pages deal primarily with the expansion of the Celts to the south-east, which is widely reflected in Greek sources and was destined to exert a formative influence on the classical perception of the Celts.

In the fourth century BC the historian Ephorus of Cyme (quoted by Strabo *Geography* 4, 4, 6) described the Celts as 'friends of the Greeks' (*Philhéllēnes*). This view is supported in the first century BC by an anonymous description of the coasts of Europe, which gives prominence to the adoption by the Celts of Greek customs and their friendly relations with the Greeks (Pseudo-Scymnus, *Periplus Europae* 183ff.). This positive evaluation of relations between the Celts and Greeks probably rests on sources from the sixth century BC, now lost to us, which stressed the harmony between the Greek colony of Massalia and the Celts of southern Gaul. However, by the third century BC at the latest, the Greek perception of the Celts had undergone a fundamental change. In the fourth century BC Aristotle had already described the Celts as unruly and not amenable to government (*Eudemian Ethics* 1229b 25–30 and *Politics* 1327b 23–7). Plato, his mentor, disapproved of their drunkenness (*Laws* 1, 637d), the poet Callimachus described them as 'latter-day Titans', meaning enemies of the gods, in the third century BC (*Hymn to Delos* 171ff.), and an epigram in *Anthologia Graeca* (7, 492) castigates them for their 'wanton high spirits, which recognise no authority'. One decisive factor in this altered perception of the Celts was the raids by rapacious Celtic bands in the Balkans and Greece. Another was the use of Celtic warriors as mercenaries in armed conflict between the peoples of the Mediterranean.[1] As early as the fifth and fourth centuries BC, Celtic tribes had advanced into the homeland of the Venetic and Illyrian tribes on the upper Adriatic and in the Balkans. The tyrant Dionysius I of Syracuse secured their support when preparing to strike at the rich Italian trading states of the northern Adriatic during his war against Carthage in 386 BC. When in 369 BC

Dionysius brought his own troops to support the Spartans in the war against Thebes, there were Celtic mercenaries among them. They also played an important part in the following decades in the wars between Carthage and Syracuse, and were deployed by the tyrant Agathocles of Syracuse against the city of Carthage itself, during his invasion of North Africa in 310–307 BC. In 335 BC Alexander the Great sought to harmonise relations with the Celts during his Balkan campaign, as Strabo reports, referring to one of Alexander's most important field commanders:

> Ptolemy, the son of Lagus, says that during this campaign some Celts who lived about the Adriatic joined Alexander for the sake of establishing friendship and hospitality. The king received them kindly and asked them when drinking what it was that they most feared, thinking they would say himself, but they replied that they feared nothing, unless it were that Heaven might fall on them, although indeed they added that they put above everything else the friendship of such a man as he.
>
> (*Geography* 7, 3, 8)

After Alexander's death in 323 BC, Celtic attacks on his collapsing empire became increasingly frequent. Having conquered Thrace, Macedonia and Illyria in 280 BC, the Celtic raiders attacked Thessaly and Greece from Thrace one year later. The Greeks succeeded only with difficulty in holding back their attempts to sack the Temple of Apollo at Delphi until the onset of winter forced the invaders to withdraw. After costly battles in a fighting retreat, the Celts finally withdrew from Greece and Macedonia and established themselves in various parts of the north Balkan area. Some of them founded the kingdom of Tylis, so named after its capital, on Mount Haemus in Thrace. The Scordisci tribe settled on the lower Sava and there founded their capital Singidunum, on the site of present-day Belgrade.[2] The expulsion of the Celts from Greece, however, led to no interruption in the Hellenic kings' practice of deploying Celtic mercenaries. The Macedonian king Antigonus Gonatas, who in 277 BC decisively defeated the Celts at Lysimachea, employed them in battle against his rival Pyrrhus, who for his part also hired them and allowed them to plunder the royal Macedonian tombs at Aigai.

When King Ptolemy II (Philadelphus) was at war with his brother Magas, Antigonus Gonatas lent him several thousand Celtic mercenaries, who, following a rebellion, were imprisoned on an island in the Nile and perished there. More and more Celtic troops were recruited in the kingdom of Tylis, with which the Ptolemaic kings of Egypt maintained good relations. The regions settled by the Celts in northern Italy constituted another source from which Carthage raised mercenaries for the assault on Rome and its allies during the Punic Wars.

The extent to which the armed conflicts of the fourth and third centuries BC influenced the perception of the Celts in the classical period and thus also in the early Christian era is only now becoming fully apparent, for the results of modern archaeology, along with a critical reading of the Greek and Latin texts, compel us to revise this picture in many respects. In their descriptions of the Celts classical authors were inclined to blend real observations with literary clichés and mythic perceptions. A typical example is the idea, first set forth in the fourth and third centuries BC in the work of Timaeus of Tauromenion, that the Galatians (that is, the Celts) were descended from Galatos, a son of Polyphemus (the cyclops outwitted by Odysseus in Homer's *Odyssey*), and the water nymph Galatea.[3] If the name Galatea could serve to explain the origin of the name of the Galatians, the genealogical connection with the uncouth giant Polyphemus offered a possible explanation of the supposedly typical characteristics of the Celts, which included extraordinary physical strength and limited intellectual powers. The first attempts at a stylised presentation of the Celts in literature modelled on Homer's Cyclops can be seen in the work of Callimachus and the *Anthologia Graeca*, mentioned above. The attempt emerges more clearly in the writings of Polybius, in whose view the Celts of northern Italy were a completely uncivilised people who slept on beds of leaves raked into heaps (*Histories* 2, 17, 8–12). Just as Homer showed Polyphemus as slow-witted and obtuse (*The Odyssey* 9, 361 and 442), Strabo also emphasises the foolishness and simple-mindedness of the Celts, which enabled cleverer peoples to take advantage of them (*Geography* 4, 4, 2 and 5). Aristotle had already declared that the intelligence of the northern races was quite undeveloped (*Politics* 1327b 23), and the Apostle Paul may be referring to such views in chapter 3 of his Epistle to the Galatians when he addresses the Christian Celts of Asia

Minor, who were uncertain in their faith, with the words, 'Oh, you foolish Galatians!' Even the *Astérix* comic books of the twentieth century adhere to the traditional classical view of the Celts, showing the Gauls as good-natured, childlike ruffians.[4] By contrast, a more realistic appraisal is given by Diodorus Siculus (*Historical Library* 5, 31, 1), who may be taking up a remark by Caesar (*De Bello Gallico* 7, 22, 1) when he stresses the Celts' keen intelligence and ability to learn.

While the classical accounts of the Celts and their culture are therefore to be treated with great caution, there is one area at least in which these accounts show evidence of personal knowledge, keen powers of observation and a lively interest in the subject. This is the area of the Celtic style of warfare, with which the Greeks and Romans were familiar as with no other aspect of Celtic culture, on the basis of their own experience.

SHIELD, SPEAR AND SWORD: CELTIC WARFARE

Our knowledge of the armaments and combat tactics of the Celts derives from archaeological finds such as grave goods and votive offerings, indigenous pictorial representations, and illustrations showing Celtic warriors in Greek, Etruscan and Roman art, as well as the accounts of classical writers.[5] While marked regional differences, as well as dynamic changes over time, need to be borne in mind, a combination of these various sources makes it possible to venture some general statements, at least for the last third of the first millennium BC, on the arms and equipment of the Celtic warrior and the ways in which they were deployed.

The most important offensive weapon was the sword.[6] Early specimens have a pointed blade, equally suited to cutting and thrusting, on average sixty centimetres long, whereas later a cutting blade of eighty centimetres or more with a rounded point came to predominate. Metallurgical research has shown that, for improved flexibility, the blades were sometimes forged from several iron bars of varying hardness, with the hardest material used for the cutting edge. The high value placed on the sword may be seen in the fact that the blade often bears symbolic markings or stylised representations of animals, sometimes inlaid with gold. Whether these markings are merely the maker's trademark or the signature of the owner, or whether they also had a ritual or magical significance is unknown. The hilt was often in the form of an extended cross, with both faces of the hilt usually carved from wood or bone and sometimes decorated with inlaid jewellery. Frequently the pommel was shaped into the form of a head, giving the hilt a human appearance. Scabbards were usually made of iron or bronze plate, and often decorated at the opening. Pictorial representations and classical writings tell us that swords were worn on an iron or bronze chain on the right hip. The esteem in which the Celtic sword was held in the ancient world is also apparent from the fact that one of the old Celtic terms was borrowed into Latin (compare Latin *gladius*, Old Irish *claideb* and Welsh *cleddyf*) and largely displaced the native Latin *ensis*.

Another Celtic loanword is Latin *lancea* (whence Old French *lance* and Middle High German *lanze*), which originally meant a throwing spear fitted with a sling. In wagon-graves in the Marne area, archaeologists have found spears 2.5 metres long with a narrow twenty-centimetre blade, and these were presumably used by chariot-fighters as javelins. Thrusting lances with iron heads between thirty and sixty centimetres long have also been found. Another Celtic word for 'spear' was *gaisos* (whence Old Irish *gae* and Welsh *gwayw*), and this is found in the classical tradition in personal names such as *Gaesatus* ('spear-bearer') and *Gaisatorix* ('commander of the spear-men'), as well as in the term for Celtic mercenaries, *Gaesatae*.

For protection there is evidence of helmets, armour and shields. The latter were usually made of wood and covered with leather, so that in most graves only the metal fittings have survived. Generally oval in shape, the earlier shields were relatively small (fifty by forty centimetres), but later ones were almost the height of a man and weighed several kilogrammes with their iron buckles. Judging by the evidence of the grave hoards, iron or bronze helmets were relatively uncommon, but we should be aware of the great number of leather helmets, which have not survived. Similarly, metal armour was probably reserved for particularly distinguished warriors, while the majority of fighters wore leather armour, or none at all.

On the question of the practical use of Celtic arms and their effectiveness in combat, the accounts of the classical authors are the prime source of information. In the second century BC, the historian Polybius, for example, recounts how in the battle of Telamon in 225 BC all the surrounding hills resounded with the din of war-cries and trumpets, while the sight of the Gauls, many of them naked and adorned with gold armlets and torcs, filled the Romans with terror (*Histories* 2, 29). A description by Posidonius, preserved in the writings of Diodorus Siculus (*Historical Library* 5, 29), stresses the psychological effect produced by the Gaulish warriors. According to this account, before battle the Celts frequently challenged individual warriors to single combat. They would brandish their weapons, loudly proclaim their own and their ancestors' deeds of heroism, while at the same time seeking to humiliate their opponents with abuse.

An extensive report on Celtic cavalry tactics, based on older sources, is given by the Greek traveller and writer Pausanias (*Description of Greece* 10, 19ff.) in the second century AD. According to this account, the Celts' method relied on a tactical unit which they themselves called *trimarkisía* (compare Welsh *tri* 'three' and *march* 'horse'). This consisted of one mounted warrior, supported by two attendants who took no part in the initial combat but stood ready to provide a fresh mount if the first was wounded or lost. If the horseman himself was wounded, one of the attendants would help him to safety while the other took his mount and continued the fight. As Strabo notes, the Celts were so famed for their prowess as horsemen that when finally defeated they formed the best elements of the Roman cavalry (*Geography* 4, 4, 2).

Unlike the Germani, the Celts used horses not only for riding, but also to haul their light two-wheeled war chariots.[7] The Celtic name for these was *essedon*, which was borrowed into Latin in the form *essedum*. As can be seen from archaeological hoards and from pictures on coins, for example, these were very light vehicles, open at the front and rear, and drawn by two ponies. The ponies ran under a wooden yoke, to which they were harnessed on the back or withers. The Greek ethnographers paid particular attention to this use of horses, as it reminded them of the description of Greek chariots in Homer, and thus of their own history. Diodorus Siculus (*Historical Library* 5, 29), again utilising a description given by Posidonius, writes:

> In both journeys and battles they use two-horse chariots
> which carry a charioteer and a warrior. When they meet
> cavalry in battle, they throw their spears at the enemy then
> dismount and enter the fray with drawn swords.

While the chariot had fallen out of use as a tactical weapon on the
European mainland in the first century BC, in Britain and Ireland it
survived until the early Middle Ages. The fullest account of the use
of the chariot is given by Julius Caesar (*De Bello Gallico* 4, 33), who
became familiar with it during his expeditions to Britain.

> With their chariots they fight in the following manner: first
> they drive about in all directions hurling their spears and
> sowing confusion in the enemy ranks by the fear of the
> horses and the rumble of the wheels. When they have
> worked their way into the middle of the enemy cavalry they
> leap down from their chariots and fight on foot. In the
> meantime the charioteers drive their chariots a short distance
> away and station them so that the warriors can easily reach
> their comrades if it seems they will be overwhelmed by the
> enemy. Thus they combine in combat the mobility of
> cavalry and the stability of infantry. By daily practice and
> habit they reach the point of being able to gallop down a
> steep slope and slow the horses and turn them in a moment.
> They also run along the shaft, stand on the yoke and return
> at great speed to the chariot.

A further account of Celtic chariot tactics at the battle of Sentinum,
in 295 BC, was set down by the historian Livy (*History of Rome* 10,
28, 9), although his description may have been directly influenced by
Caesar's words and cannot therefore be taken as independent
testimony.

Following the military conflicts between the Celts and the Mediterranean peoples in the fourth and third centuries BC, we find the
first indications of a Celtic clientage culture.[8] According to Diodorus
Siculus, relying on Posidonius, the Celtic warriors took with them
into battle selected members of the free-born but less affluent classes
as servants, charioteers and shield-bearers (*Historical Library* 5,
29, 2). As Caesar explicitly observes, the links binding patrons

and clients were not only economic and social, but also religious in their basis (*De Bello Gallico* 7, 40, 7). Thus, Caesar writes in connection with his account of the surrender of the capital of the Aquitani:

> While the attention of our troops was engaged upon that business, Adiatunnus, the commander-in-chief, took action from another quarter of the town with 600 devotees, whom they call *soldurii*. The rule of these men is that in life they enjoy all benefits with the comrades to whose friendship they have committed themselves, while if any violent fate befalls their fellows, they either endure the same misfortune along with them or take their own lives; and no one yet in the memory of man has been found to refuse death, after the slaughter of the comrade to whose friendship he had devoted himself.
>
> (*De Bello Gallico* 3, 22, 1–3)

That military action was initiated and accompanied by religious rites is clear from an observation by Polybius that at the outbreak of war with the Romans the Celtic Insubres brought out the supposedly 'immovable' golden battle standards from a shrine dedicated to a Celtic goddess of war which the Greek historian identified with Athene (*Histories* 2, 32, 6). Caesar also mentions such effigies, writing that in 52 BC, at the start of the general uprising against Rome, several Gaulish tribes swore a solemn pledge of mutual armed support beneath the assembled battle standards (*De Bello Gallico* 7, 2, 2). It is likely that these refer to images of animals, which we know from designs on coins and from the Roman triumphal arch at Orange. The Germani possessed comparable standards, which were stored in peacetime at sacred sites. Tacitus refers to the 'images of wild beasts, brought forth from the forests and groves', with which the Batavi joined battle against the Romans during the rebellion in 69 AD (*Histories* 4, 22, 2). The iron bull, beside which the Cimbri solemnised a treaty with Rome in 102 BC, according to Plutarch, may have been such an image, fulfilling the function of a battle standard (*Life of Marius* 23, 7).

The practice of sacrificing captured armaments and prisoners, as a token of thanks for successful divine assistance in battle, is equally well attested in archaeological finds and classical literature. For example, Diodorus Siculus, no doubt following Posidonius (*Historical Library* 5, 32, 6), writes: 'They also use captives as sacrificial victims to honour their gods. Some of them even kill the animals captured in war with the human beings, or burn them or kill them by other means.' His report of an episode from the third Macedonian war accords with this:

> When the commander of the Celtic barbarians returned
> from the pursuit and had mustered his captives, he set about
> a brazen and barbaric deed. He selected the most handsome
> prisoners in the bloom of youth, crowned them with
> garlands and sacrificed them to the gods – if any god could
> accept such offerings.
>
> (*Historical Library* 31, 13)

No doubt aware of the same source, and perhaps influenced by it, Caesar writes, referring to his description of the Celtic god of war whom he calls Mars:

> To Mars, when they have determined on a decisive battle,
> they dedicate as a rule whatever spoil they may take. After a
> victory, they sacrifice such living things as they have taken,
> and all the other effects they gather into one place. In many
> states heaps of such objects can be seen piled up in hallowed
> spots, and it has not often happened that a man, in defiance
> of religious scruple, has dared to conceal such spoils in his
> house or to remove them from their place, and the most
> grievous punishment, with torture, is ordained for such an
> offence.
>
> (*De Bello Gallico* 6, 17)

The writers of antiquity paid particular attention to the Celts' practice in warfare of beheading their fallen enemies and preserving the heads as trophies. The earliest reference to this in literature comes from Polybius, who states that following the battle of Ticinus in 218 BC the Celtic auxiliaries in Hannibal's army cut off the heads of the fallen Roman soldiers (*Histories* 3, 67, 3). Diodorus Siculus gives a fuller account:

When their enemies fall they cut off their heads and fasten
them about the necks of their horses; and turning over to
their attendants the arms of their opponents, all covered in
blood, they carry them off as booty, singing a paean over
them and striking up a song of victory, and these first fruits
of battle they fasten by nails upon their houses, just as men
do, in certain kinds of hunting, with the heads of wild
beasts they have mastered. The heads of their most
distinguished enemies they embalm in cedar-oil and carefully
preserve in a chest, and these they exhibit to strangers,
gravely maintaining that in exchange for this head some one
of their ancestors, or their father, or the man himself,
refused the offer of a great sum of money. And some among
them, we are told, boast that they have not accepted an
equal weight of gold for the head they show, displaying a
barbarous kind of magnanimity; for not to sell that which
constitutes a witness and proof of one's valour is a noble
thing but it is far more bestial to continue hostility against
the dead.

(Historical Library 5, 29, 4–5)

Strabo paints a similar picture (*Geography* 4, 4, 5), making an
explicit reference to Posidonius's eye-witness account, and this may
also be presumed to have been the source for Diodorus. It is
noteworthy here that the wording of this description recalls at
several points Herodotus's account of Scythian customs, in which
he tells how the Scythians also suspended the scalps of their fallen
enemies on the reins of their horses and displayed the most
significant of their trophy skulls to their guests (*Histories* 4, 64–5).
Nevertheless it is quite clear from the archaeological finds that these
literary parallels are not a case of merely borrowing and uncritically
transferring a recurrent anthropological motif, but do in fact reflect
real correspondences in the practice of warfare in these two
cultures. A Celtic coin from the middle of the first century BC
shows on the reverse a Celtic warrior clutching in his left hand
the severed head of an enemy.[9] An early La Tène picture, from
Kärlich near Koblenz, of a horseman probably also shows a severed
head hanging from the hand holding the reins.[10] The hoard found
in the sanctuary of the settlement at Roquepertuse in the south of

France also points to the same conclusion. Furthermore, in graves explored as early as 1919–24, three monolithic columns were discovered from the second century BC with human skulls (now lost) set in niches cut into them. While the museum reconstruction of 1926 assumes that these skulls were placed on the outside of a portal to ward off danger, the new study of the burial deposits which began in 1988 brought indications that the skulls actually decorated the inside of the building (see B. Lescure in Haffner 1995, 75–84). The skulls of humans and cattle adorning a massive portal at the entrance to the sanctuary at Gournay-sur-Aronde, which has been under investigation since 1977, clearly served protective purposes (see J.-L. Brunaux in Haffner 1995, 59). The most impressive evidence to date of the Celtic practice of headhunting came in 1982 from the La Tène sanctuary at Ribe-mont-sur-Ancre. Here the archaeological investigation brought to light the bones of sixty headless warriors, who, the deposit showed, had been placed on display with their weapons on a raised platform, as human trophies.[11] The full significance of this find, however, becomes apparent only when seen against the background of our current knowledge of the Celtic religion of that era.

VICTORY MONUMENTS AND SACRIFICIAL SITES: THE OLDEST CELTIC SANCTUARIES

As the archaeological deposits show, even in pre-Celtic times sacrifices were often performed at sites with particularly outstanding landscape features. Impressive examples of this are the sites of sacrifice by burning, widespread in the Alps and the Transalpine foothills, where they stand out by being exposed at a high altitude. For example, the site at the 'Burgstall' in the South Tyrol lies on an inhospitable mountain plateau 2,500 metres above sea level and far from any human habitation. Within an area twelve metres wide and sixteen metres long, calcified and pulverised bone remnants and a mass of ceramic potsherds were found, testifying to periodically repeated votive offerings.[12] Another natural monument, which re-mains a striking sight to this day, is the sheer rock face, known as Heidentor, at the Oberburg site near Egesheim in the district of Tuttlingen, which, from the evidence of the fibulae and other small artefacts found there, served as a votive site in the late Hallstatt and early La Tène period.[13]

Caves and rock fissures made similarly attractive sacrificial sites, and some show evidence of continued use over many centuries. The 'Felsenloch' in the Veldenstein Forest in Upper Franconia, for example, was used from the early Bronze Age to the early La Tène.[14] Another sacrificial site may be the cave near Agris in western France, where several pieces of a ceremonial helmet from the fourth century BC, made of iron, bronze, gold and silver inlaid with coral, were found in 1981–6 (see J. Gomez de Soto in Moscati et al. 1991, 292–3). The custom of sinking votive gifts in water-sources, rivers, lakes, bogs and marshes, which reaches back into pre-Celtic times, is likewise well attested. At the 'Giant's Spring' at Duchcov, in northern Bohemia, a bronze cauldron was discovered at a depth of five metres, with fibulae and rings from the fourth century BC, while at a depth of nine metres lay a lance head from the Bronze Age (see V. Kruta in Moscati et al. 1991, 295). It is certain that many of the sunken sacrificial offerings were connected with homage to chthonic deities that were supposed to dwell beneath the surface of the earth, but only occasionally do the deposits help us to establish which groups of people were involved in making the sacrifices. At La Tène, for example, the typical female garments, which are so well represented at Duchcov, are absent. When Strabo reports that the Celts submerged quernstones of beaten silver in a lake near Toulouse (*Geography* 4, 1, 13), this must suggest a thanksgiving or supplicatory offering by a population of farmers.

How often a repeatedly used sacrificial site might have developed into a permanent structure for religious purposes we cannot estimate. An early example may be the sanctuary at the 'Burgwall' at Závist, on a steep hill at the confluence of the Berounka and Vltava, south of Prague, where in the sixth century BC first a place of worship was established at the sacrificial site, then a permanent settlement.[15] The Goloring near Koblenz, a circular enclosure in the middle of which a pole more than ten metres high may have been set, apparently also dates from the sixth century BC (see Röder 1948). The most important and eloquent examples of pre-Roman Celtic sanctuaries, however, date from the third to the first centuries BC and are found in modern-day France in an area stretching from the Ardennes to Picardy and from the Champagne and Ile-de-France regions as far as Normandy.

The systematic study of these, initiated barely twenty-five years ago, has extended our knowledge of pre-Roman Celtic worship in many respects, and also shed new light on the question of the continuity of this worship in Roman Gaul.[16]

Research into the *type picard* or northern French sanctuaries began in 1977 with the excavation of the sanctuary of Gournay-sur-Aronde in the department of Oise. This is to date the only cult site of its kind to be fully explored. It lay in the valley of the small River Aronde, in the territory of the Belgic Bellovaci tribe, close to the border of the Viromandui tribal area. It originally comprised a rectangular enclosure, forty-five metres long by thirty-eight wide, with an entrance in the middle of the east side, facing the river and the rising sun. The first enclosure, from the fourth century BC, was surrounded by a ditch, two metres wide and two metres deep, which was lined with timber during a substantial structural extension of the sanctuary in the early third century BC. In front of the ditch a sturdy palisade was now erected, and another ditch was dug in front of it. The entrance also underwent expansion, so that instead of a simple interruption in the ditch, a gateway was built and a large pit dug in front of it. On a gateway structure supported by six pillars, human and bovine skulls were set, and the remains of the carcasses buried in the inner ditch on both sides of the entrance. The central point of the site consisted of a sacrificial pit, three metres long and two metres wide. This was presumably covered by a wooden roof from the late third century BC.

Among the cult rituals performed within the sanctuary, animal sacrifices and ritual displays of weaponry should be distinguished. Evidence shows that the sacrificed animals were mostly cattle, pigs and sheep, but also dogs. The cattle, without exception very old by the time of their sacrifice, were killed by an axe blow to the neck or forehead, and immediately flung into the pit as an offering to the chthonic deities, without being quartered first. There they remained for about six months, until the fleshy parts had decomposed. Then the skeleton was retrieved and the skull detached, perhaps to be set in the entrance porch. The other parts of the skeleton were deposited in the inner ditch. Whereas the skeletons of oxen were found complete, of sheep and pigs only the bones of the best parts were found, and these were all of very young animals. From this we may deduce that the meat of these animals, as was the norm everywhere in antiquity, was eaten at communal sacrificial feasts. The display of armaments presumably comprised the weapons of the enemy dead found on the battlefield. Having been collected as booty, they were placed on display over the porch, or along the enclosure on the inside, and then, after the passage of a number of decades, when the leather and wooden parts had completely decayed, rendered unserviceable by bending, smashing or dismantling and buried in the inner ditch with the bones of the animals. Along with over 2,000 weapons, the ditch at Gournay-sur-Aronde also yielded some sixty human bones with cuts on them which suggested either human sacrifice or ritual manipulation of the bodies.

Unlike Gournay, the cult site of Ribemont-sur-Ancre, about fifty kilometres to the north-east, has so far been only partially excavated. Archaeological research and aerial photography indicate that this is the most important and best preserved La Tène cult site yet discovered. As at Gournay, the sanctuary consists of a square enclosure about forty metres long, surrounded by a wooden palisade that was probably more than three metres high. Unlike Gournay, however, Ribemont has no open ditch either within the enclosure or outside it. On the south-east palisade was a monumental gateway which stood like a gallery off the wall, adorned with human skulls, as at Gournay. Outside and along the palisade, over an area of about sixty square metres, several hundred weapons and over 10,000 human bones were found, although there was not a single skull among them. Closer investigation pointed to the supposition that several hundred warriors, decapitated and mummified by exposure, had been placed on display with their weapons on a covered platform. Inside the enclosure, deposits containing the partially burned bones from several hundred more human bodies were discovered, with several thousand metal objects from the La Tène period, including almost 500 lance heads.

In Gournay, as in Ribemont, the ritual display of fallen warriors had ceased by the beginning of the first century BC, but the La Tène cult sites were replaced after the Roman conquest by a Gallo-Roman temple, and the sacrificial cult continued unchanged. Similar continuity has been established in recent years at numerous other localities, where the remains of La Tène cult sites have been discovered beneath the foundations of Gallo-Roman temples. It can therefore be supposed that the religious change brought by the conquest was far less fundamental than the political, judicial and economic changes that followed the integration of Gaul into the Roman empire. In the progress of religious history, there is every indication that the decisive changes had already come about before the arrival of the Romans and may be traced back to the earlier intensive contacts between the Celts and the cultures of the Mediterranean area.

CHAPTER 4

Gaul before the Roman Conquest

OPPIDA: THE OLDEST TOWNS NORTH OF THE ALPS

In the second and first centuries BC a far-reaching change came about in the political, economic and social structures of the Celtic peoples of central Europe. One of the substantial factors in this is thought to be the decline of the Celtic mercenary system, following the rise of the Roman republic to a commanding position in the Mediterranean area. It appears that successful Celtic mercenary chieftains returned home in increasing numbers and, backed by their clients, entered into competition with the established representatives of the old tribal aristocracies. Renewed intensive trade relations with the Mediterranean cultures, an increase in craft production and, not least, armed conflict between tribes and with land-hungry Germanic peoples such as the Cimbri and Teutoni favoured the rise of fortified centres, known in Anglo-Saxon and German archaeology as *oppida* (singular *oppidum*).[1] At the same time as the growth of these town-like settlements, a change occurred in funerary rites and practices in the surrounding country, from inhumation with rich grave goods to cremation with few burial gifts or none at all. This means that the deposits and investigations of the oppida form the central source of knowledge of Celtic culture in this period.

Like the princely centres of the sixth and fifth centuries BC, the oppida were mostly situated on high ground, on bends in rivers or in similarly protected places. They differ fundamentally, however, from all sites in earlier and later centuries in their great size, sometimes occupying several hundred hectares. Another striking characteristic is the extensive fortification, and in many cases this is likely to have served a dual purpose: as well as offering protection, it also demonstrated the economic prosperity of the community. A feature of the fortification of most oppida on the right bank of the Rhine is the so-called *Pfostenschlitzmauer*. Vertical posts were set in the ground at regular intervals, with horizontal timbers laid between them and earth and stones piled up behind them. On the outside, the spaces between the uprights were faced with blocks of stone. On the left bank of the Rhine and at some sites in southern Germany, what Caesar called the 'Gallic wall' (*murus Gallicus*; *De Bello Gallico* 7, 23) is prevalent. These were built using coffer-work of exclusively horizontal beams, some laid lengthways, with cross-members laid across them, joined by nails. The inner side of the coffer-work was packed with earth and rubble and the outside clad with blocks of stone, so that in time of siege the wall was proof against fire and battering rams equally.[2]

A critical factor in the choice of site, besides a strategically favourable position, was the proximity of transport routes and the presence of mineral resources. Within the oppida one frequently finds pointers to a great variety of specialised trades which involved working with raw materials such as iron, bronze, wood, leather and glass. Iron-working, which increased greatly in scale in the second and first centuries BC, came to occupy a key position. The use of iron nails and clamps altered traditional methods of timber-frame building; iron weapons determined a tribe's offensive and defensive capabilities; agricultural implements such as spades, hoes, sickles, scythes and ploughshares determined agricultural yields; and specialised tools such as axes, saws, hammers, awls and tongs made a substantial contribution to a rise in craft output. It is probable that a large part of the output was intended for export, with both Roman and native traders playing an important part in this.

A striking indication of the economic and social change related to this is the appearance of independent Celtic coins, most likely introduced into circulation at the behest of the tribal chieftains of the day.[3] In order to mint them, molten metal (usually gold, silver or bronze) was poured into prepared moulding trays, in quantities of exactly equal weight. The blanks thus produced were then hand-pressed by hammer-blows between two dies, with the images mostly taken from Greek and Roman models. When inscriptions are in evidence, they are usually the names of tribes and members of the tribal aristocracy, and not the name of the site of minting. It is likely that many images on coins had some religious significance, but this cannot be determined since the coins bear no legends and there is no documentary evidence with which to compare them.[4] The current designations for Celtic coins, such as 'tetradrachm', 'drachma' and 'stater', are wholly borrowed from the Greek, as we do not know the native Celtic terms. Who determined the level of circulation of any coin issued, who guaranteed the standard and what role coins played in the economic cycle we can only conjecture, since the results of excavations to date and the few indications in classical sources tell us very little about the political and social structures of the oppida. There is some evidence that the inhabitants of the oppida belonged to all classes of the population, not only to a political or military elite. Whether all classes of society shared equally in the economic prosperity is less clear. It is also difficult to estimate the population density in individual oppida, since no cemeteries can be assigned to them and the number of inhabitants can only be estimated from the density of housing or the presence of kitchen waste (animal bones), for example. An additional difficulty is that it has so far been possible to investigate only a small portion of most oppida, on account of the large size of the settled area.

One of the best known oppida in France and one of the first to be studied is Bibracte, the capital of the Aedui tribe, in the department of Saône-et-Loire.[5] Situated in a strategically favourable position, with access to long-distance trading routes along the valleys of the Loire and the Saône, it occupied an area of over 130 hectares, including four hilltops, among them Mont Beuvray (821 metres). A wall over five kilometres long, interrupted by a number of gates, surrounded a town of several separate quarters, laid out according to their function, with the artisan workshops placed close to the gates. Towards the end of the first century AD, Augustus ordered that the population be resettled at the new site of Augustodunum, now Autun. In 1865 the first excavations began at Bibracte on the orders of Napoleon III, and in 1984 an international team of archaeologists resumed the investigation.

In the east of the Celtic area of settlement, on a steep hill at the confluence of the Berounka and the Vltava, south of Prague, a sanctuary was established in the sixth or fifth century BC, as well as a strongpoint fortified by earthen ramparts and palisades. In the third or second century BC, the oppidum of Závist, one of the most important eastern Celtic towns, arose on a site of 170 hectares, surrounded by a wall over nine kilometres long.[6] The finds from inside the oppidum show that a thriving iron-working industry developed, until in about 20 BC a devastating fire, possibly connected with the advance of Germanic tribes, completely destroyed the settlement. Závist, which later became overgrown with forest, has been the object of systematic study since 1963.

The best known oppidum in Germany and one of the largest sites of its kind anywhere lies due east of present-day Manching, south of Ingolstadt.[7] It extended over an area of 380 hectares on a broad alluvial plain on the south side of the Danube, and was surrounded by a wall seven kilometres long and five metres high. The site was first excavated in the nineteenth century, but the first archaeological studies were not made until 1938 and systematic research was conducted only between 1955 and 1990. The first investigations discovered a regular construction plan, laid out with variable density of building along the cardinal points of the compass. It was based on large, enclosed land-holdings, subdivided according to purpose. Thus in the agricultural quarter, we find stables, granaries and storage buildings fifty to fifty-five metres in length with two parallel naves. The structures were built entirely of wood or wattle-and-daub, and probably had roofs of reeds or straw. Flecks of paint left on fragments of clay suggest that the walls were originally painted white.

Agriculture and animal husbandry constituted the basic food sources for the population, and bone remains indicate that cattle and pigs were the dominant domesticated animals. The bones of wild animals comprise no more than 0.2 per cent of the deposits, so it is clear that hunting played hardly any role as a means of providing food. Manching was particularly rich in iron, which was extracted in the immediate and less immediate environs and smelted in the settlement, probably for domestic use above all. Craft and trade played an important part, including the manufacture and export of iron tools, textiles, ceramics, and beads and armlets made from coloured glass. The river Danube probably provided the main means of distributing wares and produce. The oldest finds have come to light close to the middle of the site and date from the third century BC. Manching reached the limit of its expansion in the second half of the second century BC, when the entire settled area was surrounded by a wall. In the second half of the first century BC, probably as a result of social and economic change during the incursions of the Romans and Germanic peoples, the town was gradually abandoned.

Among the most noteworthy recent finds at Manching is a model tree, seventy centimetres high, from the first half of the third century BC, with leaves of bronze covered with a layer of gold, in a technique previously known only in southern Italy. It is possible that it was used in cult practices, but for what precise purpose we can only guess. The same applies to the iron figure of a horse, partially plated with bronze, from the second century BC. It may have originally stood in a site of worship or shrine in the main street in the centre of the oppidum.[8] Whether all oppida had cult sites cannot be established for certain, since we can usually only conjecture what purpose the larger buildings and open spaces might have served. However, it is worth noting an observation made by Caesar, according to which the Gaulish custom was to open all military campaigns by convening an armed council of war and publicly putting to death the last man to appear (*De Bello Gallico* 5, 56, 2). This may tell us that the assembly places in the oppida served ritual and cult purposes, although the archaeological evidence does not provide proof of their sacred nature. The site known as 'La Terrasse' inside the oppidum of Bibracte on Mont Beuvray is assumed to be one such place of assembly with a religious dimension. Here a level area about eighty metres by 100 metres, enclosed in the late La Tène period by a wall and ditch, turned out to be largely devoid of deposits or evidence.[9] It is thought that at least some of the so-called *Viereckschanzen*, established in the second and first centuries BC outside the fortified settlements, also served ritual or cult purposes. *Viereckschanzen*, however, are the subject of much dispute in recent scholarship, and therefore need to be treated separately.

VIERECKSCHANZEN AND DRUIDS: LATE CELTIC CULTS AND RITES

The term *Viereckschanze* is used to designate square or roughly rectangular enclosures with sides of irregular length, marked off from their surroundings by a rampart and ditch. They are met with in a broad belt-like zone extending from the Atlantic coast of France to Bohemia, and are particularly numerous in southern Germany, between the Rhine, the Main and the Inn.[10] There is striking variation in the size of the *Viereckschanzen*: of 200 sites measured in Baden-Württemberg and Bavaria, the largest are over 1.7 hectares and the smallest less than 0.2 hectares in area. As a rule they have a single gate, often on the east side, less frequently on the south or west, and never on the north side. The topographic location varies greatly, but they are only rarely situated in markedly exposed positions. Whether the proximity of springs or watercourses, which is seen repeatedly, influenced the choice of site is not clear.

When studies began, the *Viereckschanzen* were taken to be Roman marching camps, on account of their rectangular plan. Only in the late nineteenth century, after more thorough archaeological investigation, were they mostly dated to the late La Tène. By this time the view that they were farmsteads or refuges had prevailed, giving the sites the name *Schanze* (entrenched redoubt), which remains current to this day. Fundamental to the view of the *Viereckschanzen* as cult sites was an article by the archaeologist Friedrich Drexel, published in 1931, in which he pointed out technical similarities with later Gallo-Roman temple sites and the absence of proper fortifications. Endorsement for this theory was seen in the results of an excavation conducted between 1957 and 1963 in parts of the *Viereckschanze* at Holzhausen, near Munich. Three vertical shafts were found, containing traces of organic substances which were considered to be the remains of votive offerings. In the northernmost of these shafts was a wooden stake, thought by the excavator to be a cult object, and the ground plans of post-built structures reminiscent of the shape of Gallo-Roman ambulatory temples. The archaeological investigation in 1958–9 of part of the *Viereckschanze* at Tomerdingen in the district of Alb-Hegau, produced similar results. Here too a wooden post was found in a five-metre pit (see Zürn and Fischer 1991).

Against the view of the Holzhausen and Tomerdingen stakes as cult objects stand the results from the *Viereckschanze* of Fellbach-Schmiden, near Stuttgart, where archaeological research was conducted between 1977 and 1980.[11] Here, on the north side, a shaft which was undoubtedly a well with timber casing was found, accessible by inserted rungs. Remnants of a wooden winching device gave rise to the theory that the supposed cult objects at Holzhausen and Tomerdingen were really parts of a wooden winding gear. The discovery of three wooden animal figures, apparently the remains of a religious image of a deity flanked by animals, nevertheless suggested the performance of religious rites within or around the *Viereck-schanze* of Fellbach-Schmiden. New doubts have been cast on the idea of a dominant ritual function for all *Viereckschanzen* by further excavations at the sites of Ehningen, in the district of Böblingen (1984), Bopfingen-Flochberg in Ostalb (1989–92) and Riedlingen on the upper Danube (since 1981). In these instances the absence of shafts or settlement deposits, previously held to be typical, as well as any trace of extensive building, led to an interpretation of the sites as fortified farming estates, as earlier investigators had supposed.

Perhaps more clearly than other areas of Celtic archaeology, the history of the study of the *Viereckschanzen* illuminates the problems of interpreting prehistoric artefacts. Certainty as to the function or functions of a particular set of artefacts can, in the final analysis, be provided only by extensive excavations, conducted using modern methods at a large number of sites. Extrapolations from isolated cases are just as unreliable as interpretations based on cross-cultural analogies. This also holds for interpretations that make use of classical sources, since these, while offering much information about the religion of the Celts from the first century BC, make no mention at all of *Viereckschanzen*. On the other hand, the reports of the Greek and Roman authors provide numerous pointers to another aspect of late Celtic religion, an aspect of which there is no trace at all in the archaeological evidence. This is the Celtic clergy known as Druids, who first emerge in the historical records in the period of immediately pre-Roman Gaul.[12]

What may be the beginning of classical interest in the Celtic priesthood is marked by an observation by the writer Diogenes Laertius in the third century AD. At the very beginning of his work *The Lives and Opinions of Eminent Philosophers*, he mentions the supposition of some earlier writers that philosophy had its origins among the barbarians. The Persians, he says, had their magi, the Babylonians or Assyrians their Chaldeans, the Indians their gymnosophists and the Celts their so-called Druids. This is reported by Aristotle in his *Magicus* and Sotion in the twenty-third book of his *Diadoche*. If this source is accurate, this means the Druids had attracted the attention of the classical authors even before the first century BC. An extensive account of their role and position within the framework of Celtic society, however, does not arise until Posidonius, whose statements can be reconstructed in outline from a comparison of observations in the work of the geographer Strabo, the historian Diodorus Siculus and Timagenes (the latter cited by Ammianus Marcellinus).

Diodorus mentions the Druids as a third group, after the poets (bards) and soothsayers (*Vātēs*), and describes them as highly respected theologians and philosophers, responsible for all matters of sacrificial offerings (*Historical Library* 5, 31, 2ff.). An indirect suggestion of Diodorus's view of the content of Druidic philosophy can be seen in his explanation of Celtic bravery, which he attributed to a belief in the transmigration of souls (*Historical Library* 5, 28, 6–7). Strabo gives a very similar account:

> As a rule, among the Gallic peoples three sets of men are honoured above all others: the Bards, the *Vātēs* and the Druids. The bards are singers and poets, the *Vātēs* overseers of sacred rites and philosophers of nature, and the Druids, besides being natural philosophers, practise moral philosophy as well. They are considered to be the most just and therefore are entrusted with settling both private and public disputes, so that in earlier times they even arbitrated wars and could keep those intending to draw themselves up for battle from so doing; and it was to these men most of all that cases involving murder had been entrusted for adjudication. And whenever there is a big yield from these cases, they believe that there will come a yield from the land, too. Both these men and others aver that men's souls and the universe are imperishable, although both fire and water will at some times prevail over them.
>
> (*Geography* 4, 4, 4)

Ammianus Marcellinus, who believed the Druids were organised in brotherhoods, in accordance with the teaching of Pythagoras, also draws on Posidonius in the fourth century AD (*Res gestae* 15, 9, 8). Their preoccupation with natural history, noted by Strabo, is mentioned again by Cicero, who differs from the other sources in ascribing to the Druids the pursuit of divination by means of the interpretation of signs (*De divinatione* 1, 41, 90).

Perhaps the most colourful depiction of a sacrifice performed by the Druids is contained in a note by Pliny the Elder on the sacred properties of mistletoe:

> The Druids – as their magicians are called – hold nothing more sacred than this plant and the tree on which it grows, provided that it is an oak. They choose only groves of oaks and perform no rites unless a branch of that tree is present. Thus it seems that Druids are so called from the Greek name of the oak [Greek *drus*]. Truly they believe that anything which grows on the tree is sent from heaven and is a sign that the tree was chosen by the god himself. However, mistletoe rarely grows on oaks, but is sought with reverence and cut only on the sixth day of the moon, as it is then that the moon is powerful but not yet halfway in its course. (It is by the moon that they determine the beginning of months, years and – after thirty years – a *saeculum*). In their language the mistletoe is called 'the healer of all'. When preparations for a sacrifice and feast beneath the tree have been made, they lead forward two white bulls with horns bound for the first time. A priest in white clothing climbs the tree and cuts the mistletoe with a golden sickle, and it is caught in a white cloak. They then sacrifice the bulls while praying that the god may render his gift propitious to those to whom he has given it. They believe that mistletoe, when taken in a drink, will restore fertility to barren animals, and is a remedy for all poisons.
>
> (*Natural History* 16, 249–51)

That Pliny is not the original source of this report is indisputable, as by his lifetime the Roman regime had already proscribed the Druids. His account may go back to an older Greek source and thus refer to conditions before the Roman occupation. One pointer to this is his statement that the name of the Druids is derived from the Greek word for oak (*drus*); another pointer is the allusion to the Celtic name for mistletoe as 'the healer of all', since the Latin *omnia sanans* may be seen to be a translation of the Greek botanical name *pánakes*. Support

for the assumption of a Greek source is also found in Pliny's allusion
to the great significance in the calendar of the 'generation' (*saeculum*),
since the thirty-year 'generation' (*geneá*) played an important part in
the Greek system of measuring time, but not in that of the Romans.
It is possible that Pliny's report derives directly or indirectly from
Posidonius, since the latter not only emphasised the central importance of the Druids in Celtic sacrificial rites, but also took a keen
interest in the indigenous terms for the phenomena that he observed.

Caesar's account of the Druids concurs to a large extent with the
accounts of writers who rely on Posidonius, but also offers much
additional information which is not found elsewhere. Like Diodorus,
Strabo and Ammianus Marcellinus, Caesar ascribes to the Druids
the practice of theology, philosophy and natural history, the belief in
the transmigration of souls, supervision over the sacrificial cult and
judicial functions. Furthermore, he describes them – along with the
nobility – as the most important social group, and is able to report:

> Of all the Druids one precedes who has the highest
> authority among them. When this one dies either the one
> who excels in dignity from the rest succeeds or if there are
> many who are suitable, by the vote of the Druids they
> contend for leadership, sometimes even contending with
> arms. At a certain time of the year they sit down in a
> consecrated place in the territory of the Carnutes, which
> region is believed to be the centre of all Gaul. To this place
> all come from everywhere who have disputes and the Druids
> bring forth their resolutions and decisions. It is believed the
> training for Druids was discovered in Britain and from there
> it was transferred into Gaul. And now those who wish to
> learn the matter carefully depart for Britain for the sake of
> learning. The Druids retire from war nor are they
> accustomed to any taxes. They have immunity from military
> service and are exempt from all lawsuits. So greatly are
> young men excited by these rewards that many assemble
> willingly in training and many others are sent by parents
> and relatives. They are said to commit to memory a great
> number of verses. And some remain some twenty years in
> training. Nor do they judge it to be allowed to entrust these
> things to writing although in nearly all the rest of their

affairs, and public and private transactions, Greek letters are used. It seems to me there are two reasons this has been established: neither do they wish the common people to pride themselves in the training nor those who learn to rely less on memory, since it happens to a large extent that individuals give up diligence in memory and thorough learning through the help of writing.

(De Bello Gallico 6, 13–18)

The agreement as to the role of the Druids, the mention of transmigration of souls and the observation concerning the use of the Greek script (mainly in southern Gaul) suggest that, like the authors mentioned earlier, Caesar may have relied on Posidonius. On the other hand, it cannot be denied that his account differs sharply from that of Posidonius in not showing the threefold division of the priesthood, which figures in the accounts of Diodorus, Strabo and Ammianus Marcellinus, and in placing much emphasis on the social power of the Druids. The assumption that Caesar used his own knowledge of conditions in Gaul to consciously extend, and perhaps also bring up to date, Posidonius's description, might explain these deviations. However, against that stands the fact that Caesar's account of his campaigns and diplomatic negotiations with the Gauls never mentions the Druids. The key to an understanding of the situation may be Caesar's disparaging remark that the Germani, unlike the Gauls, possessed neither a priesthood nor a particularly well-defined sacrificial system. This is not the only place in which Caesar greatly overstates the differences between the Gauls and the Germani, in order to show the Gauls' adaptability to civilisation in the best light, and it is possible that his description of the Druids was intended primarily to present the Gaulish clerics to his Roman readers as something close to the familiar *pontifices*. Like the *pontifices*, Caesar's Druids hold supreme power in all judicial and religious matters, exert considerable political influence through their control of the sacrificial system, enjoy exemption from military service and fall under the aegis of a high priest appointed to serve, like the *pontifex maximus*, for as long as he lives. The reference to decrees (*decreta*) from the Druids, who otherwise do not write, also appears to owe much to the Roman mind, as does the distinction between public and private concerns. One cannot rule out the possibility that Caesar knowingly depicted the Gaulish clerics as a counterpart to the Roman *pontifices*, again so as to lend suitable emphasis to the Gauls' ability to assimilate.

It is difficult to say what conclusions should be drawn from the references to the proscription of the Druids by the Roman authorities. As Suetonius in his biography of the Emperor Claudius reports, Roman citizens were forbidden to participate in the religion of the Druids even in the time of Augustus, long before the entire priesthood was totally banned in the middle of the first century AD (*Claudius* 25, 5). Nevertheless Tacitus was able to report that fifteen years after the death of Claudius the Druids took the burning of the Capitol when the city fell to Vespasian's troops to be a sign that world domination would now pass to the peoples north of the Alps (*Histories* 4, 54). If we are to take at face value Caesar's reports on the political influence and hierarchical organisation of the Druids throughout Gaul, this suggests that the ban by the Roman authorities should be seen as a move against a potential focus of resistance to Rome, and the prophecies of the year 69 AD may be interpreted as a late flickering of the Gallic will to freedom. Our sources make no mention of any active resistance by the Druids to Romanisation, however, and the Roman authors plausibly attribute the ban on the Druids exclusively to the incompatibility of their sacrificial practices with Roman law. While we might dismiss Caesar's reports on the hierarchy and immense political influence of the Druids as politically motivated propaganda, there is hardly any evidence to support a concerted and politically motivated anti-Roman stance by the Gaulish priesthood.

There is a further consideration: while 'Druid' in pre-Roman Gaul refers to a priest as a ministrant of a communally observed cult, the feminine form of this noun occurs in the late classical *Historia Augusta* as a general designation for Gaulish soothsayers. Thus in 235 AD a Druidess is supposed to have warned the emperor Alexander Severus in the Gaulish tongue, as he set out on a campaign, against hoping for victory or trusting his men (*Alexander Severus* 60, 6). Another Druidess is said to have prophesied to the emperor Diocletian in his youth that he would become emperor when he killed *Aper* (the boar), which meant, as it turned out, the *praefectus praetorio* of Emperor Numerian, who bore the name Aper (*Numerianus* 30, 40, 2). It is patently clear that these Druidesses shared no more than their name with the priests of the pre-Roman era. But this may also apply to some earlier recorded uses of the word, such as a remark by Pliny the Elder (*Natural History* 30, 13), where the phrase *druidas eorum et hoc genus vatum medicorumque* may have nothing to do with any exclusive priestly caste, but may instead mean, in a broad sense, 'Gallic magicians, soothsayers and witch doctors'. In view of this, it seems entirely possible that the Druids who foretold the end of Roman domination when the Capitol burned in 69 AD are more closely comparable with the late classical female soothsayers in *Historia Augusta* than with the priests of pre-Roman times.

Finally it should be added here that Caesar's remark about the Druids refusing the use of writing but using the Greek alphabet in all public and private transactions is fully confirmed by the archaeological evidence. Inscriptions show that the Celts of southern Gaul, influenced by the Greek colonies since the end of the third century BC, used the Greek alphabet in recording the vernacular.[13] So far approximately seventy inscriptions in stone and over two hundred in ceramics have been found, although most of them consist of only a few words. Of particular note are the burial and dedicatory inscriptions, which show the great influence of Mediterranean culture on the native population. The burial inscriptions usually contain only the name of the deceased, followed by the name of the deceased's father, while the dedicatory inscriptions sometimes include, besides the name of the donor and the recipient deity, additional information such as the name of the item donated. In this regard the following inscription (originally written in Greek letters), found at Vaison (Vaucluse) in 1840, is typical (Lejeune 1985, no. 153 and Lambert 1994, 84–5):

SEGOMAROS OUILLONEOS TOOUTIOUS
NAMAUSATIS EIOROU BELESAMI SOSIN
NEMETON

Segomaros, son of Villu, citizen of Nîmes, dedicates to Belisama this shrine.

Another inscription, also originally written in Greek letters, found in 1886 in Orgon (Bouches-du-Rhône) is dedicated to the god Taranus (Lejeune 1985, no. 27 and Lambert 1994, 86–7):

OUEBROUMAROS DEDE TARANOOU
BRATOUDEKANTEM

Vebrumaros gave to Taranus a tithe in gratitude.

As both these inscriptions show, Gaulish strongly resembles related
and neighbouring Indo-European languages such as Latin and
Greek. The similarities include the grammatical endings (Gaulish
-os in the nominative singular masculine corresponds to Greek -os
and Latin -us, while Gaulish -on in the nominative/accusative
singular neuter corresponds to Greek -on and Latin -um); the
vocabulary (Gaulish *dede* derives from the same root as Greek
didōmi 'I give' or *tithēmi* 'I put'); word-formation (Gaulish *toutios*
'citizen' is related to *toutā* 'tribe, community of citizens' in the same
way as Latin *patrius* 'fatherly' is related to *pater* 'father'); and its
onomastics (Greek names in *-mōros* correspond to Gaulish names in
-māros). It is noteworthy that, on the evidence of these and comparable inscriptions, the Gaulish language, like other Indo-European
languages, places the subject at the beginning of the sentence, not the
verb, like most of the modern insular Celtic languages. In general,
with regard to their word-stock and grammar, the Gaulish inscriptions continue to present numerous difficulties of comprehension,
and some of these are likely to remain unresolved, given the paucity
of texts, for some time to come.

BETWEEN ROMANS AND GERMANI: THE
DECLINE OF THE CONTINENTAL CELTS

Towards the end of the second century BC the Celtic peoples of
central Europe found themselves facing a dual threat. In the east,
Germanic tribes had occupied broad swathes of previously Celtic
territory on the right bank of the Rhine, and would in the following
period push ever further into the territory on the left bank. At the
same time, in the south the Celts were coming into conflict with the
rising republic of Rome, which, following the victorious conclusion
of the war with Carthage, the defeat of the Celtiberians in Spain and
the consolidation of Roman supremacy in Italy, was exerting increasing influence north-west of the Alps (Freyberger 1999). We owe

some vivid depictions of the cultural situation in this final phase of Celtic independence on the European mainland to the historian and philosopher Posidonius, whom we have cited many times already. One such scene occurs in his description of the prince Lovernius, who ruled the tribe of the Arverni in the mid-second century BC. According to this description (cited by Athenaeus of Naucratis p. 152 D–F), when Lovernius appeared in public he had himself driven through the country in a chariot while he tossed gold and silver to the countless accompanying Celts. He also set up spacious rectangular enclosures, in which food and drink were prepared in such quantities that all who wished could enter and make themselves at home for days on end. When, after the feasting had concluded, one poet lauded the greatness of Lovernius and at the same time lamented his own late arrival, Lovernius threw a bag of gold pieces from his chariot to the poet running along beside it. Thereupon the poet sang another song of praise to the prince, whose very chariot tracks, he said, yielded gold and largesse to mankind.[14]

The Romans had first intervened militarily in southern Gaul in 154 BC, in support of the Greek colony of Massalia. From 125 BC they again began to wage wars against Massalia's neighbours, and in 122 BC dealt a resounding defeat to the Saluvii people, laid waste their capital of Entremont and founded the town of Aquae Sextiae, the modern Aix-en-Provence. When some of the Saluvii chieftains then fled to the neighbouring Allobroges, the refusal of the latter to hand over the fugitives offered the Romans an occasion to pursue and widen the war. The historian Appian reports, again very likely relying on the historical work of Posidonius, that Lovernius's son Bituitus sent a splendidly arrayed envoy, with bodyguards, dogs and a poet, into the Roman camp to intercede on behalf of the Allobroges.[15] When his efforts proved fruitless, he openly took the side of the Allobroges but both he and the Allobroges were overcome by the Romans in August 121 BC. After this the Romans extended their sphere of influence right across southern Gaul from the Pyrenees to Lake Geneva, and established a Roman colony in Narbo, the modern Narbonne.[16]

Between 109 and 101 BC southern Gaul was threatened by the Germanic Cimbri and their allies the Teutoni and Tigurini, but Gaius Marius was able to secure the Roman transalpine possessions by decisive victories at Aquae Sextiae and Vercellae. Soon after this,

Posidonius visited southern Gaul and described at length and first-hand the appearance of the Gauls, their dress and weaponry, and the impression they made upon strangers:

> The Gauls are tall of body, fleshy and white of skin, and their hair is blond, and not only naturally so, but they also make it their practice by artificial means to increase the distinguishing colour which nature has given it. For they are always washing their hair in lime-water, and they pull it back from the forehead to the top of the head and back to the nape of the neck, with the result that their appearance is like that of Satyrs and Pans, since the treatment of their hair makes it so heavy and coarse that it differs in no respect from the mane of horses. Some of them shave the beard, but others let it grow a little; and the nobles shave their cheeks, but they let the moustache grow until it covers the mouth. Consequently, when they are eating, their moustaches become entangled in the food, and when they are drinking, the beverage passes, as it were, through a kind of strainer . . . The clothing they wear is striking – shirts which have been dyed and embroidered in various colours, and breeches, which they call in their tongue *bracae*; and they wear striped cloaks, fastened by a brooch on the shoulder, heavy for winter wear and light for summer . . . They are terrifying in appearance and speak with deep, harsh voices. They speak together in few words, using riddles which leave much of the true meaning to be understood by the listener. They frequently exaggerate their claims to raise their own status and diminish another's. They are vainglorious, violent and melodramatic, but very intelligent and learn quickly.
>
> (Cited by Diodorus Siculus,
> *Historical Library* 5, 28, 1–3 and 30, 1–31, 1)[17]

Posidonius also left a full account of the eating habits of the Gauls:[18]

> The Celts sit on dried grass and have their meals served upon wooden tables raised slightly above the earth. Their food consists of a small number of loaves of bread together

with a large quantity of meat, either boiled or roasted on
charcoal or on spits. They partake of this in cleanly but
leonine fashion, raising up whole limbs in both hands and
biting off the meat, while any part which is hard to tear off
they cut through with a small dagger which hangs attached
to their sword-sheath in its own scabbard. Those who live
beside the rivers or near the Mediterranean or Atlantic eat
fish in addition, baked fish, that is, with the addition of salt,
vinegar and cummin. They also use cummin in their drinks.
They do not use olive oil because of its scarcity and, due to
its unfamiliarity, it has an unpleasant taste to them. When a
number of them dine together, they sit in a circle with the
most powerful man in the centre like a chorus leader,
whether his power is due to martial skill, family nobility, or
wealth. Beside him sit the remainder of the dinner guests in
descending order of importance according to rank.
Bodyguards with shields stand close by them while their
spearmen sit across from them, feasting together with their
leaders. The servers bring drinks in clay or silver vessels
resembling spouted cups. The platters on which they serve
the food often are of similar material, but others use bronze,
wooden, or woven trays. The drink of choice among the
wealthy is wine brought from Italy or the region of
Massalia. It is normally drunk unmixed with water, although
sometimes water is added. Most of the rest of the population
drinks a plain, honeyed beer, which is called *corma*.

Again it is Diodorus Siculus who retails the following critical remarks
by Posidonius concerning the consumption of wine:

The Gauls are exceedingly addicted to the use of wine and
fill themselves with the wine which is brought into their
country by merchants, drinking it unmixed, and since they
partake of this drink without moderation by reason of their
craving for it, when they are drunken they fall into a stupor
or a state of madness. Consequently, many of the Italian
traders believe that the love of wine of these Gauls is their
own godsend. For these transport the wine on the navigable
rivers and through the level plain on wagons, and receive for

it an incredible price; for in exchange for a jar of wine they receive a slave, thus acquiring a cup-bearer in lieu of the drink.

(*Historical Library* 5, 26, 3)[19]

The fact that these portrayals are often cited and taken for granted in modern perceptions of the Celts and their culture should not blind us to the fact that Posidonius's account can claim validity only for the first half of the first century BC, and geographically only for the heavily Hellenised southern Gaul. It is also noteworthy that, like most classical ethnographers, Posidonius likes to give emphasis to the unusual and is not free of the general tendency to lapse into clichés, for example when commenting on the Celtic fondness for drink. Less transparent to the modern reader, but nevertheless ever present, are certain allusions that can be understood only from the author's cultural and philosophical views. Thus his mention of a small knife, kept by the Gauls in a separate scabbard next to the sword, is a reference to the similar habits of the Homeric heroes (cf. *The Iliad* 3, 271–2). Thus also, his observations concerning the fleshiness of the Gauls may be based less on reality and more on preconceived notions, for Posidonius assumed that the bodies of people living in a northerly climate would absorb moisture and thus necessarily be fleshier than those of their Mediterranean neighbours (see Malitz 1983, 187). Nevertheless, even in the fragmentary form that has come down to us, Posidonius's depictions of the Celts constitute a cultural and historical source of the first rank, with which the Greek philosopher raised an enduring monument to the Celts of central and western Europe in the last decades of their independence.

The end of this era came into view when in 58 BC Gaius Julius Caesar was appointed proconsul of the Celtic region of northern Italy and the southern Gaulish province of Gallia Narbonensis.[20] By this time Caesar already had a swift political career behind him, and was now eager to pay off his financial debts through military action and at the same time raise a powerful army that would be loyal to him personally. As early as 70 BC the Germani, led by their king Ariovistus, had crossed the Rhine and allied themselves with the Sequani against the Aedui, who were friendly with the Romans. In 61 BC, Diviciacus of the Aedui sought support from the Roman senate against the Sequani and their ally Ariovistus, who for his part, however, concluded a treaty of friendship with Rome in 59 BC and, on Caesar's recommendation, was awarded the honorary title of 'Friend of the Roman People'. The balance of power shifted when the Celtic Helvetii, under increasing Germanic pressure, attempted to migrate from their area of settlement and in the process cross the Roman province. This was the opportunity Caesar needed: on the pretext of an appeal for help – which he himself may have arranged – from Rome's allies the Aedui, Caesar moved to block the migration. He defeated them near the oppidum of Bibracte and forced the survivors back to their homeland (see Walser 1998). A renewed call for help from the Aedui now led to conflict with Ariovistus, who was defeated by Caesar in open combat in the autumn of the same year near Mühlhausen and then had to withdraw to the eastern side of the Rhine.

After the first year of war, Caesar raised the number of legions under his command from four to six and then to a total of ten in the following year. In 57 to 56 BC, from his power base in south-eastern Gaul the Roman commander launched forays against the Belgae in north-eastern Gaul, subjugated the inhabitants of the coastal region of present-day Brittany, and conducted successful campaigns against the tribes of Aquitaine in south-western Gaul. In order to secure his military position and demonstrate the strength of Roman power, he crossed the Rhine in 55 BC and entered the territory of the Ubii, who were allied to Rome. Shortly afterwards he set out on his first expedition to Britain. In 54 BC he sailed to Britain for the second time and achieved the formal subjugation of the prince Cassivellaunus, but a little later a serious rebellion broke out in northern Gaul. Led by their prince Ambiorix, the Eburones destroyed the one and a half legions – at that point about one fifth of Caesar's army – who were stationed on their territory. In 53 BC Caesar completed the bloody suppression of the rebellion, almost wiped out the leadership of the Eburones and, following successful battles against the Treveri, crossed the Rhine again in the area of the Neuwied Basin.

In 52 BC the last general uprising of the peoples of Gaul broke out. It began with the murder of Roman citizens in Cenabum, the modern Orléans. The Gauls were led by Vercingetorix, of the Arverni, who sought to deny the Roman armies their logistical base by means of a scorched-earth policy. After the loss to the Romans of the fiercely defended oppidum of Avaricum, Vercingetorix withdrew to his home town of Gergovia, inflicted a severe defeat upon the attacking Romans and forced Caesar to retreat. A little later, however, Vercingetorix and his army were trapped in the oppidum of Alesia (on Mont Auxois, near the modern Alise-Sainte-Reine) and, after several unsuccessful attempts to break out, were compelled to surrender to Caesar's troops. In 51 BC, the seizure of Uxellodunum marked the fall of the last bastion of resistance to the Romans. Vercingetorix was held in captivity for six years, and then paraded by Caesar through Rome in 46 BC, and he is thought to have been executed shortly afterwards.[21]

After putting down the last large Gaulish rebellion, Caesar established a number of colonies which served to consolidate Roman authority and provide allocations of land to his soldiers. One year after Caesar's death, and still acting on his orders, the proconsul of Gallia Transalpina founded the colony of Lugudunum, the modern Lyons, at the confluence of the Rhône and the Saône, which would later develop into the political and economic hub of Gaul. In 40 BC Gaul came under the rule of Octavian, later called Augustus Caesar, whose proconsul Marcus Agrippa settled Germanic tribes such as the Ubii on Gaulish territory in order to secure the Rhine as a border. Following mixed successes in battles against rebellious Gauls and marauding Germani, the territorial reorganisation of the regions conquered by Caesar ensued in 27 BC, with these regions now divided into three imperial provinces: Aquitania, Lugdunensis and Belgica. With the subsequent development of communications and the economy of Gaul, the era of Gallo-Roman civilisation began. This civilisation – the last branch of mainland Celtic culture – came to an end in the late classical period, following the encroachment of Germanic tribes. Before looking more closely at the history of Gaul under Roman domination, we shall turn our attention from central Europe to the Iberian peninsula, northern Italy and Asia Minor, the most important peripheral zones of Celtic culture in ancient times.

CHAPTER 5

The Celts of Iberia

BEYOND THE PILLARS OF HERCULES: THE EVIDENCE OF CLASSICAL ETHNOGRAPHY

The modern perception of the 'Celtic' character of Gaulish culture is founded principally on the testimony of the classical authors and the remarkable unity of central European La Tène art, while our picture of 'Celtic' Ireland and 'Celtic' Britain (as will be shown in later chapters) rests primarily on linguistic continuity. Matters are different, however, in the Iberian peninsula. Here La Tène ornamentation and iconography play hardly any part, and the Celtic tongue of a large part of the population died out in ancient times and survives only in inscriptions and isolated words of Spanish, Catalan, Portuguese and Basque. All the more valuable, then, are the numerous references in the works of the classical authors, who coined the collective designation 'Celtiberians' (Latin *Celtiberi*), still in use today, for the Celtic inhabitants of the Iberian peninsula.[1]

The oldest report on the Celtic tribes of the western limit of Europe is taken to be that by the Latin poet Avienus, whose account of the Spanish and Gaulish coast (*Ora maritima*), written in the fourth century AD, is based at least partly on ancient Greek sources from the sixth century BC. A precise separation of this oldest layer from later insertions and accretions is difficult, however, and the Celtic origin of several of the names of peoples mentioned by Avienus is highly debatable.[2] We are on surer ground in the fifth century BC with Herodotus (*Histories* 2, 33), who, in his description of Egypt, points to the (supposed) parallel courses of the Nile and the Danube, remarking:

> The Ister (the Danube), beginning in the land of the Celts
> and the city of Pyrene, flows through the middle of Europe,

which it divides. The Celts live beyond the Pillars of
Hercules and border on the Cynetes, who are the
westernmost inhabitants of Europe.

His sources were, no doubt, the reports of Greek traders and
seafarers, who had passed through the Straits of Gibraltar (which
they called the Pillars of Hercules) on their way to the 'tin islands' of
Britain, and visited the town of Tartessos, an important trading
centre at the mouth of the Guadalquivir.

Map 2: The Iberian peninsula in the classical period

Since the Carthaginians, in about 530 BC, after their victory in the
sea battle of Alalia off Corsica, had denied the Greeks passage
through the Straits of Gibraltar, Herodotus's report must be based
on records from the first half of the sixth century BC at the latest (see
Fischer 1972). According to later sources, the Cynetes lived in
southern Portugal, in what is now the Algarve, and the name Pyrene
was used by Aristotle to mean the Pyrenees. At another point

(*Histories* 1, 163), Herodotus refers to a king of Tartessos and friend of the Greeks called Arganthonios, which may be derived from a Celtic word for silver (Old Irish *argat*, Welsh *arian*).

The Celts appear as an important race in the mid-fourth century BC in the writings of the historian Ephorus of Cyme, who devoted to them a special ethnographic description which survives in quotations (see Dobesch 1995, 28–30). He places the Celts in the extreme west of the known world, while attributing all of the east to the Indians, the south to the Ethiopians, and the north to the Scythians. Apart from describing them favourably as 'friends of the Greeks', Ephorus also recounts certain of their peculiarities, of which the classical ethnographers were fond. These included imposing punishments on young men if they exceeded a certain waist-size, or going to fight the waves of the sea with weapons in hand. An exhaustive geographical account of the Iberian peninsula was given in the mid-second century BC by the historian Polybius in his forty-volume history of the universe. The surviving fragments of Book 34 show that this work dealt with both matters of geography and natural history, such as the land area, the movement of the tides, and the population of the peninsula and the Iberian mines, made famous earlier by Cato the Elder. In about 100 BC Artemidorus of Ephesus published his geography of the west, although surviving fragments seem to indicate that this comprised primarily an exact description of the coastline with few facts about the interior and its inhabitants.

Posidonius visited the Iberian peninsula at the beginning of the first century BC and turned his first-hand knowledge to account in his book about the seas of the world and in his sequel to Polybius's history (see Malitz 1983, 96–134). As the quotations passed on mainly by Diodorus Siculus and Strabo show, this philosopher, ethnographer and scientist of manifold interests dealt in his book not only with the world of plants and animals, natural resources and particular features of tidal movements, but also with the customs and practices of the Celtiberian people. According to Diodorus, in earlier times the Celts and the Iberians had been enemies but had later come to terms, shared the lands they once fought over and ultimately, having intermingled, accepted the name 'Celtiberian'. Diodorus also praises the hospitality of the Celtiberians, the strength and endurance of their horsemen and foot-soldiers, and the high quality of their iron weaponry. He mentions as one of their odder features the practice of using urine to wash in and clean their teeth (*Historical Library* 5, 33, 1–5 and 34, 1–2).

From the classical sources we learn that the Celtiberians were divided into numerous tribes, including the Belli, with their important settlement of Segeda in the valley of the Jalón; the Arevaci, with their capital of Numantia in the upper Duero basin, in the western part of the modern province of Soria; the Pelendones in the area between the Duero and the Moncayo; and the Berones on the upper Ebro in the locality of Briones, which was named after them.

All these tribes first impinged upon the consciousness of the Romans in the first half of the second century BC when the Romans were seeking to bolster their power in the region, after the defeat of Hannibal in the Second Punic War and the expulsion of the Carthaginians from Spain.

THE STRUGGLE FOR NUMANTIA: ROME'S WARS AGAINST THE CELTIBERIANS

In 209 BC the Romans had occupied Carthago Nova (now Cartagena), which had been founded twelve years earlier, and in 201 BC, the Carthaginians were compelled to surrender all their Spanish possessions in a peace treaty with Rome. In 180 BC, the proconsul of the province of Hispania Citerior, Tiberius Sempronius Gracchus, conquered several Celtic settlements, exacted tribute from the defeated tribes and forbade them to establish new fortified settlements. In 154 BC the Belli built a large wall round their capital of Segeda, in defiance of the agreement, and this led to war with Rome, involving not only those tribes generally termed Celtiberian, but also the neighbouring Vaccaei in the central Duero valley, the Vettones between the Tagus and the Duero, and the Lusitani. In 151 BC the Roman praetor Servius Sulpicius Galba was beaten by the Lusitani, but a year later he achieved their voluntary subjugation. Defying all agreements, Sulpicius Galba exploited his advantage to carry out a bloodbath among the defenceless Lusitani and sell the survivors into slavery. Thanks to his considerable wealth, he was able to thwart an attempt to put him on trial in Rome. One of the Lusitani who managed to escape was Viriatus, who in 147 BC took command in a war against the Romans and achieved significant military successes using a flexible guerilla strategy. In 147 BC he seized the valley of the Guadalquivir and dealt the Romans several severe defeats, and in 140 BC he forced the Roman proconsul Quintus Fabius Maximus Servilianus to capitulate. A year later, however, the peace treaty which endorsed Viriatus as ruler of the conquered regions of southern Spain and declared him 'a friend of the Roman people' (*amicus populi Romani*) was pronounced null and void by the Roman senate. After renewed fighting, Viriatus was murdered in the same year by his own countrymen at the instigation of the Roman proconsul Quintus Servilius Caepio. As a result, the leadership of the Celtiberian resistance to the Romans passed to the Arevaci, who had taken in the fugitive Belli from Segeda in 154 BC. Their eastern outpost of Numantia, at the confluence of the Duero and the Merdancho on the plain of Old Castile, became the focus and the embodiment of this resistance, and this ended only in 133 BC when Publius Cornelius Scipio Aemilianus Africanus seized and destroyed Numantia after a siege lasting several months.

After the fall of Numantia, the will of the Celtiberian tribes to resist was broken, although in the first two decades of the first century BC there was further conflict under the Roman proconsul Titus Didius and his successor Quintus Valerius Flaccus. Gradually, however, the town-like settlements were Romaniscd and Latin speech and writing steadily spread. In the years 80 to 71 BC, the whole region became deeply involved when the Lusitani again rose against the Romans, led by Sertorius, a former officer of the Roman equestrian order. In the first years of this war, Sertorius repeatedly achieved military successes against the Roman proconsuls Quintus Caecilius Metellus and Marcus Domitius Calvinus, thanks to his use of native guerilla tactics. After Pompey took command in Spain in 77 BC, Sertorius inflicted some heavy defeats on him, but from 75 BC, in spite of an alliance with King Mithridates VI of Pontus, Sertorius was increasingly forced onto the defensive. He was murdered by his own followers in 72 BC, and Pompey won the war just one year later. Between 29 and 19 BC Augustus's victories over the Astures and Cantabri in the region north of the Duero completed the subjugation of the Iberian peninsula.

CELTIBERIAN, IBERIAN, BASQUE: THE PRE-ROMAN LANGUAGES OF SPAIN

Well into the first half of the twentieth century it was thought that the language of the pre-Roman population of Spain was an early form of Basque. Only after the end of World War II did the understanding take root that Basque was not a descendant of the language of the old Iberians and that two completely different languages were in use in the early inscriptions on the peninsula: the non-Indo-European Iberian and an ancient form of Celtic.[3] On the basis of the classical term for the people, 'Celtiberians', the same name was applied to their language. However, the evidence of personal and place names shows that this language was used in an area far wider than the territory of the tribes called 'Celtiberian', for example in Asturias and Cantabria.

To write the Celtiberian inscriptions, some use was made of the Iberian syllabic script, which was widespread in the south of the country, as well as of the Latin alphabet, which was usual in Roman garrisons and administrative centres. All Celtiberian inscriptions date approximately from the period between 180 and 50 BC, so the tradition begins only with the appearance of the Romans in the region and – unlike in Gaul – comes to an end before the imperial period. The most significant Celtiberian epigraphic evidence includes the large rock inscription in Latin script at Peñalba de Villastar in the province of Teruel, which is generally taken to be a dedication to the god Lugus, and the first bronze tablet from Botorrita, discovered in 1970 during excavations at the ancient locality of Contrebia Belaisca, south of Saragossa. This latter is written in Iberian script and much of its meaning is still in dispute. In 1992 a second bronze tablet, also in the Iberian script and containing mainly personal names, was unearthed in Botorrita. The so-called Lusitanian inscriptions in the west of the peninsula are also noteworthy. These are thought to show either a particularly ancient form of Celtic or another Indo-European tongue influenced by Celtic. The best known Lusitanian linguistic monument is the rock inscription at Cabeço das Fráguas near Guarda in Portugal, which is believed to refer to a threefold animal sacrifice of the Roman *suovetaurilia* type.

When and how the Celtic language reached the Iberian peninsula and spread across it is largely unknown. Older studies in prehistory posited an earlier 'Indo-European' migration in the second millennium BC and a later 'Celtic' migration in the first half of the first millennium BC, in which the influx of Celtic settlers was linked with the expansion of the Urnfield culture. However, a contrary view now prevails: that the expansion of the Urnfield culture as a new form of burial should not be seen as constituting evidence of a migration, and therefore does not permit us to draw any conclusions regarding the introduction of a new language into the peninsula. In fact the whole region is characterised by a strikingly unified native cultural landscape, and the archaeological deposits in the Celtic-speaking territories can rarely be interpreted as new developments with recognisable origins north of the Pyrenees. To what extent Celtiberian owes its spread to the assimilation of a pre-Celtic population, and to what extent it should be attributed to the influx of Celtic-speaking newcomers can hardly be determined given the present state of our knowledge. A similar problem may be seen in the case of the Celts of northern Italy, where the results of modern research in archaeology and comparative linguistics and the statements of the classical historians all illuminate different aspects of a complex historical process.

CHAPTER 6

The Celts in Northern Italy

FROM THE GOLASECCA CULTURE TO LA TÈNE: THE EVIDENCE OF ARCHAEOLOGY

When the International Congress of Anthropology and Prehistorical Archaeology met in Bologna in 1871, the participants went on an excursion to the diggings at the Etruscan town of Marzabotto, south of Bologna. The similarity between certain of the grave goods and some hoards found in Switzerland and Champagne led the French scholar of prehistory Gabriel de Mortillet to link the Marzabotto graves with the incursion of Celtic peoples into Italy, recorded by the classical historians, towards the end of the fifth century BC and the beginning of the fourth. After over a century of intensive excavation in the regions south and north of the Alps, modern archaeology has confirmed the close relations – first noted at Marzabotto – that existed between the Celtic peoples of 'Gaul this side of the Alps' (*Gallia cisalpina*) and 'Gaul beyond the Alps' (*Gallia transalpina*) before the Romanisation of northern Italy in the third and second centuries BC. The deposits, far more than the classical writings, point to a complex relationship of co-operation and cohabitation between the Celts, the Etruscans, the Liguri and the Veneti and their respective cultures. Of particular note is the so-called Golasecca culture in the northern Italian lakes region north of Milan. The bearers of this culture clearly exercised an intermediary function between the Mediterranean south and the Celtic north, owing to their control of long-distance communication routes over the Alpine passes of St Bernard and St Gotthard.[1]

The study of the Golasecca culture, named after the site of some finds close to the southern end of Lake Maggiore, began in about 1870, but for a long time no consensus could be reached regarding the ethnic attribution of the deposits. Some researchers regarded the bearers of the Golasecca culture as Celts, while others opted for the Liguri or assumed a mixed 'Celtoligurian' population, falling back on an expression used in classical ethnography. New excavations and studies of older finds showed that inscriptions in a Celtic tongue, the so-called Lepontic, were made near Lake Como as early as the sixth and fifth centuries BC. But the question of when and how its speakers came to this region is one on which opinions differ to this day. In the territory of the Golasecca culture, fibulae of a kind typical of central European West Hallstatt culture occur as early as 600 BC. It might therefore appear at first sight that these finds confirm Livy's statement dating a first migration of Celtic peoples to Italy early in the sixth century BC (*History of Rome* 5, 34). However, we should bear in mind that Livy's account is not supported by other documentary sources, and that the archaeological data do not suggest an influx of newcomers at the turn of the sixth century BC. Instead, the archaeologists have pointed out that the characteristic features of Golasecca culture can be traced back to the thirteenth century BC without any significant interruption. Only at this period, the beginning of the so-called Canegrate culture in pottery and metal-working, can we identify innovations of any importance that have Transalpine counterparts and point to close relations between the two regions. In the centuries that followed, the Golasecca culture turned increasingly towards the culture of its southern neighbours, while also serving as an intermediary between the Mediterranean world and the regions north of the Alps, following the increase in Etruscan trade with the north from the eighth century BC. This is demonstrated by numerous artefacts exported from the Etruscan trading centres of Vetulonia and Felsina (later Bologna) to the territory of both the Golasecca and the West Hallstatt cultures. We may assume that in addition to finished products, raw materials such as amber, coral and tin and comestibles such as wine, oil and salt were also traded.

As in the Iberian peninsula, we cannot precisely determine to what extent the spread of the Celtic language in the region of the northern Italian lakes results from a process of assimilation, or to what extent this may be attributed to the immigration of Celtic-speaking people. In either case it is noteworthy that individual finds, such as the parts of a sword-belt, show the presence of Celtic outsiders in northern

Italy as early as the fifth century BC, although nothing more can be deduced about their activities or their relations with the native population. While it is possible that we are dealing with members of marauding warrior bands who had crossed the Alps on their own initiative, they may equally well have been enlisted mercenaries. The great Celtic migrations of about 400 BC, archaeologically attested by the products of La Tène crafts, apparently formed only the culmination of a complex and much longer process of infiltration that probably began centuries earlier.

CELTS, ETRUSCANS AND ROMANS: THE LITERARY EVIDENCE

The Celtic-speaking population of northern Italy before the fourth century BC is known to us only from archaeological hoards and a few inscriptions, but from the subsequent period there is literary evidence of several large tribes, most of whose names are also recorded from the Celtic regions north of the Alps. At the southern limit lived the Senones, whose territory lay on the east coast of Italy between the Utens (Uso) and the Aesis (Esino). In Gaul itself their name first occurs in Caesar's accounts, in which the Senones lived south of the Belgae, between the middle Loire and the Seine. The Senones who migrated to Italy are known from archaeological evidence at the burial grounds of Montefortino d'Arcevia and Santa Paolina di Filottrano, and from the richly furnished warrior tomb at Moscano di Fabriano in the upper Esino valley. The Adriatic coast between the mouth of the Po and the Apennines, according to Polybius and Livy, was inhabited by the Lingones. This name, which endures to this day in the name of the town of Langres, appears in Caesar's work as the name of a tribe in the region between the Senones and the Sequani. To the west of the Italian Lingones dwelt the Boii, whose territory extended from Bononia (previously the Etruscan Felsina, and now Bologna), to Mutina (Modena) and Parma, and was bounded in the north by the Po. North of the Po, between the rivers Oglio and Adige, lived the Cenomani, with their centres at Brixia (Brescia) and Verona, and west of the Cenomani were the Insubres, with their capital of Mediolanum. While the name of the Insubres is known only from Italy, that of the Cenomani also occurs in Gaul as the name of a tribe in the region of the modern Maine, between the Loire and the Seine.

In about 390 BC, a few years after expelling the Etruscans from the plain of the Po, the Celts pushed west against Rome from the territory of the Senones, defeated a Roman army on the Allia and seized the city on the Tiber. According to the heavily embroidered later tradition, the Romans succeeded in defending the Capitoline Hill against all assaults and buying the withdrawal of the besieging Celts by paying a huge ransom. After this the Celts continued to play an important role in conflicts within Italy, for example as allies of the tyrant Dionysius I of Syracuse, who, after conquering the region in 386 BC, asserted his influence in the area of the northern Adriatic and established bases in Ancona and the Dalmatian islands. Of the military conflicts with Rome, the later Roman historians recounted a number of legendary episodes. Livy, for example, writes that in about 360 BC the Roman Titus Manlius Imperiosus, after triumphing in single combat against a Celtic warrior, cut off the head of his vanquished foe, put on his twisted neck-ring (Latin *torques*) and thus received the nickname Torquatus (*History of Rome* 6, 42, 5). Livy also tells how Marcus Valerius was able to defeat a physically superior Celtic warrior in single combat, with the aid of a raven that landed on his helmet, and on the strength of this received the epithet Corvus (*History of Rome* 7, 26, 1–5).

In 295 BC the Senones, who were in alliance with the Umbrians, Samnites and Etruscans, were beaten for the first time by the Romans near the Umbrian town of Sentinum. In 285 BC they enjoyed greater success against a Roman army, with a successful assault on the town of Arretium (Arezzo), which was allied to Rome, but they then suffered a decisive defeat at Roman hands the following year, and the Romans proceeded to found the colonies of Sena Gallica (Senigallia) and Arminium (Rimini) on the Adriatic coast north of Ancona in 283 and 268 BC. In 283 BC at Lake Vadimone, near Bomarzo, the Romans retained the upper hand over the combined Etruscans and Boii, who were forced to sue for peace. Soon after the end of the First Punic War (264–241 BC), new tensions developed between the Roman Republic and its Celtic neighbours. In 232 BC Rome annexed the territory of the Senones, parcelling it out to citizens of Rome by drawing lots, and this prompted the Boii and Insubres to form an alliance against the Romans, who, for their part, formed their own alliance with the Veneti, the Samnites, the Etruscans and the Cenomani. In 225 BC the Boii and Insubres suffered a crushing defeat at the town of Telamon in Etruria, and a year later the Boii submitted to Rome. In 222 BC, at the battle of Clastidium (Casteggio), the Romans again routed the Insubres, seized their capital of Mediolanum, and in 218 BC founded the colonies of Placentia (Piacenza) and Cremona on Celtic territory.

When the Second Punic War (218–201 BC) broke out, Celtiberians fought alongside the Boii and Insubres in the army of the Carthaginian commander Hannibal, who, after crossing the Alps, defeated the Romans in three battles, on the Trebbia (218 BC), on Lake Trasimeno (217 BC) and at Cannae (216 BC). However, with the Romans' recapture of Carthago Nova (209 BC), their victory over Hannibal's brother Hasdrubal near Sena Gallica (207 BC), and Hannibal's recall to Carthage (203 BC), the fortunes of war changed to favour the Romans. After the final defeat of the Carthaginians at Zama (202 BC), they moved decisively against the Celts of northern Italy. In the years 197–194 BC they struck at the Insubres and in 193 BC at the Boii, and the vanquished remnants then fled Italy and settled in Bohemia, which later took its name from them (Latin *Boiohaemum*). In 190–189 BC, with the dispatch of more colonists to Placentia and Cremona and the establishment of a new colony in Bononia, the Romans laid the foundations for a lasting Romanisation of the Celtic territories of northern Italy.

GAULISH AND LEPONTIC: THE CELTIC INSCRIPTIONS OF NORTHERN ITALY

Apart from the Celtic place names and personal names which Greek and Latin literature has preserved, the language of the Celts of northern Italy is known from a number of brief inscriptions, in which comparative linguists distinguish a Lepontic group and a Gaulish group.[3] Both the Lepontic and Gaulish inscriptions are written in a form of north Etruscan script, the so-called Lugano alphabet. But whereas the Lepontic inscriptions from the region of the northern Italian lakes begin in the sixth or fifth centuries BC, the oldest Gaulish inscriptions are from the period after 400 BC, after the Celts had driven the Etruscans out of the plain of the Po. Some of the problems which these inscriptions still pose for researchers may be illustrated by the following examples.

This inscription on a vessel from Ornavasso, referring to a burial offering, is one of the latest samples of Lepontic, from the second or first century BC (see Lambert 1994, 21 and Solinas 1995, no. 128):

laTumarui: saPsuTai: Pe:
uinom: našom

To Latumaros and Sapsuta;
wine from Naxos

Here -*ui* and -*ai* can easily be recognised as the Celtic equivalents of the Latin dative endings -*o* (masculine) and -*ae* (feminine); the element -*pe*, meaning 'and', corresponds to the Latin -*que* (Greek *te*, Sanskrit -*ca*, found in Celtiberian in the form -*cue*); and the Celtic word *uinom* for wine is borrowed from the Latin *vinum* (Irish *fín*, Welsh *gwin*). However, the following stone inscription from Vergiate, thought to date from the beginning of the fifth century BC, is much less clear (see Lambert 1994, 21 and Solinas 1995, no. 119):

PelKui: Pruiam: Teu: KariTe: išos: KaliTe: Palam

In this case it is clear that the first four and the last three of the total of seven words form two phrases of parallel structure. In the first, the subject is the noun *Teu*, and in the second the pronoun *išos* is the subject. *KariTe* and *KaliTe* function as verbs, while the two nouns *Pruiam* and *Palam* (whose ending corresponds to the Latin accusative in -*m*) stand as direct objects of the two verbs. In *PelKui* we can recognise the dative of the personal name *PelKos* (probably pronounced *Belgos*), while in *Teu* the personal name *Dēvū* can be discerned (from an older form *Deivō*). (The spelling of these two words illustrates a typical feature of the Lugano alphabet: it makes no distinction between the voiceless consonants *p*, *t*, and *k* and their voiced counterparts *b*, *d*, and *g*.) However, both verbs and both direct objects lack any plausible etymology, so the meaning of the sentence remains obscure.

By contrast, the two large Gaulish inscriptions in stone at Todi and Vercelli are easier to understand since a Latin translation is supplied. The inscription found at Todi in Umbria in 1839 consists of a single sentence, not fully preserved in its Latin version, saying: 'Coisis, the son of Drutos, built the tomb of his brother Ategnatos, the son of Drutos' (see Lambert 1994, 74–6).

> [ATEGNATEI.DRVTEI.F.]
> . . . COI]SIS
> DRVTEI.F.FRATER
> EIVS
> MINIMVS.LOCAV-
> IT.ET.STATVIT
>
> ATEKNATI.TRUT-
> IKNI.KARNITU
> ARTUAŠ KOISIS.T-
> RUTIKNOS

As a comparison of the versions shows, the Latin sentence is fuller than the Gaulish. The single verb *karnitu* in the Gaulish is matched by two Latin verbs, *locavit et statuit,* and the description of Coisis as younger brother of the deceased Ategnatos (*frater eius minimus*) does not appear at all in the Gaulish. The rendering of the Latin expression *Druti f(ilius)* by *Drutiknos* is typically Celtic. The element *-cno-* also serves to indicate the name of a person's father. Thus, besides the god Taranus, we can recognise his son by the name of Taranucnos, and in a dedication found in 1894 in Genouilly the names of a father and son occur side by side as *Aneuno(s) Oclicno(s)*, 'Aneunos, son of Oclos', and *Lugurix Aneunicno(s)*, 'Lugurix, son of Aneunos' (see Lambert 1994, 86–7 and 94). The verb *karnitu* in the inscription cited above may be derived from the Celtic word that denotes a heap of stones in Irish and Scots Gaelic, in the form *carn,* and has been borrowed into English as *cairn.*

A longer Latin text with a shorter Gaulish rendering also appears in an inscription from Vercelli found in 1960 in a gravel pit on the bank of the Sesia (see Lambert 1994, 76–9 and Ch. Peyre in Verger 2000, 155–206). It had been carved into a block of stone measuring 1.5 metres by about seventy centimetres, which had probably served as one of four such stones marking the limits of an area of a sacred site. The longer and better preserved text in Latin reads:

FINIS
CAMPO.QVEM
DEDIT.ACISIVS
ARGANTOCOMATER-
ECVS.COMVNEM
DEIS.ET.HOMINIB-
VS.ITA VTI LAPIDES
IIII.STATVTI SVNT

End
Of the field which
Acisios
Argantocomaterecos
Donated to be the shared property
Of gods and men,
Where four stones
Have been placed.

From the perspective of cultural and religious history, the translation of the Latin expression *communem deis et hominibus* by the compound adjective *dēvogdonion*, 'belonging to gods and men', is of particular interest, as it contains the old Celtic words for 'god' (*dēvos*, whence Irish *día* and Welsh *duw*) and 'man' (*gdonios*, whence Irish *duine* and Welsh *dyn*) in their oldest surviving forms. Here we may note that Celtic *gdonios* is related to Greek *chthon*, so the Celts, like the Romans and Germans, described men as 'earthly' (compare Gothic *guma* and Latin *homo* 'man', and Latin *humus* 'earth'). The fact that the adjective *dēvogdonios* has been attested nowhere else, and was completely unknown until the chance discovery of the inscription at Vercelli, clearly shows the extent to which our knowledge of the Celtic world is dependent on the current state of research. Some major surprises may yet await us in the soil of the once-Celtic-speaking regions.

CHAPTER 7

The Celts in Asia Minor

MERCENARIES AND SETTLERS: THE HISTORY OF THE GALATIANS

While the beginnings of the Celtiberians and the Celtic inhabitants of northern Italy are lost in the twilight of prehistory, the movement of the Celts into their easternmost areas of settlement on the Anatolian plain lies exposed to the clear light of Hellenistic historiography.[1] The history of the Galatians (as the Celtic inhabitants of Asia Minor are known in modern usage, as distinct from that of classical antiquity) begins soon after the establishment of the kingdom of Bithynia in north-western Asia Minor at the beginning of the third century BC. After the death of the founder of the kingdom in 280 BC, his eldest son and successor Nicomedes I invited Celtic mercenaries into the country to join in the struggle against his younger brother Zipoetes. After the defeat and execution of Zipoetes in 277 BC, these mercenaries first lingered restlessly in the regions bordering on Bithynia, but gradually settled down. According to the classical sources, the Celts of Asia Minor were divided into three tribes: the Tolistoagii, the Tectosages and the Trocmi. The Tolistoagii, whose name also appears in the form Tolistobogii, settled in the west, near Pessinus and Gordium, while the Tectosages settled in the central area around Ancyra (Ankara), and the Trocmi in the east on the right bank of the River Halys (the modern Kızıl Irmak near Tavium). Each of the three tribes was divided into four territories, known as tetrarchies, each ruled by a tetrarch (*tétrarchos*), a judge (*dikastēs*) and a commander of the army (*stratophýlax*), with two assistants (*hypostratophýlakes*). The twelve tetrarchs together had a 'council of 300', which assembled in a site known as a *drunémeton*. For the political offices and functions of the Galatian tribes, only the

Greek names have come down to us, but the term *drunémeton*, passed on by Strabo *(Geography* 12, 5, 1), evidently stands for a Celtic word meaning an 'oak sanctuary' (in the sense of a sacred grove). Here we may note that the element *dru-* 'oak' also figures in the name of the 'oak-knowing' Druids, but the classical sources contain no reference whatever to any Galatian Druids. Whether their existence in Asia Minor may be assumed nonetheless is not clear (see Schmidt 1994, 26).

As mercenaries in the service of the Hellenistic rulers, the Galatians again played a vital role after a decisive defeat by King Antiochus I of Syria in the so-called 'elephant battle' in 275 BC. In about 250 BC, Ziaelas, a son of King Nicomedes I, conquered a large part of the kingdom of Bithynia with the help of the Tolistobogii; in about 240 BC King Antiochus Hierax, with Galatian support, defeated his elder brother and rival Seleucos II at Ancyra, and in 217 BC King Ptolemy IV of Egypt defeated King Antiochus III of Syria with the support of Celtic auxiliaries. Under Antiochus II (261–246 BC), a 'Celtic tax' was levied as tribute on the Galatians, but King Attalus I of Pergamum (241–197 BC) refused to pay it. In a battle near the source of the Caice (now Bakır Çay) close to Pergamum, he routed the Galatians and as a result received the honorific title *sōtēr*, or 'saviour'. Attalus I then brought the Celtic tribe known as the Aegosages from Thrace to Greece and settled them on the Hellespont.

After Antiochus III of Syria had conquered more areas of Asia Minor in the first decade of the second century BC, and had also dominated Thrace after crossing the Hellespont, the Romans intervened to protect the Greek towns of Asia Minor. In 190 BC Antiochus was beaten at the battle of Magnesia, and in 188 BC he renounced all his conquests in Asia Minor in the Treaty of Apamea. Since the Galatians had also fought the Romans at Magnesia, the Roman supreme commander, Gnaeus Manlius Vulso, launched a punitive expedition against them. During this expedition the main strongholds of the Tolistobogii on Olympus and of the Tectosages and Trocmi on Mount Magaba, east of Ancyra, were stormed by the Romans, and large numbers of Galatians perished or were sold into slavery. The main beneficiary of the peace of Apamea was Eumenes II of Pergamum, who received almost the whole of Seleucid Asia Minor. Again, he gained the upper hand in the war that followed against the Galatians, who were allied with Prusias I of Bithynia and Pharnaces I of Pontus, and he celebrated his successes in about 180 BC by building an altar to Zeus in Pergamum.

In 133 BC, by an instruction in the will of the last King Attalus III, the empire of Pergamum became a possession of Rome and was made the province of Asia in 129 BC. In the conflict between the Romans and King Mithridates VI of Pontus, the Galatians first joined with the Romans, but then recognised the superiority of Mithridates and gave many hostages from among the tetrarch nobility. After the first significant Roman victory at Chaironeia, Mithridates had a large part of the Galatian nobility put to death, but then had to formally relinquish Galatia in the peace of Dardanos in 85 BC. After the death of Mithridates in 63 BC, Pompey placed each of the three Galatian tribes under the rule of a single tetrarch as part of the new political order in Asia Minor. Deiotarus, who in 86 BC had escaped Mithridates's purge and supported all the Roman commanders against the king of Pontus, continued to rule over the Tolistobogii, while his son-in-law Brogitarus received dominion over the Trocmi and Castor Tarcondarius became tetrarch of the Tectosages. After the death of Brogitarus, the Roman senate granted the tetrarchy of the Trocmi to Deiotarus in 52 BC, and he ruled the whole of Galatia after the assassination of the tetrarch Castor in 44 or 40 BC. After Deiotarus's death, his grandson Castor succeeded him, and he in turn was succeeded in 36 BC by his erstwhile record-keeper Amyntas, who since 39 BC had ruled the kingdom of Pisidia in the area of the western foothills of the Taurus Mountains. When Amyntas was killed in battle against a Pisidian mountain tribe in 25 BC, Augustus made the Galatian client state a Roman province.

GALATIAN NAMES: THE CELTIC LINGUISTIC HERITAGE IN GREEK RECORDS

With the incorporation of the Galatian state into the Roman empire, Augustus had laid the foundations for the complete Romanisation of the Galatians. One of the foremost features of the Galatian culture, which survived into the late classical period, according to the documentary and literary evidence, is its Celtic language (see Schmidt 2001 and Freeman 2001). As might be expected, given the central European origin of the Galatian tribes, we are dealing here not with an independent member of the mainland Celtic family, as in the case of Celtiberian in the Iberian peninsula and Lepontic in northern Italy, but rather with a variant of Gaulish. Unlike Gaul, however, Asia Minor has as yet yielded no inscriptions with continuous text in Celtic, so our knowledge of Galatian rests above all on names and isolated loan-words in Greek, and less frequently Latin, texts. The compound personal names of the Galatian nobility display a striking similarity to Gaulish compound personal names, which are known to us in great numbers from inscriptions and literary sources.[2]

Of the Galatian personal names which have already occurred, *Deiotaros* and *Brogitaros* should be mentioned first, although their meaning remains unclear. The second element -*taros* may represent the Celtic word for 'bull' (Gaulish *tarvos*, Welsh *tarw*), while the first element *Deio-* may be connected to the word for 'god' (Gaulish *dēvos*, Irish *día*, Welsh *duw*). The component *brogi-* is clearly the Celtic equivalent of English *march* and German *Mark* in the sense of 'boundary, borderland' (*Irish bru(i)g*, Welsh *bro*). It appears in the name the Welsh have for themselves, *Cymry* (from *kombrogī*), as well as in the Gallic tribal names *Allobroges* and *Nitiobroges*, which, according to the meaning of their components, mean respectively 'those living in foreign parts' (compare the Germanic runic inscription *aljamarkiR*, 'foreigner') and 'those living in their own territory' (compare Sanskrit *nitya-*, 'own').

Also typically Celtic are the Galatian personal names ending in -*rix* (corresponding to Latin *rex* 'king'), of which numerous examples are also attested from the Celtic regions of central and north-western Europe. For example, from the early imperial period we know *Ateporix*, a member of the tetrarch nobility, whose son *Albiorix* held the office of high priest in Ancyra in Tiberius's time. While the name *Albiorix*, which is attested in southern Gaul as the name of a god, contains an old Celtic word for 'world' (Middle Welsh *elfydd*, 'land, world'), *Ateporix* contains, following the emphatic prefix *ate-*, the Celtic designation for 'horse' (Irish *ech*, 'horse' and Welsh *ebol*, 'foal'). Here we should note that the elements -*rix* and -*maros* may have been interchangeable in many compounds. If *Albiorix* occurs as the name of a Galatian deity and as a personal name, the Galatian personal name *Ateporix* has an exact equivalent in the Gaulish name for a deity, *Atepomaros*. The Galatian personal names *Zmertorix* and

Zmertomaros, the first element of which appears in the name of the Gallo-Roman goddess Rosmerta, also show the two forms in parallel. The Celtic word for 'horse', mentioned above, which also appears in the name of the originally Gaulish horse-goddess *Epona*, is seen again in the names of the two tetrarchs *Eporedorix* and *Eposognatos* ('friendly with horses'). The first of these was also the name of a noble from the Aedui tribe in Gaul during the time of Caesar. Between *epo-* and *-rix*, it contains the word *reda*, which meant a four-wheeled cart and also occurs in the Gallo-Roman term *paraveredus*. The latter originally meant a post-horse on a by-road (as distinct from *veredus*, a post-horse on a main route), and was borrowed in the early Middle Ages into German, where in the form *Pferd* it displaced the older native terms *Ross* (steed) and *Gaul* (nag). *Paraveredus* was also borrowed into Old French as *palefroi*, and from there passed into English as *palfrey*. The Celtic precursor of Latin *veredus* is thought to have developed into Welsh *gorwydd* 'steed', and *veredus* itself even passed via Greek into Arabic, where the word *barīd* came to designate the intelligence service of the Abbasid caliphs. Of Galatian names ending in *-rix*, *Gaisatorix* merits special attention, since it contains the term 'lancer' (from Celtic *gaisos* 'lance').

When the Galatian language died out we do not know, but it must have survived in rural areas of the Roman province, at least, into the third or fourth century AD. This is supported, for example, by Saint Jerome, who remarked that the Galatians spoke almost the same language as the inhabitants of Trier, although this remark was most probably based on an observation by the ecclesiastical writer Lactantius and not on personal experience (see Maier 1997, 124 with further references).

THE DYING GAUL: THE CELTS IN CLASSICAL ART

If the Celtic inhabitants of Asia Minor left behind no noteworthy works of art or pictorial representations of their own, their presence inspired Hellenistic artists to produce a number of significant images of them. These were to exert a decisive influence on the perception of the Celts in classical antiquity and beyond this in the modern era.[3]

The earliest images of the Celts to come from the Mediterranean cultural region are from northern Italy. They include an illustration of a battle between Italic and Celtic warriors on a bulbous two-handled vase from southern Etruria, which has been dated to the first quarter of the fourth century BC. In this imperfectly preserved picture a total of four people may be seen: on the far right, sprawling on the ground, lies a naked Celt upon whom a vulture has alighted. A second Celt, clad in a short cloak, is riding away over him, followed by another naked warrior on foot. While the horseman is looking to his right, the Celt, armed only with his sword and shield, is looking back over his shoulder as he runs, seeing that he is being pursued by a bearded Italic warrior, also armed with a sword and shield.[4] A similar scene is shown on a stele on an Etruscan tomb at Bologna, from about the same period: an armoured Italic horseman with raised sword is leaping from right to left upon a naked Celt, also armed with a sword, who is taking cover, in a standing position, behind his shield (see colour illustration in Moscati et al. 1991, 60).

The best known and most impressive pictorial representations of Celts from classical times have their origins in Asia Minor, where Kings Attalus and Eumenes II of Pergamum, after their victories over the Galatians, erected monumental, larger-than-life bronze statues to the vanquished. Originally placed on the acropolis of Pergamum, only a few figures from this group have come down to us in marble copies from the Roman imperial period. These include the celebrated 'Dying Gaul', which is held in the Capitoline Museum in Rome, and show a mortally wounded Celtic warrior slumped over his shield and war trumpet as he awaits his end. Another group of figures, now in the Terme Museum in Rome, shows a Celtic warrior with his wife overtaken by their pursuers after defeat in battle and now voluntarily choosing death rather than captivity. The man, who is wearing only a short, flapping cloak, is supporting his wife, as she sinks to the ground, with his left arm; turning his head back towards his pursuers, he is plunging his sword into his carotid artery with his right hand.

The terracotta frieze discovered in 1896, from an Italic temple in Civitalba near Sassoferato probably built about the year 160 BC after the Roman victories over the Boii and the Galatians, displays the influence of the Pergamum depictions of the Celts.[5] It shows a group of Celtic warriors put to flight while sacking a Mediterranean sanctuary by the gods that dwell in it. The goddesses Artemis and Athene, armed with a bow and spear respectively, can still be recognised, although the figure of Apollo has not been preserved. The Celts, whose chieftain is standing in a war-chariot drawn by two horses, may be recognised by their elongated shields, torcs and moustaches, as well as their straggly hair, combed back from the forehead to the neck.

Mention should also be made of some depictions of Celts on coins struck in Rome soon after the middle of the first century BC, following Caesar's conquest of Gaul.[6] One denar shows the bearded head of a man who can be identified by his hair-style as a Gaul, and on the reverse a Celtic chariot, in which a warrior with shield and spear sits beside the charioteer. Another denar coin shows the head of a woman in mourning, with her long hair undone, who can clearly be identifed as a Gaul from the accompanying typically Celtic war trumpet, or carnyx; on the reverse is a female deity with lance and stag. Other denar coins feature Gauls in chains and captured weapons on the reverse, including the typical trumpets and elongated shields.

When we view the classical depictions of the Celts in their entirety, it becomes clear that they reflect the viewpoint of a military adversary rather than a detached observer. The apparent realism of the classical artists goes hand in hand with unconcealed propagandist intent, which places disproportionately strong emphasis on the wild and warlike aspect. What would become the definitive manifestation of this artistic tradition in the longer term is most visible in the art of the empire of Pergamum, and these depictions of the Celts may have been used by later ethnographers such as Posidonius when they wrote their own descriptions.

CHAPTER 8

Gallo-Roman Culture

FROM AUGUSTUS TO CLOVIS: THE HISTORY OF THE PROVINCES OF GAUL

Just as the Galatians of Asia Minor clung to much of their cultural identity after the establishment of the Roman province of Galatia, the Celtic tribes of Gaul preserved many features of their native cultural heritage after the Roman conquest. From the blend of indigenous and foreign traditions, there emerged an independent Gallo-Roman culture which would endure for close to half a millennium, stretching from the Pyrenees to the Rhine and from the Atlantic to the Alps.[1] Unlike in Britain, where the old Celtic tongue reasserted itself after the Roman withdrawal, the Gaulish language increasingly yielded to Latin as time passed, and this, following annexations of land by Germanic tribes, gradually evolved into French.

From a political perspective, even after the establishment of the three Gaulish provinces in 27 BC and despite the progress of Romanisation, Gaul continued to be troubled by regional uprisings and incursions by Germanic marauders from the territory on the right bank of the Rhine (Urban 1999). In 16 BC the Roman governor Marcus Lollius suffered a severe defeat against the combined Sugambri, Usipetes and Tencteri. In AD 21 the Treveri and Aedui rose in rebellion at the same time and were subdued only with the intervention of the legions stationed in northern Germany. As rich graves from the Augustan period show, as early as the last decades of the pre-Christian era Rome was already taking pains to make the Gaulish nobility amenable to their new rulers by extensively conferring Roman civil rights. In pursuance of this policy, in AD 48 the

Emperor Claudius granted full civil rights to all the Gaulish nobility, against the opposition in the Senate of the urban Roman and Italian aristocracy.

Renewed trouble erupted twenty years later when the Aquitanian noble Julius Vindex, by this time governor of the province of Gallia Lugdunensis, rebelled against Nero and won the support of numerous Gaulish tribes. When Vindex was defeated by the commander of the north German legions in a battle at Vesontio (Besançon) and proceeded to take his own life, the uprising collapsed. Unrest continued, however, as the Roman officer Julius Civilis, from the Germanic tribe of the Batavi, led his people into rebellion in the turmoil following the death of Nero. With Julius Classicus and Julius Tutor of the Treveri and Julius Sabinus of the Lingones, he set about establishing an independent Gallo-Germanic empire. After continuing struggles along the Rhine border, with fluctuating fortunes on both sides, the Batavian rebellion was crushed by Roman troops in AD 70, during the reign of Vespasian. In the last two decades of the first century AD, under the Emperor Domitian, the border with Germany along the Rhine was secured by the construction of a *limes*, or fortified frontier, while along the left bank of the river the two provinces of Germania Superior and Germania Inferior came into being.

Although the Gaulish provinces enjoyed a long period of internal peace in the first half of the second century, soon after mid-century the Emperor Marcus Aurelius had to fend off an attack by the Chatti. In AD 197 Gaul became the arena of conflict between the Emperor Septimius Severus and his rival Clodius Albinus, which left the provincial capital Lugudunum sacked and reduced to ashes. In AD 233–4 the Germanic Alemanni first broke through the Roman frontier defences, thrusting into the Saarland and lower Alsace, across the Rhine as far as the territory of Gaul. Thrown back by the Emperor Maximinus Thrax, in AD 260 the Alemanni again overran the Roman territory on the right bank of the Rhine and pushed through the Burgundy gap to the lower Rhône. At the same time the Franks on the lower Rhine forced their way into Gaul and campaigned as far as southern Gaul and Spain. As a reaction to these expeditions, in AD 259, following a victory over the Franks, the army commander Postumus was appointed emperor. After the conquest of Cologne in AD 260, he formed the Germanic and Gaulish provinces into a separate empire, which later included Spain and Britain and lasted until AD 273.

In AD 284 Diocletian came to the imperial throne, having worked his way up from private soldier to commander of the imperial guard. He carried out a thorough reorganisation of the entire Roman empire, having first appointed his friend Maximian to share the throne with him in AD 286. To Maximian fell the task of dealing with the so-called Bagaudae in Gaul. These were impoverished farmers and herdsmen who had resorted to armed insurrection out of economic hardship. In AD 293 Diocletian and Maximian adopted Galerius and Constantius, prefects of the guard, and named them as their successors and joint regents. Gaul, with Spain and Britain, fell to Constantius, who chose Trier as his seat of government. In the course of a far-reaching division of the territory of the whole empire into twelve administrative regions (the so-called *dioeceses*), on Gaulish soil there arose in AD 297 the *Dioecesis Galliarum*, with eight provinces, and the *Viennensis Dioecesis*, with five. Further divisions increased the number of provinces to a total of seventeen in the second half of the fourth century, while the two *dioeceses* of Gaul were amalgamated between AD 418 and 425.

After several years of conflict following the abdication of Diocletian, Constantius's son Constantine reigned in the west from AD 312 and over the entire Roman empire from 324. When he died in 337, there was renewed confusion over the succession. Constantine's younger son Constans reigned in the west from 340, but he was overthrown in 350 by Magnentius, a senior officer, and perished during his flight to Spain. In the struggle against Magnentius, Constans's brother Constantius II called on the help of the Germanic peoples, who proceeded to advance deep into the interior of Gaul. With a decisive victory over the Alemanni near Argentorate (Strasbourg) in 357, Constantine's nephew Julian restored the Rhine border, and Emperor Valentinian then secured this between 365 and 375 by means of alliances with the Germani, and the systematic consolidation of fortified positions.

The final collapse of the frontier system came in 406, when the Germanic Vandals and Suebi, with the Alans, crossed the Rhine at Mainz, while the Franks invaded Gaul from the north and the Burgundians from the south. As there was no prospect of driving out the invaders or of keeping them out of the imperial territory in the long term, measures were stepped up to settle them on an amicable basis within the borders of the Roman empire and integrate them into the Roman army as confederates. Thus the Burgundians, for example, immediately after crossing the Rhine, received territory between Mainz, Alzey and Worms and, following their defeat in 436 at the hands of the Roman general Aetius and his allies the Huns, they were settled along the Rhône. Having roamed the Balkans and Italy, the Visigoths founded an empire in south-western Gaul in about 418 that reached its greatest extent about 475, with Tolosa (Toulouse) as its capital. The greatest success was achieved by the Franks, who settled the region west of the lower Rhine towards the end of the third century and were recruited into the Roman army in great numbers. In the fourth and fifth centuries the Salian Franks settled in what is now southern Belgium between Liège and Tournai, while the Rhenish Franks occupied the lower Rhine. In the second half of the fifth century, the Frankish king Clovis eliminated the remnants of Roman rule in northern Gaul, defeated his co-sovereign, and seized territory from the Alemanni and Visigoths to create a Frankish empire which would have a crucial influence upon the further political and cultural development of the West.

DEDICATORY INSCRIPTIONS AND MAGIC FORMULAE: CELTIC TEXTS FROM ROMAN GAUL

When Clovis defeated the last Roman ruler Syagrius and thus brought all of northern Gaul between the Somme and the Loire under his control, Gaul could look back on half a millennium of assimilation of Roman culture. During this time, changed administration and power structures, the development of urban centres, innovations in craft, trade and communications, to say nothing of the adoption of a southern mode of life, had irrevocably altered the face of Gaul. The foundations of Roman authority were formed by old tribal associations, whose importance is clear from the fact that in the late classical period the old tribal names displaced the official Roman names of many large cities and survive to this day in the French forms of these names. The names of the *Ambiani* (whence *Amiens*, formerly *Samarobriva*), the *Carnutes* (whence *Chartres*, formally *Autricum*), the *Parisii* (whence *Paris*, formerly *Lutetia*) and the *Remi* (whence *Reims*, formerly *Durocortorum*) are typical examples (see Dauzat and Rostaing 1979). Until the late classical period the Celtic inhabitants of Roman Gaul preserved not only their tribal names, but also their traditional Gaulish language, of which our knowledge has increased substantially in the last three decades, thanks to the sensational discovery of longer inscriptions (see Lambert 1994).

Most Gaulish inscriptions, which as a result of Romanisation are in the Latin script, are of a dedicatory nature. The great majority of them come from central Gaul and were inscribed, it is thought, during the first 100 years after the Roman conquest. A typical example is the following, which came to light in 1839 at Mont Auxois, the site of the ancient Alesia (see Lejeune 1988, L-13, and Lambert 1994, 98–101):

MARTIALIS . DANNOTALI
IEVRV . VCVETE .SOSIN
CELICNON ETIC
GOBEDBI . DUGIIONTIIO
VCVETIN
IN ALISIIA

Martialis (son) of Dannotalos,
dedicated to Ucuetis this
building, together
with the smiths who do honour
to Ucuetis
in Alesia.

Recent excavations lead us to suppose that this inscription refers to a shrine to the god Ucuetis who, according to the evidence of a Latin inscription found subsequently, was worshipped there with a goddess named Bergusia (see Martin and Varène 1973).

While the majority of the fifteen or so Gallo-Roman dedications found to date are brief, fragments of a longer Gaulish inscription were discovered in 1897 near Coligny in the south of France (see Duval and Pinault 1986). The inscription is a remnant of a Gaulish calendar, showing on a bronze tablet a period of five solar years. The basic unit of measurement of time was the lunar year, with 355 days (seven times thirty, and five times twenty-nine). The difference

between the lunar year and the solar year was made up by inserting a
thirty-day leap-month every thirty months, or two and a half years.
The five-year cycle shown on the calendar covers sixty-two indivi-
dually named months, each of which is divided into two halves of
fifteen plus fifteen, or fifteen plus fourteen days. We may assume that
the calendar, with the statue of a deity found with it, was displayed in
a sanctuary and used for cult purposes, among others. For a long time
it was thought to date from the first century AD, but today is
considered to have originated no earlier than the end of the second
century.

The Coligny calendar, so-called after the place where it was
discovered, remained for a long time the longest Gaulish inscription,
until in January 1971, during excavations at the Gallo-Roman
sanctuary at Source-des-Roches de Chamalières near Clermont-
Ferrand, a lead tablet was found with an inscription in Gaulish
consisting of 336 letters, thus exceeding in length all previously
known Gaulish texts (see Lambert 1994, 150–9). The Gaulish text of
another lead tablet, which served as the lid of a funerary urn, found
in August 1983 during the archaeological investigation of a Gallo-
Roman cemetery at l'Hospitalet-du-Larzac (Aveyron), was much
longer again (see Lambert 1994, 160–72). Both these inscriptions
were evidently appeals to chthonic deities, and many of the words
and expressions used in them occur in similar form more than half a
millennium later in the Irish and Welsh literary monuments of the
Middle Ages. A key concept in both texts is the word *bricta* or
brictom, meaning 'magic', which is attested in the same meaning in
Ireland as *bricht* and in Wales as the second element of the word
lledfrith. Moreover, the expression *bnanom brictom*, or 'women's
magic' from the Larzac inscription has an exactly corresponding
phrase in an Old Irish Christian blessing which is applied *fri brichtu
ban*, or 'against women's magic', but the parallel cannot be seen as
either an example of the continuity of a magic formula or as anything
typically Celtic. Since magic spells are seen as the preferred weapon
of the physically weak, in many traditional cultures a particular
ability in this area is often attributed to women (especially older
women). What exactly *bricht* meant in pre-Christian times we cannot
fully gather from the medieval sources, as the descriptions in
narrative literature have plainly fantastic elements, and the constantly emphasised link with the Druids may only reflect the

Christian perspective of this genre. A further bridge between the traditions of the mainland and insular Celts is provided by the god Maponus, who is invoked in the Chamalières inscription. This deity is also known from several Latin dedications in northern England and lives on in the medieval Welsh tradition under the name of Mabon (see Maier 2001, 94–9). In spite of the numerous new words and grammatical forms which have become known to Celticists from these texts, differing interpretations exist of both inscriptions, so that at present not even a partially reliable complete translation can be provided.

We do not know exactly when the Gaulish language died out but, in the fifth and sixth centuries at the latest, large parts of the population must have understood it insufficiently or not at all (see Lambert 1994, 10–11). Late evidence of its use comes in about AD 400 from the compendium *De medicamentis*, compiled by the medical writer Marcellus Empiricus, from Burdigala (Bordeaux). As the author explains in the introduction to his work, his sources were not only the information from older medical literature, but also popular domestic remedies which he had learned from ordinary people. These are partly notes on the use of herbal medications and partly magic formulae and directions for the performance of magical procedures, some of which are wholly or partially preserved in Gaulish (see Meid 1996).

INTERPRETATIO ROMANA: ASPECTS OF GALLO-ROMAN RELIGION

The fact that some religious and magic Gaulish texts could be cited in the previous section is thanks to the wide dispersal of the Roman alphabet – without doubt one of the most significant innovations in the process of Romanisation. Generally speaking, with regard to Gallo-Roman religion, the archaeological investigations of the past thirty years show clear continuity from the immediate pre-Roman period to the Roman period. Although the Druids and certain sacrificial practices were proscribed under the Romans, the rural population, in particular, continued to seek out many of the old cult sites even after the conquest, and in time replaced them with stone-built temples after the Roman fashion (see Fauduet 1993a and

1993b). An important aspect of religion about which the sources from Roman Gaul provide information is the Celtic pantheon, of which pre-Roman evidence is largely absent. However, it is accessible to us almost exclusively through the inscriptions and sculptures in stone of the most thoroughly Romanised part of the population, and the picture thus obtained should not be generally applied to the whole population of Roman Gaul, and should on no account be projected back to the pre-Roman era.[2]

Gods and goddesses had a significant role to play as givers of fertility, a function which must have been of vital importance for the predominantly agrarian Gallo-Roman civilisation. This applies particularly to the mother-goddesses known as matrons (Latin *Matronae/Matres/Matrae*), whose cult is known to us from over 1,100 dedicatory inscriptions and stone sculptures, mostly from the second to the fourth centuries AD (see Bauchhenss and Neumann 1987). The matrons are most often depicted as a seated group of three richly attired women, holding flowers, fruits, cereals and the like in their hands. Both married and unmarried women (the latter indicated by their unbraided hair and absence of bonnets) are shown as matrons. In the inscriptions these goddesses have Celtic and Germanic names, the latter frequently being derived from the names of peoples, tribes or places.

The healing function of Celtic deities is also well attested, and there is now abundant and compelling evidence of this (see Bourgeois 1991–2, Landes 1992 and Chevallier 1992). For example, at the remains of a large spring-source sanctuary at Hochscheid in the Hunsrück-Eifel, there is living accommodation, a bath-house and other buildings, besides a Gallo-Roman ambulatory temple with statues of the divine couple Apollo Grannus and Sirona (see Weisgerber, G. 1975). Another important shrine of pilgrimage to the Gallo-Roman goddess Sequana was excavated in 1836–42 near the source of the Seine, some thirty kilometres north-west of Dijon. There, in 1963–7, archaeologists found approximately 200 unusually well preserved wooden votive offerings, mostly depicting people but in some cases limbs or internal organs (see Deyts 1983). A similar spring-source sanctuary existed west of Clermont-Ferrand at Chamalières, where several thousand wooden votive offerings were found in 1968–71.

That the Celts pictured their gods to themselves as mostly having human form emerges most clearly from anthropomorphic cult images, many of them from Roman times but a small number from an earlier date. Here the procedure now known as Interpretatio Romana, in which the names of indigenous and Roman deities were treated as equal, is typical. In dedicatory inscriptions the two names are often set side by side. Where the Roman name is found alone, occasionally the added word *Deo* or *Deae* (To the god . . ./ To the goddess . . .), unusual in the case of Roman deities, tells us that the donor had an indigenous deity in mind. The decisive factor in juxtaposing two deities was their accord in some particular area which is not always apparent. The nature or function of an indigenous deity can be only approximately determined with the aid of Interpretatio Romana.[3]

Family connections may be seen in the world of gods, just as in the life of humans. The earliest evidence in literature is offered by Timaeus of Tauromenion (see Diodorus Siculus, *Historical Library* 4, 56, 4). By his account, the Celts of the seaboard regions worshipped Castor and Pollux, since legend had it that they had come to them from the sea. This is confirmed by the great popularity of Castor and Pollux in the Gaulish and Germanic provinces of the Roman empire. As in other cases, the cult known in the imperial period may derive from indigenous models (see Duval, P.-M. 1976, 86–7 and Maier 1997, 96). At the same time, the practice of linking male and female deities as divine couples was particularly widespread in Roman Gaul. In many cases both partners bear the names of Roman deities, in accordance with Interpretatio Romana, but in a combination that is unusual. There are also inscriptions in which both partners bear Celtic names, for example *Sucellus* and *Nantosuelta*, *Borvo* and *Damona*, and *Ucuetis* and *Bergusia*. Where only one of the pair keeps a Celtic name, this is usually the goddess, while her partner often takes a Roman name in addition to or instead of his native Celtic name. Typical examples are the couples *Mercurius* and *Rosmerta*, *Mercurius Visucius* and *Visucia*, and *Apollo Grannus* and *Sirona*. It is possible that this treatment of names served to make plain the subordinate position of the indigenous goddess to the alien Roman god (see Green 1989, 45–73 and Maier 1997, 131–3).

Another feature of many gods from Roman Gaul is a particular connection to certain domestic and wild animals, expressed partly in images and partly in the names of the gods and goddesses. Some typical examples are set out below.

The bear appears occasionally in the iconography of pre-Roman times, on Gaulish coins, for example. Old Celtic names for the bear occur in the names of the goddesses *Andarta* and *Artio* (Welsh *arth*, 'bear'), perhaps also in the name of the god Matunus (Old Irish *math*, 'bear'). One of the two known inscriptions to the goddess Artio refers to a bronze figurine about twenty centimetres tall shown in a sitting position in front of a bear. In early Celtic society, the image of the bear as the epitome of strength was so powerfully felt that the Irish word *art* continued to be used in the sense of 'chief' or 'warrior' long after the word had gone out of use as a designation for the bear (which had died out in Ireland during the Bronze Age at the latest).[4]

An important role was also played by the stag, by whose antlers many essentially anthropomorphic devotional images of the pre-Roman and Roman periods may be recognised. The earliest evidence is a rock painting from Val Camonica in northern Italy, which has been dated to the fourth century BC. It shows a figure larger than life-size, wearing a long shirt-like garment and with antlers on its head, next to a human figure with hands held high. From its raised right arm hangs a torc and under the left arm, which is also raised, a snake is coiled. The picture of an upright figure with arms raised and antlers on a fragment of painted vase from Numantia and the well-known design on the silver plating of the Gundestrup cauldron also originate in pre-Roman times. The Gundestrup cauldron shows a figure, wearing a torc that identifies it as a deity and with antlers on its head, sitting cross-legged amidst animals. The raised right hand holds another torc, and twined round the raised left hand is a snake with the head of a ram.[5] Images from Roman times show gods (sometimes with their characteristic attributes, the torc and serpent) standing or sitting cross-legged. The bronze statuette of a deity recovered in 1845 from the River Juine at Bouray, about thirty-five kilometres south of Paris, wearing a torc and sitting cross-legged, with legs that end in hooves, may be a variant on this kind of figure. The serpent so often featured and the image of a horned god with a sack full of coins, which appears on a Gallo-Roman frieze from Rheims, have prompted the theory that all such figures relate to a chthonic god of wealth and plenty, in which the antlers may be seen as symbolic of strength or of annual renewal. The name of the horned god is supplied only by the partially preserved image on the so-called pillar of the Nautae of the Parisii, on which an inscription from the time of the Emperor Tiberius mentions Cernunnos (see Maier 1997, 69–70 and 205; also Duval, P.-M. 1989, I, 433–62).

Unknown in the iconography of the Hallstatt period, the boar appears in many images from the Roman and immediately pre-Roman period, for example on Gaulish coins, as part of the helmet decoration in a design showing a Celtic warrior on the Gundestrup cauldron, and as a votive offering in Gallo-Roman temples. As the presumed attribute of a god, the boar is found with the sandstone figure of a nameless deity from Euffigneix (Haute-Marne), which has been dated by its style to the first century BC. As a mount for the goddess Diana, who was paired with the Gaulish goddess Arduinna, the boar appears with a Gallo-Roman bronze figure which may come from the Ardennes. The Gallo-Roman god *Mercurius Moccus*, whose name is identical with the Celtic word for 'pig' (Irish *mucc*, Welsh *mochyn*), is recorded in inscriptions.[6]

Unlike the boar, the bull has an important role as far back as the Hallstatt period. Among the names of deities found in inscriptions, the goddess *Damona*, whose name may be derived from the term meaning 'ox' (Irish *dam*, 'ox, cow') merits special mention. The dedications show that she was venerated singly, but also as the partner of the gods *Borvo*, *Albius* and *Moritasgus*. The name of the goddess *Sirona* may be compared here, if its derivation from a word for 'bull' is correct. The most striking instance of the bull as symbol or incarnation of a god is provided by the 'bull with three cranes' (*Tarvos Trigaranus*), whose name and image are shown on the pillar of the Nautae of the Parisii, like those of the god Cernunnos. The relief shows a bull standing behind a tree, with three cranes on its head and back. Beyond the bull can be seen some branches, perhaps representing another single tree or a whole forest. This picture has a parallel in the relief on a stele from Trier, where a bull's head and three birds can be seen in the dense foliage of the top of a tree. In the lower part of the picture a man dressed as a workman is walking with an axe in his hand, as if to cut down the tree. This may have a bearing on the god Esus, who is shown in similar fashion on the pillar of the Nautae, right beside the bull with the three cranes, but the mythological significance of these images remains obscure (see Maier 1997, 90 and 261–2; also Duval, P.-M 1989, I, 463–70).

Names which are applied without distinction to both deities and parts of the natural environment are typical of the pantheon of Roman Gaul. This aspect is striking in the case of numerous names of rivers, which appear in inscriptions as the names of gods, including the Rhine (*Rhenus*), the Seine (*Sequana*), the Yonne (*Icauna*), the Marne (*Matrona*) and the Saône (*Souconna*). Other geographical names which occur in Roman times as names of deities are the native names of the Black Forest (*Abnoba*), the Ardennes (*Arduinna*) and the Vosges (*Vosegus*). It is also noteworthy that many gods bear toponymic names. Aulun has its god *Alaunius*, Besançon has *Mars Vesontius*, Bouhy has *Mars Bolvinnus*, Cimiez has *Mars Cemenelus*, Luxeuil has *Luxovius*, Vence has *Mars Vintius* and Vouroux has *Mars Vorocius*. One particular feature of the Gaulish gods shows clearly in these toponymic personal names: the degree of regional affiliation. Here it should first of all be pointed out that the great majority of the names of divinities appear no more than once in inscriptions or are known exclusively from inscriptions from a single region or from a single locality. Of particular note is a regional connection in the case of the god Belenus, named by Tertullian as the god of the province of Noricum, while Herodian and the *Historia Augusta* name him as the tutelary god of the town of Aquileia. These statements are confirmed by the dedicatory inscriptions for Belenus, one of which originates in the eastern Alps, while almost all others were discovered in or near Aquileia (see Maier 1997, 33–4).

At the same time there are cases in which the same name appears in inscriptions in widely separated areas but this should not necessarily be taken to imply that the deity in question had any supra-regional importance. For example, a dedication found in Rome and another from Gey, near Düren, both to *Arduinna*, can be explained by the fact that, according to the inscription on the Roman monument, the donor was a *civis Remus* from the homeland of the goddess, serving in the Praetorian Guard in Rome. Similarly, *Mars Leucetius/ Loucetius* was venerated chiefly in the tribal area of the Treveri in Mainz, Worms and Wiesbaden. Of four inscriptions found outside this area, in Bath in Britain, in Grosskrotzenburg, Strasbourg and Angers, three certainly – and the fourth possibly – come from a Treverian donor. In cases of dedications mentioning the same divine name from widely dispersed localities, we also need to bear in mind that names with self-evident meanings could have been applied quite independently in different places. This may be the case, for example, with the name *Anextlomāros*, which, according to its etymology (Old Irish *anacul* 'protection'; *már* 'great'), must denote a god as a great or powerful protector. Dedications to deities of this name are known from South Shields in the north of England, Avenches in western Switzerland and possibly from near Le Mans in France, without there necessarily being any connection between them. The fact that the names of many gods are also recorded as personal names, and were therefore probably understood less as designations for any individual deity than as respectful epithets, prominently supports the multiple use of such formations. The alternative suggestion, that the people concerned were named after a god or goddess, seems less likely. Many locally popular deities (such as *Belenus* in the environs of Aquileia) play no part at all in the personal names of the region, while on the other hand personal names like *Camulus, Camula, Camulata, Camulatucus, Camulianus, Camulinius, Camulogenus* and *Camulognata* are much more common and widespread than the few dedications to *Mars Camulus* might suggest.

Of the prehistory of Gallo-Roman religious cults, very little is known since the scarce observations found in the Greek classics about the Celtic gods give no information about the geographical range of the cults in question, and instead of native Celtic names of deities give only those of classical mythology. For this reason, the picture provided by Caesar of the Gaulish gods on the eve of Romanisation is of particular and enduring note:

> Among the gods, they worship Mercury above all others. There are more numerous images of him than of any other god; they declare him the inventor of all the arts, the guide for every road and journey, and they deem him to have the greatest influence for all money-making and traffic. After him they set Apollo, Mars, Jupiter and Minerva. Of these deities they have almost the same idea as all other nations: Apollo drives away diseases, Minerva supplies the first principles of arts and crafts, Jupiter holds the empire of heaven, Mars controls wars.
>
> (*De Bello Gallico* 6, 17, 1–2)

If we attempt an interpretative exploration of the author's intention within the framework of his contemporary readers' mental horizons, Caesar's picture of the Gaulish pantheon clearly conforms to his tendency to shift the religion of the Gauls towards Roman religion and at the same time to mark it off as clearly as possible from the religion of the Germani: while the Celts have a hierarchically ordered pantheon, in which each god and each goddess has a counterpart in the Greco-Roman pantheon, their neighbours across the Rhine know nothing, even from hearsay, of personal gods (that is, gods in human form) (*De Bello Gallico* 6, 21, 2). Accordingly, the Celts – like the Romans – have a highly developed sacrificial system and a privileged clergy (the Druids), while the Germani make do without any Druids and place no special value on sacrificial practices. These differences in matters of religion correspond closely to the general level of civilisation since the Germans, according to Caesar, spend their entire lives hunting or in training for war, attach little importance to agriculture and sustain themselves, like nomads, mainly on milk, cheese and meat.

It is now generally accepted that this schematic opposition is a product of politically and militarily motivated propaganda, intended to highlight the capacity of the Gauls to assimilate against the sombre background of Germanic primitivism, and written with an eye to the Roman commander's plans for conquest. The prejudices that Caesar is opposing here show in Cicero's oration *pro Fonteio* in 69 BC, in which Cicero perpetuates the Hellenistic cliché of the godless, pagan Gauls as the scourge of civilised humanity, the opposite of Caesar's description. The fact that Mercury was indeed the most frequently represented deity in Roman Gaul does not in any way mean that Caesar was right, or that there was any visible continuity in the historical development of religion. It seems far more plausible that in Roman Gaul it was precisely the most Romanised part of the population – those whose religion found enduring expression in graven monuments – who reified the idea that Caesar was the first to propagate. Accordingly, the markedly local and regional nature of the great majority of Gaulish cults should not be taken as marking the dissolution or collapse of a largely unified pre-Roman pantheon. On the contrary, we should view the process of Interpretatio Romana and the supra-regional dissemination of particularly popular deities as a secondary standardisation of the original variety of localised cults. With the spread of Christianity in Gaul, however, the old Celtic divinities, even in their new Roman garb, passed swiftly into oblivion. Henceforward they would survive only in the lore of the insular Celts, who preserved their language after the end of the classical period and the mass migration of peoples.

PART II

The Insular Celts of the Middle Ages

CHAPTER 9

The Early Celts of Ireland and Britain

EXPLORERS, CONQUERORS AND HISTORIANS: THE EVIDENCE OF THE CLASSICAL SOURCES

We owe the earliest reports on Britain and Ireland to Greek seafarers who reached the 'tin islands' in the North Sea, known as Kassiter-ides, on their trading voyages beyond the Straits of Gibraltar in the sixth century BC.[1] The Roman poet Avienus made use of their sketches in his work *Ora maritima*, where he gives a description – incompletely preserved – of the coasts from Britain to the Black Sea in the fourth century AD. The Latin author betrays his dependence on a great number of older Greek sources by mentioning, for example, the traditional name for Ireland, 'the Sacred Isle' (*sacra insula*). All the evidence suggests that this is a rendering of the Greek expression *Hierā nēsos*, which arose because of the phonetic similarity between the Greek name of Ireland *Iernē* (Old Irish *Ériu*, Modern Irish *Éire*) and the Greek word *hieros* 'sacred'. For Britain, Avienus used the name 'the Isle of the Albions' (*insula Albionum*), which is derived from an indigenous term (compare Old Irish *Albu*, 'Britain', Modern Irish *Alba*, 'Scotland').

In the second half of the fourth century BC, the Greek seafarer and geographer Pytheas of Massalia reached Ireland and Britain on a voyage of discovery to northern Europe. Unfortunately, his book *On the Ocean* (*Peri Okeanu*), like the comprehensive description of the coasts by the politician and geographer Artemidorus of Ephesus from around 100 BC, has not survived. More detail on Britain did not come until the two expeditions undertaken by Julius Caesar to the south-east of the island in 55 and 54 BC. In his account of these campaigns, we find an extensive geographical excursus, which contrasts in stereotyped terms the low level of civilisation of the inhabitants of the interior with the high culture and advanced civilisation of the coastal dwellers (*De Bello Gallico* 5, 12–14).

Whereas Caesar's expeditions went no further than a demonstration of military might, the army dispatched by the Emperor Claudius in AD 43 conquered large areas of Britain, which was now incorporated into the Roman empire as the province of Britannia. Detailed accounts of the campaigns of the first century AD are given by the historian Tacitus in his *Annals* and in *Agricola*, a biographical tribute to his father-in-law Gnaeus Julius Agricola. During his governorship, between AD 77 and 84, the Romans drove north as far as Scotland and their fleet circumnavigated the island (see Hanson, W. S. 1991). In the period following, the northern border of the province of Britannia ran alternately between Carlisle and Newcastle and the Firth of Clyde and the Firth of Forth, while Ireland succeeded in permanently retaining its independence of the Roman state. The geographical work of the mathematician and astronomer Ptolemy, which records numerous Celtic names from both Ireland and Britain, dates from about AD 150 (Parsons and Sims-Williams 2000). A collection of ethnographic curios from these parts is contained in a geographical study written in about AD 200 by the Roman writer Julius Solinus, who relied principally on the *Natural History* of Pliny the Elder and the work of the geographer Pomponius Mela from the first century AD.

The spread of Christianity to Britain shows in the names of some ecclesiastical dignitaries who signed the enactments of the Council of Arles in AD 314. In the decades that followed, the historian Ammianus Marcellinus reports repeated attacks by the Picts of Scotland against the northern border of the province of Britain, while the Irish, known by the term Scots (*Scoti*), and the Germanic Saxons raided the coasts of the island. During the fifth century the Roman troops finally withdrew from Britain and left its Celtic inhabitants, Romanised in varying degrees, to an uncertain fate.

FROM NAVAN FORT TO MAIDEN CASTLE: IRON AGE HOARDS AND ARCHAEOLOGICAL SITES

For the modern traveller, the traces of the Roman occupation of Britain are to be seen in the countryside and in numerous museums. Remains in larger cities such as Canterbury, London and Colchester, as well as the elaborate defensive positions on Hadrian's Wall between Carlisle and Newcastle and the Antonine Wall between the Firth of Clyde and the Firth of Forth, even today communicate to the observer a lasting impression of the southern civilisation and mode of life which was stamped upon the face of the island in the first five centuries after the birth of Christ. The paucity of Roman remains in Ireland stands in striking contrast to this. There the archaeological exploration of graves, settlements and cult sites has so far yielded only modest finds, such as potsherds, coins, fibulae and jewellery, which presumably reached Ireland by trade routes.[2]

If we leave aside the hoards from Roman times, the archaeological legacy of the Iron Age inhabitants of Ireland and Britain essentially falls into three categories of deposit, each yielding very different results according to the period and region. While the deposits and investigations in settlements supply data about the everyday life of the population, the graves and cult sites communicate a picture of the belief systems, the social organisation and the high status of crafts, which is apparent above all in votive and devotional offerings made of precious metals. However, as on the continent, many of the finds in Britain and Ireland come from older excavations which were either not documented at all or documented insufficiently. This places severe limits on any archaeological interpretation.[3]

A vital source of knowledge of the material culture is provided by deposits which have emerged during the archaeological exploration of hill forts from the second half of the first millennium BC in the south and west of England.[4] These sites usually extended over an area of at least five hectares and were protected on all sides by a rampart and ditch, and their interior was densely settled over a period of several hundred years. On occasion the excavations have also produced evidence of cult sites, which may have been a feature of all these settlements. The largest hill fort of this kind is the site of Maiden Castle in Dorset. Traces of human presence in the Neolithic, the fourth and third millennia BC, have been found here, but the oldest fortifications, with rampart and ditch, date from about 600 BC. In the second century BC Maiden Castle achieved its greatest flowering, with an area of over forty-five hectares, but it increasingly declined in importance over the following centuries and was completely abandoned soon after the Roman conquest of Britain. There is a similar Irish site at Dun Aengus on Inishmore, the largest of the three Aran Islands, fifteen kilometres out from Galway Bay. The site covers no less than 4.5 hectares on the edge of a sheer cliff 100 metres above the Atlantic, and was protected on three sides by walls which even today are up to four metres thick and high. Unlike the hill forts of England and Wales, Dun Aengus and similar Irish sites have as yet yielded no substantial traces of human habitation, so their date of origin, function and duration of use cannot be determined with certainty.

The archaeological study of graves and burial offerings, as well as the exploration of settlements, provides information on the material culture of the centuries preceding and following the birth of Christ, but in this respect too Iron Age Ireland is markedly poorer in evidence than neighbouring Britain.[5] In Ireland the practice of cremation was dominant at first, which meant that grave goods were limited to a few personal effects such as fibulae (brooches). In the first few centuries after the birth of Christ, cremation was gradually replaced by burial, perhaps as a result of the influence of Roman Britain. The burial customs of pre-Roman Britain show pronounced regional variations, and some collections of deposits have given their names to the material culture of a particular region. Thus, south-east England has the so-called Aylesford-Swarling culture, which is distinguished by cremation graves with fairly rich burial offerings. Usually up to a dozen such graves are found together, but large cemeteries with over 400 graves are also known. While the majority of these graves date from the decades before and after the birth of Christ, the burials of the so-called Arras culture in east Yorkshire are from the fourth and third centuries BC. Its characteristic feature is the inhumation of the uncremated body beneath a tumulus in a field of barrows. The grave goods include clothing, ceramics and weapons, and in some cases also two-wheeled war-chariots. As in the case of the Aylesford-Swarling culture, scholarly opinion differs on the similarities with contemporary burials in northern France: these may perhaps result from an influx of settlers from these regions, but it is possible that only some details of burial customs were adopted from the mainland Celts.

The grave goods offer only limited information about the pre-Christian religion of the insular Celts. A vision of earthly life continuing after death is supported by the fact that in many cases the dead were buried with characteristic tokens of their status, as well as offerings of food. What myths and rites were involved remains largely unknown, owing to the absence of contemporary documentary sources. It is certain that the Celts of Britain and Ireland had personal gods and goddesses, whose names, character and functions may be partially reconstructed from the dedicatory inscriptions of Roman Britain as well as Irish and Welsh medieval literature. The worship of these deities found tangible archaeological expression in the establishment of cult sites and in the sacrifice of material goods, animals and humans.

As in the Celtic shrines of northern France, recent investigations in Roman Britain have provided evidence that a number of Roman temples were built on the sites of earlier pre-Roman shrines. A particularly impressive example is the round, stone Roman temple on Hayling Island, on the south coast of England, which replaced an older pre-Roman wooden structure.[6] In Ireland, recent broad-acre excavations are showing that a number of prominent prehistoric sites that are described in medieval literature as royal centres from a legendary past, must in fact have been pre-Christian cult sites. These include Tara (Temair) in County Meath, Knockaulin (Dún Ailinne) in County Kildare and Navan Fort (Emain Macha) west of the city of Armagh.[7] In all three cases, a religious or ritual function may be deduced from the sacrificial remnants, the presence to some extent of elaborate wooden structures and the absence of any evidence of long-term habitation. Some of the traces of human presence reach back as far as the Neolithic period. The distant contacts that the builders of these sites maintained are strikingly shown by the discovery at Navan Fort of the skull of a Barbary ape, which found its way from the North African coast to the north of Ireland some time in the last centuries before the birth of Christ (Raftery 1994, 61–2 and 79).

Some human skulls and four elaborately decorated bronze trumpets recovered from Loughnashade in 1798 may be connected to cult rituals in and around Navan Fort (Raftery 1994, 165–6 and 185). In many comparable sites, however, the existence of similar structures is unconfirmed or insufficiently documented, and one may only surmise a connection with ritual. This applies, for example, to the large cache of iron and bronze items in a bog near Lisnacrogher in County Antrim, found by accident during peat-cutting work towards the end of the nineteenth century (Raftery 1994, 184–5). The gold model of a boat, with rowing bench, mast and movable rudder, found in 1896 with other gold artefacts at Broighter on the shore of Lough Foyle in Northern Ireland, is generally taken to be an offering to the sea-god.[8]

Some of the most beautiful and best known specimens of Celtic crafts from pre-Roman Britain have come down to us thanks to the custom of ritually sinking valuable artefacts in rivers (Jope and Jacobsthal 2000). These artefacts include the richly decorated bronze facing of a wooden or leather shield, found in the River Witham near Lincoln, two bronze shield-bosses recovered from the Thames at Wandsworth, and another bronze shield facing and bronze helmet from the Thames at Battersea and Waterloo Bridge (Brailsford 1975). Numerous gold and silver torcs and other precious-metal artefacts found, partly by chance and partly during systematic excavations, between 1948 and 1991 on a farm near Snettisham in Norfolk date from the first century BC (see I. M. Stead in Haffner 1995, 100–10). A comparable votive site of supra-regional significance was unearthed in 1942–3 at Llyn Cerrig Bach on the west coast of Anglesey while a military airfield was being laid out. In addition to a great number of animal bones, many metal objects, including swords, spearheads, shield bosses and parts of chariots and harness, were found, dating from the second century BC to the Roman conquest soon after the middle of the first century AD. All had been thrown into the lake as votive offerings (see S. Green in Moscati et al. 1991, 609).

When it comes to forming a historical picture of the Celts, all these finds have one egregious drawback: from them we can tell neither the language nor the ethnic affiliation of their creators. The fact that they are generally termed Celtic rests above all on the absence of any clear interruption between them and the Celtic-speaking cultures of Roman times and the early Middle Ages that might indicate major changes in the composition of the population. Here it is worth noting that there is no evidence of such an interruption in earlier centuries either, in particular for the period of transition between the Bronze and Iron Ages. That the Celtic language came to Britain and Ireland from the European continent and completely replaced the languages previously spoken there is certain. When and how this occurred remains largely a mystery, and the sub-division of the insular Celtic tongues and their place within the Celtic family are matters of dispute to this day.

P-CELTIC, Q-CELTIC: THE INTERPRETATION OF THE EARLIEST LINGUISTIC EVIDENCE

As the personal names and names of regions, localities, rivers and peoples in ancient texts show, a Celtic language was spoken in large parts of Britain and Ireland before the beginning of any native written sources. The Greek name for Ireland, *Ierne*, for example, can be traced back to the Old Celtic *$\bar{I}$werjū* (Old Irish *Ériu*), which represents a cognate of the Greek *pieira* ('fertile land') with a typical loss of initial *p*. The Greek name for Britain, *Albiōn*, corresponds to the first element of the name of the Gallic god Albiorix and the Middle Welsh *elfydd* ('world, land'). The latter, in view of the historically related Latin *albus* ('white'), probably had an original meaning of a 'light' or 'bright' world of the living (as opposed to the dark underworld of the dead) (see Rivet and Smith 1979, 248; also Meid 1991). The Roman term *Britannia* is derived from *Britanni*, the name of the inhabitants, which in Greek sources appears with an initial *p* as *Prettanoi*. That this Greek form is close to the original form of the name is demonstrated by the later Welsh names *Prydain* ('Britain') and *Prydyn* ('land of the Picts'), which can be traced back to an original **Pritani* or **Priteni*. This last in its Irish form **Quriteni* produced *Cruithin* ('Picts') (see Rivet and Smith 1979, 280–2).

A comparison of **Priteni* and **Quriteni*, *Prydyn* and *Cruithin*, also illustrates a striking difference within the insular Celtic language. As in all Celtic tongues, in both Goidelic (Irish, Scots Gaelic and Manx) and Brythonic (Welsh, Cornish and Breton), the initial and inter-vocalic *p*, inherited from Indo-European, disappears. But whereas in Goidelic the labiovelar *k^w*, also inherited from Indo-European, was at first preserved then simplified to *k* (written as *c*), in Brythonic a new *p* arose. The continental Celtic languages show the same change. The Celtic cognate of Latin *-que* ('and'), for example, appears as *-Cue* in Celtiberian but in Lepontic as *-pe*. The Celtic cognate of Latin *equus* ('horse') appears in Gaulish personal names in the form *epo-*, while in the Coligny calendar the older form *equos* still occurs. The fact that in early Christian Ireland, *p* in Latin loanwords was replaced by *k* can be seen in terms such as *cruimther* ('elder', *presbyter*), *cásc* ('Easter', *pascha*), *corcur* ('purple', *purpura*) and *cland* ('offspring', *planta* 'plant'), while in later loanwords such as *purgatóir* (*purgatorium*), *persan* (*persona*), *pardus* (*paradisus*), *epscop* (*episcopus*), *peccath* ('sin', *peccatum*) and *póc* ('kiss'; *osculum pacis*, 'kiss of peace') it was preserved. The name of the country's patron saint, *Patrick* (*Patricius*), was borrowed twice, appearing in the earliest sources as *Cothrige*, but later in the form *Pátraic* (in its modern spelling *Pádraig*).[9]

The regularity with which the insular Celtic languages either preserved the sound k^w or developed *p* in its place led earlier scholars to distinguish Q-Celtic and P-Celtic as two originally distinct variants within Celtic. More recent studies have shown that the significance of this difference has been exaggerated, and an original difference between the two branches, Goidelic and Brythonic, now seems questionable. Differences in phonetics, morphology and sentence structure, which we have been able to establish between Goidelic and Brythonic since the Middle Ages, are probably of comparatively recent origin and, given the present state of our knowledge, cannot be projected back into prehistoric times before the advent of literacy.

The extent to which the influence of pre-Celtic languages may account for some of the characteristic differences between the insular and continental language groups is a question which has as yet been insufficiently studied. Apart from the many words of obscure etymology in the vocabulary of insular Celtic, this is mainly a matter of differences in sentence structure, such as the placing of the verb before the subject or describing actions by means of the verb 'to do' and a verbal noun. As typological research has shown, many features by which insular Celtic differs both from Gaulish and from the other early Indo-European languages have precisely corresponding features in the Hamitic languages of North Africa, such as Berber and ancient Egyptian, and the Semitic languages such as Hebrew and Arabic. Since the archaeological evidence shows clear continuity in the prehistoric population of Britain and Ireland, these correspondences may perhaps be explained by the hypothesis that when the

Celts reached Britain and Ireland they found a numerically far superior population of North African origin. This adopted the language of the new elite but, owing to the inertia of established speech habits, wrought radical changes in the form of that language. A parallel to this may perhaps be seen in the history of English in Ireland, where it largely displaced Irish as the language of the elite, but at the same time was strongly influenced by it.[10] However, the details of how the Celtic 'takeover' and the gradual intermingling with the old-established population came about will probably long remain in that darkness that was dispelled only partly by the introduction of the Latin language and script following the advent of Christianity.

CHAPTER 10

Ireland after the Conversion to Christianity

ISLAND OF SAINTS: THE EARLY IRISH CHURCH

'To the Irish believers in Christ, Palladius is being sent as the first bishop ordained by Pope Celestine.' Thus the contemporary chronicler Prosper of Aquitaine reports in the year AD 431, giving us the first historic date in Ireland's past.[1] How many of the Irish had by then converted to Christianity, where these Christians lived and what had moved them to forswear their old gods, is completely unknown to us. It is highly likely that British captives who were carried off to Ireland brought Christianity with them. Above and beyond this, it must be supposed that Irish settlers in the south-west of Wales were exposed to the new religion and spread their knowledge of it in their continuing contact with their old homeland. Of the subsequent fate of Bishop Palladius and the success or failure of his mission, the sources have nothing to communicate. Instead, subsequent tradition attributes the conversion of Ireland to Saint Patrick alone, about whose life and work historical scholarship can report few certain facts.[2]

The earliest mention of Patrick is contained in two of his own writings, entitled *Confessio* and *Epistula ad Coroticum* (Letter to Coroticus). *Confessio* is a confessional document with an autobiographical slant, written by Patrick for reasons unknown to us, presumably in his declining years, and justifying his work in Ireland. *Epistula* is an open letter in which Patrick, as Bishop of the Irish, calls the Briton Coroticus to account for abducting Irish Christians into slavery.[3] In addition, we have two hagiographical works concerning

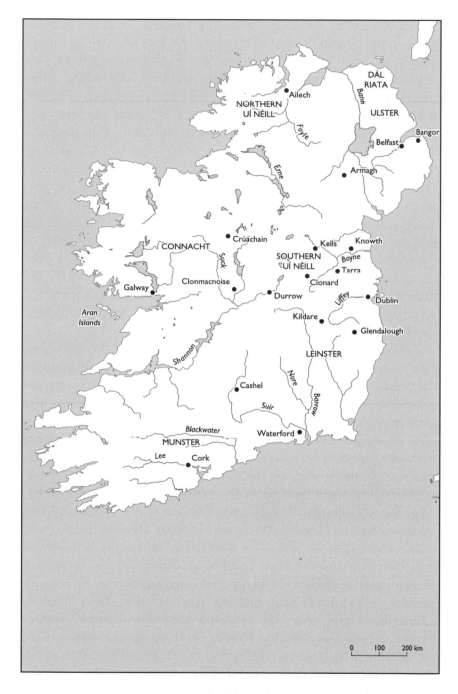

Map 3: Ireland in the Middle Ages

Patrick written by the Irish clerics Muirchú and Tírechán in about 670, and the biography *Bethu Phátraic* (The Life of Patrick), mostly written in Irish in about 900 and also known by the title *Vita Tripartita* on account of its three-part structure.[4] According to his *Confessio*, Patrick came from a family of Romanised British Celts and was kidnapped at sixteen by Irish pirates. He spent six years as a slave in Ireland before managing to escape on board a ship. Inspired by a vision, he returned to Ireland in order to spread Christianity there. This scant information aside, we know hardly anything about Patrick. There is broad agreement that he was active in the fifth century AD, but we know neither the year of his birth nor that of his death. Nor do we know the place of his imprisonment in Ireland, the purpose or duration of his sojourn on the European continent, or the extent of the area of his mission. Although legend attributes the conversion of almost the whole island to the saint, this is clearly due to an anachronistic perspective which simplifies and foreshortens the actual historical events, while glorifying them in the light of later developments.

Following the continental model, Patrick organised the early Irish Church on the basis of bishoprics, of which Armagh later acquired the greatest importance. In the sixth century, however, this organisation was relegated to the background by the establishment of a great number of monasteries.[5] The independent abbots, who were often responsible for the administration of the surrounding estates as well, now came to be among the most important bearers of ecclesiastical authority. Among the most prominent founders of monasteries whose work dates from the period between AD 500 and 650 were Búithe, who died in 521, the founder of the monastery that bears his name (Monasterboice, or Mainistir Búithe); Brigit, who died in about 524, the founder of the twinned monastery and convent in Kildare; Columba (Colum Cille), who died in 597, the founder of the monasteries of Derry, Durrow and Iona; and Kevin (Coemgen), founder of the Glendalough monastery, who died in about 618. But, with isolated exceptions, the early founders of monasteries remain beyond our reach as historical figures. Our complete ignorance of the life of Saint Brigit, whose cult spread throughout Ireland from the seventh century and even reached the European mainland with the Irish missionaries, is typical. As the oldest biography of Brigit, compiled in about 650 by a hagiographer named Cogitosus, contains hardly any historical facts, we may assume that even by this date there was no precise memory of her life in Kildare, and that the figure of the saint had become merged with that of a Celtic goddess of the same name.[6]

A clear impression of the strict monastic discipline is conveyed by the penitentials, typical of the early Irish Church, with their comprehensive coverage of possible lapses and the means by which to expiate them (published with English translations in Bieler 1963). Yet by the eighth century a certain degree of secularisation of the monasteries may be observed, expressed in the close intermeshing of ecclesiastical and political interests and in the participation of the monasteries in armed confrontation and even battles between different monasteries. This was chiefly because many of the great monasteries enjoyed an advantageous position on land and water trading routes, as well as being the proprietors of large estates built up through donations, and thus became centres of dynamic economic development. They therefore functioned as landowners, receiving tribute and services from dependent farmers, and as patrons of learning and the arts. The Ardagh hoard, discovered in 1868, and the Derrynaflan altar-set hoard, found in 1980, are significant testimony to the influence of the Church upon the crafts of the time.[7]

The great number of churches founded and their close connection with the social elite lead one to suppose that the pre-Christian belief went into swift decline soon after their foundation. Those elements of the old cults, rites and myths that escaped complete oblivion were given a new Christian sense or eked out a twilight existence in the shadow of the official religion, as a grudgingly tolerated superstition. In Ireland, as in all the Celtic lands, the introduction – in several stages – of a Latin-influenced culture of writing played a decisive role in this transformation.[8] Before adopting the Latin alphabet, the Irish had invented the so-called Ogam script, in imitation of Latin writing habits, which in its oldest known form distinguished twenty sounds with the aid of dots and marks on a straight horizontal line.[9] The earliest evidence of the use of this script is approximately 300 brief inscriptions in stone, found in various parts of Ireland, as well as Wales, Devon, Cornwall and the Isle of Man. Historical linguistics allows us to deduce that most of these inscriptions date from the fifth and sixth centuries. This means that they contain the earliest specimens of the Irish language, although most of them offer no more than the names of people and tribes. While some medieval Irish tales report that the Ogam script was also used to inscribe written communications on wood, it is probable that these were no more than contemporary perceptions projected back into the remote past. Whether the Ogam, like the Germanic runes, was used for magical practices is doubtful, according to our present state of knowledge, and although an understanding of the sound value of the symbols remained alive in Ireland into modern times, the Ogam was completely displaced by the Latin alphabet soon after the coming of Christianity.

Since Ireland never became part of the Roman empire, Latin served purely as the language of religion. The main object of extensive study was the Bible, known in the Old Latin version and Jerome's translation, as well as the writings of the Church fathers. Exegetical works with a particular taste for historical interpretation of the Bible testify to an active engagement with the Scriptures, as may also be seen from the many Old Irish glosses on the Latin text.[10] Side by side with this, written in blank spaces in the margins of the surviving manuscripts of learned content, are numerous lyric poems dealing with the monastic life of fulfilment and the beauty of creation, as well as the conflict between the joy of life and the ascetic ideals of the authors.[11]

In connection with the calculation of the date of Easter, orderly records eventually arose of the investiture and death of kings, the founding and destruction of monasteries, wars, failed harvests and similar events. The records later formed comprehensive chronicles, including the 'Annals of Ulster' (*Annála Ulad*), which are of particular value as a historical source.[12] Other areas of monastic scholarship were liturgical and hymnological texts, texts about the kingship such as the Old Irish 'Mirror of Princes' *Audacht Morainn* (The Legacy of Morann), and lives of the saints, the oldest of which, written in Latin, date from the second half of the seventh century.[13] Other examples of the variety of style and content of Old and Middle Irish religious literature are the elegy to Columba (*Amra Choluim Chille*), probably written about AD 600 by the poet Dallán Forgaill, and the poem *Immram Brain* (The Voyage of Bran) from the early eighth century. The latter, like *Navigatio Sancti Brendani*, written in Latin, tells of the eventful voyage of the eponymous hero to fabulous islands beyond the world of men. Mention should also be made of two other poems written in the eighth century, by the cleric Blathmac mac Con Brettan, about the life of Christ; and the tale *Fís Adamnáin* (The Vision of Adamnán), from the ninth or tenth centuries, with its account of the hero's journey through various parts of the other world.[14] The self-confidence with which the early Irish Church looked back on the pagan past shows in the calendar of saints and martyrs of the cleric Oengus mac Oengobann (*Félire Oenguso*), from the early ninth century, which names a saint for each day of the year in 365 four-line stanzas and contrasts, in its introduction, Ireland's Christian present with its pagan past:[15]

Dún Emna ro tetha
acht mairde a clocha;
is rúaim iarthair betha
Glend dálach Dá Locha.

The fort of Emain Machae has melted away,
all but its stones;
thronged Glendalough is the sanctuary
of the western world.

ISLAND OF KINGS: ECONOMY AND SOCIETY

Among the most valuable works that provide information about social life in Ireland in the seventh and eighth centuries are legal texts in the vernacular. Many of them stem from a collection known as *Senchas Már* ('The Great Tradition').[16] The texts are treatises and compendia for the instruction of specialists in traditional indigenous justice, which was known as *fénechas* to distinguish it from the Latin-language ecclesiastical law. The oldest of these texts date from the period between the mid-seventh and mid-eighth centuries, but have mostly come down to us in manuscripts from the fourteenth to sixteenth centuries, with later notes in the margins, insertions and commentaries. The Irish legal scholars (plural *brithemain*, anglicised as *brehon*) interpreted indigenous law above all as an oral tradition, so the act of recording it in writing may well be seen as a reaction by the indigenous schools against the introduction of the written ecclesiastical law. Here the compilation of ecclesiastical law in the *Collectio Canonum Hibernensis* early in the eighth century played an important role.[17]

A characteristic feature of early Irish society was the close integration of the individual in the family group or *fine* (sept), and the individual's status as a member of a particular clan (*túath*, plural *túatha*). Of the various kinds of *fine* named in the law-texts, the *derbfine*, whose members could trace their lineage back to one and the same great-grandfather, was the most important. These kinship groups owned land in common (*fintiu*) and in certain circumstances assumed responsibility for the transgressions or debts of the individual members of the group. The leader of the *fine* was known as *agae fine* or *cenn fine*. He was chosen on the basis of his power, social standing and personal merits and represented in public the interests of the *fine*.

The law-texts use the term *túath* to denote both a group of people and the area inhabited by that group, so it may be translated as 'tribe' or 'petty kingdom'. It is thought that in early and mid-medieval Ireland there were at least 150 such kingdoms, with an average number of perhaps 3,000 members per *túath*. The great majority of the Irish population no doubt spent their entire lives within the boundaries of their *túath*, outside which the individual generally enjoyed no rights, with only the educated classes being able to move about freely. The word *túath* goes back to an older form *teutā*, which is found in several Indo-European languages meaning 'people', and appears in Gaulish, for example, in the name of the deity *Teutates*. The adjective *diutisc*, which in later times came to signify 'German' (deutsch), is derived from the Old High German *diot*.

Compared to modern times, early medieval Irish society was not egalitarian, but had a strict hierarchical structure. At the head of each *túath* stood a king (*rí*), to whom every free member of a clan owed obedience and the payment of a certain tribute.[18] When offensive or defensive action was required, it was incumbent upon him to call out a force of able-bodied men (*slógad*) and in peacetime to convene the political assembly (*óenach*). The king represented the interests of his *túath* externally, concluding treaties of friendship (*cairde*) with kings of neighbouring tribes, or recognising a stronger neighbouring ruler as over-king (*ruiri*) by accepting gifts, paying tribute or producing hostages. Just like the clerics, the poets (*fili*) and those who, as masters (*flaith*), had dependent vassals (*céili*) under them, the king belonged to a particularly privileged stratum, defined in the law-texts as *nemed*. We may take it as likely that the prominent position of this stratum originally had a religious foundation, since the basic Old Celtic form *nemeton* originally denoted a (pre-Christian) shrine. Those who did not belong to this class were counted as either free (*sóer*) or unfree (*dóer*), and several degrees of 'unfreedom' were distinguished, ranging from dependent tenants (*fuidir*) who could be evicted at any time, to slaves (*mug*) with no rights at all. The great importance of slavery emerges clearly from the fact that in the law-texts the word for 'female slave' (*cumal*) is often used as a unit of value, for example to determine a price or a fine. Of crucial importance for the social, and therefore also legal, position of the individual was his 'honour price' (*lóg n-enech*), which determined the scale of the compensation owing to him if his rights were abused or if the value of his word was disputed. The honour price applied only to free men. In the case of offences against women, the compensation was paid to her husband, and where slaves were involved their master was the recipient.

A characteristic feature of early medieval Irish society was that it was predominantly rural.[19] The great majority of the population lived in individual homesteads, and town-like settlements developed only rarely, in the environs of the great monasteries. Cultivation and animal husbandry formed the basis of economic life, and the law-texts indicate that barter played only a subordinate role. There are, however, occasional suggestions in the documents that in trading settlements on the southern and eastern coast of the island such commodities as wool, skins and hides were exported and luxury goods such as wine or fine cloth imported. Of crucial importance in feeding the population were the cultivation of various cereals, such as barley, oats, wheat and rye, and animal husbandry, in which cattle served less as providers of meat than of milk. Hunting for large and small game must have been practised mainly for pleasure, but fishing, both on the coasts and in fresh water, had great economic importance.

ONE COUNTRY, FIVE PROVINCES: ASPECTS OF POLITICAL HISTORY

In the medieval view, Ireland consisted of five 'provinces', termed in indigenous sources 'fifths' (*cóiced*, plural *cóiceda*). Their traditional names were Connacht (*Connachta*), Ulster (*Ulaid*), Leinster (*Laigin*), Munster (*Mumu*) and Meath (*Mide*), of which the first three names (like the names of the Germanic tribes *Schwaben*, *Bayern* and *Sachsen*) could denote both the regions and their inhabitants. Behind this division lies the fiction that all the country's great dynasties were descended from a single common ancestor, whose descendants had shared Ireland out, like brothers, when they had first settled there.[20]

In the west of the island lay the province of Connacht, whose name is derived from that of the legendary King Conn Cétchathach ('Conn of the hundred battles'). By tradition, three Connachts (*teóra Connachta*) were distinguished, each linked with the clans of Uí Briúin, Uí Fiachrach and Uí Maine, and descended from three brothers of King Niall Noígiallach ('Niall of the nine hostages'). Niall Noígiallach himself is held to be the ancestor of the extremely successful and extended dynasty of the 'sons of Niall' (Uí Néill), who began spreading their authority northward and eastward from the west of Ireland in the fifth century. In the north lay the province of Ulster, whose western regions lay in the direction of the main thrust of the Uí Néill. Here the main dynasties were the Dál Fíatach, Dál nAraide and Dál Riata, who since the sixth century had been extending their power into the territory of the west of Scotland. The province of Leinster, with the basins of the Liffey, Barrow and Slaney at its heart, took in the east of the island. Its natural borders were formed by the great bogs of the Irish midlands to the west, the forests on the far side of the Liffey to the north, and to the south the uplands west of the Barrow. It is possible that the province originally reached much further north and also included the territory north of the Liffey and the royal seat of Tara. The Uí Chennselaig in the south and the Uí Dúnlainge in the north of Leinster appear in the historical period as the most important dynasties competing against each other. The south-west of Ireland formed the province of Munster with the royal seat of Cashel (Irish *Caisel*, from Latin *castellum*). In the early Middle Ages Munster maintained close relations with both Britain and Visigoth Spain, and it was ruled from the seventh century until the early tenth century by the large Eóganachta dynasty, which claimed descent from Eógan Már, one of the legendary second-century rulers. Meath ('the middle'), whose name survives in the names of the modern counties of Meath and Westmeath, counted as the fifth province. In Meath stood the Hill of Uisnech, which was reckoned to be the middle point of Ireland. It was ruled by the dynasty of the Clann Cholmáin, a branch of the Uí Néill, which became a potent political force in central Ireland from the mid-eighth century.

By about the mid-seventh century, the idea appears in literary sources that the 'King of Tara' (*rí Temro*), as 'High King' (*ardrí*), had held the highest rank from time immemorial and was therefore of higher standing than all other kings.[21] In the political reality of the time, this idea could have played only a secondary role, as the law-texts mention the petty king (*rí túaithe*), the over-king (*ruiri*) and the provincial king (*rí cóicid*) but are silent about any superior high king. In later times, prominent representatives of the successful dynasties strove ever harder against competing rulers to press their claim to the title of High King. The important role of the Church as landowner meant that those dynasties in which a clerical branch had been able to secure, over several generations, an influential ecclesiastical office, such as abbot of one of the great monasteries, were especially well placed to bolster their position. Prominent contenders for the dignity of High King were first the Uí Néill kings, then from the mid-eighth century several rulers from the Eóganachta dynasty of Munster. A marked shift in power relations within Ireland came about, however, soon after the appearance of the Vikings, who first assailed the shores of Ireland in 795. This is covered in the next chapter.

CHAPTER 11

Ireland in the Time of the Vikings

THE STRUGGLE FOR SUPREMACY: VIKINGS AND NATIVE RULERS

Is acher in gaíth in-nocht,
fu-fūasna fairggae findfolt:
ni ágor réimm Mora Minn
dond láechraid lainn ūa Lothlind.

Bitter is the wind tonight: it tosses the ocean's white hair;
I fear not the coursing of a clear sea by the fierce heroes
from Lothlend.

Thus wrote an unknown ninth-century Irish monk in a blank space in a manuscript now kept in the monastery of Saint Gall (Stokes and Strachan 1901–3, II, 290). After the Vikings had attacked and pillaged monastic houses on the west coast of Ireland in 795, they soon extended their raids to cover the whole coastline, and the north and east of the island were the most affected.[1] The coveted prize in these assaults was not only liturgical utensils and reliquaries in precious metals, but livestock and provisions, which one could expect to find in monastic settlements on account of their high population density and economic power. In the first four decades, the raids were effected by small, highly mobile bands, but from 830 ever larger fleets of Viking ships began to appear and make their way into the interior via rivers like the Liffey, the Boyne and the Shannon. From 840 the Vikings began to establish permanent coastal bases, of which Dublin proved the most important in the long term. If the establishment of these fortified settlements made the Vikings more vulnerable to Irish counter-attacks, they also had the effect of letting the Irish grow accustomed to the presence of the Norsemen, and they increasingly sought to exploit this presence in their own disputes and for their own ends. Thus, in the latter half of the ninth century, the Vikings began to appear increasingly as the allies of Irish kings, while they focused their main thrust to a greater extent on the Irish Sea, north-west England and the newly discovered Iceland. In many parts of Ireland, by the beginning of the tenth century, Vikings had become allied and intermarried with the Irish, adapted to their way of life and even converted to the Christian faith. They undoubtedly exerted greatest influence on the development of trade and seafaring, but the effects of Viking settlement on literature and art should not be underestimated.[2] By this time major raids within Ireland had become rare, but with the growth of the kingdom of Wessex in England, the foundation of the Duchy of Normandy and the gradual conclusion of the settlement of Iceland, Ireland from 914 was again afflicted by plundering bands of Scandinavian pirates. Only in the second half of the tenth century did the indigenous Irish rulers increasingly gain the upper hand in the resulting conflicts.

Until the mid-tenth century the struggle for supremacy in Ireland was waged, with varying fortunes, by the Uí Néill dynasty in the north and the Eóganachta dynasty in the south. But in the last two thirds of the tenth century, the rise of the Dál Cais dynasty, which had its home in Munster, reached its completion, and this dynasty displaced the Eóganachta from their dominant position in the south and was soon contesting the high kingship. Its most important ruler was Brian Boru (Brian Bóruma), who put an end to the centuries-old dominance of the Uí Néill in the north, and from 1002 ruled almost all of Ireland. In 1014 his forces achieved a decisive victory at the battle of Clontarf, in which he himself was killed, against the Vikings who were allied to the king of Leinster. The political and military achievement of Brian Boru, who was buried in Armagh, contributed substantially to the popularisation of the notion of a unified national kingdom of Ireland. In the following period, provincial kings from all parts of the island attempted, with varying degrees of success, to press their own claims for the high kingship, in the sense of a kingdom embracing the whole island. One of the most powerful kings of his day was Toirdelbach Ua Conchobair (Turlough O'Connor), who reigned over Connacht from 1106. In his fifty-year rule he had to resist above all the claims of the kings of Leinster. In 1166 Toirdelbach's son Ruaidrí succeeded to his throne, while Diarmait Mac Murchada (Dermot Mac Murrough) was forced to flee Leinster ahead of his opponents. As he could find no allies in Ireland, Diarmait sought in exile the support of the Anglo-Norman aristocracy, whose armed incursions into Ireland in 1169 would open a new chapter in the history of the island. Before proceeding to a fuller treatment of later events, the following sections deal with two aspects of early medieval Irish culture that are of particular significance in cultural history: the rise of a rich vernacular literature and the effects of Irish missionary work on continental Europe.

ATTACHMENT AND SEPARATION: THE PAGAN PERIOD IN LITERATURE

One of the greatest achievements of the Irish monastic culture that distinguished the Irish Church well into the twelfth century is the setting-down of an extensive narrative literature describing the time before and during the conversion to Christianity. An important precondition for this was the fact that the pre-Christian poets (*filid*), the guardians and bearers of the culturally relevant and distinctive tradition (*senchas*), were able to preserve their elevated social position under the new religion. Until recent times, the peculiar style and content of this literature lent currency to the theory that the stories were originally pagan and had acquired no more than a veneer of Christianity. At the same time the absence of comparable texts from continental Celtic antiquity or medieval Wales often caused specifically Irish tales to be seen as epitomising Celtic narrative tradition as a whole. Although it remains beyond dispute that much early and middle-Irish narrative material does indeed date back to pre-Christian times, and in some cases has close counterparts in the reports of the classical authors on mainland Celtic culture, some clarification is called for to avoid misunderstandings in the interpretation of the evidence.

If we first take the hard facts about pagan beliefs, culture and society in the texts that have come down to us, it may quickly be seen that few of these originate in a time before Christianity had taken hold as the sole religion of the Celtic-speaking inhabitants of western Europe. On the contrary, the great majority of reports on religious and social matters before the conversion come from a time when Christianity had several centuries of history in all the Celtic lands to look back upon. Whether an accurate picture of the old pagan culture still survived at this time must, in view of the numerous anachronisms and projections of Christian notions and institutions into the past, seem questionable in the extreme. Even if we accept the dubious proposition that the memory of pre-Christian religious beliefs, rites and myths endured in the early and high Middle Ages, the value of the literatures of the insular Celts as religious-historical sources depends entirely on whether the extant texts really refer to them. This very idea, so long taken for granted, has increasingly been called into question of late, since recent research into narrative has shown that medieval Irish literature drew on oral transmission to a far lesser extent than was thought a generation ago. The influence of Christian and Latin scholarship, on the other hand, is now held to be much greater than was generally the case in times of romantic theories of continuity and rampant nationalism. It may, moreover, be assumed that the preoccupation with the past in medieval Ireland had nothing to do with a love of antiquity for its own sake, and much more to do with lending legitimacy to the aspirations to property and power of the patrons of these works. The fact that many of the stories seem distinctly cumbersome to the modern reader led earlier scholars to adopt the view that the medieval authors wrote with open-hearted honesty and respectful reverence for the oral tradition. Today, by contrast, emphasis is placed on the medieval historians' and jurists' capricious unconcern, which led them to update the traditions of various historical eras as they saw fit, and to distort, falsify and fabricate in the process. We may therefore dismiss out of hand the notion that, in the course of this continual reinterpretation of the pagan past, any concern was evinced for the authenticity of the facts. A comparison with the Old Norse documents on the religion of the Norsemen, often only slightly more recent, shows more convincingly that both the Irish and the Icelanders viewed the pre-Christian culture through the prism of Christian theology. Thus, even if the ancestry of many materials and motifs in the works that have come down to us really does reach back into pre-Christian times, every individual case must be meticulously examined to ensure that mythical elements and fable are filtered out.

The most important works of vernacular literature that tell of the history of Ireland before and during the coming of Christianity are contained in large manuscript collections from the eleventh and twelfth centuries. Pride of place belongs to *The Book of the Dun Cow* (*Lebor na hUidre*), which is thought to have been written in the late eleventh century in the monastery of Clonmacnoise. It contains sixty-seven imperfectly preserved parchment folios and has been kept since 1844 in the library of the Royal Irish Academy in Dublin.[3] *The Book of Glendalough* (*Lebor Glinne Dá Loch*), which used to be known by its shelf mark in the Bodleian Library, *Rawlinson B 502*, dates from the period around 1130.[4] The most comprehensive collection of old Irish manuscripts is the so-called *Book of Leinster* (*Lebor Laignech*), which was originally known as *The Book of Nuachongbáil/Oughaval* (*Lebor na Núachongbála*). It numbers 187 parchment folios, of which ten are kept in the Franciscan Library in Killiney and the rest in the library of Trinity College, Dublin.[5]

From a later period, the fourteenth century, come *The Book of Ballymote* (*Leabhar Bhaile an Mhóta*, in the library of the Royal Irish Academy since 1785), *The Book of Lecan* (*Leabhar Leacáin*, now in the libraries of Trinity College, Dublin and the Royal Irish Academy), and *The Yellow Book of Lecan* (*Leabhar Buidhe Leacáin*, now in the library of Trinity College, Dublin). For an overview of the variety of content in Old and Middle Irish narrative literature, the classification of the stories into various cycles, standard since the nineteenth century, serves the purpose well. It is customary to distinguish an Ulster Cycle, a Finn Cycle, a Historical Cycle and a Mythological Cycle, but many stories may be assigned to more than one category and a number of important works stand outside them.

The Ulster Cycle comprises a group of stories set at the time of the birth of Christ.[6] They are known as the Ulster Cycle because the northern Irish province is the home of the protagonists. The heroes are King Conchobor mac Nessa and his nephew Cú Chulainn, who are opposed by King Ailill and Queen Medb from the province of Connacht. In this cycle the longest and most important tale, to which some further stories may be assigned as 'pre-tales' or prefatory tales (*remscéla*), tells of a cattle raid in Cuailnge (*Táin Bó Cuailnge*).[7] It recounts how Ailill and Medb raise a large army and lead it from their home of Cruachain in Connacht to Cuailnge in Ulster to carry off the famous bull named Donn Cuailnge. As the grown men of Ulster are suffering one of their recurrent bouts of debility, only the boy Cú Chulainn can resist the foe. In a series of battles he halts the advance of the enemy army again and again, but is unable to prevent the theft of the bull. Thanks to his determined resistance, however, the campaign is drawn out so long that the warriors of Ulster are at length able to enter the fray. As the intruders withdraw they are dealt a crushing defeat and only a few survive to take the stolen bull back to Connacht.

Other important stories from the Ulster Cycle are *The Tale of Mac Dathó's Pig* (*Scéla mucce meic Dathó*), which tells of the struggle for pre-eminence between the warriors of Ulster and Connacht at a banquet, and the tragic tale *The Destruction of Da Derga's Hostel* (*Togail Bruidne Da Derga*). The hero of the latter is young Conaire Mór, the son of Queen Mes Buachalla and an unknown man who took the form of a bird and was intimate with her before her marriage. After the death of the old king, Conaire is chosen, with the aid of a pagan rite, to be king. At first his reign is richly blessed, but his foster-brothers cause trouble by pillaging the land. By omitting to administer sufficient punishment, Conaire breaks the precept of 'the justice of the ruler' (*fír flathemon*) and forges his own downfall: in the hostel of his friend Da Derga he is attacked by his foster-brothers and killed after a fierce struggle.

The tales known as the Finn Cycle or Ossianic Cycle are those that deal with the legendary Finn mac Cumaill and his followers, the Fianna (see Murphy 1955, Nagy 1985 and Ó hÓgáin 1988). These tales are set in the reign of King Cormac mac Airt at the beginning of the third century AD, and have as their central characters, besides Finn himself, the leader of the Fianna, his son Oisín and Oisín's son Oscar. Most of the stories in this cycle, which in early times played only a minor role but has gained in popularity since the late Middle Ages, deal with hunting adventures, love and warfare. The longest work of this kind, uniting various episodes in a single frame story, is *The Conversation with the Elders* (*Acallam na Senórach*), in which Oisín and his nephew Caílte, together with some surviving veterans of Finn's warrior band, in their old age meet Saint Patrick and his entourage. As they travel through Ireland together, the saintly figures discover the myths and legends that pertain to particular places and salient points of the landscape.

While the stories from the Ulster and Finn Cycles are comparatively closely linked by their central characters, the Historical Cycle (or Kingly Cycle) is more a collection of cycles, each centred on an outstanding ruler from the period between the third century BC and the eleventh century AD (see Dillon 1946). Among the most prominent of these kings are Labraid Loingsech, who is said to have ruled the province of Leinster in the fourth and third centuries BC; Conn Cétchathach and his grandson Cormac mac Airt, who, according to legend, ruled the whole of Ireland in the second and third centuries AD; and Diarmait mac Aeda Sláine, Domnall mac Aeda and Mongán mac Fiachna, the seventh-century rulers also known from contemporary sources. Whatever the conventional modern term 'Historical Cycle' might lead one to expect, these tales treat not only the genuine historical past, but also the past of myth and legend.

Unlike the works mentioned so far, the tales of the Mythological Cycle have elves and fairies rather than mortals at the focus of events. In Irish these central figures are mostly known as *fir/mná/áes síde* 'men/women/people of the *síd*', because they used the manmade grave-mounds (*síd*) of the pre-Celtic population of Ireland as their dwellings.[8] Many tales identified the *áes síde* with the wonder-working Túatha Dé Danann, whom the medieval Irish regarded as an aboriginal race that had arrived from Asia long before, but whom modern scholarship sees as figures from pre-Christian Irish mythology elevated to historical status. The most significant tale of the Mythological Cycle is the *Tale of the Battle of Mag Tuired* (*Cath Maige Tuired*), which recounts the struggle between the Túatha Dé Danann and the demonic Fomoire.[9]

Two large compilations stand outside the cyclical categories generally accepted today. These are *Dindshenchas* (*Place-Name Lore*), and *Lebor Gabála Érenn* (*The Book of Invasions*). *Dindshenchas*, which is extant in three different versions, is a collection of legends that elucidate place-names, although the majority of the tales most likely rely on medieval scholarly speculation and only a few on local oral tradition.[10] *Lebor Gabála Érenn* is a fictitious history of Ireland, compiled in the eleventh century, beginning with the creation of the world and describing the fluctuating fortunes of Ireland and its inhabitants from first settlement by a grand-daughter of Noah until the date of writing.[11] Much space is occupied by six consecutive waves of immigration, and the Irish are said to be the descendants of the last wave, the sons of Míl. Like the tales of the Mythological Cycle, *The Book of Invasions* displays the efforts of the medieval clergy to bring the pre-Christian history of Ireland into accord with the Biblical story. Its authors make use of indigenous myths and legends alongside material and motifs from the Old Testament and the classics, and, whilst disassociating themselves from Ireland's pagan past, show a clear sense of pride and attachment to it.

HARBINGERS OF THE MIDDLE AGES: THE IRISH MISSION IN EUROPE

'Get thee out of thy country, and from thy kindred, and from thy father's house, into a land that I will shew thee.' Thus, according to the Old Testament, did God instruct Abraham (*Genesis* 12: 1). 'He that loveth father and mother more than me is not worthy of me,' said Jesus to his disciples, in the Gospel according to Saint Matthew (10: 37). From these and similar points in the Bible, and from the traditional Irish punishment by exile (*indarbe*), the early Christians of Ireland developed the ascetic ideal of *peregrinus pro Christo* or *deorad Dé*, of 'banishment for Christ's sake', of the exile who, in striving after religious perfection, turns his back on the safety and security of his home to serve God in foreign parts.[12]

Ireland's first great missionary, to whom we shall return in connection with the conversion of Scotland, was Columba (Colum Cille). His younger contemporary was Columbanus, known as Columba the Younger to distinguish him from Colum Cille.[13] Born in about 543 in Leinster, Columbanus received his education in the northern Irish monastery of Bangor, and travelled from Ireland to France in 590. In the solitude of the Vosges, under the protection of King Childebert II of Burgundy and Austrasia, he founded his first monastery in the ruins of the Roman fortress of Anagrates

(Annegrey). The number of novices grew so rapidly that a second, larger monastery soon arose a few miles away on the site of the old Luxovium (Luxeuil). For the monks, who lived in both monasteries according to the Irish tradition, Columbanus wrote a monastic code and a book of penitentials, while letters, sermons and poems by him, derived from classical models, are also known. After Childebert's death, Columbanus was banished by Childebert's son and heir for criticising his way of life. He went to the court of the king of Neustria, from there to Metz and up the Rhine to Lake Constance, and finally to Italy. There, at the invitation of the King of the Lombards, he founded another monastery at the remote site of Bobbio in the Apennines, and died there on 23 November 615.

One of the pupils of Columbanus was Gall, whose Irish origins are not entirely certain. Together with Columbanus he travelled to the area of Lake Constance, where they parted company and Gall settled on the upper Steinach. After his death in about 650, a local cult of sainthood and pilgrimage developed, followed in the early eighth century by the founding of the monastery of Saint Gall. Although the first known scribes at the monastery of Saint Gall were Alemanni, this monastery played a major role, from the middle of the ninth century, in spreading the Irish cultural heritage on the continent. Evidence of this may be seen in the numerous manuscripts still held in the library of the monastery of Saint Gall. The nearby Reichenau monastery, whose founder Pirmin was Spanish rather than Irish, also came under Irish influence in this period.[14]

The Irish monk Kilian, who was martyred in about 689 with his companions Coloman and Totnan at Würzburg, travelled as a missionary to eastern Franconia and Thuringia.[15] In 752 Burchard, whom Boniface had ordained as first bishop of Würzburg, ordered that the holy relics be transferred to his cathedral. There a lively cult soon developed, which in the ninth century reached as far as Ireland. To this adoration of Kilian at Würzburg, we also owe the famous manuscript, with glosses in Irish, of the text of the epistles of Paul, which is said to have reached the town with ninth-century Irish pilgrims.

The name of Saint Virgil (Fergil) is linked with the diocese of Salzburg.[16] After leaving his Irish homeland in about 742, he travelled in 745 with a recommendation from Pepin III to Duke Odilo of Bavaria, who appointed him to the vacant diocese of

Salzburg. There, on papal orders, he organised the mission to the Slavs of Carantania and in 774 had the first Salzburg cathedral built. In 1181, in the course of construction of the cathedral of Archbishop Conrad III, the lost tomb of Virgil, who had died in 784, was discovered. He was canonised in 1233.

Two other factors which, from the end of the eighth century, repeatedly drew Irish monks from their homeland to the European mainland were the pillage of Irish and Scottish monastic houses by the Vikings and the flowering of continental centres of learning during the reforms of Charlemagne. Among the most important Irish scholars active in the Carolingian empire in the ninth century were: Dungal, who, as a monk in the Saint-Denis Monastery, wrote a study of the 810 eclipse of the sun, as well as a defence of the worship of images; Dicuil, who left a treatise on astronomy and an important work on geography (*Liber de mensura orbis terrae*), in addition to his poetry *De Grammatica*; the poet, grammarian and theologian Sedulius Scottus; and the mystic Johannes Scottus Eriugena (c. 810–77), highly educated in philosophy, who translated into Latin the 'Heavenly Hierarchy' by the Pseudo-Areopagite and other Greek writings, wrote commentaries on the Gospel according to Saint John and on Martianus Capella and Boethius, and in his main work *De divisione naturae* (*On the Division of Nature*) – officially condemned as heresy in the thirteenth century – confessed to a pantheistic understanding of the unity of creator and creation.[17] Here it should be noted that the use of the appellation *Scot(t)us* (the Irishman) for the last two writers reflects early medieval usage. Latin *Scot(t)us* denoting a 'Scotsman' is found only in later times, after the immigrants from Ireland known as *Scot(t)i* had given their names to the north of Britain. This means that the term still means 'Irish' when applied to the chronicler Marianus Scotus (1028–82), who was active in Fulda and Mainz, while the philosophical scholar Johannes Duns Scotus (1266–1308), who taught in Paris and Cologne, did indeed come from Scotland.

After the late ninth century, Irish theologians no longer exerted any significant influence on the intellectual life of central Europe, but over 200 years later a new wave of Irish influence begins with the founding of the so-called Scottish monasteries (see Hammermayer 1976). This was a particularly privileged group of Benedictine monasteries (including Regensburg, Würzburg, Nuremberg, Erfurt,

Constance, Eichstätt and Vienna), which maintained close relations with Ireland for hundreds of years and were only taken over by German Benedictines at the close of the Middle Ages. By this time the Irish Church had undergone far-reaching changes which had much to do with its ever-closer ties to the English Church.

CHAPTER 12

Ireland from the Coming of the Normans to Colonisation

IRELAND, ENGLAND AND THE ANGLO-IRISH: POLITICAL DEVELOPMENTS

When King Diarmait Mac Murchada was driven out of Ireland in 1166 and sought the support of Henry II of England, he obtained, in exchange for recognition of Henry's supremacy, his permission to raise auxiliary troops within Henry's kingdom. Diarmait proceeded to enlist the Earl of Pembroke, Richard FitzGilbert (dubbed Strongbow), as his most important ally, and in 1167 he ventured a return to Ireland at the head of an Anglo-Norman, Welsh and Flemish mercenary army. Three years later, after variable fortunes in battles with the forces of the High King, Richard FitzGilbert himself led an expeditionary force to Ireland and there married Diarmait's daughter Aoife (Eve). Taking up his ally's earlier promise, after Diarmait's death FitzGilbert claimed the kingdom of Leinster in the early summer of 1171, and thanks to the superiority of his troops he was able to make good his claim against all resistance from both the High King and his own Irish subjects. The strong position he thus won for himself awoke the suspicion of Henry II, who set sail for Ireland with his army a few months later to secure his own influence there. At the synod of Cashel in 1172, the Anglo-Normans and several Irish rulers acknowledged the supremacy of the English king, who proceeded to place Dublin directly under his crown and Leinster and Meath in the fief of Richard FitzGilbert and Hugh de Lacy. On his return to England in 1175, Henry II concluded, through his governor Hugh de Lacy, the Treaty of Windsor with Rory O'Connor, the High King. By this treaty, Rory recognised

Henry's overlordship and agreed that Ireland would be divided into an Anglo-Norman region and another region ruled by the Irish High King. Two years later, when Henry named his youngest son John, then ten years old, as Lord of Ireland (*Dominus Hiberniae*), he created the Lordship of Ireland, which would endure until 1541, though varying in extent (see Lydon 1972 and Flanagan 1989).

In the century that followed, despite the division of Ireland prescribed in the Treaty of Windsor, the Anglo-Norman liegemen of the King of England extended their dominion at the expense of the indigenous rulers, especially in the south and west, until they controlled over two-thirds of the island. In the conquered regions they built castles, founded towns, bestowed fiefs upon their followers and thus installed the English system of rule, administration and law.[1] These conquests were made easier by quarrelling among the Irish, and they took place in largely unplanned fashion and without the approval of the English crown, from whose control the Irish possessions repeatedly threatened to slip away. From the thirteenth century the Irish rulers moved to compensate for the military inferiority of their forces by engaging mercenaries from the Hebrides, the so-called *gall-óglaigh* (anglicised as *galloglasses*). Thus, by the beginning of the fourteenth century the Anglo-Norman expansion had mostly ceased, largely owing to quarrels among the barons, the numerical superiority of the Irish population and the inability of the English king to exert any influence.

The vulnerability of the possessions of the English crown in Ireland became apparent in the war with Edward Bruce, brother of the King of Scots Robert Bruce. After landing in Ireland in 1315 with an invasion force, he was crowned King of Ireland a year later at Dundalk, before perishing in battle in October 1318 near the site of his coronation (see McNamee 1997). In addition to the lawlessness and pillage brought by the war, the English settlers suffered repeated crop failure and plague in the decades that followed, and many of them returned to England. The English kings observed with suspicion and concern the conduct of many members of the Anglo-Irish nobility, who either abandoned their Irish estates for their lands in England, Wales and France, or, if they chose to remain in Ireland, increasingly adopted the dress, speech and way of life of the native population (see Nicholls 1972 and Simms 1987). In reaction to this, a parliament convened in 1366 enacted the Statutes of Kilkenny, which, with measures for increasing the effectiveness of the defence of border regions, contained precise instructions concerning a strict separation of Anglo-Irish from Irish. The Statutes forbade inter-marriages and adoption, along with the wearing of Irish dress and the use of the Irish tongue. In spite of the draconian penalties laid down in the Statutes for those who violated them, the blending of the Irish and Anglo-Irish population proceeded further in the fourteenth and fifteenth centuries, and the area under English dominion in the east of the island, known as 'The Pale', after its frontier posts, became ever smaller.

Fundamental changes took shape when Henry VIII, in the course of his efforts to create a centralised state, achieved recognition as head of the Irish Church in 1536, and in 1541 assumed the title of 'King of Ireland', after suspending the Lordship.[2] In view of his international isolation, Henry must have feared that, in the event of war, Ireland could become a bridgehead for his foreign, Catholic opponents, so he sought to extend his influence and integrate all Irish rulers into the English legal system by conferring English titles upon them. After Henry's death in 1547 this system, known as 'surrender and regrant', was abandoned, and from the latter half of the sixteenth century the crown increasingly pursued a policy of colonisation, in which rebellious Irish and Anglo-Irish were systematically replaced by loyal English settlers. Only in the seventeenth and eighteenth centuries would the adverse consequences of this plantation, com-bined with the effects of the Reformation, become fully apparent.

ALIGNMENT WITH ROME: THE IRISH CHURCH AND THE NORMANS

In seeking a better understanding of the history of Ireland in the modern age, we must consider the effects of the English Reformation on the neighbouring island, but we also need to look at the history of the Irish Church from the end of the Age of the Vikings. As early as the second half of the eleventh century, in parallel with the Gregorian Church reforms on the continent, the beginnings of a fundamental renewal of the Irish Church may be discerned, and the impetus for this came both from Rome itself and the Archdiocese of Canterbury. That the Irish monasteries of this period still enjoyed great renown as centres of learning is demonstrated by the example of the Welsh nobleman Sulien, who received his training at the monastery of Glendalough and later held the office of bishop of Saint David's. Among the most significant changes set in train soon after his time was the establishment of territorially defined bishoprics. These had been known in Ireland since the days of Saint Patrick, but since the sixth century they had been of secondary importance owing to the monastic organisation of the Church. After a first reform synod had met in Cashel in 1101 on the initiative of the King of Munster, a second reform synod met in Ráith Bresail ten years later. This second synod decided to divide the whole island into two ecclesiastical provinces – Cashel and Armagh – each with twelve bishoprics and archbishoprics, although they initially left aside several bishoprics, including Dublin. The territorial reorganisation was concluded in 1152 at a synod which met first at Kells then at Mellifont, presided over by a papal legate sent from Rome. This synod restructured the whole Irish Church under the primacy of Armagh, with four archbishoprics in Armagh, Tuam, Dublin and Cashel. An accelerated drive to build diocesan stone churches on the continental model was related to this.

One of the participants in the reform synod at Ráith Bresail was Cellach, of the Uí Sinaich family, who since 1106 had been the first cleric for 200 years to unite in one person the offices of Abbot and Bishop of Armagh. One of the most important reformers of the first half of the twelfth century was his successor Malachy, to whose influence the first Augustinian and Cistercian establishments in Ireland may be attributed. In Clairvaux, while travelling to Rome, he made the acquaintance of Saint Bernard, who became his close friend and wrote an account of Malachy's life after he died in 1148. In *Vita Malachiae*, Bernard painted a dismal picture of the deplorable state of the Irish Church and the persistence of pagan customs, and this picture would have its effect on the papal view of the situation: in 1155 Pope Hadrian IV, who was of English birth, called on King Henry II of England in the papal bull *Laudabiliter* to conquer Ireland in order to expand the frontiers of the Church and take the truth of the Christian faith to an uncivilised and benighted people. A similarly negative view of Ireland is given by Giraldus Cambrensis (Gerald de Barri, Gerald of Wales), the youngest son of an Anglo-Norman nobleman and a mother of Welsh origin, born in Wales in

1146. Following theological studies in Gloucester and Paris, he was chaplain at the court of Henry II from 1184 to 1194, and wrote a description of Ireland (*Topographia Hiberniae*) and an account of the Norman conquest of Ireland (*Expugnatio Hiberniae*), as well as two books about his travels in Wales (*Itinerarium Cambriae* and *Descriptio Cambriae*) (see Boivin 1993). With the growth of the Anglo-Norman area of settlement and influence and the increasing feudalisation of the native Irish rulers, the alignment of the Irish Church towards Rome moved ahead, in spite of rivalries between the indigenous Irish and Anglo-Norman clergy. After the Cistercian and Augustinian orders, the Dominicans set foot on the island in 1224 and the Franciscans followed in 1231.

Just as Henry VIII's policy of 'surrender and regrant' met with broad approval in Ireland, his policy on the Church was at first welcomed by the Irish and Anglo-Irish nobility, since, after the dissolution of the monasteries, the English crown bestowed large estates upon many of them. Unlike England, however, where different social and economic conditions prevailed, opposition soon arose in Ireland to the changes in Church doctrine, the liturgy and the veneration of saints which were introduced after the death of Henry VIII by his son Edward VI. Many in Ireland therefore welcomed the change of direction with regard to the Church in the reign of Mary Tudor (1553–8), and rejected the renewed turn towards Protestantism under her successor Elizabeth I. In many places the general resistance to the Reformation and adherence to Catholicism furthered the ethnic and cultural fusion of Irish and Anglo-Irish (who were now called 'Old English' to distinguish them from the newly arrived Tudor colonists). The fact that the 'New English' overwhelmingly supported the Reformation increasingly lent the conflicts between them and the majority population the character of a religious war from the seventeenth century on. The consequences of this would mark the history of Ireland to the present day.

TRADITION AND INNOVATION: IRISH LITERATURE IN THE LATE MIDDLE AGES

For the history of Irish literature, the Church reforms of the eleventh and twelfth centuries and the coming of the Anglo-Normans had been of great importance.[3] Until then, literature had largely been practised in the great monasteries, but from the twelfth and thirteenth centuries it lay more and more in the hands of notable scholarly families, who specialised in particular fields of the historical and literary tradition, under the patronage of the nobility. While some families produced more historians and genealogists, others were distinguished by their legal scholars or achieved fame thanks to their poets.

Among the best-loved indigenous subject matter in Irish literature of the late Middle Ages are the tales of the legendary Finn mac Cumaill and his followers, mentioned in the previous chapter. Their markedly fable-like nature chimed well with a widespread literary current at the period, whereas the previously popular tales of the Ulster Cycle and the Historical Cycle had lost much of their relevance and topicality, owing to the changed political and social conditions. Typical of the Finn legends of the Anglo-Norman age is *Tóraigheacht Dhiarmada agus Ghráinne* (The Pursuit of Diarmaid and Gráinne), which is famed for its closeness to the Tristan saga. It tells of the tragic love of the young Gráinne, who is married to an elderly Finn, and the warrior Diarmaid Ua Duibne. Imitations of this story in other works of Irish literature show that it was circulating as early as the ninth or tenth centuries, although it has come down to us only in a version from the fifteenth century (see Ní Shéaghdha 1967). At this period, ballads about Finn and his Fianna also became widespread. Sixty-nine of these have been preserved from the period between the twelfth and early seventeenth centuries, in a manuscript from about 1627 known as the *Songbook of Finn* (*Duanaire Finn*).[4]

Long before the arrival of the Anglo-Normans, foreign literary material had been translated or rewritten. In this way a history of Alexander the Great (*Scéla Alaxandair*) had appeared in the tenth century, based on the *Historiae adversus paganos* by the late classical historian Orosius.[5] The Odyssey of Aeneas (*Imtheachta Aeniasa*) is the title of a version of Virgil's *Aeneid*, while a Latin tale of the siege of Troy, *De excidio Troianorum*, thought to be by Dares of Phrygia, became popular in a free Irish re-working known as *Togail Troi* (*The Destruction of Troy*) (see Poppe 1995 and Myrick 1993). The popularity of this foreign subject-matter grew with the spread of Anglo-Norman influence in Ireland, as tales of Charlemagne and King

Arthur and the Holy Grail were translated into Irish, along with works such as Lucan's *Bellum Civile* (*In Cath Catharda* in Irish) (see Williams and Ford 1992, 134–45).

As the Anglo-Irish adopted the Irish tongue and culture and the old-established Irish nobility became feudalised, the ideal of courtly love also took hold in Irish literature from the fourteenth century.[6] An early example of the love poetry inspired by this ideal (*dánta grádha*) is by Earl Gerald Fitzgerald (Gearóid Iarla, 1338–98), the first Irish poet of Anglo-Norman descent known to us by name. However, professional bardic poets, who composed and performed on official occasions after years of training at a bardic school under the patronage of the nobility, played a much greater role than those who wrote poetry when the inclination or opportunity arose.[7] The 2,000 or so surviving poems of this genre demonstrate that these professional poets composed according to well established metrical rules in a formal and highly conservative literary language (although some also left less formal personal verses in addition to official poems written for accessions to the throne or the marriages of aristocratic patrons). Thus, for example, the poet Muireadhach Albanach Ó Dálaigh from the first half of the thirteenth century wrote not only praise-poems for Irish and Anglo-Norman nobles, but religious verse invoking the Virgin Mary and a lament on the death of his wife, who had given him eleven children in twenty years of marriage. He received the nickname Albanach ('the Scot') because he had lived for a long time in Scotland, and later became known as the ancestor of the MacMhuirich family of poets. His personal biography mirrors the close political, social and literary relations that bound the Celtic-speaking regions of Ireland and Scotland in the late Middle Ages and early modern age. The origins and history of these relations, which are expressed in family ties within the nobility, in common features in the organisation of the Church, and in the existence of a unified literary language, are the subject of the next chapter.

CHAPTER 13

Scotland from Irish Settlement to the Reformation

SCOTS AND PICTS: ASPECTS OF POLITICAL HISTORY

As far back as the third century AD Irish settlers from the region of the later County Antrim had crossed the North Channel and settled in the west of Scotland. In their own language they called themselves 'the Gaels' and gave this name to their new homeland, the 'Gaelic coast' (Scots Gaelic *Earraghaidheal*, English *Argyll*). Latin sources, however, termed the newcomers Scots (*Scot[t]i*), and thus the part of Britain north of the Cheviots and the Tweed later received the name of Scotland.[1] A turning point in the history of these Irish colonists came in about AD 500 when their ruler Fergus Mór mac Eirc, of the royal house of Dál Riata, moved to Scotland (see Bannerman 1974 and Anderson 1980). An early high point in the power of the new kingdom was reached under Fergus's grandson Aedán mac Gabráin, who in 574 was anointed king in the monastery of Iona by its abbot Columba (Colum Cille). With the diplomatic support of Columba, he reinforced his position by an alliance with the king of the northern Uí Néill and achieved military successes from the Isle of Man in the south to the Orkneys in the north. The kingdom of Dál Riata suffered a painful setback, however, under Aedán's grandson Domnall Brecc, who acceded to the throne in 629. In 637 he lost the battle of Mag Rath, against the northern Uí Néill, who had been allied to the ruler of Dál Riata, and was killed in 642 in the battle of Strathcarron against the Brythonic Celts from the Strathclyde area.

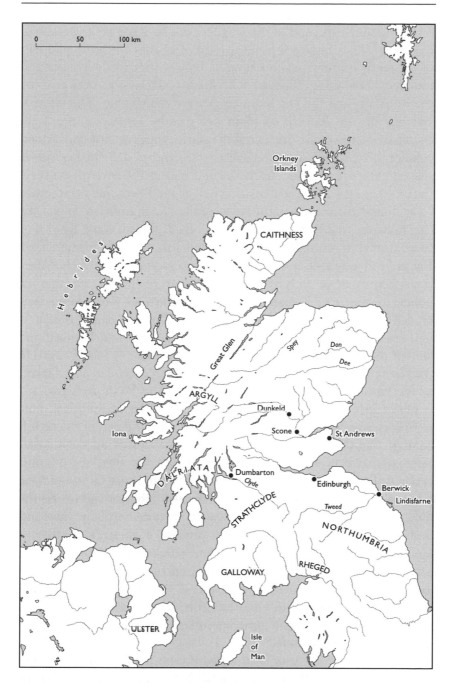

Map 4: Scotland in the Middle Ages

To the north and east of the kingdom of Dál Riata lay the realm of the Picts.[2] They emerged into the light of history in the second half of the sixth century, when Columba paid a visit to their ruler and initiated their conversion to Christianity. Relations between the Pictish rulers and the Dál Riata kings were changeable. The internal stability of the Pictish kingdom set narrow limits on the Irish colonists' expansionist drive, and the sources suggest not only armed conflict, but also alliances to ensure peace and to defend themselves against external enemies. In the second half of the seventh century, the Picts and the Dál Riata Irish, as well as the Brythonic Strathclyde Celts, found themselves in the realm of the Northumbrian Angles. In 685, however, the Pictish ruler Brudei mac Bili dealt King Egfrith of Northumbria a resounding defeat in the battle of Nechtansmere near Forfar, and was able to consolidate the kingdom of the Picts. After three centuries of cultural exchange and reciprocal exertion of political influence, Kenneth mac Alpin, the Dál Riata king, succeeded in uniting the two kingdoms in 843. With the establishment of new centres of secular and clerical power in Scone and Dunkeld, he shifted the focal point of his kingdom some distance to the east. He died in 858 as king of a united Scotland, which extended as far south as the line between the Firth of Forth and the Firth of Clyde.

One factor that exerted considerable influence on political, cultural and linguistic conditions in Scotland from the end of the eighth century was the Norwegian Viking raids. After sacking the Lindisfarne monastery on the Northumbrian coast in 793, the Vikings reached the monastery of Iona, then the Welsh coast in 795 and the Mull of Kintyre and the Isle of Man in 797. Whereas in Ireland the Vikings established towns and engaged in commerce, in Scotland and on the Isle of Man they seized possession of large swathes of land and colonised them.[3] This applied particularly in the Orkneys and Shetlands, the Caithness region and the northern tip of Scotland and the Hebrides, which, as a result of the influx of Norwegian settlers, would henceforth bear the Scots Gaelic name of *Innse Gall* ('the island of foreigners'), although in later times the Gaelic tongue again asserted itself there.[4]

English-speaking communities had established themselves in the area south of the Firth of Forth and the Firth of Clyde in the seventh and eighth centuries. In 1018 the Scottish king Malcolm II defeated a Northumbrian army at the Battle of Carham and thus secured the south-east border of Scotland along the Tweed. In 1040 Malcolm's successor Duncan I was murdered by his rival Macbeth, but after Macbeth's death in 1057 Duncan's son Malcolm III succeeded to the Scottish throne. (Shakespeare's version of events during the reign of Macbeth, which is said to have been first produced in the summer of 1606 at the court of King James of Scotland, is more legendary than historically authentic.) During the reign of Malcolm III, the influence of the English language and culture spread. After the ruler's marriage to Margaret, the daughter of the English king, the recognition of the supremacy of William the Conqueror and the influx of English-speaking traders and Anglo-Norman noblemen, this influence extended further, mainly into the Lowlands but also along the whole of the east coast (see Barrow 1980). After the extinction of the Scottish royal house in 1286, Edward I of England backed John Balliol as king and accepted his allegiance for the whole of Scotland. Resistance to the English king was led by William Wallace, later hailed as a hero of the struggle for freedom, who was executed in August 1305, following his defeat at Falkirk in 1298. In 1314 the Anglo-Norman noble Robert Bruce restored the independence of Scotland with his victory at Bannockburn (see McNamee 1997).

In 1371 the House of Stuart acceded to the throne of Scotland. During its tenure, the gulf between the economically prosperous, heavily anglicised Lowlands and the traditionally structured Gaelic-speaking Highlands deepened further. Early evidence of this is provided by the chronicler John of Fordun, who in about 1380 described the English-speaking Lowland and coastal population as civilised, dependable, peaceful and devout, and that of the Gaelic-speaking Highlands and islands as savage, 'given to rapine', 'ease-loving' and cruel.[5]

One significant area of tension between the kingdoms of Scotland, Norway and England was the Hebrides, where a Scandinavian dynasty of sea-kings had established itself after the centre of political power in Scotland had shifted to the east in the ninth century.[6] In about 1156, Somerled, who could trace his ancestry back to a follower of King Kenneth mac Alpin, reached out from his power-base in Argyll to claim lordship over the southern Hebrides. The northern Hebrides were still controlled by Scandinavian rulers, until in 1266 Norway ceded the Hebrides to Scotland by the Treaty of Perth, and their rulers at least formally accepted the jurisdiction of the Scottish crown. At the battle of Bannockburn, Somerled's descendant Angus Óg MacDonald of Islay supported the Scottish king Robert Bruce with his own interests in mind, and his son John was able, by deft manoeuvring between England and Scotland, to consolidate his hold over the Hebrides. From 1354 he introduced the Latin title *Dominus Insularum* (Scots Gaelic *Rí Innse Gall*, 'Lord of the Isles') and made the Hebrides a focal point of Gaelic culture, with close connections with Ireland. His successors increasingly came into conflict with the Scottish crown. In 1462 John MacDonald sought to achieve greater independence from England by an agreement with Edward IV of England, and in 1493 the Lordship of the Isles was abolished by James IV of Scotland. After this the crown intensified its efforts to establish its position in the Hebrides and western Highlands, until finally in 1609, in the Statutes of Iona, some of the most eminent nobles of the region were compelled to pledge their allegiance formally to the crown and the Church, and to relinquish certain privileges that were detrimental to the central authorities. Attempts were still being made in the first half of the seventeenth century to revive the power and the title of Lord of the Isles, but these were successfully suppressed by the central government.

During his twenty-five-year reign (1488–1513), James IV not only restored to the crown its authority over parliament and the nobles, but also secured for his descendants the right to succession in England, by marriage to Margaret Tudor, a daughter of Henry VII. Under his son James V (1513–42), there was renewed conflict with the nobility, who embraced the Reformation that had already triumphed in England. In 1560, under the leadership of John Knox, a pupil of the Geneva reformer Calvin, the nobility founded the Church of Scotland. After Mary Stuart had been forced to renounce the crown in 1567, this became the established state church under James VI (later James I of England). In the same year the first printed book appeared in Scots Gaelic, John Carswell's *Foirm na n-Urrnuidheadh*, a translation of the Book of Common Prayer, with an expanded translation of Calvin's short catechism (see Thomson, R. L. 1970). In the history of the Church in Scotland, the beginning of the Reformation brought with it such momentous change that at this point a glance back to the beginnings of Christianity in Scotland is called for.

RULERS AND SAINTS: EARLY CHRISTIANITY IN SCOTLAND

The decisive impetus for the conversion of Scotland stemmed from the monastically oriented Irish Church, in particular from Columba (Colum Cille). Born in about 520 in the north of Ireland, the great-great-grandson of the founder of the Uí Néill dynasty, Columba founded the Derry monastery in 546 and those at Durrow and Kells in later years (see Herbert 1988, Bourke 1997 and Lacey 1997). In about 565 he went with some companions to the kingdom of the Picts and founded a monastery on the island of Iona, where he was buried on his death in 597. King Oswald of Northumbria had a particular connection with Iona, finding refuge there after the death of his father and accepting baptism there. When in 634 he succeeded in winning back his kingdom, he sought support from Iona to convert Northumbria to Christianity, and in 635 Abbot Aedán founded the monastery of Lindisfarne on a little island off the coast.[7] An early example of monastic scholarship can be seen in the writings of Adamnán, who was born in about 624 and from 679 until his death in 704 served as ninth abbot of Iona. From his pen came a book about the Holy Places of Palestine, *De locis sanctis*, and a historically valuable biography of Columba, *Vita Columbae* (see Anderson 1991 and Sharpe 1995).

In the seventh century came a controversy over the correct calculation of the date of Easter, and in this the Celtic churches of Ireland, Scotland and Wales differed sharply from the general practice elsewhere in the Latin western world. At the Synod of Whitby, convened in 664 by King Oswiu of Northumberland, the supporters of the Roman system won their case, but the unified reckoning system was not implemented everywhere at once. While the Irish church gradually adapted in the course of the seventh century, those in the territory of the Picts and in Iona did not adopt the Roman reckoning until 716, and Wales clung to the old system until 768.

At the same time as the Viking raids, from the end of the eighth century, the monastic reform movement known as the 'Clients of God' (Irish *Céli Dé*, anglicised as *Culdees*) was gaining ground. Its aims were stricter discipline and a renewal of the ascetic ideal. One of the centres of this movement was Iona, but St Andrews, Abernethy, Brechin and other less important churches also felt the influence of *Céli Dé*. A fundamental renewal came with the introduction of continental monastic orders, including the Benedictines, Augustinians, Cistercians and Premonstratensians, who since the end of the eleventh century had established themselves mainly in the English-speaking south-east of Scotland and determined the shape of the Church until the end of the Middle Ages.

Christianity provided a crucial impetus to the arts, of which notably metalwork, monumental sculptures in stone and illuminated manuscripts have come down to us. Bronze and silver reliquaries are early samples of metalwork, as is a collection of richly decorated silver bowls, clasps and other objects found hidden under the floor of a church on the small Shetland island of St Ninian's, probably placed there at the time of the Viking raids in about 800 (see Small et al. 1973). Examples of sculpture, especially in the sphere of influence of the Lordship of the Isles, are much more numerous. The monumental crosses decorated with figures and ornaments, which, as in Ireland, bring together the tradition of eastern Christian art and Germanic and Celtic elements, are of particular note. This tradition was embraced, as the Latin inscriptions in the Western Highlands and the Hebrides show, mainly from the late thirteenth century to the first half of the sixteenth century, but one of the earliest and most beautiful examples of the tradition is the Ruthwell Cross in Dumfriesshire, from the late seventh or eighth century, with a runic inscription in the Northumbrian dialect of Old English (see Steer and Bannerman 1977; also Harbison 1992). Pictish sculptors, unlike those of Ireland and the north of England, did not carve free-standing crosses, but instead chiselled ornate crosses in large slabs of rock, which they then adorned with geometric symbols and pictorial representations of humans and animals (see Close-Brooks and Stevenson 1982).

A blend of early eastern Christian, Germanic and Celtic elements is also found in the early medieval illuminated manuscripts, whose ornamental style is strongly influenced by metalwork and shows no less than the sculptures in stone the close cultural relations between Ireland, Scotland and Christian Northumbria (see Nordenfalk 1977 and Henderson 1987). In the second half of the seventh century *The Book of Durrow*, named after the place where it was later kept, was produced in Iona or Northumbria. Another precious possession of the library was *The Book of Kells*, from the second half of the eighth century, also kept there since 1661, and for which a Scottish origin may be posited.[8] *The Book of Deer*, which was held in the Monastery of Deer in north-eastern Scotland until it found its way to Cambridge University library in 1715, is a gospel-book from the tenth century. Its special importance lies in some notes appended in Gaelic, which represent the first example of continuous text in this language on Scottish soil (see Jackson 1972 and Forsyth 2002).

The art of building in stone also reached Scotland with Christianity and classical civilisation. Although the first monastery in Iona was built of wood, craftsmen from Northumbria brought the new technique to north-east Scotland in the early eighth century. One of the most beautiful surviving monuments of that period is the round tower of the Brechin monastery near Forfar, built to an Irish pattern in about 1000 and standing twenty-six metres high. Early specimens of Roman architecture may be found in churches built since the end of the eleventh century, when continental monastic orders were introduced.[9]

SEVEN TONGUES, SIX NATIONS: THE LANGUAGES OF SCOTLAND IN THE MIDDLE AGES

In his history of the English Church, completed in 731, the Benedictine monk known as the Venerable Bede wrote that Britain had five languages and four nations. Although the Anglo-Saxons, Britons, Scots of Irish descent and Picts each had their own language, all these peoples were, he claimed, united by the use of Latin as the medium for the study of the Scriptures. If we consider the entire medieval period, the number of peoples with their own language increases in Scotland since the Norwegian Vikings brought Old Norse and the Normans introduced Norman-French to the court.

The language of which we have least knowledge is Pictish, of which the earliest inscriptions known to us date from the seventh to ninth centuries. It was previously thought that, like Basque in Spain and France, Pictish was a pre-Indo-European language, which served only for restricted purposes and died out shortly after the last inscriptions were incised. If this were the case, one could venture no statements concerning the structure of Pictish or its possible relation to other languages, owing to the scarcity of evidence. Nowadays, however, the prevailing scholarly view is that the supposed pre-Indo-European Pictish was merely the most northerly branch of a Brythonic tongue which was closely related to Cumbrian in southern Scotland and the north of England, and to Welsh (see Forsyth 1997, Price 2000, 127–31). Whereas the Celtic tongue of Pictland is thought to have died out in the ninth century, Cumbrian survived until about 1100. Unlike Welsh, Cornish and Breton, these two daughters of the old Brythonic tongue are known only from single words, mostly the names of people and places (see Price 1984, 146–57).

The most important language of commerce in the area north of the Firth of Forth and Firth of Clyde from the ninth century was Scots Gaelic, which the Irish settlers had introduced into Scotland.[10] However, since the oldest continuous texts date from the twelfth century, the early history of the language can be reconstructed only in broad outline from place-names and indications in Latin sources of its use. Before the twelfth century, Scots Gaelic must have differed little from Irish, but texts from the modern period display characteristic deviations, which may be due to the influence of Brythonic Celtic on Gaelic. For example, in Gaelic, as in Welsh, a continuous present develops (Gaelic *Tha mi a' dol* and Welsh *Rydw i'n mynd*, English *I'm going*), while the old present takes on future meaning in both languages.

Gaelic was also greatly influenced by Old Norse, which had reached the country with the Vikings at the end of the eighth century. This is shown by numerous loan-words from the areas of seafaring and fishing, including *acair* 'anchor' (Old Norse *akkeri*), *stiùir* 'rudder' (Old Norse *stýri*) and *trosg* 'cod' (Old Norse *þorsk*), but primarily by characteristic features of the pronunciation and the sentence intonation of some Gaelic dialects. The previously broad geographical range of Old Norse may still be seen today in place-names of Scandinavian origin, which are especially numerous in the Hebrides.[11]

The significant role of Latin as the medium of classical culture and the Christian faith is apparent from the many Latin loan-words which (sometimes by way of Brythonic) entered the Irish language at an early date and survive to this day in Scots Gaelic. These include specifically Christian concepts, such as *aingeal* 'angel' (Latin *angelus*), *aoine* 'fast' (Latin *ieiunium*), *beannachd* 'blessing' (Latin *benedictio*) and *diabhal* 'devil' (Latin *diabolus*), and concepts from the culture of writing, such as *leabhar* 'book' (Latin *liber*), *litir* 'letter' (Latin *littera*) and *sgoil* 'school' (Latin *schola*).

The use of Norman French in Scotland was always restricted to a relatively small aristocratic circle, but Lowland Scots, or Lallans, grew in importance from the late Middle Ages as the language of the court and the flourishing trading towns. Scots loan-words are therefore common in Gaelic, although in the early period the ultimate origin of some borrowings is often difficult to establish, owing to the high proportion of French and Latin words in English. The oldest Gaelic loan-words in Lowland Scots are thought to be those related to the mission of the church of Iona in Northumbria. From this period we have *clugge* 'bell', *dry* 'magician' (Druid) and perhaps also *stær* (from Latin *historia*). Later loan-words are found in early sources and documents dealing with social structures, the law and the topography of the Gaelic-speaking Highlands, including some terms which are still current today: *loch* (first recorded 1375), *glen* (first recorded 1489), *bog* (first recorded 1505), *cairn* (first recorded 1535) and *strath* (first recorded 1540). The term Gaelic first occurs in 1596, as the Celtic tongue of the Highlands and the Hebrides was usually called *Irish* in English and *Erse* in Scots.

The Isle of Man was a melting pot of different Celtic dialects, in which place-names, inscriptions and literary evidence from the early and later Middle Ages point to the use of both Goidelic and Brythonic forms of insular Celtic. In addition, Old Norse, which took hold in the ninth century in the wake of the Viking raids, and Norman French, whose influence on linguistic development is related to the Norman conquest of Ireland, both played an important role on the island. As a brief bilingual inscription from about AD 500 shows, Latin, as the language of the Christian Church, had taken hold in the island centuries before. In the second half of the fourteenth century at the latest, a local form of Irish became the accepted colloquial language and after the Reformation achieved the status of a literary language. Besides translations of the Bible and liturgical and catechetic works, ballads were recorded from the eighteenth century. During the nineteenth century, however, English – the language of economic progress – steadily gained the dominant position, particularly in the towns. The last speaker of Manx, Ned Maddrell, died on 27 December 1974 at the age of 97 (Broderick 1999, R. L. Thomson in Price 2000, 58–67).

CHAPTER 14

Wales from the Romans to the Normans

CELTS AND ANGLO-SAXONS: THE HISTORY OF BRITAIN IN THE EARLY MIDDLE AGES

If Celtic Scotland owes its distinctive cultural identity to the influx of Irish-speaking colonists and the contribution of the Picts and long-established Brythonic Celts, this is even more emphatically the case in Celtic Wales. Here, the inhabitants held fast to their ancient language and culture in the mountainous regions in the west of the island, having been cut off from the rest of Celtic Britain by the Anglo-Saxon conquests.[1]

Since the fifth century, Germanic tribes had been settling permanently in Britain in great numbers. The Jutes settled in the south-east, in present-day Kent and on the Isle of Wight and the coastal area facing it. The Saxons occupied the whole area south of the Thames, while the Angles claimed the lands north of the Thames to beyond the present Scottish border, as far as the Firth of Forth. About the territorial boundaries and internal organisation of the Celtic kingdoms which arose simultaneously in the north and west of Britain, we have insufficient information, owing to a lack of contemporary documents. In the far south-west, in present-day Cornwall and Devon, lay the kingdom of Dumnonia, from which Celtic settlers colonised Brittany, on the coast opposite. North of the Bristol Channel and the Severn Estuary, in the south of what is now Wales, lay the kingdom of Dyfed in the west and Brycheiniog in the east, whose rulers saw themselves as the descendants of Irish settlers. The north-west of Wales, with the Isle of Anglesey and the region of Snowdonia, belonged to the kingdom of Gwynedd, while the kingdom of Powys took shape in the north-east and in the central area of present-day Wales. To the north, from Lancashire through the Lake District and beyond the Scottish border as far as Galloway and Dumfries stretched the kingdom of Rheged. Its northern border met the kingdom of Strathclyde, which had its main fortress at Dumbarton Rock on the north bank of the Clyde near Glasgow, and in the east it adjoined the territory of the Gododdin, whose capital was Din Eidyn, later Edinburgh.

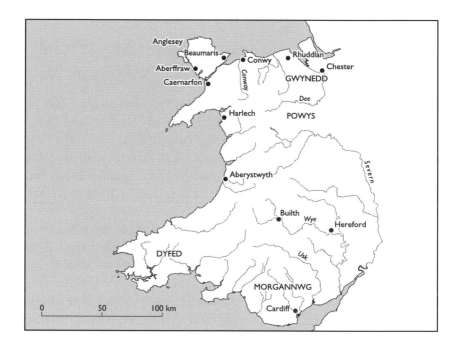

Map 5: Wales in the Middle Ages

In 577, after the battle of Deorham near Bath, the Severn Valley, with the towns of Gloucester, Cirencester and Bath, fell to the Saxons as they pushed westwards. With this defeat, the land link between the Celtic tribes of Wales and their southern neighbours in Devon and Cornwall was permanently broken. In 615 the King of Powys was beaten by the Northumbrian Angles at the Battle of Chester, so the Celts of Wales were now cut off from their kinsmen to the north. The seal was finally set on their territorial isolation in 654 by the victory of the King of Bernicia over the combined forces of the King of Mercia and several Celtic princes in the Battle of Winwaed Field, near Leeds. In 638 the kingdom of the Gododdin had submitted to the assaults of the Angles after losing the principal Gododdin stronghold of Din Eidyn, while at the same time the kingdom of Rheged had come under Northumbrian control through a dynastic marriage. Of the Brythonic kingdoms outside Wales only that of Strathclyde preserved its independence until the eleventh century. By this time all the others had collapsed under the Anglo-Saxon onslaught and would survive only in memory.

Like Ireland, early medieval Wales comprised a large number of competing kingdoms, and this made for long-term difficulties in establishing any concerted defence against the advance of the Anglo-Saxons. In the mid-seventh century, the east of the kingdom of Powys passed to the neighbouring kingdom of Mercia, but at the same time the kingdom of Gwynedd in the north-west of Wales was able to extend its power. According to *Historia Brittonum*, compiled in about 830, the inhabitants of what became Wales called on Prince Cunedda from the lands of the Gododdin in northern Britain for help in defending their country against invaders from Ireland. His great-grandson Maelgwn Gwynedd reigned over the kingdom of Gwynedd from his court in Degannwy near Conwy in the first half of the sixth century. A signal success in the defensive struggle against the Angles was achieved by King Cadwallon ap Cadfan, who, backed by an alliance with the pagan King Penda of Mercia, defeated King Edwin of Northumbria at the Battle of Heathfield near Doncaster in 632. After a start had been made on an earthen fortification to secure the Welsh border during the reign of King Ethelbald of Mercia (716–57), his successor Offa (757–96) had a rampart built with a defensive ditch in front of it, stretching for more than 200 kilometres, with few interruptions, from Prestatyn in North Wales to Sedbury on the Severn Estuary in the south. Known as Offa's Dyke, with some deviations it marks the approximate line of the Welsh border even today.

A great stride along the way to a united Wales was taken in the mid-ninth century by Rhodri Mawr, who succeeded his father on his death as King of Gwynedd in 844. When his uncle died in 855 he became King of Powys and defeated the Danish Vikings in a sea battle off the coast of Anglesey. Following the death of his brother-in-law in 872 his rule extended over the Kingdom of Seisyllwg, but this success was short-lived, as on his death in 878 his kingdom was divided among his six sons. As a direct consequence of the ensuing rivalries, several Welsh rulers accepted at least formally the supremacy of King Alfred the Great of Wessex (871–99), whose defensive struggle against the Danes and reorganisation of state structures and education laid the foundations for a united English kingdom.

The most outstanding Welsh ruler of the tenth century, in the eyes of his contemporaries and of posterity, was Rhodri's grandson Hywel ap Cadell, known as 'the Good' (Hywel Dda). He first reigned over the Kingdom of Seisyllwg, which he had inherited from his father. After the death of his father-in-law Llywarch ap Hyfaidd, the last ruler of Dyfed, he united the two territories in the newly created Kingdom of Deheubarth in 904 and in 942 secured sovereignty over Gwynedd. By acknowledging the overlordship of King Athelstan of Wessex, he succeeded in ensuring many years of peace with his Anglo-Saxon neighbours. As the first King of Wales, Hywel had coins issued with his name on them and set about codifying traditional Welsh law. Although his law code is known only from manuscripts written between the twelfth and eighteenth centuries and containing many additions and amendments, the code bears his name to this day (*Cyfraith Hywel Dda/The Law of Hywel Dda*).[2]

After Hywel's death, Wales was afflicted for decades by internal disputes and wars with the English and the Vikings, and none of its rulers was able to provide lasting stability. Only Gruffudd ap Llywelyn succeeded in uniting large areas of Wales under his rule from 1039. When Gruffudd was killed in 1063 by his own countrymen in the struggle against Harold of Wessex, Wales lost the most powerful ruler it had ever had. Three years later Harold himself fell in battle against his rival William of Normandy, whose invasion in 1066 would open a new chapter in the history of England and Wales.

THE LEGACY OF ROME: THE EARLY HISTORY OF CHRISTIANITY IN WALES

Pan darffo heddwch Rhufain
fe saif tangnefedd ein Harglwydd;
Offrwm beunyddiol offeiriaid Crist
yw meini saerniaeth ein dinas,
A chredo ddisyflyd yr Eglwys
balmanta undod gwareiddiad.

When Rome's armistice passes,
the peace of our Lord will endure;
the daily worship of the priests of Christ
are the stones with which our city will be built,
and the unswerving creed of the Church
will pave the way for a unified culture.

Thus does an eye-witness comment on the departure of the Roman legions from Britain in the radio play *Buchedd Garmon*, by the modern Welsh playwright Saunders Lewis (1893–1985), first broadcast in 1937.[3] In reality, the Christianity of the Romanised Britons following the Anglo-Saxon conquest would display far greater vitality than Roman law, urban culture or the Latin language. In Wales, in contrast to Gaul, Latin gave way to various Celtic and Germanic dialects soon after the end of Roman rule.[4]

The British Church of the early Middle Ages, like the Church in Gaul, had an episcopal structure which originated in the era of Roman occupation. But it was strongly influenced by the monastic movement, which had spread from the Near East and overtaken Gaul in the late classical period, to flourish in post-Roman times in Ireland and Britain. One of the first British theologians of more-than-regional importance was the monk Pelagius, who went to Rome in 384 and remained active there as a lay ascetic until the Visigoth invasion in 410. His rejection of the Augustinian doctrine of original sin and his emphasis on free will led to the condemnation of 'Pelagianism', which was branded as heresy in the Western Roman Empire in 411 and in 431 in the Eastern Empire. As the Venerable Bede reports in Chapters 17–21 of Book One of his history of the

English Church, Bishop Germanus of Auxerre and Bishop Lupus of Troyes travelled to Britain in 429, successfully opposed the Pelagian doctrine and helped the Christian Britons to achieve a significant military victory over the heathen Saxons.

Later sources describe the fifth and sixth centuries, when the most important missionaries, founders of monasteries and men of the Church lived, as 'the age of the saints'.[5] Their influence can typically be seen in the numerous surviving place-names consisting of the element *Llan-*, denoting the enclosure of a monastery, and the name of the founder. One of the earliest Welsh saints was Dyfrig (Dubricius), who is said to have had a particularly close connection with the south-east of Wales. The memory of Saint Cadog, to whom tradition attributes the founding of the monastery at Llancarfan, is linked with the same region. So too is the legend of Illtud, who, as a pupil of Bishop Germanus of Auxerre, is reputed to have founded the monastery of Llanilltud Fawr (Llantwit Major). The figures of Saint Teilo, the founder of Llandeilo Fawr in Carmarthenshire, and Saint David (Dewi Sant) – later the patron saint of Wales – are associated with the south-west of the country. Tradition ascribes to Saint David the founding of Saint David's Monastery (Tŷ Ddewi) in Glyn Rhosyn, which later became an episcopal see and from the twelfth century drew great numbers of pilgrims.[6] Beuno and Deiniol are linked with sites in north Wales, the former being particularly revered in Anglesey and Llŷn, and the latter credited with establishing the Bangor-in-Arfon monastery, as well as having a special connection to the Bangor-is-Coed monastery further east.

Like the early medieval Irish Church, the Welsh Church departed from the general Roman practice in some particulars of its organisation, its liturgy and especially in its calculation of the date of Easter. The Benedictine monk Augustine, who was sent to England by Pope Gregory I in 596, did not succeed in removing these deviations, despite his other outstanding successes as a missionary. Only in about 768 did the Welsh adopt the Roman method of reckoning the date of Easter, the last of the Celtic churches to do so. Other special features, such as the right of priests to marry, were not relinquished until later centuries in many places.

As in Ireland, the Church in Wales maintained a rich culture of writing, and it continued to use Latin as the traditional language of communication and administration even after the end of Roman rule.

It was described as 'our language' (*nostra lingua*) in the sixth century by the monk Gildas who, in his treatise *De excidio Britanniae* (On the Ruin of Britain), castigated the moral decay of his fellow-countrymen.[7] The earliest account in Latin of the history of Britain and its inhabitants, wrongly attributed to a cleric by the name of Nennius and today generally known as *Historia Brittonum*, probably dates from about 830 (see Dumville 1994). A chronicle from the mid-tenth century, from Saint David's monastery, is one of the sources of the twelfth- and thirteenth-century texts collectively known today by the name applied by the first publisher, *Annales Cambriae* (see Hughes, K. 1973). From the early Middle Ages, clerics used the Latin script to set down vernacular texts and thus laid the ground for the rise of a native Welsh literature.

TALES FROM THE OLD NORTH: THE EARLIEST WELSH LITERATURE

The earliest evidence of the Welsh language comes from the late sixth century, when the Celtic dialect of the inhabitants of Wales had become sufficiently distant from the closely related Cornish, Cumbrian and Breton dialects to be regarded as a language in its own right. The period until the end of the eighth century was the age of Early Welsh, known mainly from names in inscriptions and in Latin texts.[8] Welsh literature is traditionally seen as having its beginnings in the works of the so-called 'Early Poets' (*Cynfeirdd*) Aneirin and Taliesin, who, according to *Historia Brittonum*, lived in the late sixth century in the region of the Gododdin and in Rheged, the 'Old North' of Celtic Britain. Whether the poetry which appears under their names in more recent manuscripts and in modernised language really dates back to this early time has justifiably been called into question in recent research. *The Book of Aneirin*, from the second half of the thirteenth century, attributes to the bard Aneirin the heroic poem *Y Gododdin*, which tells of the downfall of a select band of mounted warriors of the Gododdin tribe in their campaign against the town of Catraeth, the modern Catterick in Yorkshire. Preserved in two versions with a total of over 1,400 lines, the poem sheds much light on the warrior ethos of the stratum of society that it was created to celebrate.[9] In medieval Wales, Aneirin's contemporary Taliesin was seen as the author of a great number of different poems, but their content and language suggest that, at most, eleven praise-poems and a lament on the death of Owain, the son of Prince Urien of Rheged, can be ascribed to the historical Taliesin. The remainder of the poems attributed to him presuppose the conventionalised figure of a legendary sage from a bygone era and certainly could not have arisen before the tenth century.[10] *Moliant Cadwallon*, a praise-poem for King Cadwallon of Gwynedd, killed in battle against Oswald of Bernicia in 633, may date from the early seventh century, but the earliest extant manuscript is from the seventeenth century (see R. G. Gruffydd in Bromwich and Jones 1978, 25–43).

Old Welsh, which survives not only in names but also in explanatory glosses in Latin and Old English manuscripts, is dated to the period between the late eighth century and the mid-twelfth century. The few continuous texts that survive from this period include the so-called *Surexit Memorandum*, a judicial note in a Latin evangeliary from the eighth century, known variously as *The Book of Saint Teilo*, *The Book of Saint Chad*, or *The Lichfield Gospels*, after the town where it was later held (see Jenkins and Owen 1984). Another Old Welsh text is the *Computus* fragment, a partially preserved discourse in twenty-three lines on calendar calculation, thought to be from the early tenth century. Of Old Welsh poetry in contemporary manuscripts (and therefore without later accretions and alterations), only the so-called *Juvencus-Englynion*, two anonymous poems of three and nine stanzas, have come down to us in a manuscript with the poetry of the late Latin poet Juvencus (see T. A. Watkins in Gruffydd, R. G. 1982, 29–43).

Other poems, probably written at that time, have reached us in more recent manuscripts and in a modernised form of language. The seven-stanza poem *Edmyg Dinbych Penfro*, which joins a praise-poem for the fortress of Tenby in Pembroke with a lament on the death of the resident ruler, dates from the late ninth century. A prophetic poem from about 930, *Armes Prydein*, sets forth in over 200 lines a vision of a Welsh alliance with Cornwall, Brittany, Ireland and the Vikings of Dublin to drive the Anglo-Saxons out of Britain, and is noteworthy evidence of the conflicts between the Celts and Anglo-Saxons (Williams, I. 1972). Two cycles of poems about the legendary characters Llywarch Hen and Heledd originate in the ninth or tenth centuries. They set out in the form of dialogues or monologues the dramatic high points of tales unknown to us, whose plots may have been related in prose or were assumed to be known.[11] According to the saga, Llywarch Hen was a cousin of King Urien of Rheged, who lived in the north of Britain in the late sixth century, although later tradition links him with places and landscapes in North Wales. In the so-called *Cân yr Henwr* (Song of the Old Man), Llywarch portrays himself as a lonely old man, ailing and weighed down by sorrow. In other stanzas he laments the death of his twenty-four sons, who went to war on his orders and were killed. Heledd was said to be the sister of King Cynddylan, who ruled over the Kingdom of Powys in the seventh century. In the poem *Ystafell Gynddylan* (The Hall of Cynddylan) she depicts the desolation at the royal castle, which was destroyed by the enemy after the death of the king. Where once warm fires and candles burned, darkness now reigns, and in place of singing there is silence. In other stanzas, Heledd laments the death of her brothers, the devastation of the country and her own fate, which has delivered her defenceless into enemy hands. Repeatedly she blames herself for complicity in the fall of the royal house, but the surviving stanzas shed no light on the precise meaning of the lines in question.

The beginning of the Middle Welsh period, from which we have the first substantial literary monuments, is considered to be the first half of the twelfth century. Their preservation is owed to a number of extensive compilations from the thirteenth to the fifteenth centuries, including *The Black Book of Carmarthen* (*Llyfr Du Caerfyrddin*), *The Book of Aneirin* (*Llyfr Aneirin*), *The Book of Taliesin* (*Llyfr Taliesin*), *The White Book of Rhydderch* (*Llyfr Gwyn Rhydderch*) and *The Red Book of Hergest* (*Llyfr Coch Hergest*) (see Huws 2000). Most of these were produced in Welsh monasteries, although the oldest of the texts contained in them often go back to events connected with the names of legendary heroes from the Celtic north of Britain. To the Welsh, these 'men of the north' (*Gwŷr y Gogledd*) include the poet Myrddin, who, according to legend, was a liegeman of King Gwenddoleu who went mad at the Battle of Arfderydd in 573, sought refuge in the forests of Scotland in fear of Gwenddoleu's opponent Rhydderch Hael, and received in isolation the gift of prophecy.[12] The oldest evidence of this legend, which in many respects recalls the Irish tradition surrounding King Suibhne Geilt, is found in some stanzas preserved in *The Black Book of Carmarthen*. From the twelfth century on, under the name of Merlin, Myrddin would become widely known beyond Welsh literature and continue to inspire German-speaking poets and playwrights right down to the modern age – from Dorothea von Schlegel to Ludwig Uhland, Karl Immermann and Tankred Dorst.[13] The essential prerequisite for this was the adaptation of Welsh traditions by the Anglo-Normans, whose changing relations with the Welsh principalities are the subject of the next chapter.

CHAPTER 15

The Union of Wales and England

FROM DIVISION TO ANNEXATION: POLITICAL DEVELOPMENTS

Soon after his victory over Harold II at the Battle of Hastings and his
coronation at Christmas 1066, William I subjugated the whole of
England and granted to some of his most loyal vassals the fief of three
earldoms on the Welsh border round the towns of Hereford, Shrews-
bury and Chester. In the decades that followed, the new masters
undertook, with varying degrees of success, forays into 'Wales
proper' (*Pura Wallia*), as the still existing Welsh kingdoms of
Gwynedd, Powys and Deheubarth would now be known, as distinct
from the 'Welsh marches' (*Marchia Walliae*), the area dominated by
the Norman nobility.[1] The Normans achieved their greatest military
successes in the south of the country, where they managed to gain
control of large areas of coastal territory after the death of King Rhys
ap Tewdwr of Deheubarth in 1093.

The Norman conquest brought to the affected regions a number of
major changes in land-holding and economic practices. The new
authorities secured their possessions by building simple castles,
situated at strategically favourable sites and fortified by stockades,
ramparts and ditches. Protected by the castles, walled towns grew up,
and in these Norman traders and artisans settled, enjoying privileges
in law. Outside the towns, especially in the lowland regions of the
south and east, new forms of agriculture were practised on broad
manorial estates, while in the less fertile mountain regions the old-
established population clung to their traditional livelihood.

The Norman influx also brought far-reaching changes for the

Church, which was now divided on the continental model into the four dioceses of Bangor, Saint David's, Llandaff and Saint Asaph. The bishops were often of Norman extraction and were directly subordinate to the Archbishop of Canterbury. Among the continental orders that established themselves in Wales, under the protection of the new masters, foremost were the Augustinians and the Cistercians. Augustinian priories arose at Llanthony Prima (1103), Carmarthen (1148) and Haverfordwest (1200), and during the thirteenth century existing monasteries in Penmon, Bardsey and Beddgelert joined the order. The first Cistercian abbey arose at Tintern in 1131, followed by another foundation at Margam (1147). Two other monasteries at Neath and Basingwerk also joined the Cistercian order in 1147. Whitland Abbey was opened in about 1140, and substantial daughter-houses were established in Strata Florida (Ystrad Fflur 1164), Strata Marcella (Ystrad Marchell, c. 1170) and Cwm Hir (1176). Daughter-houses of the Abbey of Strata Florida arose in Llantarnam (1179), Llanllŷr and Aberconwy (1186).

As centres of culture and learning, the new monasteries enjoyed the protection not only of the Normans, but also of the Welsh princes, who, after initial territorial losses, successfully defended their position against the Normans in the twelfth century. The kingdom of Deheubarth attained the zenith of its power under Rhys ap Gruffudd (1132–97), while Powys experienced a late flowering under Madog ap Maredudd (d. 1160) (on Rhys ap Gruffudd see Jones and Pryce 1996 and Turvey 1997). Gwynedd, whose rulers Gruffudd ap Cynan (c. 1055–1137) and Owain ap Gruffudd (c. 1100–70) managed to reinforce their position by means of astute diplomacy, achieved clear supremacy (on Gruffudd ap Cynan see Maund 1996). Gwynedd reached the summit of its power under Llywelyn ap Iorwerth (1173–1240), by far the most powerful Welsh prince of his time. In the Treaty of Montgomery in 1267 his grandson Llywelyn ap Gruffudd (c. 1225–82) claimed the title of Prince of Wales in exchange for his recognition of the overlordship of the English king, but he came increasingly into conflict with the crown of England after the coronation of Edward I in 1272.[2] A first war in 1276–7 ended in defeat for Llywelyn, and under the Treaty of Aberconwy he had to cede a considerable part of his territory and sphere of influence. In 1282 Llywelyn's younger brother Dafydd, who had previously taken the side of the English king, unleashed a new rebellion, during which Llywelyn was killed on 11 December 1282 in a skirmish at Cilmeri. After this, Dafydd took over the leadership of the rebellion, but was captured in June 1283 and executed for high treason in October of the same year.

O laith Llywelyn cof dyn ni m'daw.
Oerfelawg calon dan fron o fraw.

Poni welwch-chwi'r môr yn merwinaw-'r tir?
Poni welwch-chwi'r gwir yn ymgweiriaw?
Poni welwch-chwi'r haul yn hwylaw-'r awyr?

Since Llywelyn is slain, my mortal wit fails me.
The heart's gone cold, under a breast of fear.

See you not the sea stinging the land?
See you not the truth in travail?
See you not the sun hurtling through the sky?

More than any other document of the era, these lines by the poet Gruffudd ab yr Ynad Coch from his lament on the death of Llywelyn ap Gruffudd convey an idea of the impact made on his contemporaries by the demise of the last of the Welsh princes.[3] In 1284 in the Statute of Rhuddlan Edward I decreed the territorial reorganisation of the subjugated principality, and it was divided into a northern and a southern half with administrative centres in Caernarfon and Carmarthen respectively. In 1283, on the orders of the king, construction began of the immense castles of Caernarfon, Conwy and Harlech. Under their protection, fortified towns quickly sprang up, but the native inhabitants were forbidden to reside in these and could not enter them bearing arms. In 1301 Edward I transferred dominion over the principality to his son, later King Edward II, and to this day every heir to the British throne bears the title of Prince of Wales.

In the fourteenth century Wales enjoyed a period of internal security and economic prosperity, and many members of the lower-ranking nobility found positions in the administration or the army of the English king. Nevertheless the social, economic and judicial discrimination against the Welsh produced enduring dissatisfaction with English rule, dissatisfaction which was deepened by the deteriorating economic situation following a sharp fall in the population caused by the plague of 1348–9. Widespread insurrection was sparked when Owain Glyndŵr (c. 1354–1416), a descendant of the kings of Powys and Deheubarth, was proclaimed Prince of Wales by a small group of supporters on 16 September 1400. Angered by the draconian punitive measures adopted by the English crown, broad sections of the population supported the rebels, who seized the castles of Harlech and Aberystwyth in 1404. In the same year Owain Glyndŵr convened a Welsh parliament in Machynlleth and was crowned Prince of Wales in the presence of French, Scottish and Castilian envoys. In 1406, however, the English king regained the military advantage. When Harlech and Aberystwyth were recaptured in 1408, the revolt came to an end, although the English forces never succeeded in capturing Owain Glyndŵr.[4]

The decades which followed were marked by economic recovery, but also by increasing lawlessness as a result of a decline in public order. Great hopes were awakened at the end of the Wars of the Roses, when, after the Battle of Bosworth Field in 1485, Henry Tudor (1457–1509), a Welshman, ascended the English throne as Henry VII. But as the king appointed many of his supporters to high office in London or rewarded them for their services with landed estates in England, many Welsh noblemen became more and more alienated from their fellow-countrymen. The inability of the crown to deal with the lawlessness that had arisen from its loss of authority, together with Henry VIII's efforts to establish the strongest possible central control, ultimately led, as in Ireland, to a new territorial reorganisation. In 1536 and 1543 the special status of the Principality and the marches was annulled and the whole of Wales was divided into twelve counties with the right of appropriate representation in the English parliament. English became the official language of administration and the judiciary, and English law became equally binding on the Welsh and English alike.

CELTIC TRADITION AND COURTLY IDEALS: MIDDLE WELSH LITERATURE

For the history of Welsh literature the presence of the Anglo-Normans was of great significance as, on the one hand, the conquerors brought with them new literary material and forms and, on the other, disseminated traditional Celtic material far beyond the borders of Wales. The literary works of the twelfth to fifteenth centuries reflect not only the military conflicts of the period, but also a lively cultural exchange.

In poetry, soon after 1100, with the restoration of the Kingdom of Gwynedd under Gruffudd ap Cynan, the age of the 'Poets of the Princes' (*Beirdd y Tywysogion*), began. This period harked back to recognised models from sagas and poetry in a consciously old-fashioned, alliterative linguistic mode, praising living rulers and lamenting the dead, while also handing down to posterity lyrically tinged personal lines.[5] To distinguish these poets from the 'Early Poets' (*Cynfeirdd*) Aneirin and Taliesin, the authors of these works are often termed 'the Fairly Early Poets' (*Gogynfeirdd*). This designation was also applied to those poets who continued to write in traditional metrical and linguistic forms after the death of the last Welsh prince in 1282 and until the end of the fourteenth century. The earliest member of this group known by name is the poet Meilyr (Meilyr Brydydd). As court poet, he was a liegeman of King Gruffudd ap Cynan, just as his son Gwalchmai ap Meilyr served Gruffudd's son and successor Owain ap Gruffudd. Hywel ab Owain Gwynedd, a bastard son of the prince, was the first poet to compose poetry of courtly love on the French model. Cynddelw Brydydd Mawr was considered the poet of greatest significance among the Poets of the Princes. In his work he glorified not only the rulers of Powys, his homeland, but also the princes of Gwynedd and Deheubarth. Whereas the poet Llywarch ap Llywelyn (Prydydd y Moch) celebrated the rise of Gwynedd under Llywelyn ap Iorwerth, only two generations later the poet Bleddyn lamented the death of both grandsons of Llywelyn, and these deaths marked the end of the age of the Poets of the Princes. The last major exponent of their art was Gruffudd ap Maredudd ap Dafydd, whose work created a monument to his Anglesey homeland and the local Tudor family of Penmynydd in the second half of the fourteenth century.

While the Poets of the Princes wrote mainly in the traditional forms of the *awdl* and the *englyn*, their successors in the service of the lesser nobility, the so-called *Beirdd yr Uchelwyr* (Poets of the Gentry), favoured a new form, the *cywydd*, from the first half of the fourteenth century.[6] Here every poem consisted of rhyming couplets with a fixed number of syllables (usually seven), with various patterns of consonantal correspondence (*cynghanedd*). The greatest poet of this era, if not of Welsh literature as a whole, is generally considered to be Dafydd ap Gwilym (c. 1320–70), who blended elements of native and courtly Anglo-Norman literature to create a new unity of these components.[7] Well-versed in foreign poetic forms such as the aubade, the serenade and the pastourelle, Dafydd was also familiar with works such as *Le Roman de la rose*. Using a combination of French loan-words and the rich vocabulary of traditional Welsh poetry, he achieved a hitherto unrivalled expressive power in his poetry. One of his contemporaries was Iolo Goch, who was among the first to write praise-poems in the form of the *cywydd* to glorify the English king and various Welsh nobles. Among the most important 'gentry poets' of the fifteenth century were Siôn Cent, Lewys Glyn Cothi and Dafydd ab Edmwnd. One of Dafydd ab Edmwnd's nephews and pupils was Tudur Aled, on whose death in about 1525 the tradition of praise-poetry rapidly waned.[8]

The range of Middle Welsh prose literature is much narrower, but its content is remarkably varied. Educational religious writing, of which much has come down to us in *The Book of the Anchorite* (*Llyfr Ancr Llanddewibrefi*), a manuscript from the mid-fourteenth century, comprises a high proportion of it. Hagiographies, accounts of visions and exegetical treatises have been preserved, as well as translations of Biblical, apocryphal and pseudo-epigraphic works.[9] The text known as *Ymborth yr Enaid* (*The Nourishment of the Soul*) is not a translation, but was written in Welsh in about 1250 as part of a treatise on spirituality and mysticism, by an unknown Dominican friar (see the critical edition by Daniel 1995). Many other historical documents have survived, including *Ystorya Dared*, a translation of the Latin *Historia Daretis Phrygii de Excidio Troiae*; *Brut y Brenhinedd*, an adaptation, preserved in several versions, of *Historia Regum Britanniae* (History of the Kings of Britain) by Geoffrey of Monmouth; and *Brut y Tywysogion*, the translation of a lost Latin chronicle of the Welsh princes of the period from 682–1282.[10] Works of a lighter nature translated from Norman French into Welsh from the early twelfth century include stories about Charlemagne, the anonymous epic *La Geste de Boun de Hantone* and the *Bestiaire d'amour* by Richard de Fornival.[11]

Unlike in Ireland, where the rich manuscript tradition has preserved an immense wealth of indigenous stories in prose, from medieval Wales we have only eleven adaptations of traditional narratives. That many more stories of this kind were previously current can be seen from the collection known as *The Triads of the Isle of Britain* (*Trioedd Ynys Prydain*). This groups together three well-known names from each saga or story under a common heading and briefly explains the tradition associated with each heading. Many of the names that occur are either unknown anywhere else or known only from a few allusions.[12]

Since Lady Charlotte Guest (1812–95) first translated and published them in 1838–49, the eleven surviving prose narratives have been collectively known by the title of 'The Mabinogion', although this name (the plural of the word *mabinogi*, of uncertain meaning) occurs only once in the manuscript and has every appearance of being a scribal error. The tales of Pwyll, the Prince of Dyfed (*Pwyll Pendefig Dyfed*), Branwen, the daughter of Llŷr (*Branwen ferch Lŷr*), Manawydan, the son of Llŷr (*Manawydan fab Llŷr*) and Math, the son of Mathonwy (*Math fab Mathonwy*), found in the *White Book of Rhydderch* as well as the *Red Book of Hergest* in the same series, are known as 'The Four Branches of the Mabinogi' (*Pedair Cainc y Mabinogi*).[13] The *Four Branches* refer to various places, mostly in the north and south-west of Wales, in a pre-Christian past which cannot be more precisely defined, and depict the fabulous adventures of a large number of characters whose lives are often only loosely connected. They are probably the work of a single author from the twelfth century, who uses materials and motifs from fables, sagas and pre-Christian myths which had been handed down orally over a long period, and were written for the entertainment of a medieval audience of gentry.

The tale of Lludd and Llefelys (*Cyfranc Lludd a Llefelys*), in which the Brythonic King Lludd and his brother Llefelys liberate their country from three seemingly insuperable afflictions, and the tale of the dream of the Roman Emperor Macsen (*Breuddwyd Macsen Wledig*), which tells how Macsen wooed the Brythonic princess Elen, also belong to the Mabinogion. For the further development of European literature and culture, however, the remaining five tales are perhaps the most important. At their centre stands the legendary figure of Arthur, who would spread the Celtic narrative tradition far beyond the borders of the Celtic-speaking world as the epitome of courtly culture in the twelfth century.

ARTHUR: THE CELTIC CONTRIBUTION TO WORLD LITERATURE

The Arthurian tradition rests on Welsh and Breton stories from the second half of the first millennium and draws together memories of historical figures from the sixth century, the motifs of fables and names from pre-Christian mythology.[14] Arthur appears in the ninth century in *Historia Brittonum* as the victorious commander (*dux bellorum*) in twelve battles against the invading Saxons, but in the Welsh tradition these few historical outlines are largely overlaid by features from sagas and fables. The short and sometimes obscure poems *Pa ŵr yw'r Porthor?* (Who is the Gatekeeper?) and *Preiddeu Annwfn* (The Spoils of Annwfn) portray Arthur as the leader of a band of fearless warriors with all manner of fabulous powers and qualities.[15] These warriors also accompany Arthur in the story of Culhwch and Olwen (*Culhwch ac Olwen*), the oldest prose narrative of the Arthurian cycle, telling of Culhwch's courtship of Olwen, the daughter of the giant Ysbaddaden Bencawr.[16] Here Arthur appears as the cousin of Culhwch, whose step-mother has decreed that Culhwch can marry nobody but Olwen. With Arthur and his followers, Culhwch makes his way to Ysbaddaden's castle and, after performing a series of seemingly impossible feats, wins the hand of Olwen.

A completely new picture of Arthur is painted in about 1137 by Geoffrey of Monmouth (in Latin, Galfridus Monemutensis), in his *Historia Regum Britanniae*.[17] Relying on the work of Gildas, Bede's history of the English Church, *Historia Brittonum* and the oral traditions of Wales and Brittany, Geoffrey tells the story of the kings of Britain from the beginning to the Anglo-Saxon conquest. He does so in such a way as to provide a quasi-historical foundation for the Anglo-Norman kings' claim to power in the twelfth century. In Geoffrey's account, the mythical ancestor of the kings of Britain is the great-grandson of Aeneas, the Trojan Brutus – from whom the British Isles took their name – who arrives in Britain following various adventures on his travels through the countries of the

Mediterranean. The true hero of the work, however, is Arthur, depicted by Geoffrey as a powerful feudal lord and a worthy match for the Roman empire. Although some historians of the generations immediately following castigated Geoffrey for his fanciful elaboration on the tradition, his account met with broad approval. In about 1155 the Anglo-Norman poet Wace used it as the basis for his epic in verse *Roman de Brut*, which in turn was translated into English by the cleric Layamon in about 1200.

While Geoffrey and Wace introduced the figure of Arthur from the Celtic tradition into Latin and Anglo-Norman literature, it was the Old French poet Chrétien de Troyes, with his novels in verse *Erec et Enide, Lancelot ou le Chevalier à la charrette, Yvain ou le Chevalier au lion* and the unfinished *Perceval ou le Conte du Graal*, who became the true founder of courtly Arthurian literature between 1160 and 1190.[18] Unlike his predecessors, Chrétien largely stripped the legendary figures of their historical and geographical references and placed not Arthur himself, but in each case a single knight from his entourage in the foreground of a predominantly fairy-tale plot. How these knights are tested and prove their worth forms the focus of the events, for which Arthur's court merely provides a glittering backdrop. Here Chrétien was skilfully updating the traditional narrative stock with his treatment of contemporary social and philosophical ideas, and this suggests he had a broad education and precise knowledge of various strata of society. As *matière de Bretagne*, and side by side with the national historical epics and the literature of classical antiquity, the Arthurian stories would swiftly come to enjoy astonishing popularity throughout Europe. At the same time, they offered poets a perfect opportunity to project into an undefined past the ideals and aspirations of contemporary courtly society, and thereby lend them a quasi-historical grounding.

Chrétien's novels in verse *Erec et Enide, Yvain* and *Perceval* have exact counterparts in Middle Welsh literature in the three prose narratives *Owein* or *Iarlles y Ffynnawn, Peredur fab Efrawg* and *Gereint fab Erbin*.[19] In Welsh scholarship, on account of their closeness to the French novels, they are collectively known as 'The Three Romances' (*Y Tair Rhamant*), and they clearly draw on the courtly social ideal of the twelfth century in their descriptions of material and spiritual culture. Marked differences in style, structure and treatment of plot suggest that these three stories are the work of different authors, who each transferred their French models in thoroughly independent, and in some degree arbitrary, fashion. The satirical tale of the dream of Rhonabwy (*Breuddwyd Rhonabwy*) is no such free translation, being originally written in Welsh. In it the eponymous hero Rhonabwy is transported in his dream from shabby, squalid lodgings to Arthur's splendid camp.[20] Unlike the Three Romances but like *Culhwch ac Olwen*, *Breuddwyd Rhonabwy* alludes precisely to specific places in Wales and Cornwall, and here too the influence of Anglo-Norman culture is clearly reflected, especially in the language of the narrator.

In the German-speaking world the Arthurian tales took hold towards the end of the twelfth century (see Gottzmann 1989; also Mertens 1998). Between 1180 and 1205, Hartmann von Aue translated the verse novels *Erec et Enide* and *Yvain* into Middle High German. In his *Iwein* he adhered closely to the Old French model, but in *Erec* he expanded substantially on Chrétien's novel and modified the details. Chrétien's *Perceval* was translated by Wolfram von Eschenbach, who introduced the legend of the Grail into German literature in about 1200, in his epic *Parzival*, approximately 25,000 lines long. The saga of Tristan (Welsh *Drystan*), which survives only in fragments in the older Welsh tradition, was refashioned in about 1180 by Eilhart von Oberge and soon after 1200 by Gottfried von Strassburg.[21]

Since the early nineteenth century, Arthurian literature has experienced a renaissance which continues to this day.[22] The Romantic return to the Middle Ages has produced numerous retellings of stories, tone poems, paintings and films, especially in the Anglo-Saxon world but also in the German-speaking world, while the development of Germanic, Romance and Celtic studies has prompted scholarly research into medieval literary works. From this it emerges that, with regard to the Celtic sources of Arthurian writing, the English, French and German authors usually took only names and motifs from the Celtic tradition, rather than entire stories (see Frappier 1978 and Bromwich 1983). Both Welsh and Breton stories served as sources, and these became known to the French and Anglo-Norman writers through bilingual intermediaries. Since the traditional Welsh and Breton sources have been largely lost, however, often only the names of the characters survive, whereas many of the typical motifs appear only in Irish literature, which is better preserved. The significant Breton contribution to the rise of Arthurian literature provides good reason for us to turn here to the history and culture of a region which was settled from Britain in the early Middle Ages.

CHAPTER 16

Brittany from Prehistory to the Union with France

THE LAND ON THE SEABOARD: FROM THE EARLY SETTLERS TO 'BRITANNIA MINOR'

The earliest evidence of human habitation in Brittany reaches back to Palaeolithic times.[1] After the early hunters and gatherers, in the fifth millennium BC came the first tillers of the soil and domesticators of animals, who left behind the many standing stones (menhirs) and burial chambers (dolmens) still in evidence today. In the second half of the third millennium BC the use of bronze implements began, and tin mining enabled the inhabitants of Brittany to benefit from a significant economic and cultural upturn. With the advent of the Central European Iron Age in about 700 BC, the old trading and cultural links along the Atlantic seaboard declined in importance, to the point where the Iron Age culture of Brittany seems backward compared to the flourishing communities of central and eastern Gaul. Only in the last centuries BC can a steep rise be seen in trading relations both with Britain and central and southern Gaul. Archaeological deposits also point to a marked increase in the population and the formation of small tribal kingdoms. An impressive specimen of the religious art of this period is the stone figurine of a deity, about forty centimetres tall, with lyre and torc. Found in the fortified settlement of Paule in 1988, it dates from about 100 BC.[2]

In 57 and 56 BC Julius Caesar conquered 'the land of the sea' (*Aremorica*), as Brittany would henceforth be called by the Romans, using its Gaulish name.[3] Following Augustus's reorganisation of the territory captured by Caesar, Brittany became part of the province of Gallia Lugdunensis. In the regions of the five tribes (*civitates*) known

by the Latinised names Redones, Namnetes, Veneti, Coriosolites and
Osismi, important urban centres grew up at Condate (later Civitas
Redonum, now Rennes), Portus Namnetum (now Nantes),
Darioritum (now Vannes), Civitas Coriosolitum (now Corseul)
and Vorgium (now Carhaix). Intensive coastal navigation and a
well-developed road network now linked Brittany with the whole
of the Roman Empire. The blend of the indigenous and Roman
religious attitudes, typical of Gaul as a whole, shows clearly in the
head of a bronze statuette of the goddess Minerva, found at Kerguilly
(Finistère) in 1913 (see Maier 1997, 195–6).

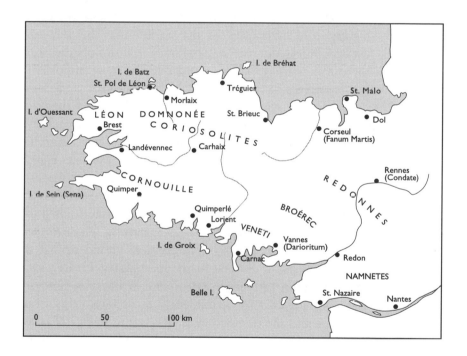

Map 6: Brittany in the classical period and the Middle Ages

The progress of Romanisation suffered a setback in the second half
of the third century AD with pirate raids and incursions by Germanic
hordes. The resulting unrest, pillage and destruction led to the
rebuilding of Rennes, Nantes and Vannes on a reduced ground-
plan with town walls as fortification. Corseul was abandoned in
favour of Aletum (now Saint-Malo), while Brest and Quimper

assumed the functions of Carhaix. Of lasting consequence for the subsequent history of the region and its culture was the immigration of British Celts, probably initiated by the Romans in the late third and fourth centuries AD to defend depopulated areas. Under pressure from the Irish and Anglo-Saxons at home, they settled in Aremorica in numbers in the fifth and sixth centuries. From the sixth century the areas of the Osismi, Coriosolites and Veneti came to be known as *Britannia*, after their old homeland, or, to distinguish them from the island of Britain, *Britannia minor*.[4]

Four Breton principalities are known from the sixth century: Léon in the north-west, Domnonée on the north coast, Cornouaille in the south-west and Vannetais, also known as Broérec, in the south-east. The early history of Christianity in the region may be seen in numerous hagiographies, but the hagiographical tradition did not begin until the ninth century. They record that the most important founders of monasteries, Samson (Dol), Paulus Aurelianus (Saint-Pol-de-Léon), Briocus (Saint-Brieuc) and Winwaloë/Guénolé (Landévennec), arrived from Christian Britain in the sixth century to support their expatriate kinsmen in establishing the Church. Typical components of toponyms such as *Plou-* (Welsh *plwyf* 'parish', from Latin *plebem*), *Tre-* 'hamlet' (Welsh *tre* 'village') and *Lan-* (Welsh *llan* 'monastery') testify to the wide area over which these early churches were founded.[5] In the west and north of Brittany the Church was of a largely monastic nature, while in the east the Gallo-Roman Church of the late classical period persisted within the archbishopric of Tours, with episcopates in Rennes, Vannes and Nantes. As in Ireland, Scotland and Wales, the Church in Brittany was distinguished by certain features of the liturgy, the ordaining of bishops and the calculation of the date of Easter. These differences began to disappear gradually from the late seventh century.

THE BRETONS AND THE FRENCH: ASPECTS OF POLITICAL HISTORY

In the east of Brittany the Frankish Merovingians ruled. Their supremacy may have been formally acknowledged by the Breton princes, but was widely ignored in border disputes and more particularly in their internal affairs. Gregory of Tours reports that in the second half of the sixth century the Breton ruler Waroc captured the town of Vannes and laid waste the environs of Rennes and Nantes. For the following century and a half, however, relations between Franks and Bretons are mostly obscure, owing to the absence of documentary sources. It is only at the beginning of the Carolingian period that detailed information again becomes available.[6]

It is possible that Vannes and the surrounding regions were seized by Pepin III 'the Short'. For the year 778 the chronicler Einhard (in the ninth chapter of his *Vita Caroli Magni*) first mentions 'the Breton March', as the region of the three Frankish earldoms of Nantes, Rennes and Vannes was henceforth known. The reason it is mentioned is the death of the 'Prefect' (Praefectus) of the March, Hruodlandus, the same Roland who would later become the central figure of the Old French and Middle High German 'Song of Roland'. For subsequent decades the annals repeatedly report the campaigns of Charlemagne and his son Louis the Pious, who, however, enjoyed no lasting success. Finally Louis appointed the Breton noble Nominoë Duke and *missus imperatoris* for the whole of Brittany. As long as Louis was alive, Nominoë remained loyal to the Frankish Empire, but in 840 he came into conflict with Louis's son and successor Charles the Bald. In 845 Charles submitted to Nominoë and in 851 to Nominoë's son Erispoë. The latter ruled over the whole of Brittany, including the earldoms of Rennes and Nantes and the area surrounding Retz, to the south of the Loire estuary. While rendering homage to the West Frankish king, Erispoë was recognised as king by Charles. When Erispoë was murdered by his cousin Salomon in 857, Charles the Bald was obliged to accept the change of power and granted to the new ruler the fief on new lands between the rivers Mayenne and Sarthe. In 874 Salomon was murdered following a conspiracy of Breton and Frankish nobles, and his lands divided between the rulers Gurvant and Pascweten. After their death, Pascweten's brother and successor Alan I managed once more to restore the kingdom in 888 but on his death in 907 the activities of the Danish Vikings plunged the country into a deep crisis.

By 843 the Normans had attacked the town of Nantes and established themselves firmly in southern Brittany at the mouth of the Loire. In 847 they defeated Nominoë and attacked Angers in

872. In 911 Charles III gave their leader Rollo (Hrolf) charge of Normandy, after his conversion to Christianity, and the pressure on Brittany was increased in subsequent decades to the extent that many monks and nobles fled to the interior of France or across the sea to Britain. The fugitives at the court of the English king Athelstan included the stepson of Alan I. His son Alan II (Alain Barbe-Torte) succeeded, with the help of the English fleet, in recapturing Nantes in 937, while Athelstan could claim to have achieved the unification of England by his victory over an alliance of Danes, Scots and Welshmen.

By the time Alan II returned, the Breton rulers had long lost their once close connection with their land of origin, thanks to the Anglo-Saxon conquests, and had aligned themselves increasingly towards the empire of the Franks. By the first half of the ninth century, on the initiative of Louis the Pious, the Benedictine code was introduced in several Breton monasteries, including that of Redon, founded in 832. At the same time the whole of Brittany outside the old Gallo-Roman bishoprics of Rennes, Vannes and Nantes was divided into dioceses, while at the political level the institution of the earldom was introduced. As feudal lords of several earldoms, the Breton rulers adopted the title of duke (*dux*) from the time of Alan II, while the dignity of kingship declined in importance.

The following centuries were marked by rivalries within Brittany among the princely houses of Nantes, Rennes and Cornouaille, and by conflicts with powerful neighbours like the dukes of Normandy and the counts of Blois and Anjou. With the shift of the political centre of gravity to the French-speaking east of Brittany, the adoption of feudal structures of the French type, and the influence of the great monasteries on the Loire, old Breton traditions lost their importance.[7] In the second half of the twelfth century, Brittany came under the rule of Henry II of England. However, after a crisis over the succession at the beginning of the thirteenth century, Pierre de Dreux (known as Mauclerc), a French prince of the Capetian line, attained the dukedom in 1213. Under the ruling house he established, which reigned until 1341, the state structure, the economy and the judiciary were modernised, power was centralised, and links with France were further developed.

Brittany suffered severe ravages during the first decades of the Hundred Years' War, until the house of Montfort managed to decide the struggle for the dukedom in its favour. After this, Brittany experienced a period of political advancement and economic prosperity, while England and France exhausted themselves in military conflict until the mid-fifteenth century. With the resurgence of France under Charles VII, however, the dukes of Brittany found themselves increasingly tied to the King of France, in whose service Breton troops played a vital role in the decisive battles against the English in 1450–3. After Louis XI had come to power in 1461, tensions increased between the French king and Duke Francis II of Brittany, who lost his most powerful ally, Charles the Bold of Burgundy, in 1477. Following the crushing defeat of the Bretons in the battle of Saint-Aubin-du-Cormier and the death of the duke in 1488, Francis's daughter Anne attempted to secure the succession through an alliance with Austria. Her union with Maximilian of Habsburg, achieved in 1490, was dissolved under French pressure the following year. In December 1491 Anne married Charles VIII of France and, after his death in 1499, his successor Louis XII. Their daughter Claude married Francis of Angoulême, the heir to the French throne. This joining of the Breton and French states and dynasties came to completion in 1532, when Francis I proclaimed the 'union in perpetuity' (*union perpétuelle*) of Brittany and France.

NAMES, GLOSSES AND POEMS: THE EARLY EVIDENCE OF BRETON

When Brythonic Celts migrated to Brittany in the late classical period, they brought with them their insular Celtic tongue, from which the Breton language, closely related to Cornish and Welsh, would later evolve.[8] Whether Gaulish was already completely extinct by this time is not known, and there have been attempts to explain dialect differences within Breton by the influence of Gaulish in some regions. Even at the time of its widest reach, however, the Breton language never extended as far east as Nantes or Rennes, so that in a political sense Brittany always included areas where only French was spoken.

From the Old Breton period (between the sixth and eleventh centuries) almost all that has come down to us is explanatory glosses to Latin texts and names of people and places. Important sources are collections of registry documents (compilations, or cartularies), such as those preserved for the monasteries of Redon and Landévennec. No continuous texts have reached us from that period. This is due partly to the dominance of Latin as a written language, and partly to the cultural and economic decline that followed the Norman invasions, and the fact that the nobility were turning more and more towards French culture.

The existence of an extensive oral tradition is demonstrated above all by the adaptations of Celtic saga themes in Old French literature, including in particular the fairy-tale-like Arthurian narratives, which even in 1200 were distinct in *matière de Bretagne* from the pseudo-classical *matière de Rome* and the pseudo-historical *matière de France*. There is a Celtic backdrop to the novels in verse, known as *Lays*, of the poet Marie de France (c. 1130–1200), a native of France who lived at the court of Henry II of England and whose work often alludes to Breton models (see Rieger 1980, 130–1 and 314–15). The very term for this genre *lays* (*lais*) is Breton, having originally been the designation for songs of the Breton harpists (cf. Irish *laíd* 'poem, song'), which are structured in stanzas.

From the period around 1350 come a few lines of love poetry left by a Breton scribe in the margin of a Latin manuscript:

> *An guen heguen am louenas*
> *An hegarat an lacat glas.*

The blonde girl with the friendly face makes me glad,
the beauty with the blue eyes.[9]

Whether the scribe was trying his skill as a poet or quoting a widely known folk-song is not known, as no comparable Breton texts from the Middle Ages have survived. All that has reached us is a dialogue in verse between King Arthur and Guinglaff the Sage (*An dialogue etre Arzur, roe d'an Bretounet ha Guynclaff*) and religious dramas which include one about the destruction of Jerusalem, the passion and resurrection of Christ and the life of the Breton saint Nonne. The first Breton-French dictionary, the *Catholicon* by the cleric Jehan Lagadeuc, was produced in about 1464. It was printed at Tréguier in 1499 and contains approximately 5,500 entries.[10]

Mention should also be made of the Celtic language of Cornwall, which is more closely related to Breton than to Welsh.[11] The toponymic evidence (*pen-* 'head, end, point', *Porth-* 'harbour', *Tre-* 'hamlet') indicates that as early as the twelfth century its range had been largely restricted to the western part of the peninsula, and that it retreated further in later times. While Old Cornish (tenth–twelfth centuries) is known mostly from several hundred entries in a Latin-Cornish glossary, from the Middle Cornish period (thirteenth–sixteenth centuries) we have some extended religious poems and plays in verse, including the dramatic trilogy *Ordinalia*, over 8,000 lines long, on the themes of creation, the history of Israel and the passion of Christ. Another late medieval work is *Beunans Meriasek*, a play about the Breton saint Meriasek. When the Welsh scholar Edward Lhuyd visited Cornwall in about 1700, the entire population was already bilingual, and in the second half of the eighteenth century English had completely replaced Cornish. However, by the late seventeenth century the language had caught the interest of antiquaries, and after the decline of the Cornish tin and copper mines in the late nineteenth century this interest grew as enthusiasm for English diminished. In an effort to revive the Celtic tongue, Henry Jenner published a manual of Cornish in 1904, and in 1928 a poetry contest, or *gorsedd*, on the Welsh model was introduced. In 1967 a Cornish Language Board was established, and in 1987 this advocated the promotion of 'Common Cornish' (*Kernewek Kemmyn*), based on the extensive literary texts of the Middle Ages. What the place of Cornish will be in the decentralised Britain of the present and near future remains to be seen (P. Payton in Price 2000, 109–19).

PART III

From the Reformation to the Present

CHAPTER 17

Ireland from Colonisation to Emancipation

NATIVES AND SETTLERS: IRELAND IN THE EARLY MODERN PERIOD

The modern history of the Celts begins with the gradual incorporation of the Celtic-speaking regions of western Europe into the orbit of the expanding English and French monarchies. The loss of political independence was accompanied by the disappearance of independent legal and social systems, and consequently the history of the Celts since the sixteenth century is above all a history of the Celtic languages and literatures, and of the rediscovery of their medieval predecessors and the Celtic culture of antiquity.

In spite of all chronological parallels and general tendencies, the transition from the Middle Ages to the modern era was by no means uniform in the Celtic-speaking regions, and was influenced by differing social, economic and geopolitical conditions. In the sixteenth century Wales was annexed by England and claimed for the Reformation without armed conflict, while in Ireland the Counter-Reformation held sway and the English crown placed more and more reliance on the forced settlement of loyal English and Scottish settlers to secure its military conquests.[1] The first of these 'plantations' took place in the reign of Mary Tudor (1553–8) in the area of Leix and Offaly and extended the English sphere of influence from its traditional centre around Dublin into the heart of the country. Mary's successor Elizabeth I presided over further plantations in Munster after an uprising, in which Spanish and Italian mercenaries participated, against English rule in 1579–83 had severely affected the entire province. As in its overseas possessions, the crown granted the land confiscated from the rebels to speculators who would place English settlers on it.

Three years after the defeat of the Spanish armada in 1588 Elizabeth I founded Trinity College, Dublin, the first university in Ireland, to advance the cause of the Reformation in Ireland. The last bastion of traditional Irish society was now Ulster, where Hugh O'Neill, the Earl of Tyrone, had been steadily developing a position of power since 1585.[2] In 1595, with his ally Red Hugh O'Donnell, he rose against the crown, but after initial successes and the dispatch of a Spanish expeditionary force, he suffered a devastating defeat at the Battle of Kinsale in 1601 (Silke 2000). After Red Hugh O'Donnell had left for Spain in 1602 and died there, Hugh O'Neill submitted to Elizabeth's successor James I in 1603 and left his country permanently in 1607, together with Hugh O'Donnell's successor Rory and other Irish nobles. With this 'Flight of the Earls', not only the power base of the indigenous Irish rulers, but also the Irish judicial and social order, handed down from the Middle Ages, came to an end.

The fact that Hugh O'Neill and his companions had kept their departure secret provided the crown with a welcome opportunity to present the Flight of the Earls as treason and to seize their large estates. These were transferred partly into the hands of collaborators of the crown, and partly to English and Scottish entrepreneurs to promote further plantations, with the result that the proportion of English and Scottish Protestants in Northern Ireland rose sharply. The social tensions thus created were discharged in 1641 in a rebellion, in which the old-established population of the north of the island killed thousands of colonists and seized some of the most important towns and garrisons.[3] A little later, when civil war broke out in England between King Charles I and his parliament, Irish and 'Old English' fought side by side in the Kilkenny Confederation, on the basis of their shared Catholic faith, against the Puritan-dominated parliament. They were overwhelmed in 1649–50 by the violent advance of Oliver Cromwell's troops, and the final suppression of the Irish rising in 1652 was followed by further extensive expropriations, leaving the greater part of the country in Protestant hands.[4]

With the Restoration of the monarchy in 1660, Charles II came to the throne, but Catholic Irish hopes for change in land-ownership conditions came to nothing. When Charles's successor James II set about re-establishing Catholicism in England, Parliament invited his son-in-law William of Orange to England from the Netherlands in 1688, whereupon James fled to France. His attempt to win back the throne from Ireland failed when he and his army of Catholic Irish and French supporters were decisively defeated by the forces of William III on 12 July 1690 in the Battle of the Boyne (Doherty 1998 and Simms, J. G. 2000). As a result of the Treaty of Limerick, concluded in 1695, the political, economic and judicial discrimination against Irish Catholics was intensified by a range of penal laws. Thus the eighteenth century fully favoured the Protestant ascendancy and, while bringing a certain political stability, this period was also marked by general economic stagnation and widespread poverty.[5]

Although the penal laws were relaxed in 1778, radical political tendencies gained new impetus in the wake of the French Revolution of 1789, when the republican-inclined United Irishmen, in collaboration with the clandestine Catholic 'Defenders' and the French government, began to work towards the complete separation of Ireland from England. Determined counter-measures by the British government led once more to armed insurrection in 1798. This time, however, despite the landing of a French expeditionary army, the rising was put down by government troops within a matter of months.[6] In order to bind Ireland more firmly to Britain, the British prime minister William Pitt achieved the union of the Irish and British parliaments by the Act of Union in 1800. However, full civic equality for the Irish Catholics, for which Pitt had pressed, foundered largely on the opposition of King George III. The political leadership of the Irish Catholics was now taken up by the solicitor Daniel O'Connell (1775–1849), who initiated a mass movement in 1823 when he founded the Catholic Association, and eventually achieved the admission of Catholics to Parliament and public office with the passage of the Catholic Emancipation Act in 1829. With the political mobilisation of the Catholic majority, Protestant dominance gradually declined through the nineteenth century, while the Irish national consciousness became more closely identified with Catholicism of an increasingly Roman variety.[7]

POETS AND SCHOLARS: IRISH LITERATURE IN THE SEVENTEENTH AND EIGHTEENTH CENTURIES

With the political decline of the native Irish rulers at the time of the Elizabethan conquests, the social role of the traditional learned families diminished, as did the literature they supported. At the same time English-speaking writers like Richard Stanihurst (1547–1618), Edmund Spenser (1552–99) and John Davies (1569–1626) emphasised the moral and cultural superiority of Protestant England over Catholic Ireland.[8] Whereas the bardic poets of the period between the twelfth and sixteenth centuries had celebrated the Irish and 'Old English' aristocracy as guarantors of the legitimate political order, their successors in the seventeenth and eighteenth centuries, after the decline of the established aristocracy, sought refuge in hopes for the future and political wishful thinking. Their preoccupation with history would no longer serve to sanction existing conditions, as before, but rather it would provide an effective counterweight to the new English colonists' negative image of Ireland, and give a grounding in the past for the political and social change that they longed to see in the future.[9]

One of the last bardic poets of the late sixteenth century was Tadhg Dall Ó hUiginn (1550–91), who in one of his poems called upon his noble patron Brian Ó Ruairc to struggle relentlessly against the English.[10] The political upheavals that followed are mirrored in the work of the poet Dáibhí Ó Bruadair (c. 1625–98), which includes in equal measure satirical verse aimed at the new settlers, praise-poems for the Catholic nobility, political propaganda for James II and bitter complaints at the material penury of the poet in a changed world.[11] Similar themes are found in the work of the poet Pádraig Haicéad (died 1654), who left behind lyric poetry in the tradition of courtly love poetry (*dánta grádha*), as well as political propaganda for the Kilkenny Confederates.[12] The poetic genre of the *aisling* (vision) is characteristic of Irish political poetry after the final victory of William III. The typical aisling of this period depicts an encounter between the poet and a woman of celestial beauty who in conversation reveals herself to him as Erin (Ireland), bitterly laments the absence of her lawful wedded husband, the banished king of the house of Stuart, and finally foretells the return of the rightful ruler. Among the most important practitioners of this form of political poetry are Aodhagán Ó Rathaille (c. 1670–1729), Seán Clárach Mac Domhnaill (1691–1754) and Eoghan Rua Ó Súilleabháin (1748–84), on whose death the traditional form of the aisling fell into decline in the changed political situation.[13] The establishment of seats of spiritual learning on the European continent was of great significance for Irish literature after the defeat of James II and the introduction of the penal laws. The Franciscan College of Saint Anthony of Padua in Louvain was of particular importance.[14] Founded by Philip III of Spain in 1606, it owed its existence to the initiative of the Franciscan theologian Flaithrí Ó Maoilchonaire (Florence Conry, c. 1560–1620), who in 1601 had accompanied the Spanish expeditionary army to Ireland and would in 1609 be ordained in Rome by Pope Paul V as Archbishop of Tuam. Highly respected as an authority on the writings of Saint Augustine, in 1616 he published the devotional text *Desiderius* or *Scáthán an Chrábhaidh* (The Mirror of Piety), a translation of a Catalan work entitled *El Desseoso*.[15] Two other Irish scholars who made their way to Louvain in 1607 were Giolla Bríghde Ó hEódhasa (Bonaventura O'Hussey, c. 1575–1614), who published the catechistic work *An Teagasg Críosdaidhe* (The Christian Doctrine) in Antwerp in 1611; and Aodh Mac Aingil (Hugh Mac Cathmhaoil or Mac Caghwell, 1571–1626). The latter had travelled to Salamanca with Hugh O'Neill's son Henry in 1600 and, after completing his theological studies, had been admitted to the Franciscan Order there in 1603. In addition to *Scáthán Shacramuinte na hAithridhe* (Mirror of the Sacrament of Penance), published in Louvain in 1618, he wrote a Latin work about the philosophy of Johannes Duns Scotus. In 1623 he went to Rome, where he was appointed Archbishop of Armagh shortly before his death.

The theologian Hugh Ward (Aodh Mac an Bhaird, 1593–1635) was active in Louvain from 1616, and on his initiative Mícheál Ó Cléirigh (c. 1590–1643) and other Irish scholars set about compiling a systematic collection of Irish and Latin texts bearing on the history of the Church. On the basis of this collection, the Franciscan John Colgan (c. 1592–1658) published *Acta Sanctorum Veteris et Maioris Scottiae seu Hiberniae* in 1645, about all those Irish saints whose day fell in the first quarter of the calendar year. Brigit (1 February), Patrick (17 March) and Columba (9 June) were omitted since Colgan devoted a special volume to them, entitled *Trias Thaumaturga*, in 1647. Since both works make full use of manuscripts which have since been lost, they are treated today as primary sources. The same applies to the collection of Irish annals known as *The Annals of the Four Masters* or *Annals of the Kingdom of Ireland* (Annála Ríoghachta Éireann), which Mícheál Ó Cléirigh compiled between 1632 and 1636 with the aid of indigenous scholars in the northern Irish Franciscan priory of Bundrowse. Its sources included a historically valuable biography of Red Hugh O'Donnell (died 1602), written by Mícheál Ó Cléirigh's cousin Lughaidh Ó Cléirigh in about 1616.[16] Another Irish historian who, from exile, attempted to defend traditional Irish culture against the assaults of Anglo-Irish authors was Philip O'Sullivan Beare (c. 1590–1634), whose outline of the history of Catholic Ireland (*Historiae Catholicae Iberniae Compendium*) appeared in Lisbon in 1621. Mention should also be made of the philosopher John Toland (1670–1722), who wrote *A Critical History of the Celtic Religion and Learning* (written 1718–19, published 1726), in addition to his main works *Christianity not Mysterious* (1696) and *Pantheisticon* (1720).[17]

THE GAELIC HERITAGE: FROM ANTIQUARIANISM TO CELTIC STUDIES

Among the Catholic scholars who sought to preserve the Gaelic heritage in their Irish homeland under the more difficult conditions of the new age, Dubhaltach Mac Fhir Bhisigh (c. 1600–71) stands out. Later generations have him to thank for the transcription and translation of historically important texts, especially genealogies.[18] One of his pupils was the cleric John Lynch (c. 1599–1673), who first taught classics in Galway, then in 1652, when Galway surrendered to the Parliamentary forces, moved to France. There ten years later he published *Cambrensis Eversus* in Latin, to counter the negative picture of Ireland given by Giraldus Cambrensis. Lynch's Irish pupils included Roderick O'Flaherty (1629–1718), who had also been introduced to the tradition of bardic poetry by Dubhaltach Mac Fhir Bhisigh and whose chronology of Irish history, *Ogygia, seu Rerum Hibernicarum Chronologia*, written in Latin, was printed in London in 1685 with the assistance of a prominent patron. The best known and most influential account of the history of Ireland up to the death of the last High King Rory O'Connor in 1198 is *Foras Feasa ar Éirinn* (The History of Ireland) by the Catholic cleric Geoffrey Keating (Seathrún Céitinn, c. 1580–1650).[19] Himself a descendant of the Anglo-Norman conquerors (the name Céitinn is derived from Mac Étienne, that is, FitzStephen), Keating saw his work less as one of compiling the legacy of a culture in decline and more as the basis for an accommodation and understanding between the 'old Gaels' (*Sean-Ghaedhil*) and the Anglo-Irish 'old foreigners' (*Sean-Ghaill*), in the face of the threat presented by the 'new foreigners' (*Nua-Ghaill*), the new English colonists.

That some members of the Protestant elite also took an interest in the history of Gaelic Ireland is shown by the example of Sir James Ware (1594–1666), a government official who had transcriptions of Irish texts made by Dubhaltach Mac Fhir Bhisigh and wrote a *Historie of Ireland*, published in 1633. This criticised the thoroughly unfavourable view of Ireland set forth in Edmund Spenser's *View of the Present State of Ireland*, which had been written in 1596 but was first published only in Ware's book. It was not until the last third of the eighteenth century that the Protestant elite of the country developed a positive interest in the history and culture of Gaelic Ireland, thanks to the Europe-wide interest in the supposedly Celtic poetry of Ossian (to which we shall return in connection with the history of Scotland), the heightened self-assurance of the Irish Protestants, and the relaxation of the anti-Catholic penal laws (McLoughlin 1999). Here a decisive role was played by the classicist Charles Vallancey (1721–1812), the founder of the periodical *Collectanea de Rebus Hibernicis* (1770–1804), the Catholic scholar Charles O'Conor (1710–91), the author of *An Account of the Ancient Government, Letters, Science, Religion, Manners and Customs of Ireland* (1753, 2nd edn 1766), and the translator Charlotte Brooke (c. 1740–93), the publisher of the influential anthology *Reliques of Irish Poetry* (1789). One of the first collections of traditional Irish melodies was published by the organist Edward Bunting (1773–1843) under the title *General Collection of the Ancient Music of Ireland* (1792).

The newly awakened interest in Ireland's Celtic past found eloquent expression in the founding of the Royal Irish Academy (1785), which in the nineteenth century would become a focus for philological, archaeological and historical research in Ireland (see Ó Raifeartaigh 1985). Among the outstanding scholars of the period who were linked with the Academy were the archaeologist George Petrie (1789–1866), the poet and critic Samuel Ferguson (1810–86) and the philologist James Henthorn Todd (1805–69). Pioneering studies in palaeography, philology and history were produced by John O'Donovan (1809–61), who between 1848 and 1851 compiled a bilingual edition of *The Annals of the Kingdom of Ireland*, and Eugene O'Curry (1796–1862), who in 1855 was appointed to the chair of Irish history at the newly established Catholic University of Dublin.

The rise of comparative Indo-European linguistics in the first half of the nineteenth century was of major significance for the subsequent history of this literary and historical research. After its founder Franz Bopp (1791–1867) had demonstrated in 1838 that the Celtic languages belonged to the Indo-European family of languages, Johann Kaspar Zeuss (1806–56) laid the foundations of modern Celtic studies with his *Grammatica Celtica*, published in 1853.[20] One of the first specialists in this field was the lawyer Whitley Stokes (1830–1909) who, working with John Strachan (1862–1907), published a two-volume edition of the earliest Irish linguistic documents *Thesaurus Palaeohibernicus* in 1901–3 and, with Ernst Windisch (1844–1918), produced a five-volume series of Irish texts (1880–1905). A vital role in developing Celtic studies in Ireland was also played by Windisch's pupil Kuno Meyer (1858–1919). In 1896 Meyer and Ludwig Christian Stern (1846–1911) founded the *Zeitschrift für celtische Philologie*, and between 1900 and 1907 he collaborated with Whitley Stokes on the publication of the *Archiv für Celtische Lexikographie*. It was Meyer's initiative that the School of Irish Learning opened in Dublin in 1903, the forerunner of the Dublin Institute for Advanced Studies established in 1940.[21]

CHAPTER 18

Ireland from Emancipation to 1945

FROM THE UNION TO INDEPENDENCE: ASPECTS OF POLITICAL HISTORY

The political and economic problems that led to armed insurrection by the United Irishmen in 1798 were not resolved by the Union of Great Britain and Ireland, which came into effect on 1 January 1801. Large sections of the Irish population continued to believe that their country was run solely in the interests of the Protestant minority, while in England, as before, the neighbouring island was seen as a kind of colony. Tension was further heightened by the steady growth in population, which led to agricultural land being divided into smaller and smaller and finally non-viable rented holdings. Meanwhile the landowners mostly preferred to dispose of their profits outside Ireland, thereby draining the island of much-needed capital. State counter-measures, such as creating employment by developing a national rail network, were mooted on more than one occasion, but always rejected on the basis of the laissez-faire policy of the dominant economic liberalism. Viable industries developed almost exclusively in the north-east of the island, while the population of the remainder depended almost entirely on agriculture, especially potato-growing. In 1840, dissatisfaction with the Union led to the formation of the Repeal Association, with members drawn principally from the Catholic camp. In contrast, the Presbyterians of the industrial centres in the north-east feared the economic consequences of any termination of the Union with England and now aligned themselves with the political position of the Protestant landowners. The adherents of the Young Ireland movement, which had grown out of the weekly *Nation*, established in 1842 by Charles Gavan Duffy (1816–1903) and Thomas Davis (1814–45), represented a highly romantic nationalism, without religious affiliation, which pressed for the dissolution of the Union. Initially, the Young Irelanders made common cause with Daniel O'Connell, who in 1829 had achieved the admission of Catholics to Parliament, but they parted company with him in 1845–6 because of his demands for complete non-violence and his untrammelled linking of nationalism and Catholicism (Sloan 2000).

As the supporters and opponents of O'Connell tussled on the political stage, Ireland was afflicted by a catastrophic famine, dwarfing in scale all previous famines, owing to the failure over several years of a great part of the potato harvest.[1] It is estimated that up to one million people starved or died of disease, and about the same number emigrated to America. When the country began to recover from economic and political exhaustion, bitterness over the inadequate measures adopted by the British government to alleviate the famine contributed largely to growing demands for home rule, in the form of a national parliament subordinate, however, to Britain. The revolutionary ideology of Young Ireland now found a successor in the Irish Republican Brotherhood, founded in 1858, and its American arm, the Fenian Brotherhood. In the years that followed, the moderate lawyer Isaac Butt (1813–79) sought to bring together conservatives and liberals, Catholics and Protestants in a new movement, through his Home Government Association (later renamed the Home Rule League), founded in 1870.[2] His successor, Charles Stewart Parnell (1846–91), with his policy of the New Departure, sought an alliance with both the Republican Brotherhood and the Land League, which had been founded in 1879 to press for improved conditions for tenant farmers. In 1886 the first Home Rule Bill foundered on Liberal disunity and the opposition of the Conservatives. The latter called especially on the northern Irish Protestants, who were economically dependent on England, to resist any moves of this nature. The resulting conflict culminated in 1912 when the House of Commons passed the Home Rule Bill. The Ulster Protestants responded by raising the armed units of the Ulster Volunteer Force, and the southern Irish nationalists countered with their Irish Volunteers.

The outbreak of World War I in August 1914 blocked the

implementation of the Home Rule Bill. The radical wing of the Irish nationalists subsequently proclaimed the Irish Republic on Easter Monday 1916 and took up arms against the British, but the rising was put down by British troops within a few days. Although the leaders' recourse to violence had accorded with the wishes of only a small minority, the execution of most of them caused a significant shift in public opinion, and the proponents of a complete separation of Ireland from England now had wide support. The main beneficiary of the changed political situation was the Sinn Féin ('Ourselves Alone') party, founded in 1907. Under the leadership of Eamon de Valera (1882–1975), the party won a landslide election victory in January 1919 and convened an Irish parliament, the Dáil Éireann. After a two-year guerilla war it achieved the establishment of the Irish Free State (*Saorstát Éireann*) with the status of a dominion within the British Empire, in January 1922 following the conclusion of the Anglo-Irish treaty. However, partition excluded six counties in the north, and the government of these remains an unresolved problem to this day.[3] As soon as the Irish constitution came into force and British troops were withdrawn, open civil war broke out between the adherents and opponents of the island's partition, which the adherents of the treaty finally concluded in their favour in May 1923. In late summer of the same year Ireland joined the League of Nations, and, with the passage of the Statute of Westminster in December 1931, Ireland achieved a large measure of autonomy, like the other dominions of the British Empire. In 1932 Eamon de Valera, an avowed enemy of the Anglo-Irish treaty, was elected President of the Executive Council of the Dáil. Under his rule, links with Great Britain were further cut back, to the point where Éire, as the Irish state was renamed in 1937, was able to assert its neutrality successfully in World War II.

LANGUAGE AND IDENTITY: THE ROLE OF IRISH IN SOCIETY

Although the Kilkenny Statutes of 1366 had sought to restrict the area of Irish language use in favour of English, Irish remained the language of the old aristocracy and the sole means of communication of a large part of the population until the end of the sixteenth century. This changed in the course of the seventeenth century when extensive expropriations, a steady influx of English-speaking settlers, and repressive penal laws undermined the dominant position of Irish. English took over as the language of the Protestant landlords, of government and local administration, of commerce and the law and, with the political and economic decline of the old Catholic elite, Irish lost its social prestige and was able to maintain its position only in the lower strata of society. The status of English as the language of government and law meant a knowledge of it was an absolute necessity for the impoverished rural population, for the preservation and protection of their already eroded rights. At the same time, the use of written and spoken English provided the Catholic middle and upper classes with a welcome opportunity to demonstrate their loyalty to the regime and thus to work for a relaxation of the penal laws. The use of English as the language of education hastened the decline of Irish, particularly after the establishment of state primary schooling in 1831. In addition, the Great Famine of 1845–8 led to a sharp reduction in the number of speakers in the second half of the nineteenth century because the effects of the famine – in terms of death and emigration – were felt most deeply among the Irish-speaking rural population.

The first measures to counter this decline were taken in 1876 with the founding of the Society for the Preservation of the Irish Language. From this sprang the Gaelic Union (*Aondacht na Gaeilge*) in 1880, with its influential bilingual cultural journal *Irisleabhar na Gaedhilge* (*The Gaelic Journal*). The Gaelic League (*Connradh na Gaeilge*), founded in 1893 by Douglas Hyde (1860–1949), Eoin MacNeill (1867–1945) and others, promoted the Irish language as an integral component of the national heritage, setting aside political and sectarian differences, and was of fundamental importance in cultural politics.[4] It found its most responsive audience among the English-speaking urban middle class, while its influence on the Irish-speaking rural population was limited. Among its most important activities were organising language courses, cultural festivals and campaigns to bolster the position of Irish in the education system, but they also included the publication of Irish books and the bilingual cultural magazine *An Claidheamh Soluis* (The Sword of Light). After the founding of the Ulster Volunteer Force and the Irish Volunteers, the Gaelic League became more and more involved in politics, and in 1915 its president Douglas Hyde announced his resignation. Many members joined Sinn Féin after the failure of the 1916 Easter Rising and, when the Free State was established in 1922, assumed posts in the government, whose programme allocated a prominent place to the maintenance and promotion of the Irish language. To this end the state publishing house An Gúm ('The Plan') was set up in 1925, to issue state-sponsored textbooks, original works in Irish and Irish translations of foreign literature. In spite of all the measures introduced since then, including improvements in education, economic support for backward rural regions and the inauguration of Irish-language radio and television broadcasting, the *Gaeltacht*, as the Irish-speaking regions are collectively known, has continued to shrink, to the point that the survival of the Irish language is far from assured even today (see Ó Huallacháin 1994 and Ó Riagáin 1997).

PATHS TO MODERNITY: IRISH LITERATURE IN THE NINETEENTH AND TWENTIETH CENTURIES

Given the political ascendancy of English-speaking Protestants in the eighteenth century, that period was a time of cultural impoverishment in the history of Irish writing, in which opportunities to print or disseminate hand-written contemporary Irish literature were severely limited. With the development of a Romantic sensibility at the end of the eighteenth and beginning of the nineteenth century, when broad sections of the public began to take a renewed interest in Irish-speaking culture, the focus at first was on collecting and preserving oral material and on publishing and translating medieval texts. Efforts to establish an economically viable modern Irish literature did not occur until the last third of the nineteenth century, by which time the Irish-speaking population had been so reduced by the Great Famine that, for the first time ever, the survival of the language was in doubt. Moreover, just as in previous centuries, modern Irish was seen primarily as the language of a culturally and economically backward population, while the well-to-do urban reading public overwhelmingly spoke English.

One of the first Catholic clerics to set about vigorously establishing a modern Irish literature was John MacHale (1791–1881), who was appointed Archbishop of Tuam in 1834. In addition to poems and devotional writings in Irish, he published translations of the *Irish Melodies* of Thomas Moore (1779–1852), the *Pentateuch* and the *Iliad*. The Gaelic League, which had Irish books printed in its own publishing house from 1900, gained extensive influence in the business of literature. One of the writers it promoted was Peadar Ó Laoghaire (Peter O'Leary, 1839–1920), who made translations and wrote an autobiography *Mo Sgéal Féin* (My Own Story), in addition to original stories and adaptations of old Irish literary works. From the present-day viewpoint, however, the works of Pádraic Ó Conaire (1882–1928), who published many short stories and the bleak novel *Deoraíocht* (Exile), influenced by French Naturalism, seem more modern. The work of the teacher Pádraig Mac Piarais (Patrick Henry Pearse, 1879–1916), who wrote poetry and short stories in Irish and published the journal *An Claidheamh Soluis*, also owes a debt to contemporary trends.[5]

The founding of An Gúm as the state publishing house, in the wake of the establishment of the Irish Free State, seemed to promise Irish writers a new opportunity for support, but the publishers' markedly conservative policy proved an impediment to modern and experimental writing. Undoubtedly among the most important works published in the first years of An Gúm is the autobiography *An tOileánach* by Tomás Ó Criomhthain (1856–1937). In prose as unadorned as it is vivid, this describes the harsh life of fishermen on the remote island of Great Blasket, off the south-west coast of Ireland. The autobiographical writings *Fiche Blian ag Fás* (1933) by Muiris Ó Súilleabháin (1904–50), and *Peig* (1933) and *Machtnamh Seana-Mhná* (1939) by Peig Sayers (1873–1958), may be compared to it in their unvarnished descriptions of rural life in Irish-speaking Ireland. Under the pseudonym 'Máire', Séamus Ó Grianna (1889–1969) wrote fictitious tales of rural life in Northern Ireland, and his younger brother Seosamh Mac Grianna (1901–90) left many translations, as well as stories, literary criticism and an autobiographical essay *Mo Bhealach Féin* (My Own Way, 1930).

A brilliant satire on autobiographies like *An tOileánach* and the naive enthusiasm of ignorant townsfolk for the harsh life on the land appeared in 1941 under the title *An Béal Bocht*, by the journalist and writer Brian O'Nolan (alias Flann O'Brien, or Myles na gCopaleen,

1911–66). In the following years, a number of writers sought new forms of expression, partly as a conscious reaction to the literature of the inter-war period, which was now seen as conventional. They included the writer of short stories Máirtín Ó Cadhain (1906–70), the poet, novelist and playwright Eoghan Ó Tuairisc (Eugene Rutherford Watters, 1919–82) and the poets Máirtín Ó Díreáin (1910–88) and Seán Ó Ríordáin (1916–77). Whether the Irish language will be able to exist as the medium of literature in the future remains to be seen. The same applies to its closest relative, Scots Gaelic, whose fate in the modern age is the subject of the following two chapters.

CHAPTER 19

Scotland from the Reformation to Culloden

POLITICS AND RELIGION: SCOTLAND IN THE EARLY MODERN PERIOD

After the death of Mary Tudor, her half-sister Elizabeth I, daughter of Henry VIII and his second wife Anne Boleyn, was recognised in 1558 as sovereign by the parliament of England. By restoring her father's Anglican faith as the state religion, she at once came into conflict with the Catholics, in whose eyes Mary Stuart, Queen of Scots, a great grand-daughter of Henry VII, was the rightful heir to the throne of England. Mary, the daughter of James V, had been brought up in France, had married the French King, Francis II, in 1558 and did not return to Scotland until 1561, after his death. In 1565 she married Lord Darnley who, even before the birth of their son James, killed Mary's secretary Riccio out of jealousy. Earning thus the disfavour of the Queen, he was himself murdered by the Earl of Bothwell in 1567. In the same year Mary married Bothwell, but in 1568, owing to her Catholic leanings, she was forced to flee Scotland in the face of opposition from the nobles. Imprisoned by her rival Elizabeth, she was charged with conspiracy and executed in 1587. A few years after her death, Mary Stuart was celebrated in classical drama as a martyr for the faith, while later writers who worked with the same material placed increasing emphasis on erotic motifs.

When Elizabeth, who had never married, died, Mary's son James VI of Scotland ascended the throne as James I of England, uniting the two countries in the person of the king. James's attempts to extend the royal prerogative led swiftly to conflict with Parliament, which was seeking greater independence. The conflict came to a head under his son and successor Charles I, and open civil war ensued in 1642 between the supporters of the king and those of Parliament. Under the command of Oliver Cromwell, the parliamentary army defeated the king's Scottish allies at Preston in 1648 and proceeded to execute the king and proclaim a republic in 1649. From 1653 Cromwell ruled with absolute power, backed by the constitution of the Protectorate, but after his death in 1658 his son and heir could not hold this position. In 1660 Charles II was restored as king by Parliament. However, his brother and successor, James II also came into conflict with Parliament, owing to his pro-Catholic and pro-French policies, and in 1688 Parliament called on William of Orange, husband of James's eldest daughter Mary, to take the throne of England. Under William's successor Anne, the personal union between the two countries, which had existed since 1603, became a real union in 1707 through the union of the parliaments of England and Scotland.

In accordance with the 1701 laws of succession, the throne passed to the House of Hanover after the death of Queen Anne in 1714, and this house was to remain in personal union with Great Britain until Queen Victoria came to the throne in 1837. Of far-reaching importance for the Gaelic-speaking Highlands were the attempts by the Jacobites, the supporters of James II and his successors, to help the House of Stuart reclaim the throne with Scottish and French assistance (see Lenman 1980). After a first rebellion, led by Viscount Dundee, had failed in 1689 at Killiecrankie, despite a victory over the forces of William of Orange, a second Jacobite expedition from the Highlands foundered in 1715. Within a few years, however, there was a renewal of Jacobite opposition to the regime. In 1745 the twenty-four-year-old grandson of James II, Charles Edward Stuart, landed on the west coast of Scotland and captured Edinburgh after a first victory over government forces. Shortly after this, however, the pretender's march on London came to a standstill at Derby, and in 1746 at Culloden near Inverness, in the last battle on British soil, the Scottish army was routed by the numerically superior and better equipped troops of George II, commanded by the Duke of Cumberland. Executions, expropriations, deportations and a fundamental reorganisation of the economic and social order in the Gaelic-speaking Highlands were the direct consequences of a rebellion which its leaders had unleashed more from a personal longing for power or a half-hearted loyalty to the House of Stuart than in the political, economic or cultural interests of the region.

THE WORLD OF THE CLANS: ECONOMY AND SOCIETY IN THE HIGHLANDS

Is i so an aimsir an dearbhar an tairgeanachd dhùinn,
Is bras meanmnach fir Albann fo an armaibh air thùs.
An uair dh'éireas gach treun laoch 'nan éideadh glan ùr,
Le rùn feirge agus gairge gi seirbhis a'chrùin.

Théid maithe na Galldachd glé shanntach 'sa'chùis,
Is gur líonmhor each seangmhar a dhannsas le sùnnd:
Bidh Sasannaich caillte gun taing dhaibh d'a chionn,
Bidh na Frangaich 'nan campaibh glé theann air an cúl.

This is the time when the prophecy will be fulfilled for us,
with the men of Scotland mettlesome and spirited, armed in
the van (of the battle),
each valiant man will rise in brand new garb,
with angry and fierce determination in the service of the crown.

The nobles of the Lowlands will join the cause eagerly,
and many's the slender spirited horse will prance with energy.
On that account Englishmen will be destroyed, willing or not,
and the French will be closely supporting us.

This expectation was expressed by the poet John MacDonald (Iain Dubh Mac Iain 'ic Ailein) on the occasion of the Jacobite rising of 1715 in his 'Song of the Highland Clans' (*Oran nam Fineachan Gaidhealach*), and in the stanzas following this introduction he lists by name all the clans ready to attack, and praises their qualities.[1] For an understanding of the politics as well as the social and cultural history of Celtic Scotland in the late Middle Ages and early modern period, the clan is of such fundamental importance that at this point some explanatory comment is in order.

In medieval Scotland the word *clann* first denoted a family group of high standing which could trace its lineage on the male side back to a common ancestor whose name its members bore. However, in a broader sense the word also included those socially dependent on and subordinate to this family group. In Ireland the same terminology may be seen as early as the beginning of the tenth century, when (as later in Scotland) in addition to *clann*, the synonyms *cenél* (Welsh *cenedl*) and *síl* (Welsh *hil*) were used. Two Scottish clans, *Clann Chanainn* and *Clann Morgainn*, appear in the twelfth century in the *Book of Deer*, where the leader of a clan is termed *toísech* (see Jackson 1972, 110–14). Most of the historically attested ancestors of the Scottish clans known in later times may be dated to the period between 1150 and 1350, while many leading Irish families can trace their origins back to figures from the tenth or eleventh centuries.

While the feudal system based on personal oaths of allegiance extended its domain steadily from the twelfth century, especially in the south and east of Scotland following the Norman conquest, in the Gaelic-speaking Highlands and the Hebrides the clan system, which depended on blood relationships, endured until 1745. The material basis of this economic and social order was the possession of arable and grazing land, leased by the clan leader to relatives who owed him a direct duty of obedience (Scots English *tack*). This social stratum, known in Scots Gaelic as *daoine uaisle* (nobility) and in Scots English as *tacksmen*, sub-let the land to crofters, who were economically dependent upon them. Thus the clan system not only determined the economic, political and military power of the ruling families of the western Highlands and the Hebrides, but also served as the basis of their self-perception and traditional culture, as expressed in their historical and genealogical studies, traditional legal system, medicine, music and – most importantly – poetry.

PRAISE–POEMS AND BALLADS: EARLY SCOTS GAELIC LITERATURE

The earliest specimens of Scots Gaelic literature are found in *The Book of the Dean of Lismore*, which is now kept in Edinburgh in the National Library of Scotland.[2] This is a collection of poetry in manuscript, chiefly from Perthshire and Argyllshire, mostly compiled between 1512 and 1526 from written and oral sources by the clergyman James MacGregor and his brother Duncan. The spelling is unusual in the scant regard it pays to traditional rules and in being influenced instead by the way English was written in Scotland.

The greater part of the poetry passed on to us in *The Book of the Dean of Lismore* and subsequent manuscripts provides samples of that bardic poetry already discussed in connection with late medieval Irish literature. This means that it was the work of professional poets whose task it was to praise living leaders and lament the dead in poetic forms that were linguistically, metrically and stylistically traditional. Since there was a tendency, here as in other professions, to pass on the office of bard from father to son, we know the names and writings of a large number of bardic families. The MacMhuirich bards, whose origins reach back to the poet Muireadhach Albanach Ó Dálaigh, who fled Ireland for Scotland in 1215, have the longest history. His descendant Dòmhnall MacMhuirich, who probably died in the fifth decade of the eighteenth century, is regarded as the last Scottish practitioner of this profession, which in Ireland had come to an end over 100 years earlier.

Besides the bardic poetry, *The Book of the Dean of Lismore* contains poetry of a less formal genre, including love poems or *dánta grádha* influenced by the medieval tradition of courtly love, poems of religious content and heroic ballads about Finn mac Cumaill and his Fianna, which since the late Middle Ages had also enjoyed great popularity in Ireland. Of the poets we often know little more than their names. Only occasionally, by the content of the surviving poems or from additional biographical information, is it possible to form a clearer picture of their individual personalities and their life in these turbulent times.

One eminently political poet was Iain Lom (John MacDonald, born c. 1625 and died after 1707), who, as a member of the MacDonald clan from Keppoch, could trace his ancestry back to the first Lord of the Isles.[3] In his verse he depicts the Civil War between Charles I and his Parliament as a settling of accounts between the clan of the heroes (the MacDonalds under the leadership of their chieftain Alasdair MacColla) and that of the villains (the hated Campbells of Argyll). His lament for the Marquis of Montrose, executed in 1650, compares Cromwell's persecution of the Scottish

Royalists with the oppression of the Israelites in Egypt. He rejoices at the restoration of the monarchy in 1660, and voices grief and anger at the revolution of 1688. Again in 1707, following the union of the English and Scottish parliaments, the poet pours his corrosive scorn upon all those he holds responsible for this betrayal of Scottish interests.

An Clàrsair Dall (The Blind Harpist) was the nickname of the poet Roderick Morison (Ruaidhri MacMhuirich, c. 1656–1714), one of the last professional poets and an accomplished harpist.[4] Born in Bragar on the Isle of Lewis, the eldest of six children of a prosperous *tacksman*, he travelled to Ireland to complete his musical education and in 1681 became harpist to Iain Breac, the chief of the MacLeod clan in Dunvegan on the Isle of Skye. After 1688 he fell out with his master, perhaps because of his Jacobite sympathies, and found another patron. His most famous poem, 'Song to MacLeod' (*Oran Mór MhicLeòid*), combines wistful recollection of the splendour of the house of Iain Breac, who died in 1693, with swingeing criticism of his son Ruaidhri, whom the poet accused of extravagance, neglect of his heritage and aping foreign ways while divorced from all tradition.

Alasdair Mac Mhaighstir Alasdair (Alexander MacDonald, c. 1695–1770) is generally regarded as the most eminent Scots Gaelic poet of the eighteenth century.[5] The son of a clergyman, he is thought to have studied at the University of Glasgow, like his father. It is certain that he worked as a teacher and catechist for the Society in Scotland for Propagating Christian Knowledge (SSPCK), founded in 1709. In 1745 he converted to Catholicism and joined the army of the pretender Charles Edward Stuart. Like no other poet of his time, Alasdair Mac Mhaighstir Alasdair impresses the reader with his combination of technical brilliance and multi-faceted richness in content and style. Side by side with political verse as propaganda for the Jacobite cause, he left two nature poems about summer and winter, using English-language models, and alongside the erotic licence of 'In Praise of Morag' (*Moladh Mòraig*) stands his 'Elegy for a Domestic Dove' (*Marbhrann do Pheata Coluim*), probably inspired by Catullus's ode to Lesbia's sparrow. His 'Clanranald's Galley' (*Birlinn Chlann Raghnaill*), over 550 lines long, with its vivid description of the vessel, its crew and the stormy passage across the open sea from Uist to Ireland, is considered his greatest masterpiece. By virtue of his creative innovations and confident stylistic assimilation of external literary influences, Alasdair's poem represents a first high point in Scots Gaelic literature. His poetry was published at an early date (1751) and was to serve as a model for later writers.

CHAPTER 20

Scotland from Culloden to 1945

CROFTERS, SHEEP AND TOURISTS: THE TRANSFORMATION OF THE HIGHLANDS

Following the failure of the Jacobite rising of 1745, the Gaelic-speaking Highlands faced two problems: the end of the old social order, which rested on the clan system, and a steep rise in the population, for which the traditional economy could not hope to provide. One avenue open to indigent and unemployed male High-landers was service in the British army, which first drew recruits from the Gaelic-speaking regions in 1725 and 1745. In the Seven Years' War (1756–63), the American War of Independence (1775–83) and the Napoleonic wars (1803 15) several new Highland regiments were raised and deployed on the European continent, in North America and in the British Empire's wars of conquest, for example in India. However, after the final defeat of Napoleon, the need for troops declined steeply, and more and more inhabitants of the Highlands, like those of Ireland and Wales, saw no choice but to emigrate. Their destinations were first the United States, then Canada, and from 1840 increasing numbers chose Australia and New Zealand.

The situation of the Gaelic-speaking population deteriorated alarmingly from the late eighteenth century when the landowners, with the backing of the government and the military, moved increasingly to drive the crofters and day-labourers (who had very few rights after the dissolution of the clan system), from their land in order to use it for the more profitable business of sheep-rearing. As a result of these 'clearances', broad swathes of land were left depopulated and the displaced inhabitants forced into poverty.[1] The impoverished Gaelic-speaking population found succour in the Free Church of Scotland, established in 1843, which achieved a large following in the Protestant regions of the Highlands. But only in the second half of the nineteenth century did the Highlanders succeed in developing successful ways to resist and sway public opinion to their side. Following violent unrest the government set up a committee of enquiry in 1883, headed by Lord Napier. At its recommendation, the Crofters' Holding Act was passed in 1886, ensuring a marked improvement in the rights of the crofters. Yet the number of Gaelic-speakers continued to decline in the following decades, as a result of the privileged status of English in the school system and the uninterrupted emigration of young people to the lowland industrial centres. By the mid-twentieth century, the daily use of Gaelic had become mainly restricted to the Hebrides and even there the influence of English could be felt everywhere.

In striking contrast to the modern popularity of the Highlands and the Hebrides as tourist destinations stands the fact that these regions and their culture were scarcely known outside Scotland until the late eighteenth century. In about 1695, Martin Martin (c. 1660–1719), born in Skye, wrote a description of the Hebrides with a focus on their natural and cultural history, which two generations later would move the English writer Samuel Johnson (1709–84) and his biographer James Boswell (1740–95) to travel in the region. The Welsh scholar Edward Lhuyd visited the Highlands in about 1700, and in about 1770 the naturalist Thomas Pennant (1726–98) also made the journey (see T. M. Murchison in Thomson, D. S. 1994, 132–5). The fact that soon after this more and more travellers began to visit this region for pleasure is primarily due to the imaginative powers of two Scottish writers, whom we discuss below.

'TRULY OSSIANIC SCENES': MACPHERSON, SCOTT AND THEIR AFTERMATH

When the travelling writer Ferdinand Ochsenheimer visited the ruined monastery of Allerheiligen in the Black Forest towards the end of the eighteenth century, he found 'truly Ossianic scenes . . . bare-topped mountains all around, reaching to the heavens; far below in the valley the romantic monastery, completely cut off from the rest of creation . . . Down in the precipitous depths a forest river rushes over stones and uprooted trees, and its fearsome thunder in this wilderness fills the soul with dread.'[2]

When we recall the geometrically arranged and neatly trimmed gardens so beloved of the Baroque period, and the liking of the Rococo for the pleasing and pretty, we can appreciate the distance that separates the perception of nature and scenery in those generations from that of the late eighteenth century. The newly discovered enthusiasm for undisturbed wilderness was most successfully and resoundingly expressed in *The Works of Ossian*, by the Scot James Macpherson (1736–96), of which Ochsenheimer was so strongly reminded by the sight of the ruined Black Forest monastery.[3]

Born in the village of Invertromie in the Badenoch region, Macpherson studied in Aberdeen and Edinburgh and first worked as a teacher in a village school in his home region, then as a private tutor in Edinburgh. In 1759 he made the acquaintance of the playwright John Home (1722–1808) and the theologian Alexander Carlyle (1722–1805). When they both professed an interest in Gaelic poetry, Macpherson showed them sixteen short texts which he claimed to have translated into English. With the help of Home, these texts came to the attention of the Edinburgh professor of poetry and rhetoric, Hugh Blair, on whose initiative they were published in 1760 under the title *Fragments of Ancient Poetry*. The success of this book led Macpherson to publish two further volumes of epic poetry, in which a third-century poet by the name of Ossian, Son of Fingal, was identified for the first time as the original author. *Fingal* appeared in 1762, *Temora* in 1763, and in 1765 all three books were published with a 'critical dissertation' by Hugh Blair, under the title *The Works of Ossian, the Son of Fingal*, in a two-volume set.

As we now know, Macpherson himself had written most of the 'Works of Ossian', drawing on names, episodes and motifs from various Irish saga cycles, with some stylistic borrowings from the Bible and the English poet John Milton. Although in the emotional presentation of this material he really did no more than fall in with the public taste of his day, many of his contemporaries took *The Works of Ossian* to be authentic Celtic poems of the pre-Christian era. They were widely translated throughout Europe and drew the attention of a broad reading public for the first time to the existence of the Celtic languages and literatures. This interest was intensified by the work of the Scottish lawyer, writer and pioneer of the historical novel, Sir Walter Scott (1771–1832). After publishing a series of Scottish and English border ballads in his collection *Minstrelsy of the Scottish Borders* (1802–3), he first gave shape, in his romantic novel in verse *The Lady of the Lake* (published 1810), to the contrast between the Gaelic-speaking Highlands and the English-speaking Lowlands. This contrast would also play an important part in his historical novels *Waverley* (1814), *Rob Roy* (1817) and *Redgauntlet* (1824).

For the self-perception of the Gaelic-speaking Highlands and the study of their history, language and culture, Macpherson's and Scott's popular success proved a double-edged sword. On the one hand, there was a surge of scholarly interest in Scotland's Celtic past, which only now became the subject of systematic investigation using the methodology of modern historical study. One of the pioneers was the lawyer and historian William Forbes Skene (1809–92), who published the earliest sources of Scottish history in 1867 under the title *Chronicles of the Picts and Scots*, and in 1876–80 produced his three-volume masterwork *Celtic Scotland: A History of Ancient Alban*, the first comprehensive general work on the subject. The growing interest in the maintenance of the Gaelic language and culture was further marked by the establishment of numerous learned societies, including the Gaelic Society of London (1777), the Highland Society of Scotland (1784), the Iona Club (1833), the Gaelic Society of Inverness (1871) and the Highland Association (*An Comunn Gaidhealach*, 1891). The first chair of Celtic Studies was founded at the University of Edinburgh in 1882.[4]

On the other hand, these efforts to preserve and nurture Scotland's Celtic culture became inseparably linked with a romantic misrepresentation of history which the visitor to the Highlands encounters at every turn even today.[5] The case of the Scottish national dress, the woven kilt (Gaelic *féileadh*) in tartan pattern (Gaelic *breacan*), is typical. Banned from 1746 to 1784, at the time of the Romantic enthusiasm for the Highlands in the nineteenth century, it was adopted by all those Lowland families who had previously never belonged to a clan or worn such a garment. This kind of manipulation of the past set its stamp especially on the modern face of Scots Gaelic literature which, owing to the language barrier and the absence of any close acquaintance with its social conditions and literary conventions, remained largely beyond the reach of the general public. Thus, in the Anglo-Saxon area, it was possible for writers of the so-called 'Celtic Twilight', such as William Sharp (pseudonym Fiona MacLeod, 1856–1905), to popularise a pseudo-Celtic literature which in many respects stood for the very opposite of the tradition it claimed to follow.

POETS AND COLLECTORS: MODERN GAELIC LITERATURE

For Gaelic literature the eighteenth century was a time of radical change, as the end of the clan system deprived the bardic tradition of its economic basis and social justification. In the place of professional poets came poets who wrote when the spirit moved them or the opportunity arose, poets who could embrace the bardic tradition as well as the folkloric mode in their verse, but were largely dependent on their own individual circumstances with regard to the reception, preservation and dissemination of their work.

The resulting change in the profile of the poet is reflected in the work of John (Iain) MacCodrum (1693–1779). In 1763, in a seemingly anachronistic bow to tradition, he was appointed official bard of James MacDonald of Sleat on the Isle of Skye, but his fame rests less on his praise-poems than on the verse in which he describes his environment with wit and a gift for acute observation.[6] Donnchadh Bàn Mac an t-Saoir (Duncan Bàn Macintyre, 1724–1812), born in Glen Orchy, worked as a gamekeeper. To him Gaelic literature owes some of its most successful descriptions of nature. Strongly influenced by the poetry of Alasdair Mac Mhaighstir Alasdair, he wrote not only conventional praise-poems and elegies, but also, in poems such as *Oran Coire a'Cheathaich* (Song to Misty Corrie), a vivid and precisely observed description of the landscape and wild animals around him.[7]

Reflecting the high regard in which folk poetry had been held since the second half of the eighteenth century, collectors now set about recording the store of anonymous oral material, such as songs, sayings and stories. Influential pioneers in this field were John

Francis Campbell (1822–86) from Islay, whose *Popular Tales of the West Highlands* (published 1860–2) was a comprehensive bilingual edition of Gaelic tales, and Alexander Carmichael (1832–1912), who collected a large number of prayers, blessings, oaths and songs, under the title *Carmina Gadelica*. Since 1951 the University of Edinburgh has had a School of Scottish Studies, and publishes a journal, *Tocher*, that specialises in the scholarly evaluation and publication of this type of folk material.[8]

Before the nineteenth century, prose played hardly any role as a literary form, a fact which is due in part to the lack of any generally recognised stylistic model, and in part to a degree of disdain for fiction in the world of learning and letters, which was much influenced by the Church. This meant that at first only prose writing of an edifying, homiletic or educational nature was published, most of it consisting of translations or adaptations of English-language models. Novels on the epic scale have been few in modern Gaelic writing, largely for economic reasons, while the genre of the psychological short story has been practised by Iain Crichton Smith (Iain Mac a'Ghobhainn, 1928–98).[9] Among the most important poets of the present and recent past are George Campbell Hay (Deòrsa Mac Iain Deòrsa Caimbeul, 1915–84), Sorley MacLean (Somhairle MacGill-Eain, 1911–96), Ruaridh Mac Thòmais (Derick Smith Thomson, born 1921) and Dòmhnall Mac Amhlaigh (Donald MacAulay, born 1930). The recognition that, in an age of cultural uniformity and levelling, a disadvantaged minority can protect its traditions only by consciously striving to do so led George Campbell Hay to write his *Meftah bâbkum es-sabar* (Patience is the Key to Your Door), inspired by his personal experiences in North Africa.[10]

Is cuimhne leam an Sùg el-Cheamais
sa' chaifidh dhorcha is sinn a'deasbud,
guth cianail mar ghuth chlag fo fheasgar
a mhol domh strìochdadh do'n Fhreasdal.
'Mo chridhe fhéin, is faoin bhur gleachd Ris,
's gu bheil gach toiseach agus deireadh
air an sgrìobhadh Aige cheana.'

Sgrùd a bas a làimhe 's lean e:

'Do roinn, do mhanadh, is do sgàile,
théid iad cuide riut 's gach àite.
An rud a tha san Dàn 's a sgrìobhahd
is gainntir sin a ghlais an Rìgh oirnn.
'S i 'n fhaidhidinn le sealladh ìosal
iuchair dorus ar dubh phrìosain.'

Ghin aintighearnas na gréine lasraich,
is ainneart speuran teth na h-Aifric,
gliocas brùite sgìth nam facal.

A ghliocais mar chluig mhall' an fheasgair,
chan ann dhuinne do leithid!
Oir sgrìobhadh roghainn fo leth dhuinn:
an t-sìth 's am bàs no gleachd 's a'bheatha.

Dh'fhalbh na diasan, dh'fhan an asbhuain?
Thuit na bailtean, chinn an raineach?
A bheil tom luachrach air gach stairsnich?
A shaoghail, tha sinn ann g'a aindeoin;
tha a'ghrìosach theth fo'n luaithre fhathast.

I remember at Sûq-el-Khemis,
while we argued in the dark café,
a voice, melancholy as the voice of evening bells,
that counselled me to be submissive to Providence.
'My heart own, your struggle against It is in vain,
for every beginning and ending
has been written by It already.'

He gazed at the palm of his hand and went on:

'Your portion, your destiny, your shadow –
These accompany you in every place.

'What is fated and has been written
is as a dungeon that the Divine King has locked upon us.
Patience with a down cast look,
is the key to the door of our wretched prison.'

The tyranny of the flaming sun
and the violence of the hot skies of Africa
had begotten the bruised, tired wisdom of these words.

Wisdom like the slow bells of evening, not for us is your like!
For a choice apart has been written for us:
pcacc and death, or struggling and life.

Are the full ears gone, and only the stubble remaining?
Fallen are the townships, and up has sprung the bracken?
Is here a clump of rushes on every threshold?
Oh, world, we are here and live on in spite of it;
the hot ember is under the ashes.

CHAPTER 21

Wales from Union to Industrialisation

CENTRALISATION AND ANGLICISATION: POLITICS, ECONOMICS AND SOCIETY

For Wales the union with England in 1536–42 had brought with it the loss of independent political structures and an extensive, though not yet total, realignment in the dispensation of justice and administration.[1] Nevertheless the inhabitants preserved their cultural identity and ancestral Celtic language which, although officially unrecognised, remained the sole means of communication for the great majority of the population. The advance of centralisation produced favourable results for the political and judicial stability of the country, which experienced steady economic growth and a marked increase in population, owing in particular to intensified agriculture. The main economic factor was the raising of cattle and sheep. A cottage industry turned the wool into coarse cloth and cattle were exported in great numbers to England. In some regions coal was already being mined and iron smelted although, as yet, this hardly affected the predominantly agrarian nature of the country and its economy. The main beneficiary of the political and economic development was the minor nobility: its representatives acquired, by lease or purchase, the monastic estates after the dissolution of the monasteries in 1536–9 and, at the same time, as members of parliament and justices of the peace, assumed key functions in the administration and the judiciary. The fact that in these areas, by act of parliament, only English could be used led to the increasing anglicisation of the nobility, who gradually became alienated from the lower strata of the Welsh population.

In matters of religion, following the break with Rome and the establishment of the Church of England, the population was not of one mind. Many inhabitants of rural areas continued to practise traditional forms of Catholic worship, even after the dissolution of the monasteries, the abandonment of pilgrimages and the reorganisation of the Church. However, total recusance – in the sense of formal refusal of Anglicanism or active resistance to it – took hold only temporarily in some regions, mainly in the south-east and north-east of the country. But if the pioneers of the Catholic Counter-Reformation found little backing, so too did the radical Puritans, who found greater support in the liberal-minded towns of south-east England than in rural Wales. Victory in the confessional struggle therefore went, at least in the short term, to the representatives of the Church of England. Backed by the authority of the government, the Anglican bishops initiated a complete translation of the Bible into Welsh, thus providing for the Celtic tongue of Wales a status which the government had denied it in the spheres of administration and the judiciary.

HUMANISTS AND THEOLOGIANS: WELSH LITERATURE IN THE EARLY MODERN PERIOD

With the increasing anglicisation of the Welsh nobility and the advent of new artistic genres, traditional praise-poetry diminished in importance, as in Ireland. Although in the late seventeenth century some poets still received remuneration for writing poetry in honour of noble families, few now did this to earn a living. The fact that the representatives of this venerable tradition could not keep up with the times had to do not only with the changed social and economic framework, but also with their rejection of printing, which had begun its victorious march across the whole of Europe in the second half of the fifteenth century. However, several Welsh humanists did take up the new opportunities afforded by print, and their works exerted an abiding influence on the history of Welsh literature.[2]

One of the earliest and most important representatives of Welsh humanism was Gruffydd Robert (born before 1532, died after 1598), who lived in Italy after graduating from Oxford and in 1567, influenced by the Italian humanists, published the first part of a grammar of the Welsh language, written in Welsh. The work of the humanist John Davies (c. 1567–1644), published in Latin in 1621, is comparable with this. Davies also published a Welsh-Latin, Latin-Welsh dictionary in 1632, in which he made use of preliminary work done by the lexicographer Thomas Wiliems (1545–1622). The most significant legacy of the Welsh humanists, however, and the one with the most enduring consequences, was the translation of the Bible from its original languages. In 1551, William Salesbury (c. 1520–84) published a number of translations from the Gospels and the Epistles of Paul under the title *Kynniver Llith a Ban*. After the English Parliament had ratified the decision to translate the Bible into Welsh in 1563, the first edition of the Welsh New Testament, in a translation by William Salesbury and Bishop Richard Davies (c. 1501–88) appeared in 1567. The first edition of the Old and New Testaments, translated by William Morgan (1545–1604), was published in 1588.[3]

Among the major literary accomplishments of the theological controversy in the age of the Reformation and Counter-Reformation, was, on the Catholic side, *Y Drych Cristionogawl* (The Christian Mirror), a devotional work apparently written by the priest and lawyer Robert Gwyn of Penyberth (c. 1540–1604) and first published in 1586–7. At the same time the works of Protestant writers were extremely numerous and influential. Among these the Anglicans Ellis Wynne (1671–1734) and Theophilus Evans (1693–1767) stand out, along with the translators of the Bible. Wynne was the author of *The Visions of the Sleeping Poet* (*Gweledigaetheu y Bardd Cwsc*), an adaptation of a free English version of *Sueños y Discursos de Verdades*, by the Spanish writer Francisco de Quevedo. In addition to homilies and devotional texts, Theophilus Evans wrote the historical work *Drych y Prif Oesoedd* (Mirror of the Early Centuries), first published in 1716 and re-published in 1740, an account of the early history of Britain from Roman times to the coming to Christianity.[4] At the same time some Puritan theologians were even more important than these Anglican writers for the later history of Welsh literature and culture. Pride of place in literary distinction here belongs to the mystic Morgan Llwyd (1619–59), whose allegorical *Book of the Three Birds* (*Llyfr y Tri Aderyn*; 1653) and some later writings endeavoured to prepare his fellow-countrymen for the coming of the Kingdom of Heaven on earth (see Thomas, M. W. 1988 and 1991 and Owen,

G. W. 1922). A younger contemporary of Llwyd's was Charles Edwards (born 1628, died after 1690), whose *True Faith* (*Y Ffydd Ddi-ffuant*), first published in 1667, was a classic of the new Welsh prose-writing (see the edition by Williams, G. J. 1936). The negative attitude of the Puritans towards the established Anglican Church had its logical outcome in the nonconformist movements of the Quakers, Baptists and above all the Methodists, whose influence would reach its peak in the late eighteenth and nineteenth centuries.

BARDS AND DRUIDS: THE BEGINNINGS OF WELSH ANTIQUARIANISM

The beginnings of a scholarly engagement with Welsh history and literature were put in place by the sixteenth-century humanists, mentioned above, to whom such disparate disciplines as the study of manuscripts and research into buried hoards and artefacts still retained their unity. Particular attention is merited by the cartographer Humphrey Llwyd (c. 1527–68) whose description of Britain, entitled *Commentarioli Descriptionis Britannicae Fragmentum*, was printed in Cologne in 1572 on the recommendation of his friend Abraham Ortelius. Another pioneer in this field was the historian David Powel (1552–98), whose *Historie of Cambria, now called Wales*, reprinted many times, gave an extremely influential account of early Welsh history. The English humanist William Camden (1551–1623) wrote a major work called *Britannia*, the most exhaustive compilation and critical examination of British antiquities from the prehistoric and early historic periods. First published in 1586 and reprinted six times in the lifetime of the author, this Latin-language work was translated into English in 1610 and published in revised form in 1695 and 1789.[5]

One of the first humanist collectors of Welsh manuscripts was John Price of Brecon (1502–55), who in 1546 also published the earliest printed book in Welsh, known by its first words *Yn y lhyvyr hwnn* (In this Book). The most significant collection of Welsh manuscripts was compiled by the antiquary Robert Vaughan of Hengwrt (c. 1592–1667). In 1859 this collection came into the possession of the genealogist and historian William Watkin Edward Wynne of Peniarth (1801–80) and in 1898 it was acquired by the manuscript collector John Williams (1840–1926) who bequeathed it, with his other manuscripts, to the Welsh National Library, founded in Aberystwyth in 1907.

Another milestone in the history of Celtic studies was the scholarly work of the Welsh student of the Welsh language, nature and antiquities, Edward Lhuyd (1660–1709), who studied at Jesus College and then worked for the Ashmolean Museum in Oxford from 1684 until his death (see Emery 1971). From 1697 to 1701 he undertook extensive field work in Wales, Scotland, Ireland and Brittany. In 1707 in the first volume of his never-completed work *Archaeologia Britannica*, he published the linguistic material that he had collected, including a comparative dictionary of the Celtic tongues, grammatical outlines, an Irish-English dictionary and a catalogue of Irish manuscripts. Unfortunately after these studies came a backward step later in the eighteenth century, in the form of the purely speculative association of Stone and Bronze Age artefacts with the Druids known from writings of the classical period. The attribution of Stonehenge to the Celts, still heard today outside scientific circles, was first proposed by the natural scientist and antiquary John Aubrey (1626–97), and gained wide acceptance thanks to the works of William Stukeley (1687–1765), in particular. In Wales, Henry Rowlands (1655–1723), an Anglican clergyman born in Anglesey, in his book *Mona Antiqua Restaurata*, published in 1723, popularised the notion of a close relationship between Welsh and Hebrew, and of Anglesey as a centre of Druidic culture (see Piggott 1985 and 1989).

The Romantic attitude to the Celtic past found fertile soil in the circle of Welsh patriots who from their adopted London home sought to raise the prestige of their national culture. A leading role in this was played by Lewis Morris (1701–65), originally from Anglesey, and his brother Richard (1703–79). While Lewis lent energetic support to younger Welsh poets and scholars like Goronwy Owen (1723–65) and Evan Evans (1731–88), in 1751 Richard founded the Honourable Society of Cymmrodorion, which concerned itself with the maintenance of the Welsh language, literature and culture. Similar aims were pursued by the Society of Gwyneddigion, founded in 1770, while the Society of Cymreigyddion, established in 1794, strove for political and social reform as well as supporting the maintenance of Welsh.[6] The most significant scholarly products of these activities included an edition of the poetry of Dafydd ap Gwilym, published in 1789, and a three-volume anthology published between 1801 and 1807 with the title *The Myvyrian Archaiology of Wales*, containing extracts from the earliest Welsh poetry as well as medieval chronicles. Its publishers were Owen Jones (Owain Myfyr, 1741–1814), a patron of literature, and the linguist William Owen Pughe (1759–1835), who also published a comprehensive but academically dubious Welsh-English dictionary in 1803. The most colourful personality of this circle was the stonemason, manuscript-collector and antiquary Edward Williams (Iolo Morganwg, 1747–1826). Born in Llancarfan in Glamorgan, he joined the Gwyneddigion out of romantic enthusiasm for Welsh culture, and in 1792 in London founded the Gorsedd Beirdd Ynys Prydain, a meeting-place of representatives of Welsh cultural, literary and musical life. Williams backed his efforts to present Welsh poets as the rightful heirs of the Celtic Druids by a series of brilliant literary forgeries, which his gullible supporters published, both in his lifetime and later. The fact that many of these forgeries were not recognised for what they were until the late nineteenth century illustrates both the comparative slowness of the development of academic Celtic studies, and the credulity with which a substantial audience seized on Williams's fantasy-filled picture of an idealised past.[7]

CHAPTER 22

Wales from Industrialisation to 1945

SOCIETY IN TRANSITION: INDUSTRIALISATION AND NONCONFORMISM

When Edward Williams died in 1826, Wales was in the grip of far-reaching social, economic and religious change. The principal cause of this was the Industrial Revolution, the effects of which, more than any other factor, would shape the history of the country up to the end of World War I. From the end of the eighteenth century to the mid-nineteenth century the iron-working industry was dominant in Wales, and it was mainly concentrated in Merthyr Tydfil in northern Glamorgan, where in 1830 one-third of the iron smelted in Great Britain was produced (Evans, C. 1993). The invention of the steam engine and its use in transport, together with rising demand for coal for iron-smelting, meant that from 1850 the coal-mining industry far outstripped all others. By the end of the nineteenth century the South Wales coalfield provided a living for a majority of the Welsh population and supplied a substantial proportion of the energy needs of the industrialised world. In the hitherto thinly populated valleys of Glamorgan and Monmouthshire, mining led to the development of populous industrial centres. For example, in the Rhondda and Glamorgan valleys, the population increased from less than 1,000 to 150,000 between 1851 and 1911 (Edwards, H. 1995, Williams, C. 1996).

With industrialisation came a defection by large segments of the population from the Church of England to nonconformist movements. Congregationalists and Baptists had already gained a foothold in Wales in the mid-seventeenth century, and now over

100 years later Methodism began to spread under the spiritual leadership of preacher and organiser Howell Harris (1714–73) and poet and writer William Williams (Pantycelyn, 1717–91).[12] It is difficult to overstate the influence of these nonconformists, in particular the Methodists, on the later history of Welsh culture. It led to fundamental changes in the way of life and habits of thought, created in the population at large a new political awareness, influenced the education system and enriched literature with new modes of expression. Of particular importance were the Sunday schools: not only did they reinforce an understanding of democratic structures but they also, long before Welsh was introduced in state schools and universities, cultivated a knowledge of the written language and the ability to use it, through religious instruction based on the Welsh Bible.

During World War I and the years of economic depression that followed, the iron and coal industries suffered a severe decline, as did the exporting ports of South Wales, and this marked a defining moment in the history of Welsh culture. Poverty and long-term unemployment reached previously unknown proportions and a considerable part of the population moved away to the new industrial centres of England. In place of pre-war liberalism, the socialism of the Communist Party and the Labour Party now gained popularity, while *Plaid Genedlaethol Cymru* (The National Party of Wales, later renamed *Plaid Cymru*) advocated more political independence, resistance to the spread of anglicisation, and a return to the cultural heritage of the past (see Davies, D. H. 1983). In 1936, the British government, defying all protests by the Welsh population, began laying out an air-force base and bombing range at Penyberth, on the North Wales peninsula of Llŷn, at a site of cultural and historical significance in the heart of Welsh-speaking Wales. In response, the leadership of *Plaid Genedlaethol Cymru* backed the resistance by a symbolic act of arson and received widespread approval. The Welsh National Party only gained in political weight, however, in the decades following the end of World War II under the leadership of its president Gwynfor Evans, who in 1966 was the first member elected to parliament.

CLASSICISM AND MODERNISM: WELSH LITERATURE SINCE 1800

One of the most important developments in the Welsh literature of the eighteenth century was the revival by the classicists of the bardic poetry of the past and the writing of nonconformist hymns. Both trends continued into the nineteenth century and, with the aversion that nonconformism displayed for plays and novels, contributed to the endurance of poetry as the dominant means of expression in Welsh literature. An important role was now played by the regional poetry-reading competitions known as *eisteddfodau* (singular *eisteddfod*), from which in the years 1860 to 1880, under the patronage of the Honourable Society of Cymmrodorion, grew the National Eisteddfod (*Eisteddfod Genedlaethol*), a festival of culture and music still held every year in the first week of August. The ceremonial that Edward Williams had assembled for his 'Gathering of the Bards of the Isle of Britain' made for a picturesque setting. Towards the end of the nineteenth century, the lack of originality in many hymns, the superficial sentimentality of much of the lyrics and the unfocused nature of Eisteddfod poetry, often on metaphysical topics, provoked objections from a younger generation. Conscious of the progress of the new discipline of Celtic philology and contemporary European writing, they pressed for a move away from didactic and moralising verse and a raising of standards. Their spokesman was the poet, critic, grammarian and philologist John Morris-Jones (1864–1929), who was to exert much influence on the further development of Welsh poetry (see James, A. 1987). Among the major poets of the early twentieth century whose work shows this influence were Thomas Gwynn Jones (1871–1949), William John Gruffydd (1881–1954) and Robert Williams Parry (1884–1956).

World War I and the depression that followed it had profound effects on Welsh society and literature. A sceptical attitude to traditional values and an agnostic tendency may be seen in the work of the poet, essayist and scholar Thomas Herbert Parry-Williams (1887–1975), while the poet and critic Gwenallt (David James Jones, 1899–1975) moved from Marxist atheism to Methodism, influenced by the social upheavals of the inter-war period. The leading figure in literary and cultural life, however, was the playwright, poet, critic and literary historian Saunders Lewis (1893–1985), who turned his back on his Calvinist-Methodist roots for Catholicism while politically standing for the independence of his homeland and a dominant role for Welsh. In addition to influential writing in the field of political journalism, he wrote numerous studies in the history of Welsh poetry, in which he sought in particular to interpret the work of the late medieval Poets of the Gentry in the context of the religious and social conditions of their time. He also wrote over twenty plays, refashioning material from Welsh history and legend, as well as from modern politics, from a Christian standpoint.[3]

As in all the Celtic-speaking countries, novels and stories played only a subordinate part in Wales for a long time. The first novelist of importance was Daniel Owen (1836–95), who depicted the Methodist-dominated Welsh society of his time in his novels *Rhys Lewis* (1885), *Enoc Huws* (1891) and *Gwen Tomos* (1894). The most important prose-writer of the twentieth century was Kate Roberts (1891–1985), who portrayed the harshness of life in modern Welsh industrial society in stylistically polished novels and psychological short stories.

THE FATE OF THE LANGUAGE: WELSH IN POLITICS AND CULTURE

For a large part of the Welsh population, Welsh remained the main, and often the sole, medium of communication until the early twentieth century. Nevertheless, because of the centuries-old pre-eminence of English in administrative and judicial matters and the increasing anglicisation of the nobility, Welsh had come to be seen by the Welsh people (and by their English neighbours) as a lower-class language, and a knowledge of it was in no way conducive to social advancement.[4]

In 1847, a three-volume report by a government commission gave a damning assessment of religious observance and moral and educational standards among the Welsh population, and held the prevalent nonconformism and lack of knowledge of English primarily accountable for the situation (see Roberts, G. T. 1998). The publication of these *Blue Books* (*Llyfrau Gleision*), so called because of the colour of the covers, had a profound effect upon the Welsh. While some endeavoured to deflect the charges with redoubled efforts to acquire the language and culture of England, others sought to mark themselves off the more clearly from England. One of the leading champions of greater cultural independence was historian and teacher Owen Morgan Edwards (1858–1920), who performed sterling service to Welsh education as writer, publisher and distributor of Welsh-language books and periodicals. The literary critic and columnist Robert Ambrose Jones (Emrys ap Iwan, 1851–1906), whose views had much influence on later Welsh nationalists, also called for greater political independence and a stronger position for the Welsh language. One of the greatest achievements of the nationalist movement of the late nineteenth century was the founding of the University of Wales and the National Library in Aberystwyth, as well as the National Museum of Wales in Cardiff.[5]

A new phase in the resistance to the advance of anglicisation began in 1962, when, in a celebrated radio address on 'The Fate of the Language' (*Tynged yr Iaith*), Saunders Lewis called on the Welsh people to enforce the use of Welsh in local and regional government, not ruling out civil disobedience in order to do so. In response to this, the Welsh Language Society (*Cymdeithas yr Iaith Gymraeg*) came into existence later that same year. In the 1960s and 1970s, in particular, this society attracted much attention by means of its sensational activities and achieved a lasting improvement in the position of Welsh, while provoking controversy in a largely anglicised environment.

The experience of an educated Welshman, who views his culture from a certain distance, does not necessarily appreciate the frenetic cultural activity of the nationalists yet cannot deny his roots, is perhaps best illustrated in a well-known poem by Thomas Herbert Parry-Williams:

Beth yw'r ots gennyf i am Gymru? Damwain a hap
Yw fy mod yn ei libart yn byw. Nid yw hon ar fap
Yn ddim byd ond cilcyn o ddaear mewn cilfach gefn,
Ac yn dipyn o boendod i'r rhai sy'n credu mewn trefn.
A phwy sy'n trigo'n y fangre, dwedwch i mi.
Pwy ond gwehilion o boblach? Peidiwch, da chwi,
Â chlegar am uned a chenedl a gwlad o hyd:
Mae digon o'r rhain, heb Gymru, i'w cael yn y byd.

'R wyf wedi alaru ers talm ar glwed grŵn
Y Cymry, bondigrybwyll, yn cadw sŵn.
Mi af am dro, i osgoi eu lleferydd a'u llên,
Yn ôl i'm cynefin gynt, a'm dychymyg yn drên.
A dyma fi yno. Diolch am fod ar goll
Ymhell o gyffro geiriau'r eithafwyr oll.
Dyma'r Wyddfa a'i chriw; dyma lymder a moelni'r tir;
Dyma'r llyn a'r afon a'r clogwyn; ac ar fy ngwir,
Dacw'r tŷ lle'm ganed. Ond wele, rhwng llawr a ne'
Mae lleisiau a drychiolaethau ar hyd y lle.
'R wy'n simsanu braidd; ac meddaf i chwi,
Mae rhyw Ysictod fel petai'n dod drosof i;
Ac mi glywaf grafangau Cymru'n dirdynnu fy mron.
Duw a'm gwaredo, ni allaf ddianc rhag hon.

Why should I give a hang about Wales? It's by a mere fluke
    of fate
That I live in its patch. On a map it does not rate
Higher than a scrap of earth in a back corner
And a bit of bother to those who believe in order.

And who is it lives in this spot, tell me that.
Who but the dregs of society? Please, cut it out,

This endless clatter of oneness and country and race:
You can get plenty of these, without Wales, any place.

I've long since had it with listening to the croon
Of the Cymry, indeed, forever moaning their tune.

I'll take a trip to be rid of their wordplay with tongue
and with pen,
Back to where I once lived, aboard my fantasy's train.

And here I am then. Thanks be for the loss,
Far from all the fanatics' talkative fuss.

Here's Snowdon and its crew; here's the land, bleak and bare;
Here's the lake and river and crag, and look, over there,

The house where I was born. But see, between the earth
and the heavens,
All through the place there are voices and apparitions.

I begin to totter somewhat, and I confess
There comes over me, so it seems, a sort of faintness;

And I feel the claws of Wales tear at my heart.
God help me, I can't away from this spot.[6]

CHAPTER 23

Brittany from Union to 1945

CONSERVATISM AND MODERNISATION: ECONOMIC DEVELOPMENTS

In 1532, only a few years before the union of England and Wales, the political independence of the descendants of the Celtic emigrants in *Britannia minor* also came to an end. As a province of the kingdom of France, however, Brittany experienced a period of economic prosperity, owing chiefly to maritime trade, agriculture and the domestic textile industry.[1] It lay halfway between the Iberian peninsula, England and Flanders, and the many harbours along its rugged coastline afforded favourable conditions for the export of textiles and farm produce, and for the shipment of imports bound for the interior. The economic situation deteriorated, however, when a long series of wars with England, beginning in the late seventeenth century, severely affected the Breton maritime trade and deprived domestic industries of important markets. Only a small number of larger ports profited from the changes in international politics. Lorient, for example, as a base of the East India Company, held a monopoly on trade with Asia, and Nantes, being France's second-largest trans-shipment port (after Bordeaux), held a key position in the slave trade between France, Africa and America. In contrast to this, the backward state of industry and an adherence to long-outdated methods of cultivation led to increasing difficulties in supply, which by the late eighteenth century brought famine and an overall decline in the population. The bourgeoisie of Brittany, supported by much of the rural population, took an active part in the French Revolution of 1789. Soon after, however, dissatisfaction amongst broad sections of the population with the reforms of the new regime led to counter-revolution by the *Chouans*, who were loyal to the crown. Despite repeated military defeats, these continued to terrorise the rural population, in particular, in a sporadic guerilla war of attrition that lasted until 1815 (see Sutherland, D. 1982 and Hutt 1983). Even after the fall of Napoleon, Brittany remained for decades divided into the royalist 'Whites', who relied principally on the Church, large-scale land-holding and the nobility, and the democratic and anti-clerical 'Blues', who drew most of their support from the urban intelligentsia and the merchant class.

In the nineteenth century, thanks to modernised methods of cultivation, increased use of fertilisers and the intensified cultivation of potatoes, farming became the most important occupation in Brittany. At the same time the few surviving industries declined further: Breton iron-forging, which burnt only wood, was outstripped by the British metallurgical industry, which used hard coal, while Breton cloth-manufacturing suffered from competition with cheaper cotton. The distinctively rural flavour of Brittany attracted the special admiration of the Romantics, who, in their disillusionment with social and economic development in the age of industrialisation, expressed enthusiasm for the colourful Breton feast-day attire, cattle and produce markets, pilgrimages and religious holidays.[2] Part of this tradition was the theologian and orientalist Ernest Renan (1823–92), born in Tréguier, who in an influential book on the poetry of the Celtic peoples (*Essai sur la poésie des races celtiques*), published in 1859, described the Celtic literatures as spontaneous, unspoilt and emotional. This view strongly influenced the English poet and literary critic Matthew Arnold (1822–88), in particular.[3]

An important point in the economic development of Brittany was the construction of the Rennes-Brest and Nantes-Quimper railway lines between 1851 and 1869. For the coastal regions the rail link brought great advantages, as it improved the transport of fisheries products to the Paris market and favoured the economic growth of the seaside resorts. However, agrarian central Brittany experienced a growing flight from the land with severe consequences for economic and cultural development.

Profound changes came with World War I, which cost the lives of a disproportionate number of Breton soldiers and called into question the cultural values passed on by the schools and the Church. Disturbed by the experience of war and the confrontation with other modes of life and thought, many survivors turned their backs after

1918 on the Breton language, the traditional way of life, and the economy that went with it. At the same time, dissatisfaction over the loss of traditional values produced a surge of nationalist and separatist trends. In 1927 Le Parti autonomiste breton was set up, with its journal *Breiz Atao* (Brittany Forever). With the loss of its left wing in 1931, it moved further to the right, as Le Parti national breton. When the five-hundredth anniversary of the union of France and Brittany was celebrated in 1932, the separatists used the occasion to attack a monument that had been erected in 1911 in Rennes to mark the anniversary. In 1940–4, encouraged by the Irish example, Bretons who were conscious of their culture and tradition sought support from the German occupiers, and under their protection an Institut celtique de Bretagne was founded in 1941 and Breton was permitted as a language of instruction. Soon after the allied landings in the summer of 1944, the shortsightedness of this policy became apparent: it had discredited Breton nationalism in the eyes of many and led to a severe setback when the war ended.

BRETON AND FRENCH: ASPECTS OF BILINGUALISM

Even before the union with France, Brittany had become bilingual, since Breton had never taken hold in the east, despite the extended frontiers of the duchy. In the Middle Ages the linguistic boundary ran to the west of Rennes and Nantes, but by the early modern period it had withdrawn further westward, to a line west of Saint-Brieuc and just east of Vannes. Another reason for Brittany becoming bilingual was the damage done to Breton culture in the west of the region by the depredations of the Vikings, while at the same time French was being promoted by the eastward shift of political power in Brittany and the nobility's adoption of the culture of the royal court and the neighbouring regions. From the beginning of the modern period almost the only use of Breton as a written language had been for purposes of religious instruction, and even in this sphere it never achieved the recognition in Catholic Brittany that was accorded, for example, to Welsh in post-Reformation Wales. The language of government and administration, as of education and the law, was French alone.

Until the latter half of the nineteenth century the situation was characterised by a relatively stable language boundary, with a predominantly Breton-speaking population in western Lower Brittany (*Breizh-Isel*) and a predominantly French-speaking population in eastern Upper Brittany (*Breizh-Uhel*).[4] Since then this language boundary has steadily diminished in relevance, with French expanding its range not only along the boundary as before, but also within the interior of the Breton-speaking region. One of the main reasons for this was the status of French as official language and *lingua franca*, displacing Breton above all on the coast and in the towns. Added to this was its prestige as the language of education since, with the introduction of compulsory schooling in 1882–7, no account whatever was taken of Breton – on the contrary, compulsory schooling fostered the distinctly centralising ideology of French statehood. Breton had its firmest hold among the least educated classes in remote rural areas, a fact which made for long-term difficulties in developing a unified literary language suited to the demands of modern life. Efforts were often concentrated exclusively on replacing the innumerable French loanwords by Breton neologisms, without paying due attention to the actual facts of language use.

BEYOND CHURCH AND STATE: MODERN BRETON LITERATURE

The first printeries were set up in Brittany as early as 1484–5. A major role in the Breton literature of the early modern age was played by edifying religious texts, including religious dramas about the life of Saints Barbara (*Buhez santez Barba*, 1557) and Catherine (*Buhez an itron sanctes Cathell*, 1576), the eschatological poem *Mirouer de la Mort* (The Mirror of Death), a catechism (*Doctrin an Christenien*) and collections of traditional Christmas carols (*Nouelou ancien ha devot*, 1650) and canticles (*Cantiquou spirituel*, 1642).[5] The burlesque *Amourousted eun den coz* (An Old Man's Loves) offers a rare example of a Breton comedy from the seventeenth century.[6]

Sacré Collège de Jésus, by the Jesuit Julien Maunoir, printed in Quimper in 1659, is a catechism with glossary and grammar written in Breton, and marks the beginnings of the modern Breton period.[7] The difference between Modern and Middle Breton is found less in the linguistic structure and more in a reform of the orthography, which left out many letters that were no longer pronounced and took full account of the grammatically determined changes at the beginnings of words, which are characteristic of the modern Celtic languages. The practical needs of reciprocal comprehension between Breton and French were served by bilingual vocabularies and phrasebooks, called *Colloques*. The Benedictine Dom Louis le Pelletier (1663 1733) compiled an etymological dictionary of the Breton language, which appeared in Paris in 1752.

In France in 1703 the Cistercian Paul Pézron had popularised the idea of Celtic language unity and the venerable age of Breton culture, in his book *Antiquité de la Nation et de la Langue des Celtes autrement appelés Gaulois*. At the end of the eighteenth century the growing enthusiasm for all things Celtic received new impetus from Napoleon's interest in James Macpherson's Ossianic poetry, and led to the founding of the Paris Académie celtique in 1805.[8] One of its most outstanding members was Jean-François Le Gonidec (1775–1835) who, in his Breton grammar (1807) and his Breton-French dictionary (1821), endeavoured to build a unified Breton literary language on the basis of the dialect of Léon. With the support of the Welsh antiquary and Anglican clergyman Thomas Price (Carnhuanawc, 1787–1848), Le Gonidec also produced a complete translation of the Bible, which was not published until 1866, after his death. His most eminent pupil was Théodor Hersart de la Villemarqué (1815–95), whose monumental bilingual *Barzaz Breiz* (The Poetry of Brittany) first called the attention of an audience with a literary education to Breton ballads, songs and hymns, which until then had formed a predominantly oral tradition (see Gourvil 1960 and Laurent 1989). The schoolteacher, journalist and archivist François-Marie Luzel (1821–95) published extensive collections of folk literature, including the bilingual compilations of Breton folk songs entitled *Gwerziou Breiz-Izel* (1868–74) and *Soniou Breiz-Izel* (1890), as well as a collection of Breton tales in French translation *Contes populaires de Basse-Bretagne* (1887).

The first Breton prose narratives with pretensions to literary merit also originated in the nineteenth century, and included the historical novel by Abbot Alain-Marie Inisan (1826–91), *Emgann Kergidu ha traou-all c'hoarvezet e Breiz-Izel epad dispac'h 1793* (The Battle of Kergidu and other Events in Lower Brittany during the Revolution of 1793, published 1877–8). Periodicals such as *Feiz ha Breiz* (Faith and Brittany, 1865–1944) and *Dihunamb!* (Let Us Awake! 1905–44) played an important part in the development of literary prose. François Vallée (1860–1949), who published the influential and oft-reprinted primer *La Langue bretonne en quarante leçons* in 1909, became the champion of a unified literary language based on the dialects of Léon, Trégor and Cornouaille. Jean-Pierre Calloc'h (1888–1917) was one of the most important lyric poets of the new century, while Tanguy Malmanche (1875–1953) made his name principally as a playwright.[9]

Harking back to Brittany's Celtic heritage acquired literary significance when Roparz Hémon (Louis-Paul Némo, 1900–78) founded the journal *Gwalarn* (North-West) in 1925. Translations from the Irish, by Hémon himself, and from Welsh, by his comrade-in-arms François Eliès (Abeozen, 1896–1963), were important here. Anglo-Irish, English and ancient Greek works were translated by the journalist Youenn Drézen (1899–1972) who, like the prose-writer Jakez Riou (1899–1939) and the writers mentioned above, also wrote his own novels and stories. In the years 1940–4 the Breton nationalists, under the protection of the German occupation, took their activities in educational and cultural policy to lengths previously unknown, but these came to an abrupt end with the military defeat of Germany. In 1978 Roparz Hémon died in exile in Ireland. As early as about 1930 in his poem *Pirc'hirin ar mor* (Sea Pilgrim), he had written:

Petra 'ra dit ar vro-se? Mor ha koad
A gavi forzh pelec'h. An dud? Dre-holl
Ez eus tud vat ha fall. Da gerent? Siwazh,
Gouzout a rez o deus evit da labour
Goaperezh ha dismegañs ha kasoni.
Ha sed ez out un estren 'barzh da vro![10]

What is this land to you?
Sea and forest
you can find anywhere.
The people? Everywhere
there are good people and bad.
Your parents? Alas,
you know they look upon your work
with scorn, disdain and loathing,
making you a foreigner
in your own country!

CHAPTER 24

The Celtic-Speaking Peoples from 1945 to the Present

CELTIC COUNTRIES? THE PROBLEM OF DEFINITION

In 1941 the American film-director John Ford filmed the popular novel *How Green was my Valley*, by the Anglo-Welsh writer Richard Llewellyn (Richard Llewellyn Lloyd, 1906–83), in California. When a critic pointed out that Ford had Llewellyn's Welsh miners dancing Irish jigs in his film, the director replied, 'It's a Celtic country, isn't it?' (Berry 1994, 161). This was far from being an insensitive outsider's observation since Ford, who was born Sean Aloysius O'Fearna in 1895, was of Irish extraction and six years previously had filmed Liam O'Flaherty's novel *The Informer*.

That Ireland, Scotland, Wales and Brittany are seen today by many of their inhabitants, as well as many travellers, as 'Celtic' countries is plain. The question of what, exactly, is still 'Celtic' about them today deserves closer consideration, since once-evident features of the political, social, judicial and ecclesiastical order have almost completely disappeared, and supposedly ancient 'Celtic' customs mostly turn out, on closer inspection, to be relatively new and often of primarily commercial origin. Where modern crafts resurrect 'Celtic' forms, or claim to do so, this usually means the modernisation or adaptation of La Tène style, which often has virtually nothing to do with the traditional native craft of the region in question.

Besides the lack of obvious differences between the Celtic-speaking regions and neighbouring regions, there is the inner disunity of the Celtic regions themselves, resulting from different historical preconditions. Ireland, for example, was exposed to large-scale colonial occupation in the early modern age, largely by virtue of being an island, while Wales had by this time aligned itself to a large extent with its immediate neighbour England. Another important factor in the different development of the Celtic-speaking regions was the Reformation, whose effects left a decisive mark on Wales and Scotland but not on Ireland or Brittany. Closely connected with the resulting religious differences are the economic contrasts that characterise, in particular, the continuing conflict between Catholics and Protestants in Northern Ireland.

If, despite these profound differences, Ireland, Scotland, Wales and Brittany may all be termed 'Celtic', this is due less to the overarching heritage of their shared cultural past than to the effectiveness of modern Celtic ideologies, which have rendered the adjective 'Celtic' so nebulous and enigmatic in the minds of many people that it may be filled with virtually any content. It can be argued that the causes of today's political and commercial manipulation of the Celts and their culture lie in the very vagueness of the modern concept, in an inadequate historical awareness and the widespread ignorance of Celtic languages. Objectively speaking, however, it is precisely the historically related Celtic languages that form the most prominent shared feature of the so-called Celtic lands and it is no accident that current efforts to preserve the Celtic heritage in these regions are concentrated on the languages.

ADJUSTMENT AND RESISTANCE: THE CELTIC LANGUAGES TODAY

At the beginning of the twentieth century the situation of the surviving Celtic languages, like the culture of the regions in question, varied greatly. Thanks to the iron ore and coal deposits, Welsh had weathered the economic transformations of the nineteenth century relatively unscathed, while the decimation of the Irish population by famine and emigration had greatly reduced the use of Irish. Wales also possessed a written language which had country-wide recognition, thanks to the translation of the Bible while Irish, like Breton, was still characterised by a great variety of regional dialects. These differences notwithstanding, the surviving Celtic tongues are all spoken today by minorities who constantly have to defend themselves against the overwhelming influence of English and French.[1] The oft-heard metaphor of the imminent 'extinction' of the Celtic languages might create the impression that their survival, like that of endangered plants and animals, can be ensured by a package of appropriate measures. Recent decades have shown, however, that such measures do not always bring the desired results. It is a feature of all the surviving Celtic tongues that most Irish, Welsh, Scots and Bretons today have no knowledge of them. Many others have only a limited knowledge, with the result that the use of the language has become restricted to certain contexts and topics, or to the purely oral domain. Of crucial importance is the fact that all Celtic speakers have some competence either as speakers and writers of English, in addition to Irish, Scots Gaelic and Welsh, or of French in addition to Breton. At a superficial level, the linguistic influence is apparent in the vocabulary of the Celtic tongues, since many areas of modern life are reflected in the use of foreign words and loan-translations, while many technical terms from the fields of law, poetry or traditional crafts, for example, are no longer familiar to many speakers. The influence of English and French is even more profound on the structure of the Celtic languages, which now display a large number of originally alien constructions and have also lost much of their ancient stock of idiom. In spite of all this, the Celtic languages are now enjoying a notable renaissance, which may be attributed partly to changed political configurations and partly to a nostalgia for the pre-industrial regional cultures of Europe.

NATIONALISM, REGIONALISM, FEDERALISM: POLITICAL DEVELOPMENTS

Whereas until the mid-twentieth century most of the Celtic-speaking regions were noted for some degree of economic backwardness, in the first decades following the end of World War II a wave of modernisation and rationalisation took hold. In Brittany a *Comité d'étude et de liaison des intérêts bretons* was set up as early as 1951 and it oversaw a renewal of electricity and water supply, as well as the organisation of agriculture along entrepreneurial lines. Extensive reparcelling of agricultural land has changed the face of the landscape, while the establishment of major industries has led to increased urbanisation of the whole region.[2] Scotland's Gaelic-speaking regions have also undergone far-reaching changes. There the Highlands and Islands Development Board, founded in 1965, has endeavoured to raise the standard of living and check further emigration to the urban centres by means of state subsidies for agriculture, improved electricity supply and the promotion of tourism. The constant companion of economic modernisation has been a marked increase in road and rail traffic, illustrated in Brittany by the introduction of the Atlantic Express (TGV) in 1989 and a little later in Scotland by the construction of a road bridge to the Isle of Skye.

Owing to the accelerated increase in the English- and French-speaking populations, loss of traditional village community life and the dominance of English and French in education and communications, these centrally administered measures at first had overwhelmingly adverse effects for the survival of the Celtic languages. Since economic change could be neither halted nor reversed, redoubled efforts were made to support the Celtic languages, above all by increased use in the mass media and the state schools. The highest level of state support went to the Irish language, which won an important part in public life in 1922 when the Irish Free State was founded, and again in 1949 when Ireland left the Commonwealth and became an independent republic. Breton received far less state backing, and only in 1985 was it able to find a firm place in the state school curriculum, with the founding of a national committee for regional languages and cultures. In Scotland, Gaelic, which had been banned from the education system in 1872, was at last reintroduced in 1958 and since 1979, with the establishment of *Radio nan Eilean* in Stornoway on the island of Lewis, has maintained a presence in broadcasting. Sabhal Mòr Ostaig, on the Sleat peninsula on the Isle of Skye, where regular language courses had been conducted in an adapted farmhouse since the 1960s, developed into a centre for the study and promotion of Scots Gaelic. In 1996 a Gaelic-language theatre company was formed here and in 1997 the Iomairt Chaluim Chille project came into being, to promote closer co-operation between Scotland and Ireland in educational and cultural policy (see F. Macintosh in Black et al. 1999, I, 461 note 7 and 465 note 10). Over recent decades the position of Welsh, which entered the school curriculum in 1947 and in 1982 established itself firmly in television with the founding of Sianel Pedwar Cymru

(Channel Four Wales), has visibly improved. Extensive activities in culture and cultural politics are closely connected with the integration of Welsh into the media and the education system. These include the publication of a comprehensive national biographical guide (*Y Bywgraffiadur Cymreig hyd* 1940, published 1953), the founding of the Welsh association of writers Yr Academi Gymreig (1959, with an English-speaking section since 1968), the establishment of the Welsh Arts Council (1969) and the creation of a Centre for Advanced Welsh and Celtic Studies in close proximity to the National Library of Wales in Aberystwyth (1985).

Beyond all doubt, among the most important events of the recent past in this field was the Labour Party's electoral victory in May 1997, after which the leadership intensified the search for a political solution to the conflict in Northern Ireland, and also set about dismantling centralism and reinforcing federative structures. In two referenda in autumn 1997, a majority of the populations of Wales and Scotland declared themselves in favour of devolution, and in the spring and summer of 1999 the Welsh Assembly and Scottish Parliament were ceremonially inaugurated in Cardiff and Edinburgh respectively. In summer 1999 even a solution to the Northern Irish problem seemed to have moved within reach, although the formation of a combined government of Catholics and Protestants foundered on the refusal of the Irish Republican Army to decommission its weapons in advance. Negotiations lasting some months led in mid-November 1999 to a renewed rapprochement of the opposing sides, reawakening hopes, at the start of the Third Millennium, for a speedy settlement to the disastrous conflict which began with the colonisation of Ireland nearly 500 years earlier.

Looking Back, Looking Forward: The Celts and Europe

With this survey of the most recent political, social and cultural developments in the regions which remain Celtic-speaking today, this history of the Celtic peoples comes to its conclusion. Having arrived at this point, the reader is invited to look back and reflect once more with the author on the problems of the modern term 'Celtic'.

If we compare present-day use of the term 'Celtic' with that of the term 'Germanic', we can immediately see a number of striking similarities. Both names come originally from Graeco-Roman ethnography and originally served to denote an ethnic group that was never precisely defined. Both were transferred to linguistic, archaeological and historical phenomena in the modern period, although the justice of this transfer and the precise meaning of the terms in the areas of archaeology and history are disputed to this day. Since the age of humanism, both have helped the peoples of central and western Europe to define their own identity and mark them off from their neighbours. With regard to the Celts, in Ireland, Scotland, Wales and Brittany, the term denoted primarily the survival of the Celtic languages, while in France it meant above all the history and culture of the regions before they were Romanised. In the German-speaking world, since the early nineteenth century, the term 'Germanic' has been invoked almost exclusively to establish the national identity. However, the resulting glorification of the Germanic race has had a critical reception since the end of World War II, in consequence of the perversion of this by National Socialism, and the corresponding body of thought meets with widespread disapproval today. In striking contrast to this, outside the professional milieu, any critical discussion of the term 'Celtic' and its problems has so far remained in its infancy, with the result that uninformed non-partisanship, naïveté and ideological blindness still flow easily into one another.

The serious differences between the history and emotional connotations of the terms 'Celtic' and 'Germanic' are perhaps best illustrated by the fact that 'Celtic' is possible, and to a degree even positive, in many collocations where 'Germanic' would seem unusual or even ideologically suspect. While stories of a journey through 'Celtic' Ireland might conjure up nothing more than images of a rural idyll, remarks about a journey to 'Germanic' Norway would inevitably call forth memories of occupation and oppression. Whereas one could count on approval and understanding when referring to Irish, Scottish and Breton songs as 'Celtic music', advertising a concert of Danish and German melodies as a concert of 'Germanic music' would probably produce incomprehension, if not outright indignation.

From an academic point of view, however, it must be emphasised that 'Celtic' songs are something quite different from 'Celtic' languages. If Irish, Gaelic and Breton stand in one unbroken line from the Old Celtic recorded in inscriptions, just as Danish and German derive from proto-Germanic, the traditional music of Ireland, Scotland and Brittany cannot even be traced back to the Middle Ages, let alone to any common origin. The same applies to the concept of 'Celtic' religion or 'Celtic' Christianity, which may be justified as conventional collective terms for religious phenomena in Celtic-speaking countries, but in no sense demonstrate the continuity or unity of these phenomena. It is precisely this crucial fact that is all too often overlooked. In particular, popular accounts of 'Celtic' religion often place sculptures and inscriptions from Roman Gaul side by side with specimens of literature from medieval Ireland, giving no thought to the logic of this procedure. Moreover, consideration is usually given only to a small selection of the most accessible and meaningful samples and these, being products of either Romanisation or Christianisation, say practically nothing about the religious situation in pre-Roman central Europe. Things are little different in the case of popular works and anthologies of 'Celtic' Christianity, which not only place prayers and hymns from the ninth and nineteenth centuries side by side, with no thought to their historical contexts, but also overlook some of the less fashionable aspects of the early 'Celtic' churches such as their harsh regime of penance (see D. E. Meek in Brown, T. 1996, 143–57 and Meek 2000).

The present inflationary trend in the use of the adjective 'Celtic' is therefore due firstly to a deliberately selective viewpoint, and secondly to widespread ignorance of the historical premises underlying the modern term 'Celtic', and of the Celtic languages and literatures. Whereas in antiquity the Celts were primarily the focus of collective fears, today they appear as an ideal screen on which to project individual and collective yearnings. Whereas in the political ideologies of the nineteenth and twentieth centuries they were enlisted for the glorification of national histories, with the decline of nationalism and the rejection of the Third Reich's celebration of things Germanic, the idea of Celtic culture as the secret cradle of the West has gained ground. In 1980 an international exhibition held in Steyr in Upper Austria called the Hallstatt culture 'an early form of European unity'. In 1990 a poster for the Celtic exhibition in Venice, the most lavish yet held, bore the slogan 'I Celti – la prima Europa', and in 1993 an exhibition by the Munich Prehistoric Collection (Prähistorische Staatssammlung) in Rosenheim, Bavaria, declared without hesitation the first millennium BC 'the Celtic millennium'. Typically enough, the patron of the exhibition, the Bavarian premier, felt that Celtic culture gave 'cause for pleasant contemplation' and declared that 'large parts of Europe were united by their Celtic background'. It was no accident that the reader of the exhibition catalogue learned, a few years before the introduction of the Euro, that the Celts even had a single currency. Their cultural space, however, 'though highly unified, in important ways made room for many tribes and all the individual forms of their shared legacy' (M. Streibl in Dannheimer and Gebhard 1993, XI). The fundamental meaning of the Celts for Europe, as implied here, is in striking contrast not only to the nationalist Celtic ideologies of the modern age, but also to the meaninglessness of the concepts of 'Celt' and 'Celtic' throughout the Middle Ages and to the classical view of the Celts as barbarians from the borderlands. At this point, therefore, the objective contribution of the Celts to European culture as well as their subjective role in the minds of their neighbours needs to be considered more closely.

La Tène art may be seen, with some justification, as the first significant Celtic contribution to western culture. Products of this art, characterised by an original blend of discrete cultural influences and a high level of technical skill, achieved an aesthetic effect that even today has the power to draw the observer under its spell. Typically, however, the existence of autonomous and highly developed crafts north of the Alps lay so far outside the mental horizons of the Greeks and Romans that in all of classical literature there is not one word about it. The ethnographers of antiquity evinced much more interest in the view of the Celts as an ancient peripheral people who had remained on a cultural level long since left behind everywhere else. At one end of the spectrum stand perceptions of the primeval brutality of the Celts, as expressed in numerous references to cruel and bloodthirsty sacrificial rites and in the constantly recurring charge of cannibalism. At the other, there is no shortage of examples of idealisation of the Celts who, in line with classical theories about allegedly cultureless marginal races, supposedly stood closer to an original golden age of humanity. In either case, we can plainly discern a tendency to present the Celts as 'the other' and their culture as the opposite to that of the writers.

In the Middle Ages the Celtic cultures influenced the history of Europe firstly by the Irish mission to the Anglo-Saxons and to the European mainland, and secondly by transmitting the Welsh and British Arthurian legends to the courtly poets of England, France and Germany. Here it should be noted, however, that in the Middle Ages the Irish, Scots, Welsh and Bretons did not perceive themselves to be 'Celts' and were not seen as such by their neighbours. This apart, the spiritual content which the Irish, Welsh, Scots and Bretons communicated to western culture can be termed 'Celtic' only in a narrowly circumscribed sense, even from the standpoint of today. In the case of the Irish mission the content was based on traditional Christianity, which was generally transmitted through the medium of Latin, and in the case of the re-working of Celtic material and motifs in courtly literature, *matière de Bretagne* underwent such a radical transformation at the hands of the courtly poets that the underlying Welsh and Breton tales can at best be seen as raw material.

At the beginning of the history of the Celtic image in the modern era stands the rediscovery of the classical accounts, as a result of closer study of Greek and Latin literature, along with insights into the connections linking the surviving insular Celtic languages with one another and with ancient continental Celtic. Here the reliance of writers of the modern era on the Greek and Roman ethnographers shows plainly in the fact that once again the Celts are mostly depicted as 'the other' and their culture as the antithesis of the civilisation of classical antiquity and the Christian West. The raptures that greeted not only James Macpherson's Ossian poems and the writers of the Celtic Twilight in the eighteenth and nineteenth centuries, but also the endless speculations of the early antiquaries concerning Celtic dolmens and menhirs, are symptomatic of the coexistence of uncritical enthusiasm for the Celts and profound ignorance of the surviving Celtic languages and literatures.

The beginnings of a change in the Celtic image came in the early nineteenth century with progress in comparative linguistics, Celtic philology and modern archaeology. But here the fact that the speakers of the surviving Celtic languages no longer possessed any autonomous political structures, and that state education, economic prosperity and social progress were inseparably linked with the use, or at least a knowledge, of English or French, had disastrous effects. Since none of the Celtic tongues had achieved the status of a national language, language of education or *lingua franca*, only a small minority outside the so-called Celtic regions were aware of them. Similarly the individual Celtic literatures are largely unknown outside their respective countries of origin. Whether the Celtic languages can assert themselves in future remains to be seen. Be that as it may, the study of them opens the door to a culture which has troubled, fascinated and repeatedly enriched western civilisation from prehistoric times to the present.

Notes

INTRODUCTION

1. For accounts of the Celts in the classics, see G. Dobesch in Moscati et al. 1991, 35–41; B. Kremer and R. Urban in Dannheimer and Gebhard 1993, 15–22; H. D. Rankin in Green 1995, 21–33. The earliest Greek sources are treated fully in Freeman 1996.
2. See Malitz 1983. On the relationship between tradition and innovation in Posidonius's account see also Dobesch 1995 and Maier 1996a.
3. The relationship between Posidonius's and Caesar's descriptions of the Celts is discussed in Tierney 1960 (with the relevant Greek and Latin texts and an English translation) and Nash 1976. On the perception of the Celts in the classics in general see also Kremer 1994 and Jantz 1995.
4. Recent surveys of the present state of research into the Celtic languages may be found in MacAulay 1992 and Ball and Fife 1993. See also Russell 1995 and Price 2000. On the early history of the study of the Celtic languages see Davis 1999.
5. On the archaeological term and the present state of research into archaeological sources see K. Bittel and F. Fischer in Bittel et al. 1981, 15–76; L. Kruta Poppi in Moscati et al. 1991, 42–50; G. Ruiz Zapatero in Almagro-Gorbea and Ruiz Zapatero 1993, 23–62; Fitzpatrick 1996 and T. C. Champion in Brown, T. 1996, 61–78.
6. On the ethnic origins of the Celts see L. Pauli 1980, 16–24, Fischer 1986 and Schmidt 1992.
7. On the problem of the anthropological classification of the present-day speakers of Celtic languages see Bodmer 1992.
8. On George Buchanan see J. Collis in Black et al. 1999, I, 91–107. Recent clarification of the problem of the modern term and the way it combines the perspectives of classical literature, modern linguistics and archaeology may be found in the ethnological study by Chapman 1992, the contributions in Brown, T. 1996 and the surveys of the current debate by Collis 1996, Evans, D. E. 1997, Sims-Williams 1998b and James, S. 1999. See also D. E. Evans and R. and V. Megaw in Black et al. 1999, I, 1–18 and 19–81, and Wells 2001. On the emergence and the history of a Celtic ideology in the modern age and the exploitation of this for political purposes see Dubois 1972, Viallaneix and Ehrard 1982, Asher 1993, Dietler 1994 and Maissen 1994.

9. See Wagner 1959, 1982 and 1987. See also B. Maier in Black et al. 1999, I, 152–61 and the summary of arguments drawn from linguistic typology by O. Gensler in Black et al. 1999, I, 509–10.

CHAPTER 1

1. The most recent comprehensive study is Spindler 1996. Brief summaries of our knowledge of individual regions and sites are given in the contributions to Moscati et al. 1991, 75–123. A cross-section of recent research will be found in the collection by Brun and Chaume 1997. See also Rieckhoff and Biel 2001.
2. For recent surveys see Green 1992, 5–43, P. J. Reynolds in Green 1995, 176–209 and Spindler 1996, 300–15.
3. For recent surveys see H. Reim in Bittel et al. 1981, 204–27, Kimmig 1983b, several contributions in Green 1995, 285–341 and Spindler 1996, 201–64. See also H.-J. Hundt in *Keltenfürst* 1985, 107–15 (on textiles), Schaaff et al. 1987 and Vosteen 1999 (on wagon-building). See Schmidt 1983 on early Celtic craft terms which can be partially reconstructed from later sources with the aid of comparative linguistics.
4. See Spindler 1996, 43–91. On Celtic settlement patterns in general see Audouze and Büchsenschütz 1992.
5. See the surveys by E. Penninger, K. W. Zeller and L. Pauli in *Kelten* 1980, 150–93; also Zeller 1995 and Th. Stöllner in Jerem et al. 1996, 225–43.
6. For a first introduction see Fischer and Biel 1982; also O.-H. Frey in Moscati et al. 1991, 75–92. On the more recent debate concerning the problems of archaeological interpretation see also W. Kimmig, M. K. H. Eggert, F. Fischer and P. Brun in Brun and Chaume 1997, 13–16, 287–94, 295–302 and 321–30.
7. See the summary in Spindler 1996, 54–7 and 105–9 and the more extensive coverage in Joffroy 1979. On more recent research see R. Goguey and B. Chaume in Brun and Chaume 1997, 179–84 and 185–200.
8. See Bittel et al. 1981, 390–400. On more recent research see J. Biel in Brun and Chaume 1997, 17–22.
9. See the summary by Biel 1985 and several contributions to the exhibition catalogue *Keltenfürst* 1985, 33–45 and 79–134; also the thorough treatment of drinking ware from this grave in Krausse 1996.
10. See Biel 1985, 114–17, D. Krausse-Steinberger in *Hundert Meisterwerke* 1992, 111–14, and Mac Cana 1993.

CHAPTER 2

1. See A. Haffner in Moscati et al. 1991 and the essays in *Hundert Meisterwerke* 1992.
2. See Haffner 1976. On the Waldalgesheim burial see Joachim et al. 1995.
3. In addition to Jacobsthal 1944, see the more recent surveys by Megaw 1970, Duval, P.-M. 1977, Megaw and Megaw 1989 and Stead 1996. Brailsford 1975 and Duval, A. 1989 give extended treatment of selected artefacts from the British Museum and the Musée des antiquités nationales. See Eluère 1987 on goldsmithery.

4. See Eluère 1987 and the contributions by R. Cordie-Hackenberg and H.-E. Joachim in *Hundert Meisterwerke* 1992, 171–91.
5. See Megaw 1970, no. 84, *Kelten* 1980, 282–4, Eluère 1987, 168–9 and the reflections in Fischer 1992 on how these finds should be interpreted.
6. The wide-ranging hypotheses of Jean-Jacques Hatt (in *Kelten* 1980, 52–75, for example) lack a sound basis and are unanimously dismissed by specialists. Maier 1999a offers an attempt to combine pre-Roman pictures of bulls with the evidence of medieval literature and anthropology of the modern period.
7. See Joachim 1989; on the symbolism of the leaf-crown see O.-H. Frey in Dannheimer and Gebhard 1993, 155.

CHAPTER 3

1. On Celtic mercenaries see M. Szabó in Moscati et al. 1991, 333–6.
2. On the Scordisci see B. Jovanović and P. Popović in Moscati et al. 1991, 337–47.
3. For more detail see Maier 1996a.
4. The historical and ideological background to the *Astérix* comic books is treated at length in Stoll 1974.
5. See K. W. Zeller in *Kelten* 1980, 111–32, Brunaux and Lambot 1987, A. Rapin in Moscati et al. 1991, 321–31 and J. N. G. and W. F. Ritchie in Green 1995, 37–58.
6. For more detail see Pleiner 1993.
7. See A. Furger-Gunti in Moscati et al. 1991, 356–9, B. Raftery in Tristram 1993, 173–91, Müller 1995, B. Cunliffe in Raftery et al. 1995, 31–9 and Mallory 1998.
8. See Peschel 1989 and the reflections on the military system and social structure by G. Dobesch in Jerem et al. 1996, 13–71.
9. Shown in Allen 1980, plate 22, no. 317, Nash 1987, plate 2, no. 7 and Moscati et al. 1991, 322.
10. Shown in *Kelten* 1980, 244 and Moscati et al. 1991, 136.
11. See Brunaux in Haffner 1995, 66–74, Brunaux in Verger 2000, 231–51 and M. Poux in Verger 2000, 305–35.
12. See F. Müller in Dannheimer and Gebhard 1993, 182 and fig. 147.
13. See S. Bauer and H.-P. Kuhnen in Haffner 1995, 51–4.
14. See F. Müller in Dannheimer and Gebhard 1993, 184–5.
15. See P. Drda et al. in Brunaux 1991, 199–202 and K. Motyková et al. in Moscati et al. 1991, 180–1.
16. See J.-L. Brunaux in Haffner 1995, 55–74, Brunaux 1996 and the contributions to Brunaux 1991.

CHAPTER 4

1. See F. Maier in Moscati et al. 1991, 411–24, J. Collis in Green 1995, 159–75, P. S. Wells in Arnold and Gibson 1995, 88–95 and O. Büchsenschütz in Jerem et al. 1996, 297–306. Extensive coverage is given in Collis 1984 and Audouze and Büchsenschütz 1992.

2. On Celtic fortifications see I. Ralston in Green 1995, 59–81.
3. Recent introductions to Celtic coinage will be found in Allen 1980, Overbeck 1980, Nash 1987, Gruel 1989. Summaries may be found in H. J. Kellner in Moscati et al. 1991, 451–9, B. Ziegaus in Dannheimer and Gebhard 1993, 220–7 and D. Nash Briggs in Green 1995, 244–53.
4. See Duval, P.-M. 1987 and Duval, P.-M. 1989, I, 339–90 and 623–88.
5. See J.-P. Guillaumet in Moscati et al. 1991, 519, and extensive treatment in Goudineau and Peyre 1993.
6. See K. Motyková in Green 1995, 542–3.
7. See summaries by F. Maier in Moscati et al. 1991, 530–1, W. Krämer and R. Gebhard in Dannheimer and Gebhard 1993, 107–19 and S. Sievers in Jerem et al. 1996, 321–34. Thorough documentation of the archaeological investigations has appeared since 1970 in the series *Die Ausgrabungen in Manching* [The Manching Excavations].
8. On both artefacts see Dannheimer and Gebhard 1993, 341.
9. See Goudineau and Peyre 1993, 90–3 and Haffner 1995, 37.
10. On the present state of knowledge see Büchsenschütz and Olivier 1990, Reichenberger 1993, G. Wieland in Haffner 1995, 85–99 and the contributions to Wieland 1999.
11. See Planck 1982. For a brief survey of the hoards and findings see *Keltenfürst* 1985, 341–54.
12. The best survey of the archaeological and literary sources and of the history of research in the modern age is in Piggott 1968. On the development of perceptions of the Druids in the modern age see Jones, L. E. 1998 and the richly illustrated account in Green 1997. The picture of the Druids in English literature of the sixteenth to eighteenth centuries is treated in Owen, A. L. 1962.
13. An overview of the current state of research into Gaulish inscriptions is given in Lambert 1994. The inscriptions in Greek characters are fully collected in Lejeune 1985.
14. See the annotated translation of this passage in Malitz 1983, 178.
15. Appian, *Celtica* 12, translated with commentary in Malitz 1983, 177.
16. On the Celtic culture of southern Gaul, early Roman influences and later development under Roman rule, see Rivet 1988 and Py 1993.
17. See the annotated translation of both passages in Malitz 1983, 187–8 and 193–5.
18. It is contained in this extended quotation provided by Athenaeus of Naucratis (151E–152D), greatly abridged in Diodorus Siculus (*Historical Library* 5, 28, 4). See the annotated translation in Malitz 1983, 188–9.
19. See the annotated translation in Malitz 1983, 186.
20. Caesar's campaigns in Gaul are treated at length in Goudineau 1990 and Jiménez 1996.
21. Vercingetorix as a historical figure and as the focus of ideologies in the modern period is treated in the exhibition catalogue *Vercingetorix* 1994 and Martin 2001. See also Duval, P.-M. 1989, I, 163–76 and A. Ehrard and Ch. Amalvi in Viallaneix and Ehrard 1982, 307–17 and 349–55.

CHAPTER 5

1. See A. Tovar in Schmidt 1986, 68–101, M. Almagro-Gorbea in Moscati et al. 1991, 389–405 and the contributions in Almagro-Gorbea and Ruiz Zapatero 1993.
2. See the extensively annotated bilingual edition by Schulten 1955.
3. A comprehensive and thoroughly annotated collection of Celtiberian inscriptions will be found in Untermann 1997, enriched by the dictionary of Wodtko 2000. An introduction to the present state of knowledge of the Celtiberian language is given in Jordán Cólera 1998.

CHAPTER 6

1. On the Golasecca culture see R. C. De Marinis in Moscati et al. 1991, 93–102, and Pauli 1992. On the Celts of Italy in general see D. Vitali in Moscati et al. 1991, 220–35, O.-H. Frey in Green 1995, 515–32 and Frey 1996, and D. Vitali in Verger 2000, 207–21.
2. On the process of Romanisation of northern Italy see the extensive treatment in Chevallier 1983.
3. For detailed treatment see Lejeune 1988, Solinas 1995 and Uhlich 1999.

CHAPTER 7

1. A pioneering study of the history of the Galatians of Asia Minor is given by Stähelin 1907. More recent thorough surveys will be found in Mitchell 1993 and Strobel 1996.
2. On Old Celtic personal names in general see the seminal work by Schmidt 1957 and Evans, D. E. 1967. A register of Galatian personal names is given in Stähelin 1907, 109–20.
3. On the ancients' perceptions of the Celts, see B. Andreae in Moscati et al. 1991, 61–9. The view of the Galatians in the art of Pergamum is treated at length in Künzl 1971.
4. For a colour illustration and interpretation of the group of figures see the article by B. Andreae in Moscati et al. 1991, 61–2.
5. See B. Andreae in Moscati et al. 1991, 61–3 (with illustration).
6. See B. Overbeck in Dannheimer and Gebhard 1993, 228–31 (with illustrations).

CHAPTER 8

1. On the history and culture of Roman Gaul see the surveys by Duval, P.-M. 1988, Coulon 1990 and King 1990.

2. Good general surveys are given in Duval, P.-M. 1976 and Deyts 1992. See also the relevant articles on Gallo-Roman religion in Maier 1997.

3. See Maier 1997, 158 for a summary with further references; also Duval, P.-M. 1989, I, 401–20. A detailed, regionally defined assessment of the coexistence of Roman and Gallo-Roman deities is offered by Gschaid 1994.

4. See Maier 1997, 16, 25, 32 and 190–1; also B. Maier in Zimmer et al. 1999, 121–5.

5. On the Gundestrup cauldron, thought to have been made in the Balkans in the second or first century BC, see the summary in Maier 1997, 138.

6. See Maier 1997, 19, 112–3, 196 and 224. On the Euffigneix figurine see also Duval, A. 1989, 126–7.

CHAPTER 9

1. A comprehensive compilation of classical references to Ireland and Britain in English translation, with references to further reading, is given in Rivet and Smith 1979, 37–102.

2. See the survey of hoards and the problems of interpretation in Raftery 1994, 200–19.

3. For a survey of the finds and the sites and an introduction to the extensive literature, see articles by various authors in Moscati et al. 1991, 555–617 and Green 1995, 623–700.

4. See B. Cunliffe in Moscati et al. 1991, 581–6; also I. Ralston in Green 1995, 59–81, with bibliography.

5. See I. M. Stead in Moscati et al. 1991, 587–95, Raftery 1994, 188–99 and G. A. Wait in Green 1995, 489–511 with bibliography.

6. See A. King and G. Soffe in *Sanctuaires* 1994, 33–48 and Haffner 1995, 22–3.

7. See C. J. Lyon, B. Raftery and B. Wailes in Moscati et al. 1991, 610–15 and Raftery 1994, 64–81.

8. See R. B. Warner in Moscati et al. 1991, 617 and Raftery 1994, 183–4.

9. On Latin loanwords in early Irish see the detailed treatment by D. MacManus in Ní Chatháin and Richter 1984, 179–96.

10. On the regional forms of English in the formerly Celtic-speaking areas see the collection by Tristram 1997.

CHAPTER 10

1. For a general history of Ireland see the nine-volume series *A New History of Ireland* (Cosgrove 1987, Moody et al. 1976, Moody and Vaughan 1986 and Vaughan 1989 and 1996; in progress). There are recent monographs by Foster 1989 and Lydon 1998. A concise reference work is Connolly 1998. A survey of the cultural and geographical basis of Irish history is given in Aalen et al. 1997. On the medieval history of Ireland, see Mac Niocaill 1972, Nicholls 1972 and Ó Corráin 1972, from the series *The Gill History of Ireland*; also the one-volume synopses by Ó Cróinín 1995 and Charles-Edwards 2000. Much

illustrative material with informative text, from prehistory to the early modern age, is given in O'Brien and Harbison 1996.

2. A modern account is offered by Hanson, R. P. C. 1983. For an introduction to recent scholarship, see the articles and extensive bibliography in Dumville et al. 1993. An annotated collection of historical sources on early Christianity in Ireland (in English translation) is given in De Paor 1993. On the rise of legends in the medieval and modern periods, see the survey in Ó hÓgáin 1990, 355–61.

3. Both texts published and translated by Hanson and Blanc 1978.

4. Muirchú and Tírechán published and translated by Bieler 1979. *Vita Tripartita* published (without translation) by Mulchrone 1939.

5. See the accounts of the early Irish Church in Bieler 1961, Hughes, K. 1966 and Charles-Edwards 2000.

6. See Ó hÓgáin 1990, 60–4 and the ethnographic study by Ó Catháin 1995.

7. For an introduction to early medieval Irish art see the exhibition catalogue *Irische Kunst* 1983.

8. For an introduction to the extensive recent literature on the relation between oral and written culture in early medieval Ireland, see Richter 1994, J. Stevenson in Edel 1995, 11–22 and Mac Eoin 1998.

9. See McManus 1991; also Sims-Williams 1993, Ziegler 1994 and Swift 1997. On the use of the Ogam script in medieval stories, see P. Ní Chatháin in Ní Chatháin and Richter 1996, 212–16.

10. A comprehensive edition of Old Irish glosses with English translations is given by Stokes and Strachan 1901–3. See also E. G. Quin in Ní Chatháin and Richter 1984, 210–17 and A. Breen, R. Hofman and P.-Y. Lambert in Ní Chatháin and Richter 1996, 9–16, 173–86 and 187–94.

11. See the bilingual anthology by Greene and O'Connor 1967. See also D. Ó Corráin in Ó Corráin et al. 1989, 251–67, P. Sims-Williams in Brown, T. 1996, 97–124, and P. K. Ford in Black et al. 1999, I, 162–70.

12. See Hughes, K. 1972 and Mac Niocaill 1975. Note a recent edition of *The Annals of Ulster* with English translation by Mac Airt and Mac Niocaill 1983.

13. See Sharpe 1991 on the current state of research into Irish hagiography; also J.-M. Picard in Ní Chatháin and Richter 1996, 261–74. Kelly, F. 1976 gives a thoroughly annotated edition of *Audacht Morainn* with English translation. On the liturgical and hymnological texts see M. Schneiders and J. Stevenson in Ní Chatháin and Richter 1996, 76–98 and 99–135. An annotated selection of religious texts of various genres in English translation may be found in Carey 1998. On the authors' world-view and Biblical, classical and native Irish influences on this, see Smyth, M. 1996.

14. On the linguistically and metrically difficult *Amra Choluim Chille* see Henry 1978, 191–212 and M. Herbert in Ó Corráin et al. 1989, 67–75. Blathmac's poems with English translations are given in Carney 1964, and Mac Mathúna 1985 is a bilingual edition of *Immram Brain*. On *Navigatio Sancti Brendani* and vernacular versions of this see Zaenker 1987 and Strijbosch 1995. See also Carey 1999, McCone 2000, Strijbosch 2000 and Wooding 2000.

15. Irish text and this English translation as given in Greene and O'Connor 1967, 62 and 65. On Félire Oenguso see M. Schneiders in Edel 1995, 157–69 and P. Ó Riain in Poppe and Tristram 1999, 87–104.

16. The best introduction to early Irish law is Kelly, F. 1988. On *Senchas Már* see also Breatnach, L. 1996. For a diplomatic transcription of the most important Irish law texts see Binchy 1978.

17. *Collectio Canonum Hibernensis* (Wasserschleben 1885). See also M. P. Sheehy in Löwe 1982, 525–35 and L. M. Davies in Ní Chatháin and Richter 1996, 17–35. On the relation between canonic and indigenous law see G. Mac Niocaill and D. Ó Corráin in Ní Chatháin and Richter 1984, 151–6 and 157–66.

18. On the function of the king see Ó Corráin 1978, Wormald 1986 and Jaski 2000.

19. On agriculture, animal husbandry, hunting and fishing, from the evidence of the early law texts, see Kelly, F. 1997.

20. See Byrne 1971 and 1976. On political divisions and cultural unity in early medieval Ireland see Mac Cana 1985.

21. On the history of the establishment of kingship and the individual dynasties see Byrne 1973.

CHAPTER II

1. See Etchingham 1996. A survey of the current state of research will be found in the contributions to Clarke et al. 1998.

2. On reciprocal Norse-Irish cultural influences see Sigurdsson 1988 and B. Almqvist in Ní Chatháin and Richter 1996, 139–72.

3. A pioneering diplomatic edition was published by Best and Bergin in 1929. See also Ó Concheanainn 1996.

4. For a facsimile edition see Meyer 1909.

5. See the edition by Best et al. 1954–83.

6. A general introduction and extended précis of the content of the stories (then still mostly unpublished) is given in Thurneysen 1921. On the current state of research see the articles in Mallory and Stockman 1994.

7. See the bilingual editions of the story, which has reached us in several different versions, in O'Rahilly 1961 and 1967. On recent research see the articles in Mallory 1992 and Tristram 1993; see also C. J. Hyland in Poppe and Tristram 1999, 105–22.

8. On the term 'fairy mound' and the concept, see Sims-Williams 1990.

9. For bilingual texts see Gray 1982. On the interpretation of the text see also Gray 1980–3 and Carey 1989/90.

10. For bilingual texts see Gwynn 1903–35.

11. For an (unreliable) bilingual text see MacAlister 1938–41. On the structure and transmission of the text see Scowcroft 1987–8 and J. Carey in Edel 1995, 45–60.

12. On the Irish 'Peregrinatio' and its influence on the continent before 800 see A. Angenendt in Löwe 1982, 52–79. Bieler 1961 gives a general account of the Irish influence on the continent. An introduction to recent research will be found in Löwe 1982 and Ní Chatháin and Richter 1984, 1987 and 1996.

13. On Columbanus's mission to the Franks see K. Schäferdiek in Löwe 1982, 171–202. On the poetry attributed to Columbanus see P. C. Jacobsen and D. Schaller in Löwe 1982, 434–67 and 468–93. Columbanus's theology is treated by J. P. Mackey in Ní Chatháin and Richter 1996, 228–39.

14. On the Irish manuscript tradition at Reichenau and Saint Gall see J. Autenrieth and J. Duft in Löwe 1982, 903–15 and 916–37.
15. *Kilian* 1989 and A. Wendehorst in Löwe 1982, 319–29.
16. See H. Wolfram in Ní Chatháin and Richter 1987, 415–20. On the mission to the Slavs see H. Dopsch and J. Strzelczyk in Ní Chatháin and Richter 1987, 421–44 and 445–60.
17. On Irish participation in the spiritual life of the Carolingian empire, see the articles in Löwe 1982, 735–937.

CHAPTER 12

1. See Dolley 1972, Lydon 1984, the articles in Barry et al. 1995, and Duffy et al. 2001.
2. On the history of Ireland in the Tudor period see Ellis 1985 and Brady 1994.
3. On the history of Irish literature from the late twelfth century to the early seventeenth century see S. Mac Mathúna in Price 1992, 81–100.
4. Published and translated with extended commentary by MacNeill and Murphy 1908–54.
5. Published and translated by Peters 1967. See also Tristram 1989.
6. See Ó Tuama 1988. The importance of the ideal of courtly love in Irish literature of the modern period is covered in Ó Tuama 1960.
7. See Knott 1966, 49–84, Williams, J. E. C. 1971, Breatnach 1983 and Williams and Ford 1992, 153–92. See Knott 1957 for a selection of bardic poems with introduction, commentary and glossary.

CHAPTER 13

1. On the role of the Celts in the history and culture of Scotland see the synopses by Armit 1997, Roberts, J. L. 1997, Webster, B. 1997 and the articles in Cowan and McDonald 2001; also the reference works by Thomson, D. S. 1994, Newton 2000 and Lynch 2000.
2. On recent research into the history and culture of the Picts see Laing and Laing 1995, Sutherland, E. 1994 and Nicoll 1995.
3. See Fenton and Pálsson 1984, Crawford 1987 and Ritchie 1993. For a cross-section of recent research see Batey et al. 1993.
4. The accepted English name 'Hebrides' derives from a mistaken reading of the name *(H)ebudes* used in classical writing (including Pliny, *Natural History* 4, 103) (Rivet and Smith 1979, 354–5).
5. For the quotation see Withers 1984, 22. For elucidation of the historical context see G. W. S. Barrow in Gillies 1989, 67–88.
6. For the material which follows see McDonald, A. 1997.
7. On Irish missions to the Picts and Anglo-Saxons see D. A. Bullough and M. Richter in Löwe 1982, 80–98 and 120–37; also J. N. Hillgarth, J. Campbell, I.

Wood and M. Richter in Ní Chatháin and Richter 1987, 311–31, 332–6, 347–61 and 362–76.

8. For an introduction see Brown, P. 1980 and for an introduction to recent research O'Mahoney 1994 and Werner 1997.

9. See Cowan and Easson 1976 on the history and Fawcett 1985 on the architecture.

10. See Withers 1984 and 1988, Gillies 1989, D. MacAulay in MacAulay 1992, 137–248, W. Gillies in Ball and Fife 1993, 145–227 and various authors in Thomson, D. S. 1994, 89–115. See also Ó Dochartaigh 1994–7.

11. See M. Oftedal in Thomson, D. S. 1994, 98–9 and 155. Also Graham-Campbell and Batey 1998.

CHAPTER 14

1. A monograph by Davies, J. 1994 gives a survey of the whole of Welsh history. On the early medieval beginnings see Davies, W. 1982 and 1990 and Thomas, C. 1997.

2. On traditional Welsh law see the translation with detailed commentary by Jenkins, D. 1986 and the research report by Jenkins, D. 1997.

3. As quoted in Williams, I. M. 1996, 123.

4. On the beginnings of Christianity in Britain see Thomas, C. 1981 and Watts 1991.

5. A survey of the relevant hagiographic sources is given in Henken 1987. For a cross-section of recent research into the Church in early medieval Wales, see Edwards and Lane 1992. See also Davies, O. 1996.

6. On the historical David see Bowen, E. G. 1982. Evans, D. S. 1988 gives an extended commentary on the middle Welsh Life of the Saint.

7. On Gildas, his literary work and the historical background see Lapidge and Dumville 1984, Kerlouégan 1987 and Higham 1994. Winterbottom 1978 gives an English translation of his work.

8. On linguistic history, besides the classic account in Jackson 1953, see Bammesberger and Wollmann 1990 and the study in historical phonology by Schrijver 1995. On the problems of the inscriptions as historical sources see Thomas, C. 1994.

9. Williams, I. 1938 forms the basis for more recent research. See also the introduction and translation by Jackson 1970, the bilingual editions by Jarman 1988 and Koch 1997, the articles in Roberts, B. F. 1988 and the philological and linguistic study by Isaac 1996.

10. See Williams, I. and J. E. C. Williams 1968 and A. O. H. Jarman in Jarman and Hughes 1992, 51–67.

11. See the comprehensive study (with text and translation) by Rowland 1990.

12. See A. O. H. Jarman in Bromwich and Jones 1978, 326–49, also in Bromwich et al. 1991, 117–45.

13. See Watson and Fries 1988, Goodrich 1990 and Brugger-Hackett 1991.

CHAPTER 15

1. On Welsh history in the eleventh to fourteenth centuries see Davies, R. R. 1987 and Walker 1990.
2. For a detailed biography of Llywelyn see Smith, J. B. 1998.
3. English translation from Conran 1967, 130.
4. On Owain Glyndŵr see the detailed historical monograph by Davies, R. R. 1995, the lavishly illustrated popular account by Barber 1998 and the ethnographic study by Henken 1996.
5. See C. W. Lewis and D. M. Lloyd in Jarman and Hughes 1992, 123–56 and 157–88; also Williams, J. E. C. 1994 and 1997. A selection of religious verse with translation will be found in McKenna 1991.
6. For an anthology with commentary see Bowen, D. J. 1957. See also Huws 1998.
7. See the bilingual anthology by Bromwich 1982. Fulton 1996 constitutes a bilingual edition of works from the poet's circle which were previously attributed to him.
8. See the articles in Jarman and Hughes 1997, 126–313.
9. See D. S. Evans and J. E. C. Williams in Bowen, G. 1974, 245–73 and 312–408.
10. See B. F. Roberts in Bowen, G. 1974, 274–301.
11. See Watkin 1958 and Thomas, G. C. G. 1988; also R. Reck and E. Poppe in Poppe and Tristram 1999, 289–304 and 305–17.
12. See Bromwich 1978 for a detailed commentary and translation of the *Triads*.
13. Published by Williams, I. 1951 (following the *White Book*) and Mühlhausen 1988 (following the *Red Book*, with Welsh-German glossary for students). A German translation with detailed commentary is found in Maier 1999b. See also the contributions in Maier and Zimmer 2001.
14. Lacy 1991 is a thorough reference work for the whole field of Arthurian literature and its reception and research in the modern period. See also Schmolke-Hasselmann 1998 and Barron 1998.
15. See P. Sims-Williams in Bromwich et al. 1991, 33–71. For recent editions of the poems *Pa ŵr yw'r Porthor?* and *Preiddeu Annwfn*, see B. F. Roberts in Bromwich and Jones 1978, 296–309 and Haycock 1983/84.
16. See the detailed commentary in Bromwich and Evans 1992.
17. See the edition by Wright 1985, the English translation by Thorpe 1966 and the study by Curley 1994.
18. For an introduction to recent research see Topsfield 1981 and Maddox 1991.
19. See R. L. Thomson, I. Lovecy and R. Middleton in Bromwich et al. 1991, 159–69, 171–82 and 147–57. Recent editions of all three will be found in Thomson, R. L. 1968, Goetinck 1976 and Thomson, R. L. 1997.
20. See C. Lloyd-Morgan in Bromwich et al. 1991, 183–208. The most recent edition of the text is Richards, M. 1948.
21. For the Tristan saga, see the bilingual anthology by Lacy 1998 and the articles in Crépin and Spiewok 1996.
22. See the extended treatment by Merriman 1973, Taylor and Brewer 1983, Thompson 1985 and Whitaker 1990.

CHAPTER 16

1. For a comprehensive history of Brittany from prehistoric times to the present see the series 'Histoire de la Bretagne', edited by André Chédeville (Giot et al. 1995, Pape 1995, Chédeville and Guillotel 1984, Chédeville and Tonnerre 1987, Leguay and Martin 1982, Croix 1993 and Sainclivier 1989). The period from prehistoric times to the late Middle Ages is treated in Galliou and Jones 1991. See also Delumeau 2000.
2. For illustrations see Moscati et al. 1991, 645, Dannheimer and Gebhard 1993, 278 and Haffner 1995, 17.
3. On Roman Brittany see Galliou 1991 and Pape 1995.
4. A comprehensive cultural history of Brittany from the fifth century to the present will be found in Balcou and Le Gallo 1987. The period from the fifth century to the tenth century is treated in Chédeville and Guillotel 1984. On the early settlement from Britain see Fleuriot 1982 and G. Le Duc in Black et al. 1999, I, 133–51. On social history see Davies, W. 1988.
5. On Celtic toponyms in Brittany in general see Plonéis 1989–93. The hagiographical sources are covered by Merdrignac 1985–6.
6. For extended treatment of relations between Brittany and the Carolingian empire see Smith, J. M. H. 1992.
7. The history of Brittany from the eleventh century to the early sixteenth century is treated by Chédeville and Tonnerre 1987 and Leguay and Martin 1982. A full account of Brittany in the late Middle Ages is given in Jones, M. 1988. On the history of Brittany from the fourteenth century to the present see also the exhibition catalogue *Bretagne* 1990.
8. See H. Ll. Humphreys in Price 1992, 245–75, E. Ternes in MacAulay 1992, 371–452 and J. Stephens and H. Ll. Humphreys in Ball and Fife 1993, 349–409 and 606–43. On the early evidence of the Breton language and on middle and modern Breton literature, see R. Williams in Price 1992, 276–300 and various articles in Balcou and Le Gallo 1987.
9. Breton text as cited by R. Williams in Price 1992, 277.
10. A facsimile reprint of the first edition with full introduction is given by Guyonvarc'h 1975.
11. See G. Price in Price 1992, 301–14, A. R. Thomas in MacAulay 1992, 346–70 and K. George in Ball and Fife 1993, 410–68.

CHAPTER 17

1. For extended treatment see Robinson 1984, Brady and Gillespie 1986, MacCarthy-Morrogh 1986 and Loeber 1991.
2. For extended treatment see Morgan, H. 1993.
3. For extended treatment see the articles in Mac Cuarta 1991; also Percival-Maxwell 1994, Ó Siochrú 1998, Clarke 2000 and Ó Siochrú 2001.
4. For an introduction to recent research into the history of the period 1640–60 see the articles in Ohlmeyer 1995.

5. See the articles in Moody and Vaughan 1986. On the situation of the Irish Catholics in the eighteenth century see also Power and Whelan 1990 and Ó Ciardha 2001.

6. On the political situation on the eve of the 1798 rising see Kelly, J. 1992. The relationship between Catholicism and the radical political ideologies of the time is treated by Keogh 1993. See also Dickson et al. 1993, Curtin 1994, the articles in Keogh and Furlong 1996; also Chambers 1998 and the contributions in Bartlett et al. 2002.

7. The development of political ideologies and Irish national identity at the end of the eighteenth century is treated in Whelan 1996.

8. The reaction of the political and intellectual elite to the social changes which followed the English conquests is treated in Ó Riordan 1990. On the unfavourable portrayal of Irish culture by English-speaking writers in the sixteenth and seventeenth centuries, see Hadfield and McVeagh 1994 and Bradshaw et al. 1994. On the development of Irish and British national identity in the seventeenth century see also Ross, B. 1998.

9. For extended treatment see Ó Buachalla 1994.

10. See the bilingual edition of the poet's works by Knott 1922 6.

11. See the bilingual edition by Mac Erlean 1910–17. A selection with translations may be found in Ó Tuama and Kinsella 1981, 110–23.

12. See the edition by Ní Cheallacháin 1962. For a bilingual selection see Ó Tuama and Kinsella 1981, 92–5.

13. On Aodhagán Ó Rathaille see the bilingual edition by Ó Duinnín and Ó Donnchadha 1911 and the bilingual edition of his poetry by Ó Tuama and Kinsella 1981, 140–67.

14. On the literature of the Irish Franciscans in the seventeenth century and their intellectual and historical background, see Ó Dúshláine 1987.

15. See the edition by O'Rahilly, T. F. 1941.

16. See the bilingual edition of the complete text by Walsh 1948–57.

17. See Harrison 1992 and the articles in McGuinness et al. 1997.

18. See the extended treatment by Ó Muraíle 1966.

19. See the edition with translation by Comyn and Dinneen 1902–14. Also Cunningham 2000.

20. See the extended treatment by Hablitzel 1987.

21. The life and work of Kuno Meyer are given full treatment in Ó Luing 1991. On the history of the School of Celtic Studies see the fiftieth-anniversary report *School* 1990.

CHAPTER 18

1. For extended treatment see Bourke 1993, Kinealy 1994, Portéir 1995, Morash and Hughes 1996, Ó Gráda 1997 and Clarkson et al. 2000.

2. The treatment of the Irish question in British politics since that time is covered in Boyce 1996.

3. For an introduction to the extensive recent literature on the problem of Northern Ireland see Dunn 1995, Catterall and McDougall 1996, Hennessey

1996 and Ruane and Todd 1996. The history of Northern Irish Catholicism from the seventeenth century to the present is discussed in Rafferty 1994.
4. For extended treatment see Ó Tuama 1972 and Mac Aonghusa 1993.
5. On the last two writers see the extended treatment in Ní Chionnaith 1993, Riggs 1994, Edwards 1977 and Murphy 1992.

CHAPTER 19

1. For the text of the poem see Watson, W. J. 1959, 149–55 and Thomson, D. S. 1989, 148–50.
2. See Quiggin 1937, Watson, W. J. 1937, Ross, N. 1939 and the summary by D. S. Thomson in Thomson, D. S. 1994, 59–60. A small selection of poems from various genres with English translations is given in Watson, R. 1995, 20–3, 74–7 and 102–7.
3. See Mackenzie 1964, Thomson, D. S. 1989, 118–27 and for the historical background Stevenson 1980. Three poems with English translations may be found in Watson, R. 1995, 218–29.
4. See Matheson 1970, Thomson, D. S. 1989, 150–3 and Sanger and Kinnaird 1992, 129–39. The text and translation of 'The Song to MacLeod', following Matheson, are also in Watson, R. 1995, 236–43.
5. See MacDonald and MacDonald 1924, Thomson, D. S. 1989, 157–80 and Thomson, D. S. 1996. A bilingual selection of his poetry will be found in Watson, R. 1995, 262–77.

CHAPTER 20

1. See Richards, E. 1982, Devine and Orr 1988, Dodgshon 1998 and I. Grimble in Thomson, D. S. 1994, 44–7. On the reflection of these events in Scots Gaelic literature see Meek 1995; on how they were received by public opinion in the Lowlands see Fenyö 1999.
2. Ferdinand Ochsenheimer, *Streifereien durch einige Gegenden Deutschlands*, Leipzig 1795, quoted in Max Schefold, *Der Schwarzwald in alten Ansichten und Schilderungen*, 2nd edn, Stuttgart, 1981, 102.
3. Gaskill 1995 provides a recent edition of Macpherson's Ossian. On the author, his intellectual background and the reception of his work see the biography by Stafford 1988, the collection by Gaskill 1991 and the bibliographical references in Maier 1997, 182–3.
4. On the history of scholarship in the field see T. M. Murchison and D. S. Thomson in Thomson, D. S. 1994, 269–70 and 290–2.
5. See the critical studies by Chapman 1978, Trevor-Roper 1983, Womack 1989 and Gold and Gold 1995.
6. See Matheson 1938 and Thomson, D. S. 1989, 191–4. Watson, R. 1995, 278–91 offers a bilingual selection of MacDonald's poetry.

7. See MacLeod 1952 and Thomson, D. S. 1989, 180–90. Watson, R. 1995, 306–33 offers a bilingual selection of Alasdair's poetry.
8. On the traditions of tales, legends, folk-songs, proverbs, riddles and the study of these, see A. Bruford, D. A. MacDonald, J. MacInnes and D. S. Thomson in Thomson, D. S. 1994, 77–83, 148–9, 243–4, 280–2 and 283–5.
9. On Iain Crichton Smith see the articles in Nicholson 1992 and on Scots Gaelic prose writing see K. D. MacDonald, J. MacInnes, T. M. Murchison and D. S. Thomson in Thomson, D. S. 1994, 218–19, 241–3 and 278–80.
10. For the full text of the poem (of which only about half is cited here), with English translation, see Watson, R. 1995, 632–7.

CHAPTER 21

1. On Welsh society in the early modern period see in particular Jones, J. G. 1989 and 1998 and Griffith 1996.
2. On the period treated here see Gruffydd 1997. On the influence of classical antiquity on Welsh literature see also Davies, C. 1995.
3. On the early history of Welsh Bible translation see Thomas, I. 1976 and 1988. The influence of the Bible on Welsh language and literature is covered in contributions to Gruffydd 1988.
4. See the modern editions of the three works by Bowen, G. 1996, Lewis, A. 1976 and Hughes, G. H. 1961.
5. On the rise of antiquarianism in England and Wales see Piggott 1989 and Parry, G. 1995.
6. On the background in intellectual history and politics to the efforts to preserve the past of Wales, see Morgan, P. 1983, Herbert and Jones 1988 and Thomas, P. D. G. 1998.
7. On Iolo Morganwg see Lewis, C. W. 1995 and Jenkins, G. H. 1995 and 1997b.

CHAPTER 22

1. The history of Welsh Methodism in the eighteenth century is treated at length in Morgan, D. 1988. On the life and work of Pantycelyn see Morgan, D. 1991.
2. On Welsh society and culture in the nineteenth century see Jones, I. G. 1987 and 1992.
3. On the life and work of Saunders Lewis, see Jones, A. R. and Thomas 1973; also Griffiths 1989.
4. See Jenkins, G. H. 1997a, Jenkins, G. H. 1998, Aitchison and Carter 2000, Jenkins, G. H. 2000, Jenkins, G. H. and Williams, M. A. 2000, Thomas, A. 2000 and Williams, C. 2000.
5. On the history of the University of Wales see Williams, J. G. 1993 and 1997.
6. English version by Joseph P. Clancy, quoted in Thomas, M. W. 1992, 165–6.

CHAPTER 23

1. On the history of Brittany in the sixteenth and seventeenth centuries see the detailed coverage in Croix 1981 and 1993.
2. See the detailed account in the contributions to Balcou and Le Gallo 1987, II, 7–243.
3. Renan's attitude to Brittany and Celtic culture is reviewed in Duval, P.-M. 1989, I, 187–90 and at length in Galand 1959. Balcou 1992 provides a selection of Renan's own statements, with commentary. On Matthew Arnold see Bromwich 1965.
4. On the development of the linguistic situation and the language boundary since the late eighteenth century see Broudic 1995a, 1995b and 1997. On the present role of the language in the minds of the Breton people see also McDonald, M. 1989 and Vetter 1997.
5. Le Menn 1997 provides an annotated bilingual edition of this collection of Breton canticles.
6. See the annotated editions by Hémon 1962, 1969 and 1977.
7. See Le Menn 1996 for a reprint with detailed introduction.
8. For what follows see Balcou and Le Gallo 1987, II, 247–380.
9. On Breton literature in the twentieth century see F. Morvannou and Y.-B. Piriou in Balcou and Le Gallo 1987, III, 175–252.
10. Quoted in Balcou and Le Gallo 1987, II, 206.

CHAPTER 24

1. Demographic developments in the individual Celtic-speaking regions are treated from a comparative standpoint and with the most recent statistics adduced by K. MacKinnon in Black et al. 1999, I, 324–46. See also R. O. Jones on the prospects for Welsh (Black, I, 425–56), F. Macintosh on the situation of Scots Gaelic (Black, I, 457–69) and S. Mac Mathúna on the status of Irish as a minority language (Black, I, 470–93).
2. See M. Denis in *Bretagne* 1990, 374–9, and the extensive treatment in Sainclivier 1989.

Bibliography

Aalen, F. H. A., Kevin Whelan and Matthew Stout (eds) (1997), *Atlas of the Irish Landscape*, Cork.

Aitchison, John and Harold Carter (2000), *Language, Economy and Society. The Changing Fortunes of the Welsh Language in the Twentieth Century*, Cardiff.

Allen, Derek F. (1980), *The Coins of the Ancient Celts*, Edinburgh.

Almagro-Gorbea, Martin and Gonzalo Ruiz Zapatero (eds) (1993), *Los Celtas: Hispania y Europa*, Madrid.

Anderson, M. O. (1980), *Kings and Kingship in Early Scotland*, 2nd edn, Edinburgh.

Anderson, M. O. (1991), *Adomnán's Life of Columba*, 2nd edn, Oxford.

Armit, Ian (1997), *Celtic Scotland*, London.

Arnold, Bettina and D. Blair Gibson (eds) (1995), *Celtic Chiefdom, Celtic State*, Cambridge.

Asher, R. E. (1993), *National Myths in Renaissance France: Francus, Samothes and the Druids*, Edinburgh.

Audouze, F. and O. Büchsenschütz (1992), *Towns, Villages and Countryside of Celtic Europe, from the beginning of the second millennium to the end of the first century* BC, translated by Henry Cleere, London.

Bakere, J. A. (1980), *The Cornish Ordinalia: A Critical Study*, Cardiff.

Balcou, Jean (1992), *Renan et la Bretagne*, Paris.

Balcou, Jean et Yves Le Gallo (eds) (1987), *Histoire littéraire et culturelle de la Bretagne*, 3 vols, Paris-Geneva.

Ball, Martin and James Fife (eds) (1993), *The Celtic Languages*, London.

Bammesberger, A. and A. Wollmann (eds) (1990), *Britain 400–600: Language and History*, Heidelberg.

Bannerman, John W. M. (1974), *Studies in the History of Dalriada*, Edinburgh.

Barber, Chris (1998), *In Search of Owain Glyndŵr*, Abergavenny.

Barron, W. R. J. (ed.) (1998), *The Arthur of the English. The Arthurian Legend in Medieval English Life and Literature*, Cardiff.

Barrow, G. W. S. (1980), *The Anglo-Norman Era in Scottish History*, Oxford.

Barry, Terry, Robin Frame and Katharine Simms (eds) (1995), *Colony and Frontier in Medieval Ireland*, London.

Bartlett, Thomas (1992), *The Rise and Fall of the Irish Nation: The Catholic Question, 1690–1830*, Dublin.

Bartlett, Thomas et al. (2002), *The 1798 Rebellion. A Bicentennial Perspective*, Dublin.

Batey, Colleen, Judith Jesch and Christopher D. Morris (eds) (1993), *The Viking Age in Caithness, Orkney and the North Atlantic*, Edinburgh.

Bats, Michael et al. (eds) (1992), *Marseille grecque et la Gaule. Actes du Colloque international d'Histoire et d'Archéologie du Ve Congrès archéologique de Gaule méridionale (Marseille, 18–23 novembre 1990)*, Lattes.

Bauchhenss, Gerhard and Günter Neumann (eds) (1987), *Matronen und verwandte Gottheiten*, Bonn.

Berger, Ph. (1995), 'La xénophobie de Polybe', *Revue des Etudes Anciennes* 97, 517–25.

Berry, David (1994), *Wales and Cinema. The First Hundred Years*, Cardiff.

Best, Richard Irvine and Osborn Bergin (1929), *Lebor na hUidre: The Book of the Dun Cow*, Dublin.

Best, Richard Irvine, Osborn Bergin, M. A. O'Brien and A. O'Sullivan (1954–83), *The Book of Leinster, formerly Lebar na Núachongbála*, 6 vols, Dublin.

Bew, Paul, Peter Gibbon and Henry Patterson (eds) (1996), *Northern Ireland 1921–1996. Political Forces and Social Classes*, London.

Biel, Jörg (1985), *Der Keltenfürst von Hochdorf*, Stuttgart.

Bieler, Ludwig (1961), *Irland: Wegbereiter des Mittelalters*, Olten.

Bieler, Ludwig (1963), *The Irish Penitentials*, Dublin (Scriptores Latini Hiberniae 5).

Bieler, Ludwig (1979), *The Patrician Texts in the Book of Armagh*, Dublin (Scriptores Latini Hiberniae 10).

Binchy, Daniel (1978), *Corpus Iuris Hibernici*, Dublin.

Birkhan, Helmut (1970), *Germanen und Kelten bis zum Ausgang der Römerzeit. Der Aussagewert von Wörtern und Sachen für die frühesten keltisch-germanischen Kulturbeziehungen*, Vienna.

Birkhan, Helmut (1989), *Keltische Erzählungen vom Kaiser Arthur*, 2 vols, Kettwig.

Birkhan, Helmut (1997), *Kelten. Versuch einer Gesamtdarstellung ihrer Kultur*, 2nd edn, Vienna.

Birkhan, Helmut (1999), *Kelten. Bilder ihrer Kultur*, Vienna.

Bittel, Kurt, Wolfgang Kimmig and Siegwalt Schiek (1981), *Die Kelten in Baden-Württemberg*, Stuttgart.

Black, Ronald, William Gillies and Roibeard Ó Maolalaigh (eds) (1999), *Celtic Connections. Proceedings of the Tenth International Congress of Celtic Studies*, East Linton.

Bodmer, Walter (1992) 'The Genetics of Celtic Populations', *Proceedings of the British Academy* 82, 37–57.

Boivin, Jeanne-Marie (1993), *L'Irlande au moyen âge. Giraud de Barri et la Topographia Hibernica (1188)*, Paris.

Bourgeois, Claude (1991–2), *Divona. 1. Divinités et ex-voto du culte gallo-romain de l'eau. 2. Monuments et sanctuaires gallo-romains de l'eau*, Paris.

Bourke, Austin (1993), *'The Visitation of God'? The potato and the great Irish famine*, Dublin.

Bourke, Cormac (ed.) (1997), *Studies in the Cult of Saint Columba*, Dublin.

Bowen, Desmond (1995), *History and the Shaping of Irish Protestantism*, New York.

Bowen, David James (1957), *Beirdd yr Uchelwyr. Detholiad*, Cardiff.

Bowen, Emrys George (1982), *The St David of History. Dewi Sant: Our Founder Saint*, Aberystwyth.

Bowen, Geraint (ed.) (1974), *Y Traddodiad Rhyddiaith yn yr Oesau Canol*, Llandysul.

Bowen, Geraint (1996), *Y Drych Kristnogawl*, Cardiff.

Boyce, D. George (1995), *Nationalism in Ireland*, 3rd edn, London.

Boyce, D. George (1996), *The Irish Question and British Politics, 1868–1996*, 2nd edn, London.

Bradley, Ian (1999), *Celtic Christianity. Making Myths and Chasing Dreams*, Edinburgh.

Bradshaw, Brendan (1974), *The Dissolution of the Religious Houses in Ireland under Henry VIII*, Cambridge.

Bradshaw, Brendan, Andrew Hadfield and Willy Malley (eds) (1994), *Representing Ireland: Literature and the Origins of Conflict, 1534–1660*, Cambridge.

Brady, Ciaran (1994), *The Chief Governors: The Rise and Fall of Reform Government in Tudor Ireland, 1536–1588*, Cambridge.

Brady, Ciaran and Raymond Gillespie (eds) (1986), *Natives and Newcomers. The Making of Irish Colonial Society, 1534–1641*, Dublin.

Brailsford, John (1975), *Early Celtic Masterpieces from Britain in the British Museum*, London.

Breatnach, Liam (1996), 'On the original extent of the Senchas Már', *Ériu* 47, 1–43.

Breatnach, Pádraig A. (1983), 'The Chief's Poet', *Proceedings of the Royal Irish Academy* 83, 37–79.

Breatnach, Pádraig A. (1997), *Téamaí Taighde Nua-Ghaeilge*, Maynooth.

Bretagne. Die Kultur des «Landes am Meer» 1300–1990 (1990), Vienna (exhibition catalogue).

Broderick, George (1984–6), *A Handbook of Late Spoken Manx*, 3 vols, Tübingen (Buchreihe der Zeitschrift für celtische Philologie 3–5).

Broderick, George (1999), *Language Death in the Isle of Man*, Tübingen.

Brodersen, Kai (1998), *Das römische Britannien*, Darmstadt.

Bromwich, Rachel (1965), *Matthew Arnold and Celtic Literature: a Retrospect 1865–1965*, Oxford.

Bromwich, Rachel (1978), *Trioedd Ynys Prydein. The Welsh Triads*, 2nd edn, Cardiff.

Bromwich, Rachel (1982), *Dafydd ap Gwilym. A Selection of Poems*, Llandysul (Welsh Classics I).

Bromwich, Rachel (1983), 'Celtic Elements in Arthurian Romance: A General Survey', in *The Legend of Arthur in the Middle Ages. Studies presented to A. H. Diverres by colleagues, pupils and friends*, Woodbridge, 41–55 and 230–3.

Bromwich, Rachel et al. (eds) (1991), *The Arthur of the Welsh. The Arthurian legend in Medieval Welsh literature*, Cardiff.

Bromwich, Rachel and D. Simon Evans (1992), *Culhwch ac Olwen: an edition and study of the oldest Arthurian tale*, Cardiff.

Bromwich, Rachel and R. Brinley Jones (eds) (1978), *Astudiaethau ar yr Hengerdd*, Cardiff.

Broudic, Fañch (1995a), *La pratique du breton de l'Ancien Régime à nos jours*, Rennes.

Broudic, Fañch (1995b), *A la recherche de la frontière. La limite linguistique entre Haute et Basse-Bretagne aux XIXe et XXe siècles*, Brest.

Broudic, Fañch (1997), *L'interdiction du breton en 1902. La IIIe République contre les langues régionales*, Spezet.

Brown, Peter (1980), *The Book of Kells*, London.

Brown, Terence (ed.) (1996), *Celticism*, Amsterdam.

Brugger-Hackett, S. (1991), *Merlin in der europäischen Literatur des Mittelalters*, Stuttgart.

Brun, Patrice and Bruno Chaume (eds) (1997), *Vix et les éphémères principautés celtiques. Les VIe et Ve siècles avant J.-C. en Europe centre-occidentale. Actes du colloque de Châtillon-sur-Seine (27–29 octobre 1993)*, Paris.

Brunaux, Jean-Louis (ed.) (1991), *Les sanctuaires celtiques et leurs rapports avec le monde méditerranéen. Actes du colloque de Saint-Riquier (8 au 11 novembre 1990)* organisé par la Direction des Antiquités de Picardie et l'UMR 126 du CNRS, Paris.

Brunaux, Jean-Louis (1996), *Les religions gauloises. Rituels celtiques de la Gaule indépendante*, Paris.

Brunaux, Jean-Louis and B. Lambot (1987), *Guerre et armement chez les Gaulois*, Paris.

Büchsenschütz, O. and L. Olivier (eds) (1990), *Les Viereckschanzen et les enceintes quadrilatérales en Europe celtique*, Paris.

Burillo Mozota, Francisco (1998), *Los Celtíberos. Etnias y estados*, Barcelona.

Byrne, Francis John (1971), 'Tribes and Tribalism in Early Ireland', *Ériu* 22, 128–63.

Byrne, Francis John (1973), *Irish Kings and High-Kings*, London.

Byrne, Francis John (1976), 'Die keltischen Völker', in Theodor Schieffer (ed.), *Handbuch der europäischen Geschichte*, vol. 1, Stuttgart, 449–93.

Caesar, Julius (1917), *De Bello Gallico/The Gallic war*, with an English translation by H. J. Edwards, London.

Carey, John 1989/90, 'Myth and Mythography in *Cath Maige Tuired*', *Studia Celtica* 24/25, 53–69.

Carey, John (1998), *King of Mysteries: Early Irish Religious Writings*, Dublin.

Carey, John (1999), *A Single Ray of the Sun. Religious Speculation in Early Ireland*, Andover and Aberystwyth.

Carey, John et al. (2001), *Studies in Irish Hagiography. Saints and Scholars*, Dublin.

Carmichael, Alexander (1992), *Carmina Gadelica. Hymns and Incantations with Illustrative Notes on Words, Rites and Customs, Dying and Obsolete; Orally Collected in the Highlands and Islands of Scotland*, Edinburgh.

Carney, James (1964), *The Poems of Blathmac, Son of Cú Brettan, together with The Irish Gospel of Thomas and A Poem on the Virgin Mary*, Dublin (Irish Texts Society 47).

Carr, A. D. (1995), *Medieval Wales*, Basingstoke.
Catterall, Peter and Sean McDougall (eds) (1996), *The Northern Ireland Question in British Politics*, London.
Chambers, Liam (1998), *Rebellion in Kildare 1790–1803*, Dublin.
Champion, T. C. and J. V. S. Megaw (eds) (1985), *Settlement and Society: aspects of West European prehistory in the first millennium B.C.*, Leicester.
Champion, T. C. and J. R. Collis (eds) (1996), *The Iron Age in Britain and Ireland: Recent Trends*, Sheffield.
Chapman, Malcolm (1978), *The Gaelic Vision in Scottish Culture*, London.
Chapman, Malcolm (1992), *The Celts. The Construction of a Myth*, London.
Charles-Edwards, Thomas M. (1989), *The Welsh Laws*, Cardiff.
Charles-Edwards, Thomas M. (1993), *Early Irish and Welsh Kinship*, Oxford.
Charles-Edwards, Thomas M. (2000), *Early Christian Ireland*, Cambridge.
Charles-Edwards, Thomas M. et al. (2000), *The Welsh King and His Court*, Cardiff.
Charpy, Jean-Jacques (ed.) (1995), *L'Europe celtique du Ve au IIIe siècle avant J.-C. Contacts, échanges et mouvements de populations*, Épernay.
Chédeville, André and Hubert Guillotel (1984), *La Bretagne des saints et des rois V^e-Xe siècle*, Rennes.
Chédeville, André and N.-Y. Tonnerre (1987), *La Bretagne féodale XIe-XIIIe siècle*, Rennes.
Chevallier, Raymond (1983), *La Romanisation de la Celtique du Pô. Essai d'histoire provinciale*, Rome.
Chevallier, Raymond (ed.) (1992), *Les eaux thermales et les cultes des eaux en Gaule et dans les provinces voisines*, Tours.
Clarke, Aidan (2000), *The Old English in Ireland, 1625–1642*, Dublin.
Clarke, Howard B., Máire Ní Mhaonaigh and Raghnall Ó Floinn (eds) (1998), *Ireland and Scandinavia in the Early Viking Age*, Dublin.
Clarkson, L. A. et al. (2000), *Mapping the Great Irish Famine. A Survey of the Famine Decades*, Dublin.
Close-Brooks J. and R. B. K. Stevenson (1982), *Dark Age Sculpture*, Edinburgh.
Collis, John (1984), *Oppida: Earliest Towns North of the Alps*, Sheffield.
Collis, John (1996), 'The Origin and Spread of the Celts', *Studia Celtica* 30, 17–34.
Comyn, David and Patrick S. Dinneen (1902–14), *Foras Feasa ar Éirinn. Elements of the History of Ireland*, 4 vols, Dublin (Irish Texts Society 4, 8, 9, 15).
Connolly, S. J. (1992), *Religion, Law, and Power: The Making of Protestant Ireland, 1660–1760*, Oxford.
Connolly, S. J. (ed.) (1998), *The Oxford Companion to Irish History*, Oxford.
Conran, Anthony (ed. and trans.) (1967), *The Penguin Book of Welsh Verse*, Harmondsworth.
Constantine, Mary-Ann (1996), *Breton Ballads*, Aberystwyth.
Corthals, Johan (1996), *Altirische Erzählkunst*, Münster.
Cosgrove, Art (ed.) (1987), *Medieval Ireland 1169–1534*, Oxford.
Coulon, G. (1990), *Les Gallo-Romains. Au carrefour de deux civilisations*, 2 vols, Paris.

Cowan, Edward J. and R. Andrew McDonald (eds) (2001), *Alba: Celtic Scotland in the Medieval Era*, East Linton.

Cowan, Ian B. and David E. Easson (1976), *Medieval Religious Houses. Scotland*, 2nd edn, London.

Crawford, Barbara E. (1987), *Scandinavian Scotland*, Leicester.

Crépin, André and Wolfgang Spiewok (eds) (1996), *Tristan – Tristrant. Mélanges en l'honneur de Danielle Buschinger à l'occasion de son 60ème anniversaire*, Greifswald.

Croix, Alain (1981), *La Bretagne au 16e et 17e siècles. La vie – la mort – la foi*, 2 vols, Paris.

Croix, Alain (1993), *L'âge d'or de la Bretagne 1532–1675*, Rennes.

Cunliffe, Barry (1997), *The Ancient Celts*, London.

Cunningham, Bernadette (2000), *The World of Geoffrey Keating. History, Myth and Religion in Seventeenth-century Ireland*, Dublin.

Curley, Michael J. (1994), *Geoffrey of Monmouth*, New York.

Curtin, Nancy J. (1994), *The United Irishmen. Popular Politics in Ulster and Dublin, 1791–1798*, Oxford.

Danaher, Kevin (1982), 'Irish Folk Tradition and the Celtic Calendar', in R. O'Driscoll (ed.), *The Celtic Consciousness*, Portlaoise and Edinburgh, 217–42.

Daniel, R. Iestyn (1995), *Ymborth yr Enaid*, Cardiff.

Dannheimer, Hermann and Rupert Gebhard (eds) (1993), *Das keltische Jahrtausend*, Mainz (exhibition catalogue).

Dauzat, A. and C. Rostaing (1979), *Dictionnaire étymologique des noms de lieux en France*, 2nd edn, Paris.

Davies, Ceri (1995), *Welsh Literature and the Classical Tradition*, Cardiff.

Davies, D. Hywel (1983), *The Welsh Nationalist Party 1925–1995. A Call to Nationhood*, Cardiff.

Davies, Hazel (1988), *O. M. Edwards*, Cardiff.

Davies, John (1994), *A History of Wales*, Harmondsworth.

Davies, Oliver (1996), *Celtic Christianity in Early Medieval Wales. The Origins of the Welsh Spiritual Tradition*, Cardiff.

Davies, Robert Rees (1987), *Conquest, Coexistence, and Change: Wales 1063–1415*, Oxford.

Davies, Robert Rees (ed.) (1990), *Domination and Conquest: The Experience of Ireland, Scotland and Wales 1100–1300*, Cambridge.

Davies, Robert Rees (1995), *The Revolt of Owain Glyndŵr*, Oxford.

Davies, Sioned (1995), *Crefft y Cyfarwydd. Astudiaeth o dechnegau naratif yn y Mabinogion*, Cardiff.

Davies, Sioned and Nerys Ann Jones (eds) (1997), *The Horse in Celtic Culture. Medieval Welsh Perspectives*, Cardiff.

Davies, Wendy (1982), *Wales in the Early Middle Ages*, Leicester.

Davies, Wendy (1988), *Small Worlds. The Village Community in Early Medieval Brittany*, London.

Davies, Wendy (1990), *Patterns of Power in Early Wales*, Oxford.

Davis, Daniel R. (ed.) (1999), *Foundations of Celtic Linguistics 1700–1850*, 8 vols, London.

Davitt, Michael and Iain Macdhòmhnaill (eds) (1993), *Sruth na Maoile. Modern Gaelic Poetry from Scotland and Ireland*, Edinburgh and Dublin.

Day, Graham and Gareth Rees (eds) (1991), *Regions, Nations and European Integration. Remaking the Celtic Periphery*, Cardiff.

De Hoz, Javier (1990), 'The Celts of the Iberian Peninsula', *Zeitschrift für celtische Philologie*, 45, 1–37.

Delamarre, Xavier (2001), *Dictionnaire de la langue gauloise*, Paris.

Delumeau, Jean (ed.) (2000), *Histoire de la Bretagne*, Paris.

Demandt, Alexander (1999), *Die Kelten*, 2nd edn, Munich.

De Paor, Liam (1993), *Saint Patrick's World. The Christian Culture of Ireland's Apostolic Age*, Blackrock.

Devine, T. M. and Willie Orr (1988), *The Great Highland Famine. Hunger, Emigration and the Scottish Highlands in the Nineteenth Century*, Edinburgh.

Deyts, Simone (1983), *Les Bois sculptés des Sources de la Seine*, Paris.

Deyts, Simone (1992), *Images des dieux de la Gaule*, Paris.

Dickson, David, Dáire Keogh and Kevin Whelan (eds) (1993), *The United Irishmen: Republicanism, radicalism and rebellion*, Dublin.

Diekmann, Knut (1998), *Die nationalistische Bewegung in Wales*, Paderborn.

Dietler, Michael (1994), ' "Our Ancestors the Gauls" ', *American Anthropologist* 94, 584–605.

Dillon, Myles (1946), *The Cycles of the Kings*, London.

Dobesch, Gerhard (1989), 'Zur Einwanderung der Kelten in Oberitalien. Aus der Geschichte der keltischen Wanderungen im 6. und 5. Jh. v. Chr.', *Tyche* 4, 35–85.

Dobesch, Gerhard (1992), 'Die Kelten als Nachbarn der Etrusker in Norditalien', in Luciana Aigner-Foresti (ed.), *Etrusker nördlich von Etrurien*, Vienna, 161–78.

Dobesch, Gerhard (1995), *Das europäische 'Barbaricum' und die Zone der Mediterrankultur. Ihre historische Wechselwirkung und das Geschichtsbild des Poseidonios*, Vienna.

Dodgshon, Robert A. (1998), *From Chiefs to Landlords. Social and Economic Change in the Western Highlands and Islands*, Edinburgh.

Doherty, Richard (1998), *The Williamite War in Ireland*, Dublin.

Dolley, Michael (1972), *Anglo-Norman Ireland*, Dublin.

Drda, Petr and Alena Rybová (1994), *Les Celtes de Bohême*, Paris.

Driehaus, Jürgen (1978), 'Der Grabraub in Mitteleuropa während der älteren Eisenzeit', in H. Jankuhn et al. (eds), *Zum Grabfrevel in vor- und frühgeschichtlicher Zeit*, Göttingen, 18–47.

Dubois, Claude-Gilbert (1972), *Celtes et Gaulois au XVIe siècle. Le développement littéraire d'un mythe nationaliste*, Paris.

Duffy, Patrick et al. (2001), *Gaelic Ireland c. 1250 – c. 1650. Land, Lordship and Settlement*, Dublin.

Duffy, Seán (1997), *Ireland in the Middle Ages*, London.

Dumville, David et al. (1993), *Saint Patrick, A.D. 493–1993*, Woodbridge.

Dumville, David N. (1994), 'Historia Brittonum: an Insular History from the Carolingian Age', in A. Scharer and G. Scheibelreiter (eds), *Historiographie im frühen Mittelalter*, Vienna, 406–34.

Dunn, Seamus (ed.) (1995), *Facets of the Conflict in Northern Ireland*, New York.
Duval, Alain (1989), *L'art celtique de la Gaule au musée des antiquités nationales*, Paris.
Duval, Paul-Marie (1976), *Les dieux de la Gaule*, 2nd edn, Paris.
Duval, Paul-Marie (1977), *Les Celtes*, Paris.
Duval, Paul-Marie (1987), *Monnaies gauloises et mythes celtiques*, Paris.
Duval, Paul-Marie (1988), *La vie quotidienne en Gaule pendant la paix romaine*, 3rd edn, Paris.
Duval, Paul-Marie (1989), *Travaux sur la Gaule*, 2 vols, Rome.
Duval, Paul-Marie and Georges Pinault (1986), *Recueil des inscriptions gauloises. Vol. III Les calendriers*, Paris.
Echt, Rudolf (1999), *Das Fürstinnengrab von Reinheim. Studien zur Kulturgeschichte der Früh-La-Tène-Zeit*, Bonn (Saarbrücker Beiträge zur Altertumskunde 69).
Edel, Doris (ed.) (1995), *Cultural Identity and Cultural Integration. Ireland and Europe in the Early Middle Ages*, Blackrock.
Edwards, Hywel Teifi (ed.) (1995), *Cwm Rhondda*, Llandysul.
Edwards, Nancy and Alan Lane (eds) (1992), *The Early Church in Wales and the West. Recent Work in Early Christian Archaeology, History and Place-Names*, Oxford.
Edwards, Ruth Dudley (1977), *Patrick Pearse: The Triumph of Failure*, London.
Ellis, Steven G. (1985), *Tudor Ireland: Crown, Community and the Conflict of Cultures 1470–1603*, London.
Eluère, Christiane (1987), *Das Gold der Kelten*, Munich.
Emery, F. (1971), *Edward Lhuyd F.R.S. (1660–1709)*, Cardiff.
Eska, Joseph F. (1989), *Towards an Interpretation of the Hispano-Celtic Inscription of Botorrita*, Innsbruck.
Etchingham, Colmán (1996), *Viking Raids on Irish Church Settlements in the Ninth Century*, Maynooth.
Die Etrusker und Europa (1992), Milan (exhibition catalogue).
Euskirchen, Marion (1993), 'Epona', in *74. Bericht der Römisch-Germanischen Kommission*, 607–850.
Evans, Chris (1993), *'The Labyrinth of Flames'. Work and Social Conflict in Early Industrial Merthyr Tydfil*, Cardiff.
Evans, D. Ellis (1967), *Gaulish Personal Names*, Oxford.
Evans, D. Ellis (1997), 'Celticity, Celtic Awareness and Celtic Studies', *Zeitschrift für celtische Philologie*, 49/50, 1–27.
Evans, D. Gareth (2000), *A History of Wales, 1906–2000*, Cardiff.
Evans, D. Simon (1988), *The Welsh Life of St David*, Cardiff.
Fauduet, Isabelle (1993a), *Les temples de tradition celtique en Gaule romaine*, Paris.
Fauduet, Isabelle (1993b), *Atlas des sanctuaires romano-celtiques de Gaule*, Paris.
Fawcett, Richard (1985), *Scottish Medieval Churches*, Edinburgh.
Fenton, Alexander and Hermann Pálsson (eds) (1984), *The Northern and Western Isles in the Viking World*, Edinburgh.
Fenyö, Krisztina (1999), *Contempt, Sympathy and Romance. Lowland Perceptions of the Highlands and the Clearance during the Famine Years, 1845–1855*, East Linton.

Ferdière, A. (1988), *Les campagnes en Gaule romaine*, 2 vols, Paris.

Fichtl, Stephan (1994), *Les Gaulois du Nord de la Gaule (150–20 av. J.-C.)*, Paris.

Fichtl, Stephan (2000), *La ville celtique. Les 'oppida' de 150 av. J.-C. à 15 ap. J.-C.*, Paris.

Fischer, Franz (1972), 'Die Kelten bei Herodot: Bemerkungen zu einigen geographischen und ethnographischen Problemen', *Madrider Mitteilungen* 13, 109–24.

Fischer, Franz (1973), 'ΚΕΙΜΗΛΙΑ. Bemerkungen zur kulturgeschichtlichen Interpretation des sog. Südimports in der späten Hallstatt- und frühen Latènekultur des westlichen Mitteleuropa', *Germania* 51, 436–59.

Fischer, Franz (1982), *Der Heidengraben bei Grabenstetten. Ein keltisches Oppidum auf der Schwäbischen Alb bei Urach*, 3rd edn, Stuttgart.

Fischer, Franz (1986), 'Die Ethnogenese der Kelten aus der Sicht der Vor- und Frühgeschichte', in *Ethnogenese europäischer Völker*, W. Bernhard und A. Kandler-Pálsson (eds), Wiesbaden, 209–24.

Fischer, Franz (1992), 'Gold und Geld. Gedanken zum Schatz von Erstfeld', *Helvetia Archaeologica* 23, 118–38.

Fischer, Franz and Jörg Biel (1982), *Frühkeltische Fürstengräber in Mitteleuropa* (*Antike Welt* 13, special issue).

Fitzpatrick, Andrew (1996), '"Celtic" Iron Age Europe: The Theoretical Basis', in P. Graves-Brown, S. Jones and C. Gamble (eds), *Cultural Identity and Archaeology*, London, 238–51.

Flanagan, Marie Therese (1989), *Irish Society, Anglo-Norman Settlers, Angevin Kingship: Interactions in Ireland in the Late Twelfth Century*, Oxford.

Fleuriot, Léon (1982), *Les Origines de la Bretagne. L'émigration*, 2nd edn, Paris.

Forsyth, Katherine (1997), *Language in Pictland. The case against 'non-Indo-European Pictish'*, Utrecht.

Forsyth, Katherine (ed.) (2002), *Studies in the Book of Deer*, Dublin.

Foster, Robert F. (1988), *Modern Ireland, 1600–1972*, London.

Foster, Robert F. (ed.) (1989), *The Oxford Illustrated History of Ireland*, Oxford.

Frappier, Jean (1978), 'La Matière de Bretagne', in *Grundriß der romanischen Literaturen des Mittelalters*, vol. IV, Heidelberg, 183–211.

Freeman, Philip M. (1996), 'The Earliest Greek Sources on the Celts', *Etudes Celtiques* 32, 11–48.

Freeman, Philip (2001), *The Galatian Language*, Lewiston, NY.

Frey, Otto-Herman (1985), 'Zum Handel und Verkehr während der Frühlatènezeit in Mitteleuropa', in *Untersuchungen zu Handel und Verkehr der vor- und frühgeschichtlichen Zeit in Mittel- und Nordeuropa I*, Göttingen, 231–57.

Frey, Otto Herman (1996), 'The Celts in Italy', *Studia Celtica* 30, 59–82.

Freyberger, Bert (1999), *Südgallien im 1. Jahrhundert v. Chr.*, Wiesbaden.

Fulton, Helen (1996), *Selections from the Dafydd ap Gwilym Apocrypha*, Llandysul.

Furger-Gunti, Andres (1984), *Die Helvetier. Kulturgeschichte eines Keltenvolkes*, Zürich.

Galand, R. M. (1959), *L'Ame celtique de Renan*, Paris.
Galliou, Patrick (1991), *La Bretagne romaine: De l'Armorique à la Bretagne*, Saint-Brieuc.
Galliou, Patrick and Michael Jones (1991), *The Bretons*, Oxford.
Gaskill, Howard (ed.) (1991), *Ossian Revisited*, Edinburgh.
Gaskill, Howard (1995), *James Macpherson, The Poems of Ossian and Related Works*, Edinburgh.
Gillies, William (ed.) (1989), *Gaelic and Scotland. Alba agus a'Ghaidhlig*, Edinburgh.
Giot, P.-R., J. Briard and Louis Pape (1995), *Protohistoire de la Bretagne*, Rennes.
Goetinck, Glenys W. (1976), *Historia Peredur vab Efrawc*, Cardiff.
Gold, John R. and Margaret M. Gold (1995), *Imagining Scotland. Tradition, Representation and Promotion in Scottish Tourism since 1750*, Aldershot.
Goodrich, P. (ed.) (1990), *The Romance of Merlin*, London.
Gottzmann, Carola (1989), *Artus-Dichtung*, Stuttgart.
Goudineau, Christian (1990), *César et la Gaule*, Paris.
Goudineau, Christian and C. Peyre (1993), *Bibracte et les Eduens: à la découverte d'un peuple gaulois*, Paris.
Gourvil, Francis (1960), *Théodore-Claude-Henri Hersart de la Villemarqué et le 'Barzaz Breiz'*, Rennes.
Gräber – Spiegel des Lebens. Zum Totenbrauchtum der Kelten und Römer am Beispiel des Treverer-Gräberfeldes Wederath-Beginum (1989), Mainz (exhibition catalogue).
Graham-Campbell, James and Colleen Batey (1998), *Vikings in Scotland. An Archaeological Survey*, Edinburgh.
Grassi, M. T. (1991), *I Celti in Italia*, Milan.
Gray, E. A. (1982), *Cath Maige Tuired: The Second Battle of Mag Tuired*, Dublin (Irish Texts Society 52).
Gray, E. A. (1980–3), 'Cath Maige Tuired: Myth and Structure', *Éigse* 18 (1980/81) 183–209 and *Éigse* 19 (1982/3) 1–35 and 230–62.
Green, Miranda (1989), *Symbol and Image in Celtic Religious Art*, London.
Green, Miranda (1992), *Animals in Celtic Life and Myth*, London.
Green, Miranda (ed.) (1995), *The Celtic World*, London.
Green, Miranda (1997), *Exploring the World of the Druids*, London.
Greene, David and Frank O'Connor (1967), *A Golden Treasury of Irish Poetry A.D. 600 to 1200*, London.
Griffith, William Philip (1996), *Learning, Law and Religion. Higher Education and Welsh Society c. 1540–1640*, Cardiff.
Griffiths, Bruce (1989), *Saunders Lewis*, Cardiff.
Gruel, Kathérine (1989), *La Monnaie chez les Gaulois*, Paris.
Gruffydd, Robert Geraint (ed.) (1982), *Bardos. Penodau ar y traddodiad barddol Cymreig a Cheltaidd cyflwynedig i J. E. Caerwyn Williams*, Cardiff.
Gruffydd, Robert (ed.) (1988), *Y Gair ar Waith. Ysgrifau ar yr Etifeddiaeth Feiblaidd yng Nghymru*, Cardiff.
Gruffydd, Robert (ed.) (1997), *A Guide to Welsh Literature c. 1530–1700*, vol. III, Cardiff.

Gschaid, Max (1994), 'Die römischen und die gallo-römischen Gottheiten in den Gebieten der Sequaner und Ambarrer', *Jahrbuch des Römisch-Germanischen Zentralmuseums Mainz* 41, 323–469.

Guillaumet, J.-P., (1996), *L'artisanat chez les Gaulois*, Paris.

Guyonvarc'h, Christian J. (1975), *Le Catholicon de Jehan Lagadeuc. Dictionnaire breton-latin-français du XVème siècle*, Rennes.

Gwynn, E. (1903–35), *The Metrical Dindshenchas*, 5 vols, Dublin (Royal Irish Academy Todd Lecture Series 8–12).

Hablitzel, Hans (1987), *Prof. Dr. Johann Kaspar Zeuss. Begründer der Keltologie und Historiker aus Vogtendorf/Oberfranken 1806–1856*, Kronach.

Hadfield, Andrew and John McVeagh (eds) (1994), *Strangers to the Land. British Perceptions of Ireland from the Reformation to the Famine*, London.

Haffner, Alfred (1976), *Die Westliche Hunsrück-Eifel-Kultur*, Berlin.

Haffner, Alfred (ed.) (1995), *Heiligtümer und Opferkulte der Kelten*, Stuttgart (*Archäologie in Deutschland* Sonderheft).

Haffner, Alfred et al. (2000), *Kelten, Germanen, Römer im Mittelgebirgsraum zwischen Luxemburg und Thüringen*, Bonn.

Hammermayer, L. (1976), 'Die irischen Benediktiner- "Schottenklöster" in Deutschland', *Studien und Mitteilungen zur Geschichte des Benediktinerordens und seiner Zweige* 87, 249–339.

Hanson, R. P. C. (1983), *The Life and Writings of the Historical St Patrick*, New York.

Hanson, R. P. C. and C. Blanc (1978), *Saint Patrick: Confession et Lettre à Coroticus. Introduction, texte critique, traduction et notes*, Paris (Sources chrétiennes 249).

Hanson, W. S. (1991), 'Tacitus' "Agricola": An Archaeological and Historical Study', in *Aufstieg und Niedergang der römischen Welt II* 33.3, Berlin, 1741–84.

Harbison, Peter (1992), *The High Crosses of Ireland. An iconographic and photographic survey*, 3 vols, Bonn.

Harbison, Peter (1994), *Pre-Christian Ireland. From the First Settlers to the Early Celts*, London.

Harrison, Alan (1992), 'John Toland (1670–1722) and Celtic Studies', in C. J. Byrne et al. (ed.), *Celtic Languages and Celtic Peoples*, Halifax, 555–76.

Harvie, Christopher (1991), 'The Folk and the Gwerin: The Myth and the Reality of Popular Culture in 19th-Century Scotland and Wales', in *Proceedings of the British Academy* 80, 19–48.

Haycock, Marged (1983/84), 'Preiddeu Annwfn and the Figure of Taliesin', *Studia Celtica* 18/19, 52–78.

Haycock, Marged (1994), *Blodeugerdd Barddas o Ganu Crefyddol Cynnar*, Swansea.

Hémon, Roparz (1962), *Trois Poèmes en Moyen-Breton, traduits et annotés*, Dublin.

Hémon, Roparz (1969), *Les fragments de la destruction de Jérusalem et des Amours du Vieillard (textes en moyen-breton)*, Dublin.

Hémon, Roparz (1977), *Doctrin an Christenien. Texte de 1622 en moyen-breton accompagné de la version française et du texte en breton moderne de 1677 avec préface et notes*, Dublin.

Henderson, G. (1987), *From Durrow to Kells: the Insular Gospel-books, 650–800*, London.

Henken, Elissa R. (1987), *Traditions of the Welsh Saints*, Cambridge.

Henken, Elissa R. (1991), *The Welsh Saints. A Study in Patterned Lives*, Cambridge.

Henken, Elissa R. (1996), *National Redeemer. Owain Glyndŵr in Welsh Tradition*, Cardiff.

Hennessey, Thomas (1996), *A History of Northern Ireland 1920–1996*, 2nd edn, London.

Henry, P. L. (1978), *Saoithiúlacht na Sean-Ghaeilge. Bunú an Traidisiúin*, Dublin.

Herbert, Máire (1988), *Iona, Kells and Derry. The History and Hagiography of the Monastic Family of Columba*, Oxford.

Herbert, Trevor and Gareth Elwyn Jones (eds) (1988), *The Remaking of Wales in the Eighteenth Century*, Cardiff.

Herbert, Trevor and Gareth Elwyn Jones (eds) (1995), *Post-War Wales*, Cardiff.

Herrmann, Fritz-Rudolf and Otto-Herman Frey (1996), *Die Keltenfürsten vom Glauberg*, Wiesbaden (Archäologische Denkmäler in Hessen 128/129).

Herrmann, Fritz-Rudolf and Otto-Herman Frey (1997), 'Ein frühkeltischer Fürstengrabhügel am Glauberg im Wetteraukreis, Hessen', *Germania* 75, 459–550.

Higham, N. J. (1994), *The English Conquest. Gildas and Britain in the Fifth Century*, Manchester.

Hirst, Catherine (2002), *Religion, Politics and Violence in Nineteenth-century Belfast*, Dublin.

Hughes, Garfield H. (1961), *Theophilus Evans, Drych y Prif Oesoedd yn ôl yr argraffiad cyntaf: 1716*, Cardiff.

Hughes, Kathleen (1966), *The Church in Early Irish Society*, London.

Hughes, Kathleen (1972), *Early Christian Ireland: introduction to the sources*, London.

Hughes, Kathleen (1973), 'The Welsh Latin Chronicles: Annales Cambriae and related texts', in *Proceedings of the British Academy* (1973), 233–58.

Hundert Meisterwerke keltischer Kunst. Schmuck und Kunsthandwerk zwischen Rhein und Mosel (1992), Trier (exhibition catalogue).

Hutt, Maurice (1983), *Chouannerie and Counter-Revolution. Puisaye, the Princes and the British Government in the 1790s*, Cambridge.

Huws, Bleddyn Owen (1998), *Y Canu Gofyn a Diolch, c. 1350–c. 1630*, Cardiff.

Huws, Daniel (2000), *Medieval Welsh Manuscripts*, Cardiff.

Irische Kunst aus drei Jahrtausenden. Thesaurus Hiberniae (1983), Mainz (exhibition catalogue).

Isaac, Graham R. (1996), *The Verb in the Book of Aneirin*, Tübingen (Buchreihe der *Zeitschrift für celtische Philologie* 12).

Jackson, Kenneth H. (1953), *Language and History in Early Britain*, Edinburgh.

Jackson, Kenneth (1964), *The Oldest Irish Tradition: A Window on the Iron Age*, Cambridge.

Jackson, Kenneth H. (1970), *The Gododdin: The Oldest Scottish Poem*, Edinburgh.

Jackson, Kenneth (1972), *The Gaelic Notes in the Book of Deer*, Cambridge.
Jacobsthal, Paul (1944), *Early Celtic Art*, 2 vols, Oxford.
James, Allan (1987), *John Morris-Jones*, Cardiff.
James, S. (1999), *The Atlantic Celts: Ancient People or Modern Invention?*, London.
James, Simon and Valery Rigby (1997) *Britain and the Celtic Iron Age*, London.
Jantz, Martina (1995), *Das Fremdenbild in der Literatur der Römischen Republik und der augusteischen Zeit. Vorstellungen und Sichtweisen am Beispiel von Hispanien und Gallien*, Frankfurt/Main.
Jarman, A. O. H. (1988), *Aneirin: Y Gododdin*, Llandysul (Welsh Classics 3).
Jarman, A. O. H. and Gwilym Rees Hughes (eds) (1992), *A Guide to Welsh Literature Volume 1*, rev. edn, Cardiff.
Jarman, A. O. H. and Gwilym Rees Hughes (eds) (1997), *A Guide to Welsh Literature 1282–c. 1550*, rev. Dafydd Johnston, Cardiff.
Jaski, Bart (2000), *Early Irish Kingship and Succession*, Dublin.
Jenkins, Dafydd (1986), *The Law of Hywel Dda. Law Texts From Medieval Wales translated and edited*, Llandysul (Welsh Classics 2).
Jenkins, Dafydd (1997), 'A Hundred Years of *Cyfraith Hywel*', *Zeitschrift für celtische Philologie* 49–50, 349–66.
Jenkins, Dafydd and Morfydd E. Owen (1984), 'The Welsh Marginalia in the Lichfield Gospels Part II: The "Surexit" Memorandum', *Cambrian Medieval Celtic Studies* 7, 91–120.
Jenkins, Geraint Huw (1987), *The Foundations of Modern Wales: Wales 1642–1780*, Oxford.
Jenkins, Geraint Huw (1995), 'Iolo Morganwg and the Gorsedd of the Bards of the Isle of Britain', *Studia Celtica Japonica N. S.* 7, 45–60.
Jenkins, Geraint Huw (ed.) (1997a), *The Welsh Language before the Industrial Revolution*, Cardiff.
Jenkins, Geraint Huw (1997b), *Facts, Fantasy and Fiction: The Historical Vision of Iolo Morganwg*, Aberystwyth.
Jenkins, Geraint Huw (ed.) (1998), *Language and Community in the Nineteenth Century*, Cardiff.
Jenkins, Geraint Huw (ed.) (2000), *The Welsh Language and its Social Domains 1801–1911*, Cardiff.
Jenkins, Geraint Huw and Mari A. Williams (eds) (2000), *'Let's do our best for the ancient tongue'. The Welsh Language in the Twentieth Century*, Cardiff.
Jenkins, J. Geraint (1992), *Getting Yesterday Right: Interpreting the Heritage of Wales*, Cardiff.
Jenkins, Philip (1992), *A History of Modern Wales 1536–1990*, London.
Jerem, Erzsébet, Alexandra Krenn-Leeb, Johannes-Wolfgang Neugebauer and Otto H. Urban (eds) (1996), *Die Kelten in den Alpen und an der Donau. Akten des Internationalen Symposions St. Pölten, 14.–18. Oktober 1992*, Budapest-Vienna.
Jiménez, Ramon L. (1996), *Caesar against the Celts*, New York.
Joachim, Hans-Eckart (1989), 'Eine Rekonstruktion der keltischen "Säule" von Pfalzfeld', *Bonner Jahrbücher* 189, 1–14.
Joachim, Hans-Eckart et al. (1995), *Waldalgesheim: das Grab einer keltischen Fürstin*, Bonn (Kataloge des Rheinischen Landesmuseums Bonn 3).

Joffroy, René (1979), *Vix et ses trésors*, Paris.
Johnston, D. R. (1988), *Gwaith Iolo Goch*, Cardiff.
Johnston, Dafydd (1991), *Canu Maswedd yr Oesoedd Canol. Medieval Welsh Erotic Poetry*, Cardiff.
Johnston, Dafydd (1994), *The Literature of Wales*, Cardiff.
Johnston, Dafydd (1995), *Gwaith Lewys Glyn Cothi*, Cardiff.
Johnston, Dafydd (ed.) (1998), *A Guide to Welsh Literature c. 1900–1996*, Cardiff.
Jones, Alun R. and Gwyn Thomas (eds) (1973), *Presenting Saunders Lewis*, Cardiff.
Jones, Emrys (2001), *The Welsh in London 1500–2000*, Cardiff.
Jones, Gareth Elwyn (1984), *Modern Wales. A concise history c. 1485–1979*, Cambridge.
Jones, Glyn and John Rowlands (1980), *Profiles. A Visitors' Guide to Writing in Twentieth Century Wales*, Llandysul.
Jones, Gwyn and Thomas Jones (1974), *The Mabinogion*, London.
Jones, Ieuan Gwynedd (1987), *Communities. Essays in the Social History of Victorian Wales*, Llandysul.
Jones, Ieuan Gwynedd (1992), *Mid-Victorian Wales*, Cardiff.
Jones, J. Gwynfor (ed.) (1989), *Class, Community and Culture in Tudor Wales*, Cardiff.
Jones, J. Gwynfor (ed.) (1994), *Early Modern Wales, c. 1525–1640*, New York.
Jones, J. Gwynfor (ed.) (1998), *The Welsh Gentry, 1536–1640. Images of Status, Honour and Authority*, Cardiff.
Jones, Leslie Ellen (1998), *Druid Shaman Priest. Metaphors of Celtic Paganism*, Enfield Lock, Middlesex.
Jones, Michael (1988), *The Creation of Brittany. A Late Medieval State*, London.
Jones, Nerys Ann and Ann Parry Owen (1991–5), *Gwaith Cynddelw Brydydd Mawr*, 2 vols, Cardiff.
Jones, Nerys Ann and Huw Pryce (eds) (1996), *Yr Arglwydd Rhys*, Cardiff.
Jope, E. M. and Paul F. Jacobsthal (2000), *Early Celtic Art in the British Isles*, Oxford.
Jordán Cólera, Carlos (1998), *Introducción al Celtibérico*, Saragossa (Monografías de Filología Griega 10).
Jufer, Nicole and Thierry Luginbühl (2001), *Répertoire des dieux gaulois*, Paris.
Kehnel, Annette (1998), *Clonmacnois – the Church and Lands of St Ciarán. Change and Continuity in an Irish Monastic Foundation (6th to 16th Century)*, Münster.
Keller, F. J. (1965), *Das keltische Fürstengrab von Reinheim*, Mainz.
Kelly, Fergus (1976), *Audacht Morainn*, Dublin.
Kelly, Fergus (1988), *A Guide to Early Irish Law*, Dublin (Early Irish Law Series 3).
Kelly, Fergus (1997), *Early Irish Farming. A study based mainly on the law-texts of the 7th and 8th centuries AD*, Dublin.
Kelly, James (1992), *Prelude to Union. Anglo-Irish Politics in the 1780s*, Cork.
Die Kelten in Mitteleuropa. Kultur, Kunst, Wirtschaft (1980), Salzburg (exhibition catalogue).

Der Keltenfürst von Hochdorf. Methoden und Ergebnisse der Landesarchäologie (1985), Stuttgart (exhibition catalogue)

Keogh, Dáire (1993), *The French Disease. The Catholic Church and Irish Radicalism, 1790–1800*, Dublin.

Keogh, Dáire and Nicholas Furlong (eds) (1996), *The Mighty Wave: The 1798 Rebellion in Wexford*, Dublin.

Kerlouégan, François (1987), *Le De excidio Britanniae de Gildas: Les destinées de la culture latine dans l'île de Bretagne au VIe siècle*, Paris.

Kilian. Mönch aus Irland – aller Franken Patron (1989), Würzburg (exhibition catalogue).

Kimmig, Wolfgang (1983a), *Die Heuneburg an der oberen Donau*, 2nd edn, Stuttgart.

Kimmig, Wolfgang (1983b), 'Zum Handwerk der späten Hallstattzeit', in *Das Handwerk in vor- und frühgeschichtlicher Zeit II*, Göttingen, 13–33.

Kimmig, Wolfgang (1985), 'Der Handel der Hallstattzeit', in *Untersuchungen zu Handel und Verkehr der vor- und frühgeschichtlichen Zeit in Mittel- und Nordeuropa I*, Göttingen, 214–30.

Kimmig, Wolfgang (1992), 'Etruskischer und griechischer Import im Spiegel westhallstättischer Fürstengräber', in Luciana Aigner-Foresti (ed.), *Etrusker nördlich von Etrurien*, Wien, 281–328.

Kimmig, Wolfgang et al. (1988), *Das Kleinaspergle. Studien zu einem Fürstengrabhügel der frühen Latènezeit bei Stuttgart*, Stuttgart.

Kinealy, Christine (1994), *This Great Calamity: The Irish Famine, 1845–52*, Dublin.

King, Anthony (1990), *Roman Gaul and Germany*, London.

Kinvig, Robert H. (1975), *The Isle of Man. A social, cultural and political history*, Liverpool.

Knott, Eleanor (1922–6), *The Bardic Poems of Tadhg Dall Ó hUiginn*, 2 vols, Dublin (Irish Texts Society 22–3).

Knott, Eleanor (1957), *An Introduction to Irish Syllabic Poetry of the Period 1200–1600*, Dublin.

Knott, Eleanor (1966), *Irish Classical Poetry*, Dublin.

Koch, John Thomas (1997), *The 'Gododdin' of Aneirin. Text and Context from Dark-Age North Britain*, Cardiff.

Koch, John Thomas and John Carey (eds) (2000), *The Celtic Heroic Age: literary sources for ancient Celtic Europe and early Ireland and Wales*, 3rd edn, Andover, MA.

Krausse, Dirk (1996), *Das Trink- und Speiseservice aus dem späthallstattzeitlichen Fürstengrab von Eberdingen-Hochdorf (Kr. Ludwigsburg)*, Stuttgart.

Kremer, Bernhard (1994), *Das Bild der Kelten bis in augusteische Zeit: Studien zur Instrumentalisierung eines antiken Feindbildes bei griechischen und römischen Autoren*, Stuttgart (Historia Einzelschriften 88).

Künzl, E. (1971), *Die Kelten des Epigonos von Pergamon*, Würzburg.

Kurz, Gabriele (1995), *Keltische Hort- und Gewässerfunde in Mitteleuropa: Deponierungen der Latènezeit*, Stuttgart (Materialhefte zur Archäologie in Baden-Württemberg 33).

Kurzynski, K. v. (1996), *'Und ihre Hosen nennen sie Bracas': Textilfunde und Textiltechnologie der Hallstatt- und Latènezeit und ihr Kontext*, Espelkamp.

Lacey, Brian (1997), *Colum Cille and the Columban Tradition*, Dublin.
Lacy, Norris J. (ed.) (1991), *The New Arthurian Encyclopedia*, London.
Lacy, Norris J. (ed.) (1998), *Early French Tristan Poems*, 2 vols, Cambridge.
Lagrée, Michel (1992), *Religion et cultures en Bretagne (1850–1950)*, Paris.
Laing, Lloyd and Jennifer Laing (1995), *Celtic Britain and Ireland: Art and Society*, London.
Lambert, Pierre-Yves (1994), *La langue gauloise. Description linguistique, commentaire d'inscriptions choisies*, Paris.
Landes, Christian (ed.) (1992), *Dieux guérisseurs en Gaule romaine*, Lattes.
Lapidge, Michael (ed.) (1997), *Columbanus. Studies on the Latin Writings*, Woodbridge.
Lapidge, Michael and David Dumville (eds) (1984), *Gildas: New Approaches*, Woodbridge.
Laurent, Donatien (1989), *Aux sources du Barzaz-Breiz*, Douarnenez.
Le Contel, Jean-Michel and Paul Verdier (1997), *Un calendrier celtique. Le calendrier gaulois de Coligny*, Paris.
Le Menn, Gwennolé (1996), *Les Dictionnaires français-breton et breton-français du R. P. Julien Maunoir (1659)*, 2 vols, Saint-Brieuc.
Le Menn, Gwennolé (1997), '*Cantiquou Spirituel' (1642). Premier recueil de Cantiques bretons réédité, traduit et annoté par Gwennolé le Menn avec en Annexe les airs notés précédés d'une étude par Isabelle His-Ravier*, Saint-Brieuc.
Leerssen, Joep (1996), *Remembrance and Imagination. Patterns in the Historical and Literary Representation of Ireland in the Nineteenth Century*, Cork.
Leguay, J.-P. and Hervé Martin (1982), *Fastes et malheurs de la Bretagne ducale 1213–1532*, Rennes.
Lejeune, Michel (1985), *Textes gallo-grecs*, Paris (Recueil des inscriptions gauloises I).
Lejeune, Michel (1988), *Textes gallo-étrusques, Textes gallo-latins sur pierre*, Paris (Recueil des inscriptions gauloises II, 1).
Lenerz-De Wilde, Majolie (1991), *Iberia Celtica: Archäologische Zeugnisse keltischer Kultur auf der Pyrenäenhalbinsel*, 2 vols, Wiesbaden.
Lenman, B. (1980), *The Jacobite Risings in Britain 1689–1746*, London.
Lennon, Colm (1994), *Sixteenth-Century Ireland: The Incomplete Conquest*, Dublin.
Lewis, Aneirin (1976), *Ellis Wynne, Gweledigaetheu y Bardd Cwsc*, 2nd edn, Cardiff.
Lewis, Ceri W. (1995), *Iolo Morganwg*, Caernarfon.
Lewis, Henry (1946), *Llawlyfr Cernyweg Canol*, 2nd edn, Cardiff.
Loeber, Rolf (1991), *The Geography and Practice of English Colonisation in Ireland from 1534 to 1609*, Athlone.
Löffler, Marion (1997), *Englisch und Kymrisch in Wales. Geschichte der Sprachsituation und Sprachpolitik*, Hamburg.
Lord, Peter (1998), *The Visual Culture of Wales: Industrial Society*, Cardiff.
Löwe, Heinz (ed.) (1982), *Die Iren und Europa im früheren Mittelalter*, Stuttgart.
Lydon, James (1972), *The Lordship of Ireland in the Middle Ages*, Dublin.
Lydon, James (1984), *The English in Medieval Ireland*, Dublin.

Lydon, James (1998), *The Making of Ireland. From ancient times to the present*, London.

Lynch, Michael (ed.) (2000), *The Oxford Companion to Scottish History*, Oxford.

Lynch, Peter (1996), *Minority Nationalism and European Integration*, Cardiff.

Mac Airt, Seán and Gearóid Mac Niocaill (1983), *The Annals of Ulster (to AD 1131)*, Dublin.

MacAlister, R. A. S. (1938–41), *Lebor Gabála Érenn. The Book of the Taking of Ireland*, 4 vols, Dublin (Irish Texts Society 34, 35, 39, 41).

Mac Aonghusa, Proinsias (1993), *Ar son na Gaeilge: Conradh na Gaeilge 1893–1993, Stair Sheanchais*, Dublin.

MacAulay, Donald (ed.) (1992), *The Celtic Languages*, Cambridge.

Mac Cana, Proinsias (1985), 'Early Irish Ideology and the Concept of Unity', in R. Kearney (ed.), *The Irish Mind*, Dublin, 56–78.

Mac Cana, Proinsias (1992), *The Mabinogi*, 2nd edn, Cardiff.

Mac Cana, Proinsias (1993), 'Ir. *buaball*, W. *bual* "Drinking Horn" ', *Ériu* 44, 81–93.

MacCarthy-Morrogh, Michael (1986), *The Munster Plantation: English Migration to Southern Ireland, 1583–1641*, Oxford.

McCone, Kim (1990), *Pagan Past and Christian Present in Early Irish Literature*, Maynooth (Maynooth Monographs 3).

McCone, Kim (2000), *Echtrae Chonnlai and the Beginnings of Vernacular Narrative Writing in Ireland*, Maynooth.

McCone, K., D. McManus, C. Ó Háinle, N. Williams and L. Breatnach (1994), *Stair na Gaeilge, in ómós do Pádraig Ó Fiannachta*, Maynooth.

Mac Cuarta, Brian Mac (ed.) (1991), *Ulster 1641: Aspects of the Rising*, Dublin.

MacDonald, A. and A. MacDonald (1924), *The Poems of Alexander MacDonald*, Inverness.

McDonald, Andrew (1997), *The Kingdom of the Isles: Scotland's Western Seaboard, c. 1100–c. 1336*, East Linton.

McDonald, Maryon (1989), *'We are not French!' Language, Culture and Identity in Brittany*, London.

Mac Eoin, Gearóid (1998), 'Literacy and Cultural Change in Early Ireland', in C. Ehler and U. Schaefer (eds), *Verschriftung und Verschriftlichung*, Tübingen, 99–131.

Mac Erlean, John C. (1910–17), *Duanaire Dháibhidh Uí Bhruadair. Poems of David Ó Bruadair*, 3 vols, Dublin (Irish Texts Society 11, 13, 18).

McGuinness, Philip, Alan Harrison und Richard Kearney (eds) (1997), *John Toland's 'Christianity not Mysterious'. Text, Associated Works and Critical Essays*, Dublin.

McKenna, Catherine A. (1991), *The Medieval Welsh Religious Lyric. Poems of the Gogynfeirdd, 1137–1282*, Belmont, MA.

Mackenzie, Annie M. (1964), *Orain Iain Luim*, Edinburgh (Scottish Gaelic Texts Society 8).

MacLeod, Angus (1952), *Orain Dhonnchaidh Bhàin. The Songs of Duncan Bàn Macintyre*, Edinburgh (Scottish Gaelic Texts Society 4).

Macleod, Donald J. (1934), *A Description of the Western Islands of Scotland circa 1695 by Martin Martin, Gent, Including A Voyage to St Kilda by the same author and A Description of the Western Isles of Scotland by Sir Donald Monro*, Stirling.

McLoughlin, T. O. (1999), *Contesting Ireland. Irish Voices against England in the Eighteenth Century*, Dublin.

McManus, Damian (1991), *A Guide to Ogam*, Maynooth (Maynooth Monographs 4).

Mac Mathúna, Séamus (1985), *Immram Brain: Bran's Journey to the Land of the Women*, Tübingen (Buchreihe der *Zeitschrift für celtische Philologie* 2).

McNamee, Colm (1997), *The Wars of the Bruces: Scotland, England and Ireland, 1306–1328*, East Linton.

MacNeill, Eoin and Gerard Murphy (1908–54), *Duanaire Finn: The Poem Book of Finn*, 3 vols, Dublin (Irish Texts Society 7, 28, 43).

Mac Niocaill, Gearóid (1972), *Ireland before the Vikings*, Dublin.

Mac Niocaill, Gearóid (1975), *The Medieval Irish Annals*, Dublin.

Mac Shamhráin, Ailbhe Séamus (1996), *Church and Polity in Pre-Norman Ireland: The Case of Glendalough*, Maynooth (Maynooth Monographs 7).

Maddox, D. (1991), *The Arthurian Romances of Chrétien de Troyes*, Cambridge.

Maier, Bernhard (1996a), 'Of Celts and Cyclopes: Notes on Athenaeus IV 36 p. 152A and Related Passages', *Studia Celtica* 30, 83–8.

Maier, Bernhard (1996b), 'Is Lug to be Identified with Mercury (Bell. Gall. VI 17, 1)?' New suggestions on an old problem', *Ériu* 47, 127–35.

Maier, Bernhard (1997), *Dictionary of Celtic Religion and Culture*, Woodbridge.

Maier, Bernhard (1999a), 'Beasts from the Deep: The Water-Bull in Celtic, Germanic and Balto-Slavonic Traditions', *Zeitschrift für celtische Philologie* 51, 4–16.

Maier, Bernhard (1999b), *Das Sagenbuch der walisischen Kelten. Die Vier Zweige des Mabinogi*, Munich.

Maier, Bernhard (2001), *Die Religion der Kelten. Götter – Mythen – Weltbild*, Munich.

Maier, Bernhard and Stefan Zimmer (eds) (2001), *150 Jahre 'Mabinogion' – Deutsch-walisische Kulturbeziehungen*, Tübingen (Buchreihe der *Zeitschrift für celtische Philologie* 19).

Maissen, Thomas (1994), *Von der Legende zum Modell: Das Interesse an Frankreichs Vergangenheit während der italienischen Renaissance*, Basel.

Malitz, Jürgen (1983), *Die Historien des Poseidonios*, Munich (Zetemata 79).

Mallory, James P. (ed.) (1992), *Aspects of the Táin*, Belfast.

Mallory, James P. (1998), 'The Old Irish Chariot', in J. Jasanoff et al. (eds), *Mír Curad. Studies in Honour of Calvert Watkins*, Innsbruck, 451–64.

Mallory, James P. and G. Stockman (eds) (1994), *Ulidia. Proceedings of the First International Conference on the Ulster Cycle of Tales*, Belfast.

Marco Simón, Francisco (1998), *Die Religion im keltischen Hispanien*, Budapest.

Martin, Paul (2001), *Vercingétorix*, Paris.

Martin, R. and P. Varène (1973), *Le monument d'Ucuetis à Alésia*, Paris.

Matheson, William (1938), *The Songs of John MacCodrum*, Edinburgh (Scottish Gaelic Texts Society 2).

Matheson, William (1970), *An Clàrsair Dall. The Blind Harper*, Edinburgh (Scottish Gaelic Texts Society 12).

Maume, Patrick (1993), *'Life that is Exile': Daniel Corkery and the Search for Irish Ireland*, Belfast.

Maund, K. L. (ed.) (1996), *Gruffudd ap Cynan. A Collaborative Biography*, Woodbridge.

Meek, Donald (ed.) (1995), *Tuath is Tighearna. An Anthology of Gaelic Poetry of Social and Political Protest from the Clearances to the Land Agitation (1800–1890)*, Edinburgh.

Meek, Donald (2000), *The Quest for Celtic Christianity*, Millfield.

Meek, Donald and M. K. Simms (eds) (1996), *'The Fragility of her Sex'? Medieval Irish Women in their European Context*, Dublin.

Megaw, J. V. S. (1970), *Art of the European Iron Age. A study of the elusive image*, London.

Megaw, Ruth and Vincent Megaw (1989), *Celtic Art. From its Beginnings to the Book of Kells*, London.

Megaw, Ruth and Vincent Megaw (1990), *The Basse-Yutz Find*, London.

Meid, Wolfgang (1991), *Aspekte der germanischen und keltischen Religion im Zeugnis der Sprache*, Innsbruck.

Meid, Wolfgang (1992), *Gaulish Inscriptions. Their interpretation in the light of archaeological evidence and their value as a source of linguistic and sociological information*, Budapest.

Meid, Wolfgang (1993), *Die erste Botorrita-Inschrift. Interpretation eines keltiberischen Sprachdenkmals*, Innsbruck.

Meid, Wolfgang (1994), *Celtiberian Inscriptions*, Budapest.

Meid, Wolfgang (1996), *Heilpflanzen und Heilsprüche. Zeugnisse gallischer Sprache bei Marcellus von Bordeaux*, Innsbruck.

Méniel, Patrice (1987), *Chasse et élevage chez les Gaulois (450–52 av. J.-C.)*, Paris.

Méniel, Patrice (1992), *Les sacrifices d'animaux chez les Gaulois*, Paris.

Merdrignac, Bernard (1985–6), *Recherches sur l'hagiographie armoricaine du VIIᵉ au XVᵉ siècle*, 2 vols, Rennes.

Merriman, J. D. (1973), *The Flower of Kings. A Study of the Arthurian Legend in England between 1485 and 1835*, Lawrence.

Mertens, Volker (1998), *Der deutsche Artusroman*, Stuttgart.

Metzler, Jeannot, Raymond Waringo, Romain Bis and Nicole Metzler-Zens (1991), *Clemency et les tombes de l'aristocratie en Gaule Belgique*, Luxembourg.

Meyer, Kuno (1909), *Rawlinson B. 502 in the Bodleian Library*, Oxford.

Mitchell, Stephen (1993), *Anatolia: Land, Men and Gods in Asia Minor. I. The Celts in Anatolia and the Impact of Roman Rule*, Oxford.

Moody, T. W. and W. E. Vaughan (eds) (1986), *Eighteenth-Century Ireland 1691 1800*, Oxford.

Moody, T. W., F. X. Martin and F. J. Byrne (eds) (1976), *A New History of Ireland. III. Early Modern Ireland, 1534–1691*, Oxford.

Moosleitner, Fritz (1985), *Die Schnabelkanne vom Dürrnberg*, Salzburg.

Morash, Chris and Richard Hughes (eds) (1996), *Fearful Realities: New Perspectives on the Famine*, Dublin.

Morel, J.-P. (1995), 'Les Grecs et la Gaule', in *Les Grecs et l'Occident*, Rome, 41–69.

Morgan, Derec Llwyd (1988), *The Great Awakening in Wales*, London.

Morgan, Derec Llwyd (ed.) (1991), *Meddwl a Dychymyg Williams Pantycelyn*, Llandysul.

Morgan, Hiram (1993), *Tyrone's Rebellion. The Outbreak of the Nine Years War in Tudor Ireland*, Woodbridge.

Morgan, Kenneth O. (1981), *Rebirth of a Nation: Wales 1880–1980*, Oxford.

Morgan, Prys (1983), 'From a Death to a View: The Hunt for the Welsh Past in the Romantic Period', in Eric Hobsbawm and Terence Ranger (eds), *The Invention of Tradition*, Cambridge.

Morgan, Prys (1997), *The University of Wales 1939–1993*, Cardiff.

Moscati, Sabbatino et al. (eds) (1991), *The Celts*, Milan (exhibition catalogue).

Mühlhausen, Ludwig (1988), *Die vier Zweige des Mabinogi (Pedeir Ceinc y Mabinogi)*, 2nd edn revised and expanded by Stefan Zimmer, Tübingen.

Mulchrone, Kathleen (1939), *Bethu Phátraic, the Tripartite Life of Patrick*, Dublin.

Müller, Felix (1995), 'Keltische Wagen mit elastischer Aufhängung: Eine Reise von Castel di Decima nach Clonmacnoise', in *Trans Europam. Festschrift für Margarita Primas*, Bonn, 265–75.

Murdoch, B. (1993), *Cornish Literature*, Cambridge.

Murphy, Gerard (1955), *The Ossianic Lore and Romantic Tales of Medieval Ireland*, Dublin.

Murphy, Brian P. (1992), *Patrick Pearse and the Lost Republican Ideal*, Dublin.

Myrick, L. D. (1993), *From the De Excidio Troiae Historia to the Togail Troi. Literary-Cultural Synthesis in a Medieval Irish Adaptation of Dares' Troy Tale*, Heidelberg.

Mytum, Harold (1992), *The Origins of Early Christian Ireland*, London.

Nachtergael, Georges (1975), *Les Galates en Grèce et les Sôtéria de Delphes*, Bruxelles.

Nagy, Joseph Falaky (1985), *The Wisdom of the Outlaw. The Boyhood Deeds of Finn in Gaelic Narrative Tradition*, Berkeley, CA.

Nagy, Joseph Falaky (1997), *Conversing with Angels and Ancients. Literary Myths of Medieval Ireland*, Dublin.

Nash, Daphne (1976), 'Reconstructing Posidonius' Celtic Ethnography: some considerations', *Britannia* 7, 111–26.

Nash, Daphne (1987), *Coinage in the Celtic World*, London.

Newton, Michael (2000), *A Handbook of the Scottish Gaelic World*, Dublin.

Ní Chatháin, Próinséas and Michael Richter (eds) (1984), *Irland und Europa. Die Kirche im Frühmittelalter*, Stuttgart.

Ní Chatháin, Próinséas and Michael Richter (eds) (1987), *Irland und die Christenheit. Bibelstudien und Mission*, Stuttgart.

Ní Chatháin, Próinséas and Michael Richter (eds) (1996), *Irland und Europa im früheren Mittelalter. Bildung und Literatur*, Stuttgart 1996.

Ní Cheallacháin, Máire (1962), *Filíocht Phádraigín Haicéad*, Dublin.

Ní Chionnaith, Eibhlín (1993), *Pádraic Ó Conaire: Scéal a Bheatha*, Dublin.

Nicholls, Kenneth (1972), *Gaelic and Gaelicised Ireland in the Middle Ages*, Dublin.

Nicholson, Colin (1992) (ed.), *Iain Crichton Smith. Critical Essays*, Edinburgh.

Nicoll, E. H. (ed.) (1995), *A Pictish Panorama*, Forfar.

Ní Shéaghdha, Nessa (1967), *Tóraigheacht Dhiarmada agus Ghráinne: The Pursuit of Diarmaid and Gráinne*, Dublin (Irish Texts Society 48).

Nordenfalk, Carl (1977), *Insulare Buchmalerei. Illuminierte Handschriften der Britischen Inseln 600–800*, Munich.

O'Brien, Jacqueline and Peter Harbison (1996), *Ancient Ireland: from Prehistory to the Middle Ages*, London.

Ó Buachalla, Breandán (1994), *Aisling Ghéar: Na Stíobhartaigh agus an tAos Léinn, 1603–1788*, Dublin.

Ó Catháin, Séamas (1995), *The Festival of Brigit*, Dublin.

Ó Ceallaigh, Daltún (ed.) (1994), *Reconsiderations of Irish History and Culture*, Dublin.

Ó Ciardha, Éamon (2001), *Ireland and the Jacobite Cause, 1685–1766*, Dublin.

Ó Concheanainn, Tomás (1996), 'Textual and Historical Associations of Leabhar na hUidhre', *Éigse* 29, 65–120.

Ó Corráin, Ailbhe and Séamus Mac Mathúna (eds) (1998), *Minority Languages in Scandinavia, Britain and Ireland*, Uppsala.

Ó Corráin, Donnchadh (1972), *Ireland before the Normans*, Dublin.

Ó Corráin, Donnchadh (1978), 'Nationality and Kingship in Pre-Norman Ireland', in T. W Moody (ed.), *Nationality and the Pursuit of National Independence*, Belfast, 1–35.

Ó Corráin, Donnchadh (1985), 'Irish Origin Legends and Genealogy', in *History and Heroic Tale*, Odense, 51–96.

Ó Corráin, Donnchadh, Liam Breatnach and Kim McCone (eds) (1989), *Sages, Saints and Storytellers*, Maynooth (Maynooth Monographs 2).

Ó Cróinín, Dáibhí (1995), *Early Medieval Ireland 400–1200*, London.

Ó Dochartaigh, Cathair (ed.) (1994–97), *Survey of the Gaelic Dialects of Scotland*, 5 vols, Dublin.

Ó Duinnín, Pádraig and Tadhg Ó Donnchadha (1911), *Dánta Aodhagáin Uí Rathaille. The Poems of Egan O'Rahilly*, Dublin.

Ó Dúshláine, Tadhg (1987), *An Eoraip agus Litríocht na Gaeilge 1600–1650*, Dublin.

Ó Gráda, Cormac (ed.) (1997), *Famine 150*, Dublin.

Ohlmeyer, Jane (ed.) (1995), *Ireland from Independence to Occupation, 1641–1660*, Cambridge.

Ó hÓgáin, Dáithí (1988), *Fionn Mac Cumhaill: Images of the Gaelic Hero*, Dublin.

Ó hÓgáin, Dáithí (1990), *Myth, Legend and Romance. An Encyclopaedia of the Irish Folk Tradition*, London.

Ó Huallacháin, Fr. Colmán, O. F. M. (1994), *The Irish and Irish – a sociolinguistic analysis of the relationship between a people and their language*, Dublin.

O'Leary, P. (1994), *The Prose Literature of the Gaelic Revival, 1881–1921: ideology and innovation*, Univ. Park/Pennsylvania.

Ó Luing, Seán (1991), *Kuno Meyer 1858–1919*, Dublin.

O'Mahoney, F. (1994), *The Book of Kells. Proceedings of a conference at Trinity College Dublin 6–9 September 1992*, Dublin.

Ó Muraíle, Nollaig (1996), *The Celebrated Antiquary Dubhaltach Mac Fhirbhisigh (c. 1600–1671). His Lineage, Life and Learning*, Maynooth (Maynooth Monographs 6).

O'Rahilly, Cecile (1961), *The Stowe Version of Táin Bó Cuailnge*, Dublin.

O'Rahilly, Cecile (1967), *Táin Bó Cuailnge from the Book of Leinster*, Dublin.

O'Rahilly, Cecile (1976), *Táin Bó Cuailnge: Recension I*, Dublin.

O'Rahilly, Thomas Francis (1941), *Desiderius*, Dublin.

Ó Raifeartaigh, T. (ed.) (1985), *The Royal Irish Academy: A Bicentennial History, 1785–1985*, Dublin.

Ó Riagáin, Pádraig (1997), *Language Policy and Social Reproduction. Ireland 1893–1993*, Oxford.

Ó Riain, Pádraig (ed.) (2000), *Fled Bricrenn: Reassessments*, Cork (Irish Texts Society Subsidiary Series 10).

Ó Riordan, Michelle (1990), *The Gaelic Mind and the Collapse of the Gaelic World*, Cork.

Ó Siochrú, Micheál (1998), *Confederate Ireland 1642–1649. A Constitutional and Political Analysis*, Dublin.

Ó Siochrú, Micheál (ed.) (2001), *Kingdoms in Crisis. Ireland in the 1640s*, Dublin.

Ó Tuama, Seán (1960), *An Grá in Amhráin na nDaoine*, Dublin.

Ó Tuama, Seán (1972), *The Gaelic League Idea*, Dublin.

Ó Tuama, Seán (1988), *An Grá i bhFilíocht na nUaisle*, Dublin.

Ó Tuama, Seán (1995), *Repossessions. Selected Essays on the Irish Literary Heritage*, Cork.

Ó Tuama, Seán and Thomas Kinsella (1981), *An Duanaire 1600–1900: Poems of the Dispossessed*, Dublin.

Overbeck, B. (1980), *Die Welt der Kelten im Spiegel der Münzen*, Munich.

Owen, A. L. (1962), *The Famous Druids. A Survey of Three Centuries of English Literature on the Druids*, Oxford.

Owen, Goronwy Wyn (1992), *Morgan Llwyd*, Caernarfon.

Owen, Morfydd E. and Brynley F. Roberts (eds) (1996), *Beirdd a Thywysogion. Barddoniaeth Llys yng Nghymru, Iwerddon a'r Alban*, Cardiff.

Padel, Oliver J. (1985), *Cornish Place-Name Elements*, Nottingham.

Padel, Oliver J. (1988), *A Popular Dictionary of Cornish Place-Names*, Penzance.

Pape, Louis (1995), *La Bretagne romaine*, Rennes.

Parry, Graham (1995), *The Trophies of Time: English Antiquarians of the Seventeenth Century*, Oxford.

Parry, Thomas (ed.) (1962), *The Oxford Book of Welsh Verse*, Oxford.

Parsons, David N. and Patrick Sims-Williams (eds) (2000), *Ptolemy. Towards a linguistic atlas of the earliest Celtic place-names of Europe*, Aberystwyth.

Patterson, Nerys Thomas (1991), *Cattle-Lords and Clansmen. Kinship and Rank in Early Ireland*, New York.

Pauli, Ludwig (1975), *Keltischer Volksglaube. Amulette und Sonderbestattungen am Dürrnberg bei Hallein und im eisenzeitlichen Mitteleuropa*, Munich (Münchner Beiträge zur Vor- und Frühgeschichte 28).

Pauli, Ludwig (1980), 'Die Herkunft der Kelten: Sinn und Unsinn einer alten Frage', in *Die Kelten in Mitteleuropa. Kultur, Kunst, Wirtschaft*, Salzburg, 16–24.

Pauli, Ludwig (1992), 'Die historische Entwicklung im Gebiet der Golasecca-Kultur', in Luciana Aigner-Foresti (ed.), *Etrusker nördlich von Etrurien*, Vienna, 179–96.

Percival-Maxwell, M. (1994), *The Outbreak of the Irish Rebellion, 1641*, Dublin.

Peschel, Karl (1989), 'Zur kultischen Devotion innerhalb der keltischen Kriegergemeinschaft', in F. Schlette und D. Kaufmann (eds), *Religion und Kult in Ur- und Frühgeschichtlicher Zeit*, Berlin, 273–82.

Peters, Erik (1967), 'Die irische Alexandersage', *Zeitschrift für celtische Philologie* 30, 71–264.

Piggott, Stuart (1968), *The Druids*, London.

Piggott, Stuart (1985), *William Stukeley: An Eighteenth-Century Antiquary*, London.

Piggott, Stuart (1989), *Ancient Britons and the Antiquarian Imagination*, London.

Planck, Dieter (1982), 'Eine neuentdeckte keltische Viereckschanze in Fellbach-Schmiden, Rems-Murr-Kreis. Vorbericht der Grabungen 1977–1980', *Germania* 60, 105–72.

Pleiner, Radomir (1993), *The Celtic Sword*, Oxford.

Plonéis, Jean-Marie (1989–93), *La Toponymie celtique. L'origine des noms de lieux en Bretagne*, 2 vols, Paris.

Poppe, Erich (1995), *A New Introduction to Imtheachta Aeniasa. The Irish Aeneid: The Classical Epic from an Irish Perspective*, London.

Poppe, Erich and Hildegard Tristram (eds) (1999), *Übersetzung, Adaption und Akkulturation im insularen Mittelalter*, Münster.

Portéir, Cathal (ed.) (1995), *The Great Irish Famine*, Cork.

Power, Thomas P. and Kevin Whelan (eds) (1990), *Endurance and Emergence. Catholics in Ireland in the Eighteenth Century*, Blackrock.

Price, Glanville (1984), *The Languages of Britain*, London.

Price, Glanville (ed.) (1992), *The Celtic Connection*, Gerrards Cross.

Price, Glanville (ed.) (2000), *Languages in Britain and Ireland*, Oxford.

Pryce, Huw (ed.) (1998), *Literacy in Medieval Celtic Societies*, Cambridge.

Py, Michel (1993), *Les Gaulois du Midi. De la fin de l'Âge de Bronze à la conquête romaine*, Paris.

Quiggin, E. C. (1937), *Poems from the Book of the Dean of Lismore*, Cambridge.

Rafferty, Oliver P. (1994), *Catholicism in Ulster 1603–1983. An Interpretative History*, London.

Raftery, Barry (1994), *Pagan Celtic Ireland. The Enigma of the Irish Iron Age*, London.

Raftery, Barry, Vincent Megaw and Val Rigby (eds) (1995), *Sites and Sights of the Iron Age. Essays on Fieldwork and Museum Research presented to Ian Mathieson Stead*, Oxford.

Rankin, David (1996), *Celts and the Classical World*, 2nd edn, London.

Reichenberger, Alfred (1993), 'Zur Interpretation der spätlatènezeitlichen Viereckschanzen', *Jahrbuch des Römisch-Germanischen Zentralmuseums Mainz* 40, 353–96.

Reynolds, P. (1995), 'The Food of the Prehistoric Celts', in J. Wilkins et al. (ed.), *Food in Antiquity*, Exeter, 303–15.

Richards, Eric (1982), *A History of the Highland Clearances: Agrarian Transformation and the Evictions 1746–1886*, London.
Richards, Melville (1948), *Breudwyt Ronabwy allan o'r Llyfr Coch o Hergest*, Cardiff.
Richter, Michael (1994), *The Formation of the Medieval West. Studies in the oral culture of the barbarians*, Dublin.
Rieckhoff, Sabine and Jörg Biel (2001), *Die Kelten in Deutschland*, Stuttgart.
Rieger, Dietmar (1980), *Marie de France, Die Lais*, Munich (Klassische Texte des romanischen Mittelalters in zweisprachigen Ausgaben 19).
Riek, Gustav and Hans-Jürgen Hundt (1962), *Der Hohmichele – Ein Fürstengrabhügel der späten Hallstattzeit bei der Heuneburg*, Berlin (Heuneburgstudien I).
Riggs, Pádraigín (1994), *Pádraic Ó Conaire – Deoraí*, Dublin.
Ritchie, Anna (1993), *Viking Scotland*, London.
Rivet, A. L. F. (1988), *Gallia Narbonensis: southern France in Roman times*, London.
Rivet, A. L. F. and Colin Smith (1979), *The Place-Names of Roman Britain*, London.
Roberts, Brynley Francis (ed.) (1988), *Early Welsh Poetry. Studies in the Book of Aneirin*, Aberystwyth.
Roberts, Gwyneth Tyson (1998), *The Language of the Blue Books. The Perfect Instrument of Empire*, Cardiff.
Roberts, John L. (1997), *Lost Kingdoms: Celtic Scotland in the Middle Ages*, Edinburgh.
Roberts, John L. (1999), *Feuds, Forays and Rebellions. History of the Highland Clans 1475–1625*, Edinburgh.
Robinson, Philip (1984), *The Plantation of Ulster: British Settlement in an Irish Landscape, 1600–1670*, Dublin.
Robinson, Vaughan and Danny McCarroll (eds) (1990), *The Isle of Man. Celebrating a Sense of Place*, Liverpool.
Roche-Bernard, G. (1993), *Costumes et textiles en Gaule romaine*, Paris.
Röder, J. (1948), 'Der Goloring, ein eisenzeitliches Heiligtum vom Henge-Charakter im Koblenzer Wald (Landkreis Koblenz)', *Bonner Jahrbücher* 148, 81–132.
Ross, Bianca (1998), *Britannia et Hibernia. Nationale und kulturelle Identitäten im Irland des 17. Jahrhunderts*, Heidelberg.
Ross, Neil (1939), *Heroic Poetry from the Book of the Dean of Lismore*, Edinburgh (Scottish Gaelic Texts Society 3).
Rowland, Jenny (1990), *Early Welsh Saga Poetry. A Study and Edition of the 'Englynion'*, Cambridge.
Ruane, Joseph and Jennifer Todd (eds) (1996), *The Dynamics of Conflict in Northern Ireland. Power, Conflict and Emancipation*, Cambridge.
Russell, Paul (1995), *An Introduction to the Celtic Languages*, London.
Sainclivier, Jacqueline (1989), *La Bretagne de 1939 à nos jours*, Rennes.
Les sanctuaires de tradition indigène en Gaule romaine. Actes du Colloque d'Argentomagus (Argenton-sur-Creuse/Saint-Marcel, Indre) 8, 9 et 10 octobre 1992 (1994), Paris.

Sanger, Keith and Alison Kinnaird (1992), *Tree of Strings crann nan teud. A history of the harp in Scotland*, Shillinghill Temple.

Schaaff, U. et al. (1987), *Vierrädrige Wagen der Hallstattzeit*, Mainz.

Schmidt, Karl Horst (1957), 'Die Komposition in gallischen Personennamen', *Zeitschrift für celtische Philologie* 26, 33–301.

Schmidt, Karl Horst (1983), 'Handwerk und Handwerker in altkeltischen Sprachdenkmälern', *Das Handwerk in vor- und frühgeschichtlicher Zeit II*, Göttingen, 751–3.

Schmidt, Karl Horst (ed.) (1986), *Geschichte und Kultur der Kelten*, Heidelberg.

Schmidt, Karl Horst (1992), 'The Celtic Problem: Ethnogenesis (Location, Date?)', *Zeitschrift für celtische Philologie* 45, 38–65.

Schmidt, Karl Horst (1994), 'Galatische Sprachreste', in E. Schwertheim (ed.), *Forschungen in Galatien*, Bonn, 15–28.

Schmidt, Karl Horst (2001), 'Remnants of the Galatian Language', in Ailbhe Ó Corráin (ed.), *Proceedings of the Fifth Symposium of Societas Celtologica Nordica*, Uppsala, 13–28.

Schmolke-Hasselmann, Beate (1998), *The Evolution of Arthurian Romance*, Cambridge.

School of Celtic Studies: Fiftieth Anniversary Report 1940–1990 (1990), Dublin.

Schrijver, Peter (1995), *Studies in British Celtic Historical Phonology*, Amsterdam.

Schulten, Adolf (1955), *Avieno, Ora Maritima, junto con los demás testimonios anteriores al año 500 a. de J. C.*, 2nd edn, Barcelona.

Scowcroft, R. M. (1987–8), 'Leabhar Gabhála', *Ériu* 38, 80–142 and 39, 1–66.

Sharpe, Richard (1991), *Medieval Irish Saints' Lives. An Introduction to Vitae Sanctorum Hiberniae*, Oxford.

Sharpe, Richard (1995), *Adomnán of Iona. Life of St Columba*, Harmondsworth.

Sheehy, Jeanne (1980), *The Rediscovery of Ireland's Past: The Celtic Revival 1830–1930*, London.

Shields, Hugh (1993), *Narrative Singing in Ireland. Lays, ballads, Come-all-yes and other songs*, Dublin.

Sigurdsson, G. (1988), *Gaelic Influence in Iceland*, Reykjavik.

Silke, John J. (2000), *Kinsale. The Spanish Intervention in Ireland at the End of the Elizabethan Wars*, Dublin.

Simms, J. G. (2000), *Jacobite Ireland*, Dublin.

Simms, Katharine (1987), *From Kings to Warlords. The Changing Political Structure of Gaelic Ireland in the Later Middle Ages*, Woodbridge.

Sims-Williams, Patrick (1986), 'The Visionary Celt: The Construction of an Ethnic Preconception', *Cambridge Medieval Celtic Studies* 11, 71–96.

Sims-Williams, Patrick (1990) 'Some Celtic Otherworld Terms', in A. T. E. Matonis and F. Melia (eds), *Celtic Language, Celtic Culture: A Festschrift for Eric P. Hamp*, Van Nuys, CA, 57–81.

Sims-Williams, Patrick (1993), 'Some Problems in Deciphering the Early Irish Ogam Alphabet', *Transactions of the Philological Society* 91, 133–80.

Sims-Williams, Patrick (1998a), 'Genetics, Linguistics, and Prehistory: Thinking Big and Thinking Straight', *Antiquity* 72, 505–27.

Sims-Williams, Patrick (1998b), 'Celtomania and Celtoscepticism', *Cambrian Medieval Celtic Studies* 36, 1–35.

Sloan, Robert (2000), *William Smith O'Brien and the Young Ireland Rebellion of 1848*, Dublin.
Small, Alan, Charles Thomas and David M. Wilson (eds) (1973), *St Ninian's Isle and its Treasure*, 2 vols, Oxford.
Smith, J. Beverley (1998), *Llywelyn ap Grufudd. Prince of Wales*, Cardiff.
Smith, Julia M. H. (1992), *Province and Empire. Brittany and the Carolingians*, Cambridge.
Smyth, A. P. (1999) (ed.), *Senchas: Studies presented to Francis John Byrne*, Dublin.
Smyth, Marina (1996), *Understanding the Universe in Seventh-Century Ireland*, Woodbridge.
Solinas, P. (1995), 'Il celtico in Italia', *Studi Etruschi* 60, 311–408.
Spindler, Konrad (1996), *Die frühen Kelten*, 3rd edn, Stuttgart.
Stacey, Robin Chapman (1994), *The Road to Judgment. From Custom to Court in Medieval Ireland and Wales*, Philadelphia.
Stafford, Fiona (1988), *James Macpherson and the Poems of Ossian*, Edinburgh.
Stafford, Fiona and Howard Gaskill (eds) (1988), *From Gaelic to Romantic. Ossianic Translations*, Amsterdam (Studies in Comparative Literature 15).
Stähelin, Felix (1907), *Geschichte der kleinasiatischen Galater*, 2nd edn, Stuttgart.
Stary, P. E. (1990), 'Keltische Einflüsse im Kampfeswesen der Etrusker und benachbarter Völker', in *Die Welt der Etrusker*, Berlin, 59–66.
Stead, Ian M. (1996), *Celtic Art*, 2nd edn, London.
Stead, Ian M., Jim Bourke and Don Brothwell (eds) (1986), *Lindow Man: The Body in the Bog*, London.
Steer, K. A. and J. W. M. Bannerman (1977), *Late Medieval Monumental Sculpture in the West Highlands*, Edinburgh.
Stephens, Meic (ed.) (1998), *The New Companion to the Literature of Wales*, Oxford.
Stevenson, D. (1980), *Alasdair MacColla and the Highland Problem in the Seventeenth Century*, Edinburgh.
Stokes, Whitley and John Strachan (1901–3), *Thesaurus palaeohibernicus: a collection of Old-Irish glosses, scholia, prose, and verse*, 2 vols, Cambridge.
Stoll, André (1974), *Asterix: das Trivialepos Frankreichs*, Cologne.
Strijbosch, C. (1995), *De bronnen van De reis van Sint Brandaan*, Hilversum.
Strijbosch, Clara (2000), *The Seafaring Saint. Sources and Analogues of the Twelfth Century Voyage of Saint Brendan*, Dublin.
Strobel, Karl (1991), 'Die Galater im hellenistischen Kleinasien: Historische Aspekte einer keltischen Staatenbildung', in Jakob Seibert (ed.), *Hellenistische Studien. Gedenkschrift für H. Bengtson*, Munich, 101–34.
Strobel, Karl (1996), *Die Galater. Geschichte und Eigenart der keltischen Staatenbildung auf dem Boden des hellenistischen Kleinasien*, vol. I, Berlin.
Sutherland, D. (1982), *The Chouans. The Social Origins of Popular Counter-Revolution in Upper Brittany, 1770–1796*, Oxford.
Sutherland, Elizabeth (1994), *In Search of the Picts. A Celtic Dark Age Nation*, London.
Swift, Catherine (1997), *Ogam Stones and the Earliest Irish Christians*, Maynooth.

Szabó, Miklos (1992), *Les Celtes de l'est. Le second âge du fer dans la cuvette des Carpates*, Paris.

Taylor, B. and E. Brewer (1983), *The Return of King Arthur. British and American Arthurian Literature since 1800*, Woodbridge.

Thomas, Alan (ed.) (2000), *Welsh Dialect Survey*, Cardiff.

Thomas, Charles (1981), *Christianity in Roman Britain to AD 500*, London.

Thomas, Charles (1994), *And Shall These Mute Stones Speak? Post-Roman Inscriptions in Western Britain*, Cardiff.

Thomas, Charles (1997), *Celtic Britain*, London.

Thomas, Graham C. G. (1988), *A Welsh Bestiary of Love, being a Translation into Welsh of Richard de Fornival's 'Bestiaire d'Amour'*, Dublin.

Thomas, Isaac (1976), *Y Testament Newydd Cymraeg 1551–1620*, Cardiff.

Thomas, Isaac (1988), *Yr Hen Destament Cymraeg 1551–1620*, Aberystwyth.

Thomas, M. Wynn (1988), *Llyfr y Tri Aderyn Morgan Llwyd*, Cardiff.

Thomas, M. Wynn (1991), *Morgan Llwyd. Ei Gyfeillion a'i Gyfnod*, Cardiff.

Thomas, M. Wynn (1992), *Internal Difference: Literature in Twentieth-Century Wales*, Cardiff.

Thomas, Peter D. G. (1998), *Politics in Eighteenth-Century Wales*, Cardiff.

Thompson, R. H. (1985), *The Return from Avalon. A Study of the Arthurian Legend in Modern Fiction*, Westport, CT.

Thomson, Derick S. (1989), *An Introduction to Gaelic Poetry*, 2nd edn, Edinburgh.

Thomson, Derick S. (ed.) (1994), *The Companion to Gaelic Scotland*, 2nd edn, Glasgow.

Thomson, Derick S. (1996), *Alasdair Mac Mhaighstir Alasdair*, Edinburgh.

Thomson, R. L. (1968), *Owein, or Chwedyl Iarlles y Ffynnawn*, Dublin (Medieval and Modern Welsh Series 4).

Thomson, Robert L. (1970), *Foirm na n-Urrnuidheadh: John Carswell's Gaelic Translation of the Book of Common Order*, Edinburgh (Scottish Gaelic Texts Society 11).

Thomson, Robert L. (1997), *Ystorya Gereint uab Erbin*, Dublin.

Thorpe, Lewis (1966), *Geoffrey of Monmouth. The History of the Kings of Britain*, Harmondsworth.

Thurneysen, Rudolf (1921), *Die irische Helden- und Königsage bis zum siebzehnten Jahrhundert*, Halle.

Tierney, J. J. (1960), 'The Celtic Ethnography of Posidonius, *Proceedings of the Royal Irish Academy* 60, 189–275.

Timpe, Dieter (1985), 'Der keltische Handel nach historischen Quellen', *Untersuchungen zu Handel und Verkehr der vor- und frühgeschichtlichen Zeit in Mittel- und Nordeuropa I*, Göttingen, 258–84.

Topsfield, L. T. (1981), *Chrétien de Troyes. A Study of the Arthurian Romances*, Cambridge.

Trevor-Roper, Hugh (1983), 'The Invention of Tradition: The Highland Tradition of Scotland', in Eric Hobsbawm and Terence Ranger (eds), *The Invention of Tradition*, Cambridge.

Tristram, Hildegard L. C. (ed.) (1989), 'Der insulare Alexander', in W. Erzgräber (ed.), *Kontinuität und Transformation der Antike im Mittelalter*, Sigmaringen, 130–55.

Tristram, Hildegard L. C. (ed.) (1993), *Studien zur Táin Bó Cuailnge*, Tübingen.

Tristram, Hildegard L. C. (ed.) (1997), *The Celtic Englishes*, Heidelberg.

Turner, R. C. and R. G. Scaife (1995), *Bog Bodies. New Discoveries and New Perspectives*, London.

Turvey, Roger (1997), *The Lord Rhys. Prince of Deheubarth*, Llandysul.

Uhlich, Jürgen (1999), 'Zur sprachlichen Einordnung des Lepontischen', in Stefan Zimmer et al. (eds), *Akten des Zweiten deutschen Keltologen-Symposiums*, Tübingen, 277–304.

Untermann, Jürgen (ed.) (1997), *Monumenta Linguarum Hispanicarum. Vol. IV Die tartessischen, keltiberischen und lusitanischen Inschriften*, Wiesbaden.

Urban, Ralf (1991), 'Die Kelten in Italien und in Gallien bei Polybios', in *Hellenistische Studien. Gedenkschrift für H. Bengtson*, Munich, 135–57.

Urban, Ralf (1999), *Gallia rebellis. Erhebungen in Gallien im Spiegel antiker Zeugnisse*, Wiesbaden.

Vaughan, W. E. (ed.) (1989), *Ireland under the Union, I 1801–70*, Oxford.

Vaughan, W. E. (ed.) (1996), *Ireland under the Union, II 1870–1921*, Oxford.

Vercingétorix et Alésia (1994), Paris (exhibition catalogue).

Verger, Stéphane (ed.) (2000), *Rites et espaces en pays celte et méditerranéen. Étude comparée à partir du sanctuaire d'Acy-Romance (Ardennes, France)*, Rome.

Vetter, Eva (1997), *Nicht mehr Bretonisch? Sprachkonflikt in der ländlichen Bretagne*, Frankfurt/Main.

Viallaneix, Paul and Jean Ehrard (eds) (1982), *Nos ancêtres les Gaulois. Actes du Colloque International de Clermont-Ferrand*, Clermont-Ferrand.

Villar, Francisco (1997), 'The Celtiberian Language', *Zeitschrift für celtische Philologie* 49/50, 898–949.

Vosteen, Markus Uwe (1999), *Urgeschichtliche Wagen in Mitteleuropa. Eine archäologische und religionswissenschaftliche Untersuchung neolithischer bis hallstattzeitlicher Befunde*, Rahden/Westfalen (Freiburger archäologische Studien 3).

Wagner, Heinrich (1959), *Das Verbum in den Sprachen der britischen Inseln*, Tübingen (Buchreihe der *Zeitschrift für celtische Philologie* I).

Wagner, Heinrich (1982), 'Near Eastern and African Connections with the Celtic World', in R. O'Driscoll (ed.), *The Celtic Consciousness*, Portlaoise and Edinburgh, 51–67.

Wagner, Heinrich (1987), 'The Celtic Invasions of Ireland and Great Britain: Facts and Theories', *Zeitschrift für celtische Philologie* 42, 1–40.

Wakelin, Martyn F. (1975), *Language and History in Cornwall*, Leicester.

Walker, David (1990), *Medieval Wales*, Cambridge.

Walser, Gerold (1998), *Bellum Helveticum*, Wiesbaden.

Walsh, Paul (1948–57), *Beatha Aodha Ruaidh Uí Dhomhnaill. Life of Hugh Roe O'Donnell*, 2 vols, Dublin (Irish Texts Society 42 and 45).

Wasserschleben, Hermann (1885), *Die irische Kanonensammlung*, 2nd edn, Gießen.

Watkin, Morgan (1958), *Ystorya Bown de Hamtwn*, Cardiff.

Watson, Jeanie and Maureen Fries (eds) (1988), *The Figure of Merlin in the 19th and 20th Centuries*, Lewiston, NY.

Watson, Roderick (ed.) (1995), *The Poetry of Scotland. Gaelic, Scots and English 1380–1980*, Edinburgh.

Watson, William J. (1937), *Scottish Verse from the Book of the Dean of Lismore*, Edinburgh (Scottish Gaelic Texts Society 1).

Watson, William J. (ed.) (1959), *Bàrdachd Ghàidhlig. Gaelic Poetry 1550–1900*, 3rd edn, Inverness.

Watts, Dorothy (1991), *Christians and Pagans in Roman Britain*, London.

Webster, Bruce (1997), *Medieval Scotland. The Making of an Identity*, London.

Webster, Graham (1986), *The British Celts and their Gods under Rome*, London.

Weisgerber, Gerd (1975), *Das Pilgerheiligtum des Apollo und der Sirona von Hochscheid im Hunsrück*, Bonn.

Weisgerber, Leo (1931), 'Galatische Sprachreste', in *Natalicium. Johannes Geffcken zum 70. Geburtstag*, Heidelberg, 151–75.

Welch, Robert (ed.) (1996), *The Oxford Companion to Irish Literature*, Oxford.

Werner, Martin (1997), 'Three Works on the Book of Kells', *Peritia* 11, 250–326.

Wells, Peter S. (2001), *Beyond Celts, Germans, and Scythians: Archaeology and Identity in Iron Age Europe*, London.

Whelan, Kevin (1996), *The Tree of Liberty: Radicalism, Catholicism and the Construction of Irish Identity 1760–1830*, Cork.

Whitaker, M. (1990), *The Legends of King Arthur in Art*, Woodbridge.

Whitelock, Dorothy, Rosamond McKitterick and David Dumville (eds) (1982), *Ireland in Early Medieval Europe*, Cambridge.

Wieland, Günther (ed.) (1999), *Keltische Viereckschanzen*, Stuttgart.

Wightman, Edith Mary (1985), *Gallia Belgica*, London.

Williams, Chris (1996), *Democratic Rhondda: Politics and Society 1885–1951*, Cardiff.

Williams, Chris (1998), *Capitalism, Community and Conflict: The South Wales Coalfield 1890–1947*, Cardiff.

Williams, Colin (ed.) (2000), *Language Revitalization. Policy and Planning in Wales*, Cardiff.

Williams, G. J. (1936), *Charles Edwards. Y Ffydd Ddi-ffuant*, Cardiff.

Williams, Glanmor (1976), *The Welsh Church from Conquest to Reformation*, 2nd edn, Cardiff.

Williams, Glanmor (1987), *Recovery, Reorientation and Reformation: Wales c. 1415–1642*, Oxford.

Williams, Glanmor (1997), *Wales and the Reformation*, Cardiff.

Williams, Ifor (1938), *Canu Aneirin*, Cardiff.

Williams, Ifor (1951), *Pedeir Keinc y Mabinogi*, 2nd edn, Cardiff.

Williams, Ifor (1972), *Armes Prydein: The Prophecy of Britain*, Dublin.

Williams, Ifor and J. E. Caerwyn Williams (1968), *The Poems of Taliesin*, Dublin.

Williams, Ioan M. (1996), *Dramâu Saunders Lewis*, Cyfrol I, Cardiff.

Williams, J. E. Caerwyn (1971), 'The Court Poet in Medieval Ireland', *Proceedings of the British Academy* 57, 1–51.

Williams, J. E. Caerwyn (1994), *The Poets of the Welsh Princes*, Cardiff.

Williams, J. E. Caerwyn (1997), *The Court Poet in Medieval Wales*, Lewiston, NY.

Williams, J. E. Caerwyn and Patrick Ford (1992), *The Irish Literary Tradition*, Cardiff.
Williams, J. Gwynn (1993), *The University Movement in Wales*, Cardiff.
Williams, J. Gwynn (1997), *The University of Wales 1893–1939*, Cardiff.
Winterbottom, Michael (1978), *Gildas: The Ruin of Britain and Other Works*, London.
Withers, Charles W. J. (1984), *Gaelic in Scotland 1698–1981. The Geographical History of a Language*, Edinburgh.
Withers, Charles W. J. (1988), *Gaelic Scotland. The Transformation of a Culture Region*, London.
Wodtko, Dagmar S. (2000), *Wörterbuch der keltiberischen Inschriften*,Wiesbaden.
Womack, Peter (1989), *Improvement and Romance. Constructing the myth of the Highlands*, London.
Wooding, Jonathan (ed.) (2000), *The Otherworld Voyage in Early Irish Literature. An Anthology of Criticism*, Dublin.
Wormald, P. (1986), 'Celtic and Anglo-Saxon Kingship: Some Further Thoughts', in P. E. Szarmach (ed.), *Sources of Anglo-Saxon Culture*, Kalamazoo, MI, 151–83.
Wright, Neil (1985), *The Historia Regum Britanniae of Geoffrey of Monmouth. I Bern, Burgerbibliothek Ms. 568*, Cambridge.
Zaenker, K. A. (1987), *Sankt Brandans Meerfahrt. Ein lateinischer Text und seine drei deutschen Übertragungen aus dem 15. Jahrhundert*, Stuttgart.
Zeller, Kurt W. (1995), 'Der Dürrnberg bei Hallein. Ein Zentrum keltischer Kultur am Nordrand der Alpen', *Archäologische Berichte aus Sachsen-Anhalt* I, 293–357.
Ziegler, Sabine (1994), *Die Sprache der altirischen Ogam-Inschriften*, Göttingen.
Zimmer, Stefan, Rolf Ködderitzsch and Arndt Wigger (eds) (1999), *Akten des Zweiten deutschen Keltologen-Symposiums*, Tübingen.
Zürn, Hartwig and Franz Fischer (1991), *Die keltische Viereckschanze von Tomerdingen (Gem. Dornstadt, Alb-Donau-Kreis)*, Stuttgart.

Index